Hinduism
Before Reform

HINDUISM
BEFORE REFORM

Brian A. Hatcher

▌▌▌
Harvard University Press
Cambridge, Massachusetts   London, England   2020

Second printing

Cataloging-in-Publication Data available from
the Library of Congress
ISBN: 978-0-674-98822-4

And sundry blessings hang about his throne,
That speak him full of grace.

—SHAKESPEARE, *Macbeth* IV.3

Contents

PREFACE

In one of his books A. M. Hocart remarked that to risk nothing is to achieve nothing. So here goes. In this book I risk upsetting established views of the Swaminarayan Sampraday and the Brahmo Samaj, especially concerning the lives and achievements of their respective founders, Sahajanand Swami and Rammohun Roy. I want to defy convention by treating Sahajanand and Rammohun not as modern religious reformers but as ruling lords at the head of two early colonial religious polities. This may seem problematic to some, near blasphemy to others. But I take the risk because I believe that, in reimagining the origins of the Swaminarayan Sampraday and the Brahmo Samaj, we have an opportunity to rethink the history of modern Hinduism more generally, especially as it has been framed within imperialist, nationalist, and postcolonial discourse.

I take another risk in wandering off my usual beat, which has hitherto been Bengal. If I now venture into the region of Gujarat, it is because the opportunity for comparison is too compelling to resist. Here again I hope to honor Hocart's reminder that although we must be careful, we should not be timorous. That said, whatever confidence I have in this regard owes a great deal to the encouragement and guidance I have received from numerous friends and colleagues. None of them should be held responsible for any missteps I may have made. I want to thank especially Arun Bandyopadhyay, Neilesh Bose, Arun Brahmbhatt, Avni Chag, Rosinka Chaudhuri, Catherine Clementin-Ojha, John Cort, Shomik Dasgupta, Aniket De, Amiya Dev, Amit Dey, Camillo Formigatti, Kashshaf Ghani, Jack Hawley, Ron Inden, Hanna Kim, Bhakti Mamtora, Azfar Moin, Urvi Mukhopadhyay, Thomas Newbold, Shruti Patel, Aditinath Sarkar, Subir Sarkar, Peter Schreiner, Bart Scott, Jawhar Sircar, Harald Tambs-Lyche, Robert Travers, Yogi Trivedi, Raphaël Voix, Raymond Brady Williams, Lucien Wong, and Richard Fox Young. My research has also benefited from the support and hospitality of the following institutions: American Institute of Indian Studies, Asiatic Society Calcutta, BAPS Swaminarayan Research Institute, Bodleian Library, British Library, Centre d'Études de l'Inde et de l'Asie du Sud (EHESS), King's College London, National Library Calcutta, Oxford Centre for Hindu Studies, School of Oriental and African Studies, Tarun Mitra Memorial Lecture Committee (AIIS), Tufts University, and the University of Victoria. Katherine Ulrich prepared the splendid index. I thank Sharmila Sen for taking on this project and supporting its development at every step. I dedicate the book to the memory of John and Cleo Ludwick, gone too long but still dearly missed.

✦   ✦   ✦

Just a few words on translation and transliteration: all translations are my own, unless otherwise indicated. Even where English translations are available for Sanskrit, Gujarati, or Bengali texts, I have tried to consult the original whenever possible; for Persian works I have had to rely solely on available translations. As the list of primary sources in the Bibliography reveals, there are often multiple versions of important texts that are worth attending to. I have opted not to employ diacritical marks for transliterated names and terms, since these are often a distraction for general readers and unnecessary for specialists. For Bengali I have largely followed pronunciation rather than orthography, except where current usage suggests otherwise, hence *rachanabali* and Vedanta. When it comes to the handling of names, I generally use commonly accepted forms, hence Rammohun Roy and Rabindranath Tagore.

Hinduism
Before Reform

INTRODUCTION

H ERE IS A STRANGE but telling fact: despite having emerged during
the same historical moment, the histories of the Swaminarayan
Sampraday and the Brahmo Samaj have largely been told in isolation
from each other. This is remarkable insofar as the founding figures of
these two religious polities were nearly exact contemporaries: Sahajanand Swami (1781–1830) and Rammohun Roy (1772–1833).[1] It is even
more remarkable when one considers that the Swaminarayan Sampraday
and the Brahmo Samaj might easily lay claim to being among the most
globally visible and politically consequential of Hindu organizations to
have arisen during the colonial era. How is it, then, that these two contemporaneous and influential religious polities—each featuring innovative founders and striking histories—have so far been held apart in
scholarship and critical reflection? *Hinduism Before Reform* is an attempt
to answer this question.

As we shall see, the reasons for this strange oversight are anything
but trivial. Instead they have to do with fundamental patterns in the developing discourse around Hinduism after the middle of the nineteenth
century. Chief among these patterns were teleological constructions of
religious reform and a kind of chronotopic imagining of religious progress in modern India. By this I mean to say that in the literature on
religion in colonial South Asia, the Brahmo Samaj has not only been

taken to represent the first and even quintessential expression of reformed Hinduism: more importantly, it has been figured as arising in the "here" of Bengal, which marks the triumphant "now" of empire in India. By contrast, the Swaminarayan Sampraday, even when it has been granted the status of a reform movement, typically falls short of the standard associated with the Brahmos; additionally, the Sampraday arose "out there" on the colonial fringe of Gujarat, a place necessarily redolent of the "back then" of medieval Hinduism.

This should make it all the more noteworthy that today there is a great deal of scholarly reflection on the "now" of a globally visible Swaminarayan Sampraday, which is frequently taken to represent the face of confident, if not problematic, Hindu assertion. By contrast, today the Brahmo Samaj excites little critical discussion, the very invocation of its name hearkening to a bygone colonial "then," a moment around the end of the nineteenth century when it had been the Brahmos who held center stage in conversations about religion, modernity, and pluralism. Spatial and temporal contrasts such as these alert us to the operation of significant precritical judgments encoded in the chronotopes of *here* and *now*, *there* and *then*. As I hope to show, such judgments can be accepted neither as matters of fact nor as being of little import. They point instead to the persistent work of discursive constructions regarding Hinduism in modern South Asia, constructions whose work is concealed by subtle sleights of hand. The goal of *Hinduism Before Reform* is to argue that, once we pick up on the trick, we realize there is no good reason to continue treating the Swaminarayan Sampraday and the Brahmo Samaj in isolation from each other. To the contrary, there are compelling reasons to examine them within a single analytical frame.

Surprisingly, efforts were made in this direction as early as the third decade of the nineteenth century, when colonial observers on the ground in western India—intrigued by the work of Sahajanand Swami—began to compare him with Rammohun Roy, whose name by that time was already widely known. When these early observers compared the two figures, they did so under the rubric of reform. Since that time, the term has borne immense—if unstable and precarious—weight in colonial discourse about Hinduism. In due course I plan to revisit these early conversations about Sahajanand and Rammohun, since they can be used to highlight ambiguities that would come to plague thinking about religious reform in modern South Asia. What bears noting at present is that, in the particular context of early colonial Gujarat, it proved possible for Britons to view the Swaminarayan Sampraday as a model of viable religious reform. Only later, as the century progressed, would such a verdict become less obvious. Thanks to the increasingly Bengal-centric character of late-colonial literature on Hindu reform movements in India, early comparative conversations about Sahajanand and Rammohun would be forgotten, and it would be the Brahmo Samaj that came to epitomize progressive reform.

This pattern of shifting assessments is a reminder of how important it is for us to review the history of our own second-order reflection on religious change in colonial India and to then begin the task of developing new analytical frameworks to support other kinds of conclusions about the history of modern Hinduism. *Hinduism Before Reform* attempts this task by focusing on the period of the first constitution of the Swaminarayan Sampraday and the Brahmo Samaj, a period I refer to as the era of the early colonial modern (ca. 1750–1850).[2] Careful attention to the character of early colonial modernity allows us to decouple the story of these two polities from the dominant narratives about religious reform, empire, and even the Indian nation that were to coalesce during the late colonial moment.

Precisely to avoid repeating or ratifying those dominant narratives about modern Hinduism, I have chosen to treat the Swaminarayan Sampraday and the Brahmo Samaj as religious polities rather than as religious reform movements. The category of the modern religious reform movement is too closely structured in terms of judgments about true and false religion; it presupposes a guiding narrative about modernity that makes it difficult for us to think anew about developments taking place during the early colonial moment. In the concept of religious polity we have a category that is both normatively neutral and yet also analytically precise enough to allow us to think anew about what figures like Sahajanand and Rammohun accomplished at the earliest juncture of the premodern and the modern.

That the Swaminarayan Sampraday and the Brahmo Samaj were in time forcefully drawn into developing discourse about reform and modernity is undeniable. Indeed, one of the goals of *Hinduism Before Reform* is to suggest how this happened and with what ramifications. To do this I propose to speak of the empire of reform, my own shorthand for the steady imposition, under the conditions of late colonial modernity, of normative discourse about religion, especially as such discourse supported the interests of the British imperial project in South Asia. Once they were encompassed by the empire of reform, these two early colonial religious polities were to become exemplars of two contrasting historical trajectories—one that spoke to the tenacious grip of tradition and the other to the promise of reason, progress, and freedom. Lost in such late colonial figurings of the Swaminarayan Sampraday and the Brahmo Samaj were opportunities for contemplating all that they shared at the time of their first emergence; and lost too were alternatives for thinking about the place of religion in modern and contemporary India. *Hinduism Before Reform* seeks to recover such opportunities and to propose some alternatives.

A Tale of Two Polities

The origin of the Swaminarayan Sampraday can be dated to 1802, when Sahajanand Swami placed his stamp on a community that had earlier coalesced around his late guru. The Brahmo Samaj was established in 1828 by Rammohun Roy.[3] Following the period of their first articulation, both polities were subjected to a range of similar strains and underwent a host of similar transformations. Their members debated questions of leadership and struggled with new forms of organization; the polities found themselves drawn into and reshaped by patterns of global movement and communication; and each needed to negotiate the turbulent waters of colonialism, secularism, rationalism, and nationalism. Along the way both polities became embroiled in some of the most consequential— and at times deeply contentious—matters of public life in modern South Asia, from nineteenth-century efforts at social change and political mobilization to the "saffronization" of politics in the late twentieth and early twenty-first centuries.[4] Put simply, the histories of these two polities have much to tell us about the shape of modern Hinduism and the place of religion in modern India.

Even so, there are important points of divergence, which correlate with the spatial histories of these two polities. From its inception, the Brahmo Samaj was closely linked to the expansion of the East India Company from what Peter Marshall dubbed its bridgehead in Bengal across the subcontinent; Marshall's choice of metaphor is significant, as we shall see.[5] As the material and bureaucratic tentacles of the empire extended beyond Bengal, Brahmo intellectuals were often at the forefront of new educational and professional opportunities; from Calcutta they made their way to other colonial centers like Madras and Bombay and, eventually, to the Punjab and the northwest. Simultaneously, the Brahmos began to insert themselves into international circuits of political representation and theological innovation, cultivating contacts and admirers in Britain and America.[6] They may well be thought of as the creators of the first modern transnational Hindu movement.

The Swaminarayan Sampraday has its roots in the region of Saurashtra or Kathiawar in present-day Gujarat.[7] The early Swaminarayan community was somewhat disengaged (though never isolated) from the expanding subcontinental networks of religious change; at least initially it cultivated none of the international contacts one associates with the early Brahmos.[8] However, the introduction of the indenture system after the middle of the nineteenth century meant that by the early twentieth century Gujaratis (and among them, Swaminarayanis) had begun making homes outside of India, notably in southern and eastern Africa. With the rise of midcentury decolonization movements and the ideology of Africanization, Gujarati migrants moved yet again. As a result Swaminarayanis came to settle in places like the United Kingdom, Canada, and the United States.[9] When we compare these histories of global diffusion, we can say that peak global visibility for the Brahmo Samaj came during the last quarter of the nineteenth century, whereas today the visibility of the Swaminarayan Sampraday continues to grow.

We may also point to significant differences with respect to the sociopolitical profiles of the two polities. In terms of its urban genesis, civic investments, and progressive politics, the Brahmo community has long borne a distinctively bourgeois character.[10] Brahmos were central to the rise of bourgeois nationalism, even if they have faced challenges from Gandhians and Marxists. The point is, as David Kopf noted long ago, the Brahmo Samaj is in some respect synonymous with the "modern Indian mind."[11] Indeed, Milinda Banerjee has recently pointed to the entanglement of Brahmo reform-based discourse within efforts at theorizing sovereignty in modern India and advancing a "robust political-theological concept of modern statehood."[12] In the process, it must be noted, however, that the Brahmos also benefited from their largely upper-caste Hindu and urban middle-class positionality, perpetuating rather than radically redressing persistent fractures within India's social framework. Furthermore, even Kopf noted that some of the earliest Hindu cultural nationalists, who leaned toward the symbolics and the renunciatory stylings of what is often called neo-Hinduism, emerged from the Brahmo educational matrix.[13]

Caste and class play an equally significant, if regionally distinctive, role in the development of the Swaminarayan Sampraday, which initially found traction among lower-caste groups like Kolis and Kanbis in Saurashtra before making appreciable inroads among urban and mercantile groups from central Gujarat. Not unlike the Brahmo Samaj, the Swaminarayan Sampraday has tended to support rather than contest caste ideology.[14] However, by virtue of the length of time it took for the community to gain visibility beyond Gujarat, unlike the Brahmos, the Swaminarayanis contributed little to early nationalist politics. It was really only in the latter half of the twentieth century, if not during the past quarter century, that the Sampraday came to find itself increasingly active in the global articulation of what is sometimes called public Hinduism. With prominent leadership roles granted to saffron-clad sadhus, the Swaminarayanis have at times been accused (rightly or wrongly) of rubbing shoulders with, if not abetting, the proponents of chauvinist forms of Hindu nationalism.[15]

Looking at evidence surrounding the divergent spatial, social, and political histories of the two polities, it might be fair to say that while the Brahmo Samaj helped shape the emergence of modern India during the colonial period, the Swaminarayan Sampraday is today placing its stamp on postcolonial Hindu public life in India and around the world. In this respect, the two movements have swapped their public profiles. There was a time during the late nineteenth and early twentieth centuries when, thanks to the engagement of Brahmos in colonial-era education, social change, civic life, and the arts, the Samaj might have claimed to be the "public face of Hinduism."[16] Today, however, that title better suits the Swaminarayan Sampraday, a religious community that is not merely visible but would be happy to be known as "the new face of Hinduism."[17] Overall, this striking history of similarity and divergence underscores how remarkable it is that no one has thus far thought to compare the Swaminarayan Sampraday and the Brahmo Samaj.

If the reason for this oversight has to do with the concept of reform, this is the place to point out that the story of the reform of Hinduism is the story of modern India; we sense this already from Kopf's equation of the Brahmo worldview with the modern Indian mind. Whatever Kopf may be saying about the impact of Brahmo thought on modern India, his comment is also predicated on key assumptions about religion and the Indian nation that bear investigating. For instance, if reformed religion is about finding and promoting an authentic tradition, rescuing it from error and degradation, then what does the equation of Brahmoism with the Indian mind suggest about the validity (or otherwise) of alternate modes of religious life? Do late-colonial accounts of Hinduism give pride of place to the Brahmos because they presume there is little worth saying about the sort of unreformed religion one finds in the Swaminarayan Sampraday? And do the anxieties of the postcolonial present— when religion plays a prominent a role in Indian public life (read Hindutva)—also rest on central assumptions about the relative purchase of reformed religion in contemporary life? Is this why the Swaminarayanis attract considerable critical attention, while the Brahmos have all but faded into the background?

Such questions suggest that lurking behind the divergent trajectories of the Swaminarayan Sampraday and the Brahmo Samaj is a dominant teleological narrative of reform that has swept Hinduism and even the Indian nation into its grasp. In the words of Mohamad Tavakoli-Targhi, the way we have come to think about Hindu polities like these is by inserting them into "history with borders."[18] That is to say, treatments of the Swaminarayan Sampraday and the Brahmo Samaj come to us embedded in certain self-affirming narratives that the modern West has long liked to tell about itself. And when it came to the British Empire in India, the story of the rise to power of the East India Company was always framed in terms of progress and improvement.[19] As for the Indian nation, when its imaginative project took off toward the end of the nineteenth century, it too was predicated on the values of reform, progress, and emancipation. In fact, by the early twentieth century, both imperialists and nationalists acknowledged the overriding value of reform.

To begin a new narrative of modern Hinduism that exits from such bordered and teleological histories, *Hinduism Before Reform* drops back to the early decades of the nineteenth century, when the Swaminarayan Sampraday and the Brahmo Samaj were first articulated as religious polities. To drop back to this early colonial moment is above all else an exercise in thinking "before," which I understand in two senses. To begin with, thinking before means identifying the distinctive lineaments of an early colonial moment before the heyday of British imperialism and Indian nationalism—the very moment out of which these two polities emerged. Secondly, thinking before entails the decision to critically postpone or forestall the kind of historical prolepsis that would predicate the present state of affairs in South Asia on normative assumptions about India's religious past.[20] Thinking before means asking what it might mean to contemplate the emergence of new Hindu communities (if not yet modern Hinduism) before the delineation and maintenance of the kinds of categorical and normative borders that have come to constrain our thinking.[21] This is where the category of religious polity proves its utility, since by using this category we are able to identify and compare the distinctive accomplishments of Sahajanand Swami and Rammohun Roy without yoking our conclusions to the normative discourse of religious reform. Comparing the Swaminarayan Sampraday and the Brahmo Samaj as two early colonial religious polities rather than contrasting them as two species of reform movement will open up new perspectives on the expression and governance of religious life in early colonial South Asia.

Thinking before is thus both an effort at historical reconstruction and a commitment to a reframing of our interpretive tools in the present. Focusing on the distinctive era of the early colonial and postponing the kinds of value judgments that took shape only later under the empire of reform represent a pair of strategies aimed at forestalling our habitual and often lazy recourse to problematic narratives about modern Hinduism, religious reform, and the Indian nation. Decoupling groups like the Swaminarayan Sampraday and the Brahmo Samaj from the constraining discourse and norms of reform while rethinking their emergence as religious polities is the central goal of *Hinduism Before Reform*. By doing so we will not only discover what the two polities shared by virtue of their contemporaneous origins in the early colonial moment; we will also be led to explore how the two polities differed in terms of regional context and the biographies and aspirations of their founding figures. The promise of such discoveries rests on facing certain challenges. I will ask readers to follow Sahajanand and Rammohun down some unusual paths of comparison and to think about them in some unaccustomed ways. I do this all by way of making the two men critically "homeless" in the manner enjoined by Tavakoli-Targhi.[22] What might we discover if we were to uproot Sahajanand and Rammohun from familiar bordered narratives and from the roles they have routinely been asked to occupy in critical and popular discourse around religious reform?

A Trip to Bartlett

It is important to recognize that even though the scholarly literature attests few if any explicit—not to mention extended—comparisons between the Swaminarayanis and the Brahmos, this does not mean that the two are not implicitly compared and contrasted in a variety of ways. In Chapter 9 I take up a little-discussed but important comparison of Sahajanand and Rammohun from the 1840s that allows us to detect the discursive contours of what I call the late-colonial empire of reform. But for now it is more meaningful to examine the ways that comparison around reform serves to inform contemporary discussions of religion in South Asia. To do this we need only tag along on a visit made by the classicist and ethicist Martha Nussbaum to a Swaminarayan temple in Bartlett, Illinois, west of Chicago.[23] If we attend carefully to Nussbaum's account of that visit, we can bring forward the guiding assumptions, and thereby the significant limitations, associated with the discourse of modern religious reform. As we shall see, although Nussbaum is ostensibly concerned with the religion of the Swaminarayanis, her analysis reveals a not-so-tacit debt to the ideals of Brahmo religiosity. Her visit to the Bartlett temple allows us to draw the discourse and norms around reform out into the open where they can be clearly seen and assessed.

In the summer of 2005, Nussbaum traveled to the Bartlett temple along with some of her research assistants. One of their goals was to "hear opinions about Muslims frankly expressed."[24] On the face of it, this seems a rather curious rationale for visiting a Hindu temple—that is, until one introduces the logic of communalization. In 2005 the horrific events of 9/11 remained vivid, and fears of radical Islam were at a fever pitch; Islamophobia entered our vocabulary and shaped popular and pernicious forms of backlash. At such a time, where better to look for evidence of anxieties around Islam than among a community of Hindus? This, at least, seems to have been the logic behind Nussbaum's visit to Bartlett. Nor should we forget that this was also the time when one phrase seemed to be on everyone's lips: "clash of civilizations."[25] Nussbaum registered the atmosphere of intolerance and the climate of fear; even if she rejected the idea of civilizational clash, she was worried there might indeed be a crisis. Even so, why visit a Swaminarayan temple in suburban Illinois?

To answer that question, and to get to Illinois, we need to first take a detour through a second major democracy, namely India. At this very moment, India was facing another traumatic moment in its prolonged history of religious crisis, a history stretching back at least as far as the partition of British India in 1947. In 2002, Hindu-Muslim tensions took on a particularly dire aspect when a group of Hindu pilgrims died in a fire aboard a train in the town of Godhra in the western Indian state of Gujarat. The deaths were popularly construed as an act of deliberate massacre, and blame was fixed on the Muslim community in Gujarat. Narratives were quickly concocted, accusing Muslims of seeking vengeance for the desecration of the Babri Masjid by right-wing Hindus a decade before in Ayodhya. In Gujarat, backlash against the Muslim community was immediate, sustained, and brutal.

In the ensuing weeks, Gujarat's capital of Ahmedabad was the site of a horrific anti-Muslim pogrom. The sense of horror was compounded when it became clear that the police and local politicians had aided Hindus in targeting their Muslim victims; in fact, many believed Gujarat's then chief minister, Narendra Modi, was complicit in the violence.[26] When Nussbaum turned her attention to the events at Godhra and in Ahmedabad, she realized it was not merely a story about Gujarat; it wasn't really even about India alone. She saw in all this the signs of a potential crisis facing modern democratic institutions worldwide: the tension between democracy and communalism. Her monograph, *The Clash Within*, represents an extended attempt to explore the struggle between open minds and closed worldviews. In the end, the book bears a hopeful message. Nussbaum lays special emphasis throughout on India's pluralist traditions and creative religious poetics; and politically her confidence is buoyed by the subsequent defeat of Modi's own Bharatiya Janata Party (BJP) in the elections of 2004.

What Nussbaum could not know at the time, of course, was that a decade later Modi would be sworn in as prime minister of India, riding on the popularity of the BJP's pro-Hindu platform and his purported success in bringing economic vitality to the state of Gujarat. While she could not have foreseen such developments, Modi's eventual return and meteoric rise only underscores the seriousness of Nussbaum's original concerns. The questions raised by Nussbaum in 2005 remain with us today: How significant is the threat posed to democratic life by forces of religious fanaticism, ethno-nationalism, and autocratic or (what some would call) fascist modes of political leadership? To what degree are people "prepared to live with others who are different, on terms of equal respect"? Will people inevitably choose the safety of "homogeneity" that comes through the "domination of a single religious and ethnic tradition"?[27] In the era of Donald Trump, Brexit, and the Bharatiya Janata Party, such questions cannot be ignored.

Clearly, Nussbaum's book was written as much for America as it was for India. Even so, it was Godhra that first raised the dilemma in its barest form. This explains the centrality of a section that comes early in her book, titled, "Why Gujarat?" That question can be read in several ways: Why did the events in Gujarat in 2002 take the shape they did?

Why should we look to Gujarat to understand threats to American democracy? Finally, if one of Modi's boasting points was economic development, how had Gujarat suddenly become a poster child for prosperity?[28] All these questions resonate behind Nussbaum's contention that Gujarat serves as both a bellwether of political change and a hermeneutical bridge for linking the Indian experience to developments in the United States. That is, as important as it is to understand the roots of Modi's success in Gujarat, it is just as important to appreciate the strong support he enjoys among pro-business, pro-Hindu Gujaratis in the United States. In this connection, one answer to the question, Why Gujarat?, came in the spring of 2005 when the US State Department denied Modi (who was then still chief minister of Gujarat) a visa that would have allowed him to speak at a convention of Asian-American hotel owners.[29] Anxieties over religious nationalism in India were structuring developments in the United States, even as the fault lines for potential ideological clashes were manifest in both contexts.

Now we understand the point behind her question, Why Gujarat? From the violent aftermath of Godhra, we are led to the diasporic Hindu experience in the United States. In both contexts, communalization confronts democracy. For instance, Nussbaum notes that support for Modi's proposed 2005 visit had run high among Gujaratis; from this she concludes that the US Gujarati community had by and large worked to insulate itself from core democratic values.[30] And yet she knows that Gujaratis have been far from insular; they represent a visible segment of the Indian-American business community, and among them the caste community of Gujarati Patels has enjoyed particular success.[31] Importantly, over the past two centuries, the Patels have gravitated en masse to the Swaminarayan Sampraday.[32] Given the support among what she calls the Patel "clan" for right-wing causes in Gujarat, Nussbaum concludes that the Swaminarayan Sampraday represents something like a bastion of right-wing Hinduism.[33] All this helps makes sense of her decision to visit the Bartlett Swaminarayan temple. The temple is the vital nexus between Gujarati and American Hinduism.

While Nussbaum might have turned her attention to other politicized Hindu groups active in the US—such as the Hindu Swayamsevak Sangh

(HSS), an overseas branch of the Indian Rashtriya Swayamsevak Sangh (RSS)—it was the particular constellation of religious, economic, and ethnic markers around the Swaminarayan Sampraday that set off alarm bells for her. Importantly for our purposes, the Sampraday registers for her as a sect, a closed and tightly controlled form of religious community. Unlike membership in a voluntary association such as the HSS, belonging to a sect like the Swaminarayan Sampraday evokes for Nussbaum a stronger, less negotiable, and more tightly scripted sort of commitment. This she finds troubling; but equally troubling is the relative prosperity of the Gujarati Swaminarayanis. She is aware of how the wealth of the community has helped bankroll efforts at large-scale institution building and self-representation both in India and abroad.[34] Overall then, we have the makings of what to her seems like a problem. A religious group that is closed in outlook, ethnic in orientation, flush with resources, and bent on promoting a single vision of the world. What is this if not a threat to the values of an open, pluralist, and democratic society?

The Cusp of Crisis

If this were a documentary film, one could imagine Nussbaum as the breathless narrator, speaking in a hushed and anxious tone: Follow us as we enter into "the heart of one of the most powerful subcommunities in the diaspora, the Swaminarayan sect of Hinduism, which organizes the local Gujarati community."[35] Here one gets the sense of forensic trespass, further enhanced by Nussbaum's depiction of the temple as the "primary enclave" of a highly organized, somewhat secretive, and problematically traditional "sect." Inside this sacred precinct, issues of doctrine and history are communicated with the "intense earnestness that one associates with members of authoritarian cults."[36] At times Nussbaum suggests temple volunteers might be intentionally evasive, as if shielding their cult from public scrutiny. Of course, Nussbaum is not above misdirection herself; her Gujarati Muslim assistant poses as a Hindu to avoid risking their ability to gain access; had the religious identity of her companion been revealed, Nussbaum is certain the Swaminarayanis would never have revealed what they really thought about Muslims. These are Gujaratis, after all (wink, wink).[37]

It is crucial to note how this quest to ferret out the darkest secrets harbored by Muslim-hating right-wing Hindus in the United States rests on a critique of sectarianism as delivered by an enlightened exponent of liberalism and democracy. Nussbaum is as troubled by what she takes to be the fundamentalism of Swaminarayanis as she is by their particular attitudes toward Muslims. Equally surprising, however, is how casually an accomplished scholar tosses around terms like sect, cult, indoctrination, and authoritarian. All these terms conjure the closed and blinkered world of zombie zealots. Is it too much to suggest that these are rather blunt instruments for a trained philosopher to employ? Then again, they serve Nussbaum's purpose. And they should, since they have been honed over centuries in the conceptual workshop of modernity.

Put simply, Nussbaum's portrait of the Swaminarayan sect is haunted by the specter of reform. Here I refer both to the obligatory characterization of Sahajanand Swami as a religious reformer and also to the underlying logic of reform as a kind of regulatory idea for thinking about religion. In this latter sense, reform does a lot of work: it contrasts with the closed world of the sect; it slots the Swaminarayan Sampraday into its place in the narrative of modern religion; and it gestures at a preferred path for modern democracy. Reform names a set of classically liberal assumptions about the nature of progress as improvement—a process that should be open, enlightened, progressive, and free.[38] Reform is one of those things we recognize when we see it, just as none of us will fail to notice when it becomes corrupted, delayed, or betrayed. Thanks to the empire of reform, this regulatory idea came to serve as the dominant framework for structuring narratives of religious modernity in South Asia. Although it is not often recognized, the Swaminarayan Sampraday has been given an important role to play within such narratives.[39]

Within the empire of reform, the history of the Swaminarayan Sampraday lends itself to what might be thought of as a study in contrasts between the innovative vision of a founder and the purported failures of the movement that he engendered. One version might go as follows. The founder, Sahajanand Swami, arrived in western India at the turn of

the nineteenth century; at the time he was living as a wandering renouncer (known then by the name Nilakantha Varni). After reaching
Kathiawar in present-day Gujarat, he encountered a group of disciples
who had been initiated into the Uddhava Sampraday, under the tutelage of a guru known as Ramanand Swami. Being spiritually gifted,
Nilakantha quickly earned Ramanand's blessing and was initiated into
the Sampraday under the name Sahajanand Swami. Upon Ramanand's
passing, Sahajanand went on to reveal himself not merely as Ramanand's
successor, but as the incarnate Lord himself, Swami Narayan (often
referred to in the early literature as Hari, a name for Vishnu). Sahajanand's story is easily grafted onto the paradigm of reform, since he is
said to have worked to ameliorate a range of deleterious customs that
were pervasive in precolonial Gujarat, not least female infanticide and
widow immolation.[40] Furthermore, Sahajanand could be cast as a reformer since his theology represented a brand of transcendent wisdom
that undercut the reality status of dominant caste distinctions in Hindu
society. When coupled with reports that Sahajanand cultivated friendly
ties with British officials in early colonial Gujarat, all of this fills out the
portrait of a modern reformer committed to a vision of religious and social progress.[41]

And yet, the story of the Swaminarayan Sampraday can also be
told—and in fact is often told—as one of incomplete modernity. Often
this incompleteness is signaled through metaphors that situate Sahajanand on the "cusp" of a new era; he has come up to, but perhaps not
fully entered into, the modern era. For instance, in his pioneering study,
Raymond B. Williams chose to describe the Sampraday as representing
the last vestiges of the medieval and the first glimmering of the modern.[42]
Granted, there is a great deal about Sahajanand that hearkens to premodern norms, from his guru-like authority to his conservative posture
on issues such as gender roles. What is more, the internal structure and
external social engagements of the Sampraday have been taken by observers as evidence of a community more oriented to the past than engaged in progress toward the future.[43]

The same kind of ambivalence colors Nussbaum's account as well.
She remarks favorably on Sahajanand's record as a "dedicated social
reformer" and a "progressive," developing one side of the portrait as

found in the standard literature.[44] Indeed, when it comes to his commitment to social change, Nussbaum characterizes Sahajanand the way we think of nineteenth-century American abolitionists and utopian theorists. But no sooner is Sahajanand planted on familiar interpretive ground than Nussbaum pivots to an account of the failures of Swaminarayan Hinduism. Now the same logic of progressive reform is used to indict Sahajanand for fostering the growth of a conservative, patriarchal cult that practiced the strict separation of the sexes.[45] Nussbaum thus reiterates a basic ambiguity around Sahajanand that is present already in Monier-Williams's 1885 portrait, which lauds the reformer even as it points to the lack of "the true vivifying" force of progressive reform.[46]

What Monier-Williams feared was that Sahajanand's most progressive achievements would be negated when his fledgling polity was inevitably pulled back into the hungry maw of traditional Hinduism, with its restrictive norms and ethos. Reading Nussbaum, it is almost as if Monier-Williams stands just over her shoulder; she too sees in the Swaminarayan Sampraday a cautionary tale about religious recidivism as found in Gujarat and the diaspora. In Nussbaum, the question is, To what degree does this putatively modern movement shelter profound threats to religion, modernity, and democracy? Naturally a great deal has changed since Monier-Williams's day, most recently with the success of the Gujarati economy and the increasing prosperity of diasporic Hindu communities. Nonetheless, these positive economic indicators, when paired with the rise of Hindutva politics as embodied in associations like the HSS and parties like the BJP, only heighten the potential for crisis; we are no longer pondering the passive failure of a modern movement to break with the past, but the active efforts of economically empowered agents to yoke visions of past glory to new political ends. Even so, what remains consistent from Monier-Williams to Nussbaum is the basic story of reform, not least the story of reform teetering precariously on the cusp of modernity, always at risk of succumbing to past errors.

This sense of imminent crisis is countered in Nussbaum's book by her consistent and passionate embrace of an alternative model of reform, even if the basic terms of the comparison are never stated this overtly.

To the ambiguous reforms of Sahajanand Nussbaum counterpoises the dreams and accomplishments of what we might call the liberal-Gandhian mode of reform. This is reform envisioned as open-minded, pluralist, antiauthoritarian, and committed to justice; this is reform grounded in the central liberal notion of the struggle "within the individual self."[47] The kind of religious temperament produced by such reform draws on a species of "moral imagination" that rejects the need to dominate others. The goal for anyone pursuing this alternative path of reform is to cultivate the "ability to imagine the life of people who differ from themselves."[48] We can set aside for now the irony (dare we say hypocrisy?) of Nussbaum embracing such a vision of interreligious understanding even as she goes undercover to surveil unwitting Swaminarayanis. For now what bears noting is that this alternate vision of reform in South Asian religion has its roots in the other religious polity at the heart of the present book: the Brahmo Samaj.

Brahmos and CEOs

The history of the Brahmo Samaj is familiar to many readers. It is widely known precisely because it has been so closely yoked to the story of modern India. Its founder, Rammohun Roy, has long been hailed as the "father of modern India."[49] His paternity in this regard is closely linked to his role as the founder of India's first modern voluntary associations: the "Society of Friends" (Atmiya Sabha), established in 1815, and the "Society of the Believers in the One True God" (Brahmo Samaj), established in 1828. By establishing these associations, Rammohun is said to have inaugurated the era not merely of modern associational behavior but, more substantially, of religious and social reform. Thanks to his embrace of liberal values like reason, freedom, and human dignity, it is as if he guaranteed that the Brahmo Samaj would hold pride of place in the history of India's awakening to modernity. Out of the Brahmo fold would emerge some of modern India's most compelling thinkers and artists, including two Nobel laureates, Rabindranath Tagore (literature) and Amartya Sen (economics).

The history, values, and leading lights of the Brahmo Samaj are near and dear to Nussbaum's heart. This might not be immediately apparent to readers of *The Crisis Within*, since the Brahmo Samaj is called out by name only once or twice; but attention to Nussbaum's heroes and her conversation partners, not least Tagore and Sen, indicates where she locates the best and brightest in the history of modern and contemporary India. If for Nussbaum the Swaminarayan Sampraday represents a closed, authoritarian cult, the Brahmos represent a kind of liberal poetry, more an ethic than an organization; they represent for her what is and might still be humane about modern Indian democracy.[50]

For Nussbaum, the poetry and the ethics both crystallized in the early educational experiments undertaken by Rabindranath Tagore at his forest school known as Shantiniketan. Whereas she depicts the Swaminarayan temple in Bartlett as a carefully monitored enclave, Tagore's Shantiniketan comes to life as an open and loving home. And Rabindranath is no Sahajanand; he is neither authoritarian guru nor incarnate God. When Bengalis salute Tagore as Gurudev, they celebrate his role as a "revered teacher," not as a divine leader; his is the authority to liberate, not command; he is a poet of freedom and humanity. I deliberately draw out the difference between Sahajanand and Tagore in a way Nussbaum does not; but then again she has no need to—such typologies are the stuff of the reform narrative as it has shaped reflection on religion in modern India. When coupled with Nussbaum's preference for Gandhian social justice, we have the ingredients for the realization of liberal religious modernity.[51]

Through her friendship with the Nobel economist Sen, Nussbaum establishes a personal connection to Tagore's Shantiniketan, enriched as it has been by the legacy of Sen's parentage and his own accomplishments. But Nussbaum looks for guidance to one other contemporary Indian in order to make sense of the challenges facing India. Who better to help her think through the challenges India faces in an era of neoliberal development and middle-class striving than Gurcharan Das, the former CEO of Procter and Gamble India? Das is an unabashed spokesman for the achievements of India's post-1991 economic liberalization and for Nussbaum he embodies the promise of a free and progressive India. As a man with a curious and "flexible" mind, he is the model of a very modern reformer.[52] Not only does Das advocate compassion and respect over the promotion of fear and the practice of domination, he also understands Hinduism at a "deep level." This is what sets him apart from the shallow ideologues of Hindutva.[53]

And let no one find it ironic that Das's professional life centered on the pursuit of power and profit. If anything, for Nussbaum this makes him an ideal spokesman for modern Hinduism; as her comment on the shallow ideologues reveals, she considers Das a better embodiment of modern Hinduism than Hindutva advocates who adopt the trappings of asceticism but fail to live up to the Gandhian ideal. As Nussbaum puts it, Das's business success does not detract from his reformist credentials, but marks its fulfillment. In fact, Das views reform as being about both morality and economics. As he once famously put it, call it what you will—"Protestant, Confucian, Marwari"—true reform always supports economic development.[54] Since we are free to call it what we will, let's call it Brahmo, since Das and his ethic of progress are for Nussbaum the outworking of Brahmo ideals.[55] In particular, the Brahmo vision of liberalism offers a template for religion in the age of deregulation; this is reform for an "India unbound." Rule-based religion, authoritarian gurus, and closed cults are no match for the expansive dharma of the latter-day Brahmos. Is it too much to say we witness in Nussbaum's account the victory of spirit over letter, love over law?[56]

We know this story. And for this very reason, even if Nussbaum had no intention of framing a deliberate comparison of the Swaminarayan Sampraday and the Brahmo Samaj as two versions of modern Hindu reform, her book nonetheless illustrates the persistent hold of reform-based narratives and the norms they enshrine. Whether wittingly or not, she lets us see how the religious worlds of Swaminarayanis and Brahmos tend to fare when compared as modalities of reform. And thanks to her we are now positioned to undertake another kind of comparative exercise, one that is not grounded in the sorts of assumptions she took with her to Bartlett. We can now ask: How might we compare the Swaminarayan Sampraday and the Brahmo Samaj without falling back on the discourse of reform? How might such a comparison help us think differently about modern Hinduism? And how was it that the Swaminarayan

Sampraday and the Brahmo Samaj came to be overtaken and discursively framed by the empire of reform?

Rethinking Crisis

As an exercise in exiting from familiar narrative frameworks, the critical task undertaken in this book carries obvious risks, not least the possibility of distorting, oversimplifying, or misrepresenting matters. So much has been written about religion in modern India that to trace it all to the problem of reform could easily seem not just reductive but simply wrongheaded. After all, if we focus resolutely on the problem of reform, are we not likely to overlook countless other themes and fault lines within the modern discourse around religion? Furthermore, if the goal is to rescue these two polities from the discursive clutches of reform, does success carry the risk that we might overlook meaningful dimensions of modern religious life highlighted within stories of religious progress and improvement? Finally, do we wish to turn a blind eye to the limitations or achievements of either polity merely to avoid invoking the values of reform? Are we prepared to topple Rammohun from his pedestal or to elevate Sahajanand to new heights in search of what might be a set of false equivalences?

These are all valid concerns and will need to be borne in mind as we proceed. I would say that the risks invoked here are mitigated in part by the sheer unlikelihood that we will succeed in disabusing ourselves from thinking in terms of reform. The roots go deep, not merely in South Asia but even more so in the structure of modern thought regarding religion. And we will surely find it useful in certain contexts and at certain times to invoke familiar narratives and the norms they enshrine; it is unlikely we will succeed in proving a new paternity for modern India. But if Rammohun and reform are likely to remain synonymous no matter what is accomplished here, it may be that by decoupling both his story and Sahajanand's from the yoke of reform we will gain new insights into the construction of religious worlds during a vital time in South Asian history. To bring the process of such world construction into view, however, we will need to strike at some of the load-bearing beams of reform-based discourse. This is just another way of saying we need to render Rammohun and Sahajanand homeless if we are to find in their work new ways to narrate religious modernity in South Asia.

Nussbaum's book reveals just how many load-bearing beams it takes to hold up the discourse of South Asian religious reform: progress, freedom, sect, cult, renaissance, and national awakening, to name but a few. Though it is signaled by the title of her book, one of the less visible supports in Nussbaum is the trope of crisis. One might even say that the story of reform has crisis built into it; its narrative arc presumes a reformer who confronts the challenge of getting over some cusp, overcoming a hurdle, or moving things forward against manifest resistance. Reform rests on the need for negotiating the precarious cusp. We have already seen how Sahajanand's legacy has fared when viewed in terms of the cusp of modernity. By many accounts he failed to weather the crisis of liberal faith, that inner battle for emancipation of the self that is supposed to be mirrored in an outer struggle to build forms of community that honor freedom and autonomy. But the liberal dream creates other kinds of crises, not least insofar as the desire for autonomy routinely runs afoul of the demand to honor difference. Both India and the United States struggle to find political solutions to address the proper place of religion in relation to the pursuit of public good. Nussbaum's answer is to offer Shantiniketan in place of Bartlett, but as we have seen, her decision to pry open the doors of one purported cult set the group's autonomy and the autonomy of its members at a discount.

Does Bartlett have to yield to Shantiniketan? Is there another way to approach this problem? My attempt is to develop the category of religious polity as tool for thinking about the early history of the Swaminarayan Sampraday and the Brahmo Samaj as a first step toward revisiting the larger crisis of reform. The key lies in approaching these two polities as types of association framed in relation to modes of ruling authority and guiding institutional norms—associations to which adherents subscribe out of choice and which themselves remain always open to negotiating a new kind of standing within a larger scale of religious forms. I hope to demonstrate that, approaching along these lines, we can find important new ways to compare the first emergence of these polities. I also believe that making a new beginning in this way—thinking about these polities before invoking reform—may direct us toward new paths for confronting challenges around the place of religion in India today, even if that task ultimately exceeds the scope of the present book. For now it is enough to signal how, from within the logic of reform, it must always appear as if the worlds of the Swaminarayanis and Brahmos are at odds with each other, as the ethnic challenges the universal, the communal resists the public, the world of ritual contends with a higher kind of wisdom. But is it right that such normative antinomies as these should continue to frame thinking about modern Hinduism? Is there no way out of this bind?

When operating in crisis mode, the custodians of modernity remain on the lookout for the kinds of trysts, covenants, or compacts that Hindus are led to make with political power.[57] The threat of betrayal is always in the air. Nussbaum herself worries that the key "Tagorean capacities" of critical engagement, global imagination, and empathy tend to go up in smoke when confronted by the red-hot ideology of zealots in search of political power.[58] But her own preference for Brahmo universalism blinds her to the fact that Brahmos have deployed and benefited from political power along their own path to cultural hegemony. This was already evident from David Kopf's early study of the Brahmo bourgeoisie and has only been amplified by a generation of scholars working in the wake of postcolonial and subaltern studies. The Brahmo role in shaping the modern liberal nation-state allowed that particular socioeconomic and cultural group to bypass significant engagement with the injustices and inequalities of caste, gender, and community.[59]

Once we commit to approaching these two communities as religious polities, there will be no way to avoid addressing the dynamics of power and authority as they contributed to the earliest constitution of either the Swaminarayan Sampraday or the Brahmo Samaj. Instead of treating the latter as the baseline against which deviations from true Hindu thought and practice should be measured, by placing both within a comparative framework informed by an analytic of religious polity we equip ourselves to offer a more balanced assessment of both historical origin and contemporary legacy. To my mind, there is at least a small hope that by revising our scripts in this way—away from reliance on the logic of reform—we may provide a route for Hindus themselves to escape the constraints of modern characterizations of Hinduism.

By design, this book has more to say on the topic of historical origins than on the contemporary scene. When it comes to the question of origins, my strategy is to think in terms of what we notice *before* we begin invoking the logic and tropes of reform. Earlier I spoke of engaging in an act of critical postponement, and that is the goal of *Hinduism Before Reform*: to make sure we don't begin with a vision of the past that gestures toward a predetermined future, whether in terms of modern Hinduism or of the proper place of religion in contemporary India. For this reason, in what follows I plan to hunker down in the period between 1750 and 1850, paying closest attention to the critical period from 1780 to 1830 when Sahajanand and Rammohun projected their mastery over innovative new religious polities. Only in the final two chapters do I turn to the gradual rise of the empire of reform and its critical legacy in determining subsequent reflection on modern and contemporary Hinduism.

1

BEFORE REFORM

THE STORY OF religious reform in India is mapped across both space and time. In the last half of the nineteenth century—when the discourse of reform fairly exploded into view—a number of new metaphors were coined by a range of Indian intellectuals to capture a sense of optimism around visions of national progress. We find writers describing new religious and social movements in terms of waves (*andolan*) spreading across the land, signaling an awakening (*jagaran*) toward the values of general welfare and improvement (*unnati*); others speak of a slumbering subcontinental giant entering a new age (*nava yug*), as India came to a new awareness of itself (*prabuddha Bharata*).[1] In what would become a vast literature on religious reform, the process of change is routinely imagined in terms of the dispersion of modern actors, movements, institutions, and logics outward from vital epicenters like Calcutta; progress is plotted in terms of the gradual diffusion of new initiatives in education, social reform, and political awakening. Like a drop of ink spreading on a piece of blank paper, the passage of time sees the horizon of reform expand ever outward.[2]

When one stops to think about it, a good deal of the critical terminology around colonial modernity in South Asia draws on a related set of spatial tropes. We speak of the *arrival* of Europe, the *epicenter* of colonial rule, the *spread* of English education, the *intrusion* of modernity, and the *impact* of colonialism. That all these spatial metaphors appear to us as historical descriptors may be taken as evidence of the temporo-centrism of modernity. That is, we tend to think modernity is about time and forget how much it has been charted in spatial terms as well. Even after Mikhail Bakhtin taught us to appreciate how time and space register within discourse, our standard theories of religious change in modern India continue to trade on the temporality of progressive change without giving much attention to the spatialization of our central narratives.[3] We do well, in fact, to consider how common colonial-era metaphors of reform actually work to construct modern India as a particular space with a particular history.

An important step was taken in this direction by Manu Goswami, who drew on the work of Bakhtin and Henri Lefebvre to explore how the production of the national space of Bharat (or India), relied on a kind of chronotopic imagination that drew on both South Asian and imperial conceptions of space and time.[4] Goswami's work demonstrates how the East India Company's rise to power in South Asia was not merely predicated on the economic logic of mercantile expansion; it also rested on key tropes about India as the kind of space into which British economic actors could extend their investments and deploy their military-fiscal resources. Bolstered by eighteenth-century assumptions about India as rich in wealth but politically weak, the discursive terrain was cleared in advance for the British to extend their power. Colonial maps of India—indicating vast empty interior spaces—ratified imperial projects to control, improve, and reform South Asian space.[5] While scholarship in religious studies has made strides toward understanding the discursive disciplining of religion in relation to imperialism, there is more to be said about how the spatiotemporal logics and tropics of reform have shaped—and continue to shape—reflection on religion in South Asia.

There is room to ask, in particular, how modern representations of Hinduism are implicated in the spatiotemporal imagining of India. One could say that modern Hinduism is in fact an allomorph of modern India in this respect. This is to say that representations of modern Hinduism offer another kind of a spatiotemporal mapping of India. To develop this point, I want to look briefly at two influential authors who wrote about Hinduism in the mid-twentieth century, Sarvepalli Radha-krishnan and R. C. Zaehner. Each author understands the story of Hinduism in relation to the coming-into-being of modern India in the wake of imperial rule; they each present Hinduism as a chronotope for India. We need to give some thought to influential accounts like theirs because, if the story of modern Hinduism maps onto the history of modern India, any project to rethink modern Hinduism must begin by reimagining India as well. This explains why *Hinduism Before Reform* is oriented toward the space-time of the early colonial moment. If we drop back to the early colonial it is not simply because this was the time period in which Sahajanand Swami and Rammohun Roy happened to live. More importantly, it is because by rethinking the significance of the early colonial moment we have an opportunity to rethink and rewrite the subsequent history of late colonial and postindependence India. In order to demonstrate how this may be possible, let me quickly bring forward these two influential representations of Hinduism as chronotope.

Hinduism as Chronotope

Writing in 1962, Sarvepalli Radhakrishnan felt confident enough about India's progress toward social reform to assure his readers that "we have overcome" the need for caste distinctions.[6] His claim represents the sort of thinking I want to highlight, an approach that yokes the depiction of modern Hinduism to the viability of the modern Indian nation. For Radhakrishnan, recent developments around the reform of religion had fostered an Indian public in which "it is not the color of the skin but the conduct of the person that counts."[7] When he wrote these words, he had just been named president of the Republic of India; his understanding of Hinduism gave him full confidence that the public then being created by "legislative enactments" was also perfectly "consistent with our tradition."[8] That the new president of the republic was the author of such widely read books as *The Hindu View of Life* (1927) is not unimportant.

Radhakrishnan's use of the inclusive first-person plural in the two quotations above is significant. He speaks of what "we" have overcome and the work "we" are doing to link reflection on India to "our" tradition. For a politician to speak this way might not seem all that striking; but since we are talking about a Brahmin intellectual and spokesperson for India's grand spiritual heritage, the implications are more profound. Today we understand the political import of claims like this—in relation to both official projects around national integration after 1947 and populist initiatives to promote Hindu unity (*sangathan*).[9] The politicization of Hinduism and the history of saffron politics are too familiar to need rehearsing here, as are the myriad acts of exclusion, marginalization, and fragmentation that accompanied the creation of the modern Indian nation-state.[10] Indeed, the rise of Hindu nationalism from the late imperial moment of Bankimchandra, Vivekananda, and Aurobindo through Savarkar and the Hindu Mahasabha occupies a large and secure place in today's scholarly canon and university curricula. If anything, it can be a challenge to read the proclamations of someone like Radhakrishnan without hearing in them a reminder of the unintended consequences of Hindu leaders promoting inclusivism and tolerance.[11]

That said, scholars of Hinduism still remain handicapped by a kind of "genesis amnesia," a condition that makes it difficult for intellectuals to recover the conditioning factors behind our critical categories.[12] This is not to say scholars of Hinduism have not attended to contemporary modes of criticism; that would be unfair and inaccurate. I have in mind a particular kind of failure, which we can think of as the inability to reckon with the ways historical narratives and spatial imaginings work together to generate illusions of national community.[13] Writing in the wake of the Cold War, Michael Shapiro stressed the need for new moral geographies capable of undoing the normalizing discourse of the nation-state; he called for "map alteration" to address the "structures of nonrecognition built into modernity's moral geography."[14] Shapiro's call remains salient, especially if we are to address "narrativized forms of forgetfulness" that shape persistent linkages between Hinduism and the modern Indian nation.[15]

Such linkages depend on a kind of moral prolepsis that operates like this: first, one assumes there is an Indian nation-space that exists to be reformed; next, one assumes that Hinduism is the one unitary tradition that ought to map onto this space but that has in fact hitherto failed to achieve its full identity with the Indian nation-space; finally, one assumes that what is required is a reformation of existing tradition, so that Hinduism may finally realize itself in these terms—as a nation that will in turn reflect the truest Hinduism as well as the truth of Hinduism. This, I would argue, is the very teleology that informs Radhakrishnan's views of Hinduism and the Indian public. For him, independent India had finally realized democratic inclusivity because that had been the goal of Hindu reformation all along.[16]

This kind of thinking is hardly unique to Radhakrishnan. The same logic informs another influential treatment of Hinduism, namely R. C. Zaehner's *Hinduism*, first published in 1962, the same year as Radhakrishnan's remarks on caste quoted above. The very first words of Zaehner's introduction present the case for the mapping of Hinduism onto India through a claim most will immediately recognize: "'Hindu' is a Persian word: it means simply 'Indian.' Hinduism is thus the '-ism' of the Indian people."[17] The claim is couched in terms of a familiar ambiguity promoted by the fluid phonemes in place-names like Sind, Hind, and Ind. But, for that very reason, our attention is distracted from the deeper import of the passage; Zaehner encourages us to forget—in Shapiro's terms—the kind of moral geography that would equate Hinduism and India.

From this beginning, Zaehner's narrative unfolds in equally familiar fashion: Indian history can be understood in terms of four grand phases of development, culminating in the era of modern reform when Hinduism-as-India realizes itself. If we fast-forward to the modern moment, we are reminded at once of the spatial. When thinking of modernity, Zaehner is chiefly focused on transformations taking place in the colonial era. He tells us the reformers of modern India imbibed new ideas from the West; but he also wants us to appreciate that Indians avoided the deracinating effects of cultural borrowing through their own concerted efforts at cultural preservation. Echoing the opening words of his book quoted above, he reminds his readers, "After all they were Hindus, and 'Hindu' is simply the Persian word for 'Indian.'" In other words, if the modern reformers had sought to repudiate Hinduism, it would have meant repudiating "India itself."[18]

The prolepsis here is evident: the end is present in the beginning. What falls in between is Zaehner's lively story of a nation struggling to harmonize the spiritual and the worldly, dramatized by mapping mythic characters onto historical lives. The indecisive Yudhishthira of the Mahabharata meets the conflicted modern hero Mahatma Gandhi. Both struggle—as Indians and as Hindus—to look past an obviously "degraded" dharma in order to realize a higher truth.[19] The ultimate telos for Hinduism is prefigured early on, when Zaehner informs his readers that it was to be in only the final phase of Indian history that Hindus would finally reach their goal. This they were able to do thanks to Gandhi's embrace of tradition; it was Gandhi who assured that the noble goals of Hindu reform found a place in the hearts of the "Indian people."[20] With Gandhi, both Hinduism and India reach their long-cherished goal.

Zaehner's attention to India's ability to address the threat of Western influence and deracination helps us appreciate how the chronotope of Hinduism is cast in global space. Waves of reform and awakening constitute the leading edge of global reform; India's awakening depends in part on the impelling force of European imperial expansion. Agitations within India are figured as a kind of force for change radiating from colonial metropolitan centers like Calcutta, Madras, and Bombay, the original loci for rationalization, secularization, and demystification. From them the waves of change ripple outward, upsetting the placid backwaters of tradition. It is important to appreciate how, in the process, remote places tend to become distant pasts. The spatiotemporal diffusion of reform overcomes the "yawning gap" between the "higher manifestations" of religious thought found in urban centers and the "frankly superstitious and magical practices" characteristic of the "rural masses."[21]

The approach taken by Zaehner recalls patterns around the discursive mapping of Hinduism and India that had been set in place by earlier colonial-era authors who came to speak for what I refer to as the empire of reform. A good example is Monier-Williams's *Hinduism* from 1877, which opens by calling to mind the space of Hindustan as peopled by a vast a "assemblage of beings" who, even though inhabiting a shared subcontinental space, could not be said to constitute a "nation."[22] This denial of an Indian national identity in turn echoes the thought of imperial apologists like James Fitzjames Stephen, who, just one year after Monier-Williams, drew on claims about the fractured character of India to justify imposing the stabilizing and ordering hand of empire. In Stephen the British Empire is likened to a "vast bridge" leading an "enormous multitude of human beings" from the "dreary land" of India's past to an "orderly, peaceful and industrious" future. Here we clearly see how spatial metaphors work in tandem with the teleology of imperial modernity.[23]

From Monier-Williams and Stephen we can jump to John Nicol Farquhar's 1915 monograph, *Modern Religious Movements in India*, which, even as late as the 1960s, Zaehner was content to view as a "standard work" on religious change.[24] In Farquhar too, the age of reform is yoked to a distinct spatiotemporalism; reform commences dramatically with the "penetration" of India by the West—a forceful and troubling image but one entirely consistent with the logic of empire.[25] Zeroing in on the arrival in Bengal in 1794 of the Baptist missionary William Carey, Farquhar also linked reform to the diffusion of European Christianity. In this account, Carey serves as a pebble thrown into the torpid waters of Indian religious life; he and his fellow missionaries are the ones who caused waves of reform to begin washing across the subcontinent.

It should go without saying that the tropes are not always employed consistently: images of premodern lethargy and death often go hand in hand with those of a more dynamic era of chaos and anarchy. Likewise, the advent of modernity constitutes either a stable bridge cast over troubled waters (as in Stephen) or alternatively a kind of seething "hothouse" wherein the artificial embrace of reform produces dangerous agitations in the Indian mind.[26] Nonetheless, the underlying logic is consistent: the central tropes of the empire of reform create a particular kind of moral and religious spatiotemporality within which we are compelled to situate reformers like Sahajanand and Rammohun. Not just this, but space and the time can be used to account for what differentiates them as well. For instance, P. J. Marshall's metaphor of the Bengal bridgehead echoes not only Stephen's image of the empire as bridge to the future, but also Farquhar's image of a moment of decisive colonial penetration. The spatial epicenter of the bridgehead thus marks a moment of departure, whereby it becomes straightforward to view Rammohun as a kind of forerunner while leaving Sahajanand expectantly waiting on the frontier of an older, more chaotic India.

We now have one way to understand the lack of robust comparison between Rammohun and Sahajanand. What is lost in the spatial gap between Gujarat and Bengal is any awareness of the contemporaneity of these two religious innovators. The moral geographies inherent in the imperial mapping of religious change in India thus led to a forgetting of what Rammohun and Sahajanand shared in their particular colonial moment. And forgetting seems an entirely apt concept here, because as we shall see, it was not always the case that colonial-era observers failed to pick up on the fact that these two men appeared on the scene at the same moment in time. In fact, in the first half of the nineteenth century, some British observers were drawn into overt acts of comparison regarding the work of Rammohun and Sahajanand. How that took place, and where such reflection eventually led under the empire of reform, is the concern of two chapters of *Hinduism Before Reform*. However, before turning to that we must work anew to resituate Sahajanand and Rammohun in their shared early colonial moment.

Religion before India

If we are to rethink the origins of the two polities created by these two men in a shared historical moment, then the histories of these polities must be decoupled from the teleologies of reform, empire, and the nation. We need to establish new vantage points, chart new boundaries, and follow new itineraries that might help us arrive at new "positioned sightings" that can help us theorize anew about religion in modern South Asia.[27] That is, we need alternate conceptual maps for thinking about space, identity, belonging, and meaning, maps that don't resolve into (or reduce down to) the familiar logics of the atlas or the handbook.[28] Included in such remapping are acts of critical postponement that resist the pull of stories that begin with assumptions about Hinduism or India. Abandoning the comfort of such foregone certainties, we must be willing to find our way in "a multiple and internally divided world."[29]

A useful model in this regard is Catherine Asher and Cynthia Talbot's *India before Europe*, a book that resists the appeal of familiar narratives of the modern Indian nation-state.[30] I might risk a slight alteration of their title in order to speak here about religion before India. Here the word "before" directs us to a critical moment when we might still speak of South Asian modernities before the coalescence of the idea of the Indian nation-state as patriotic frame or goal of nationalist aspiration.[31] However, as I indicated in the Introduction, to think before is not merely to indicate temporal antecedence; it is also to adopt a particular hermeneutic stance—the stance of critical postponement. That is, the goal is not so much to imagine what India was like before the rise of anticolonial resistance or communal politics as it is to imagine what religion (and Hinduism in particular) was like before the nation came to be framed in relation to such concerns.[32]

Asher and Talbot presume none of the familiar unities around the Indian nation-space, seeking instead to construe South Asia as a "pluralistic" arena wherein our ready-made, enumerated categories of religion and community find no ready home.[33] Likewise they call attention to the vitality of the early modern moment. Where once it might have been standard to invoke images of medieval decay, they speak instead of a time during which cultural energies were fueled by diverse and vibrant capillaries of trade and intellectual exchange, all of which supported innovations in art, architecture, literature, and religion. If imperialist and nationalist narratives of premodern anarchy served to justify British conquest or fuel the rhetoric around a resurgent modern Hinduism, recent scholarship on premodern South Asia encourages us to think instead of modern Hinduism as emerging—rather than divorcing itself—from premodern modes of innovation.[34]

Thanks to the rich bequest of postmodern critical theory and post-Orientalist / postcolonial thought, not to mention recent developments in global history, we are better positioned now to query the easy and self-aggrandizing dichotomizing of the premodern and the modern.[35] This is the wider critical ecology sustaining my own attempt here, which is framed more directly in terms of assisting the contemporary study of modern Hinduism to find new ways to query the operation of familiar narratives. Within this critical ecology we no longer take it for granted that the world was disenchanted after the Reformation and Enlightenment; we recognize that the ideals of religious liberalism, as consequential as these have been for structuring modern social and political life,

do not represent "our" arrival at some utopian destination but constitute instead the assertion of a particular set of claims about how society
might be ordered and politics practiced; and we no longer presume that
the secular marks a final escape from the realm of religion, any more
than we imagine rituals to be regressive, deference to religious authority
slavish, or appeals to transcendence superstitious. Insofar as this speaks
to a broad scholarly consensus today, I think we must proceed to one
further conclusion: it is time to consider more critically how the axiology
and periodization of the modern have shaped our views of Hinduism
and the Indian nation. To tackle the question of what makes Hinduism
modern is to wrestle with the conjoint problem of modernity and
reform.

My simple proposition is that we double back before India in order
to exit from the constraints of such categories, even while we keep in
view the eventual and consequential emergence of reform-based discourse in the later colonial period. This explains my resolute focus on
the early colonial modern. Without a doubt, certain patterns of categorical schematization and reification begin to occur around Hinduism
and the nation during the last quarter of the nineteenth century. But this
very fact suggests that we not be too quick to assume that the early nineteenth century was modern in the same way, or to the same degree. As
Partha Chatterjee has remarked, the historian should focus less on the
presumed rupture between premodern and modern India and pay more
attention to another kind of historical turning point, one that Chatterjee
rightly sees as "crucial"—the moment of transition from early colonial
modernity to the modernity of the late colonial.[36] To attend to this *in-
stantia crucis*, to pause at this crossroads, is not just to acknowledge the
disruptive force of imperial rule in some generic sense; it is to offer new
hope for further and more accurately historicizing South Asian colonialism itself.

The Early Colonial Modern

How then shall we think of the early colonial modern? As a period, the
early colonial modern may be thought to run from roughly 1750 to 1850.[37]

In terms of the distinctive lineaments of the age, we can associate the era with both Robert Clive's military victory over the Nawab of Bengal at the Battle of Plassey in 1757 and the East India Company's establishment in 1800 of a new institution of learning in Calcutta, the College of Fort William. Clive's victory led to fundamental changes in the practice of politics and trade in eastern India; the creation of the College of Fort William introduced into the Indian context new institutional and epistemological norms that would foster new patterns of intellectual production and social mobility. During this same period, official policies with respect to British noninterference in religion (in the era of Warren Hastings), the Permanent Settlement under Lord Cornwallis (1793), and increased missionary ambitions around the evangelization of India (especially after renewal of the EIC charter in 1813), served to empower new economic elites in South Asia, propel the rapid development of cities like Calcutta, and provide occasions for innovation in religious doctrine, ritual, and theology.[38] In the early decades of the nineteenth century, the rise of the printing press and the expansion of colonial law courts both fostered new modes of public debate and social intercourse, leading to the proliferation in time of countless associations pledged to the promotion of science, education, agriculture, and political reflection.[39] These are just a handful of distinctive features of the new colonial moment that emerged in the wake of Plassey.

The moment of the early colonial modern must be recognized for both the force of its arrival and the novelty of its bequests. Recognizing that moment and reifying it, however, are two different things. The tendency in writing on colonialism in South Asia is to miss this point and to treat the colonial period tout court, as if it represented a single era, a consistent set of ideologies, and an unchanging constellation of institutions and social formations. Some of this is, sadly, the legacy of postcolonial studies itself, which has often been content to wrestle with a straw-man colonizer made in the image of a Curzon or a Kipling. Within subaltern studies, intensive reflection on the nation, and nation-building projects after the 1880s, likewise trained most critical attention on the late colonial moment. To be sure, some notice is typically given to significant early colonial developments such as Macaulay's 1835 Minute on Education, but these are rarely read in their context as much as they are treated as proof of the deep-seated roots of colonial racism; thus the 1830s are often rapidly drawn forward into the world of the 1870s or 1880s. There is no doubt that the late colonial era witnessed the full flowering of racist, masculinist, and Christianizing imperialist policies, but we retroject such trends into the early colonial moment at the risk of missing the crucial transition between an earlier colonial era and the period of high imperialism. Put very simply, Macaulay's world was not Kipling's.

It is refreshing to see that one of the guiding voices of the early subaltern studies collective, Partha Chatterjee, has called attention to just this problem. Chatterjee's *The Black Hole of Empire* demonstrates what new insights—what new ways for periodizing South Asian modernity— emerge when one commits to bringing the early colonial modern into view.[40] When we read *Black Hole of Empire* alongside the wealth of recent scholarship around early modernity in South Asia, it becomes possible to defamiliarize the colonial era enough to shed new light on some of our cherished narratives about religious modernity in South Asia. Not only can we give greater due to the distinctive character and dynamics of the early colonial moment, but we can also lay bare the genealogy of hitherto hegemonic interpretive categories, not least the category of reform. The most trenchant way Chatterjee poses this critical challenge is by reminding us not to allow our understanding of the long nineteenth century to be "teleologically predetermined by the ascendency of the colonial modern."[41]

In making this plea, Chatterjee manages to find common ground with the late C. A. Bayly, not least those critical instincts enunciated by Bayly in his monograph, *Rulers, Townsmen and Bazaars*. There Bayly surveyed developments in several regional contexts during the eighteenth century in order to deflate popular clichés about South Asian progress. Central to the task was simply the challenge of getting past the kind of old tropes I examined briefly above. In particular, Bayly asked whether it is possible to write histories that do not presume a basic narrative of moribund South Asia yielding to the dynamic power of European modernity. He argued that in fact it was possible, and he rejected the assumption that what greeted European imperialists in South Asia was an Indian nation in decline or a subcontinent of benumbed multitudes who had yet to realize their unity. Most importantly, his review of evidence allowed him to bring into view a dynamic and diverse field of political, social, and religious movements.

Where historians had hitherto been inclined to see chaos, Bayly found evidence of emergent regional polities, active trans-regional networks, and innovative religious organizations, all of which were working to reshape the political economy and social field; he called attention to the historical contributions made by military adventurers, religious mendicants, merchants, and bankers. And within this context he of course highlighted one further emerging "new power," namely the East India Company, which had a role to play within broader processes of change. If the old consensus had been that this period witnessed nothing more than a "shuffling of the old cards," Bayly brought into view a world being made anew in relation to the rise of regional market towns, networked monasteries, and other religious sites; this was an early colonial moment, then, in which indigenous literati, commercial agents, and skilled service gentry all placed their stamp on the political economy.[42] Gone were the normative judgments about progress or decline. What we were asked to consider instead was a distinctive and consequential moment "between the heyday of the last indigenous states and the establishment of the mature colonial system after 1857."[43]

Chatterjee's *Black Hole of Empire* comes as a reminder that there is still more to be done by way of bringing this moment into view. This remains especially true in the area of religious studies, where textbook treatments of modern Hinduism remain wedded to older models of precolonial decline and a presumed colonial renaissance or awakening, imagined as a continuous process running from the advent of Rammohun Roy to the creation of modern India in 1947.[44] The question is this: What might it mean to liberate our histories of modern Hinduism from the overriding teleological trope of national awakening? How might we rethink the nature and significance of modern Hinduism if we were we to abandon normative preconceptions about premodern religious decay? Is it possible that renewed reflection on the emergence of religious polities like the Swaminarayan Sampraday and the Brahmo Samaj during the period between 1750 and 1850 might foster better understanding of the early colonial modern while also opening up new avenues for thinking about quintessentially modern problems around communalism, Hindutva, and the place of religion in Indian public life?

In raising such questions, I draw on the work of Rosinka Chaudhuri, who has helped us appreciate just what comes into view when we decide to focus on the early colonial modern as both period and episteme. One thing we come to appreciate, according to Chaudhuri, is what a remarkable moment of transition this was. In her estimation, the period between 1750 and 1850 was one in which a range of new worlds were just beginning to present themselves as possibilities within South Asia, even if this was a period that also necessarily saw certain defining lineaments of earlier worlds staring to fade from view.[45] For Chaudhuri, the challenge is to capture the creative possibilities of this period even as we pay due attention to the imminent disappearance of other lived possibilities under the conditions of an emerging imperial system. In other words, there is no attempt to divert our gaze from the onset of colonialism, but there is instead a desire to set the story of early colonialism against the backdrop of a period subject to other forces of change. Chaudhuri, like Chatterjee, makes it clear that our goal should be not to contrast the colonial with the precolonial, but to historicize the colonial itself with greater precision.

The view of things in 1880 was significantly different from the view of things in 1780, 1815, or even 1830.[46] If we are to recover the particular character of the early colonial moment, we must be attentive to the distinctive factors of economy, social intercourse, and intellectual life that affected such things as the creation of new public associations, the acquisition of authority within new civic spaces, or the maintenance of personal and professional relationships with a diverse range of contemporaries, South Asian and European. To do this we must attend to the emergence of new norms, new institutions, and new modes of sociality; and we must be mindful of the subtle passing away of equally distinctive and nontrivial forms of premodern social life, religion, and expressive culture.[47] The distinctiveness and the transiency of these forms of life can be illustrated by looking at an important early colonial space, the Calcutta Town Hall.

In the early nineteenth century, South Asian intellectuals in places like Calcutta evinced optimism about the providential character of

British rule; they were eager to think out loud about new possibilities that might flow from the opening of India to the world of free trade and liberalism. During this period Calcutta was a crucible for the exploration of novel and exciting possibilities in relation to political organization, public activity, commercial success, and general social interaction. Partha Chatterjee has demonstrated in a compelling way how a space like the Calcutta Town Hall became a kind of multicultural forum wherein the globally connected, yet locally articulated, worlds of Europeans and South Asians met, mingled, and meshed. The town hall space in this early colonial moment held out the promise of new modes of social interaction and politics. Indians and Europeans convened meetings there together; they enjoyed banquets in common; and they argued among themselves about the relative merits of proposed reforms concerning freedom of the press or the promotion of European settlement in India.[48]

Only after a series of economic and political shocks commencing in the 1830s did this rather unique world began to fracture: a global economic crisis, coupled with the local imposition of controversial new colonial legislation—not least the hated Black Acts—caused European interests and sentiments to run in conflict with those of their South Asian contemporaries and neighbors. As a result, the character of town hall gatherings necessarily changed. This once open and inclusive space came to betray new patterns of racial exclusion; shared meetings became increasingly rare. In response, local Bengali leaders gravitated to their own spaces, situated across the lines of the so-called Native Town.[49] Decades of economic downturn, followed by the shattering violence of 1857, eventually spelled the end to what we might call an era of early colonial optimism. And, just as the British after 1830 began to ascribe "cultural meaning to political domination," they simultaneously began to resort to the discourse of reform.[50]

In view of the foregoing, the discussion in these pages is structured to assist reflection on the difference between an early colonial moment that saw the creation of two dynamic new religious polities and a later colonial moment under the sway of what I call the empire of reform. It is the ongoing hegemony of the latter discursive regime that makes it so difficult to imagine the first articulation of the Swaminarayan Sampraday and the Brahmo Samaj in terms of their early colonial context. Accounts of these polities drafted from within the empire of reform encode prevailing late colonial attitudes about religion, progress, and even the nature of innovation itself. As I have shown elsewhere, when South Asian intellectuals began to work toward the articulation of new possibilities for a national future, they often sketched portraits of the past that proved most useful for distinguishing the promise of their own late colonial moment. Under the combined pressures of the belief in progress and the desire for cultural autonomy, charting new paths proved difficult without also perpetuating anxieties about an earlier colonial moment that seemed to have been compromised by patterns of cultural imitation.[51] Hoping to announce a kind of ennobling newness no longer dependent on the aping of colonial manners and values, late colonial South Asian intellectuals inadvertently made themselves complicit in framing the early colonial moment as a kind of problematic past. Some reformers, like Rammohun, were thought to have transcended the limitations of that moment, whereas others, like Sahajanand, were seen to have failed in the attempt to articulate an authentic, yet also new, Indian modernity. We have long been invited to read the story of modern Hinduism in the respective histories of these two men, strung across the space of a subcontinent, thought to be shaped by the gradual diffusion of modernity.

Exiting such chronotopic narratives requires dropping back "before reform" and thinking anew about the creation of two distinctive polities in Gujarat and Bengal. One way to do this is to destabilize our assumptions about the space-time inhabited by Sahajanand Swami and Rammohun Roy. Is it even possible to say they each operated with a consistent and unified conception of Indian national space? Does it make sense to think of them sharing a sense of an Indian homeland? Here I must part ways somewhat with Rosinka Chaudhuri, at least when it comes to thinking about another early colonial figure, the poet Henry Louis Vivian Derozio (1809–1831). Chaudhuri has suggested that in 1827, when Derozio invoked his "native land" in the poem "The Ruins of Rajmahal," it represented "one of the earliest literary expressions" of the Indian nation.[52] I read the poem—and Derozio's life more generally—less teleologically than Chaudhuri.

I would suggest that in Derozio's writings India remains as yet only an elusive and ambiguous idea at best: a "native land" but not yet a nation. India may be just coming into view for Indians at this time, but it remains as yet a shadowy thing, hung on memory and tinged with regret. And, for that matter, what would the concept of native land have meant to a marginalized Anglo-Indian poet like Derozio? Where exactly is one to locate his nation, especially when the poet forces us to toggle between a vision of past glory and radical dreams of a new dawn?[53] If anything—to trade on the title of a journal edited by Derozio—it might be best to say his remained a "kaleidoscopic" view of India—vivid and compelling to be sure, but unsettled by the shifting shapes, hues, and structures of identity, community, place, and history.[54] Derozio may seem an odd example to invoke, given the reputation he earned as mentor to the notoriously iconoclastic thinkers of Young Bengal; but I would argue that his life story as an Anglo-Indian driven from employment and often stepping carefully through various constructions of Indian space-time provides a useful reminder of the transitional character of the early colonial modern.

Much the same would have to be said of any concept of India that was operative for figures like Rammohun and Sahajanand; their India (or more properly, Bharatvarsha) could scarcely be more fixed than the fugitive native land conjured by Derozio. If Derozio's positionality vis-à-vis India seems complex and idiosyncratic, only consider the remarkable positionality of a figure like Rammohun, the precocious intellectual offshoot of a Nawabi-era service gentry family of Brahmin Hindus, who in time came to be deputed by the Mughal emperor to serve as personal envoy to the British in London. How are we to establish the contours of Rammohun's native land under such a construction? I even suggest that it is only after he reached England and delivered his testimony before Parliament on topics of Hindu law and the rights of Indian landholders—conversations shaped by global conversations about republicanism and the rights of man—that we can begin to detect a recognizable conception of India coming into view. But if this is true, then Rammohun's native land only comes into being in the discursive space created by a series of transnational conversations stretched across Europe and Asia. If he is indeed the "father of modern India," then perhaps that honorific applies only by virtue of his having helped give discursive substance to India rather than for his having defended or championed the reality of a "native India" that he and his contemporaries are supposed to have somehow already known.[55]

Partha Chatterjee has his own unique take on Rammohun's paternity in this regard. He suggests that, rather than thinking of the early colonial period in terms of the birth of modern India, we might just as well employ the language of death. As Chatterjee puts it, Rammohun's untimely death in Bristol in 1833 could in fact be viewed as marking the "unsung end" of the early colonial modern.[56] His point is not to mourn the tragic loss of a modern leader but to prompt reflection on the passing of other possible futures for an India that had yet to be. Chatterjee points in particular to the ultimate fate of Rammohun's republicanism and anti-absolutism. The South Asian prospects for such political futures were drastically constrained by the rise of the colonial modern in the decades after the 1830s, as indicated above. The period after Rammohun's death in 1833 saw the British achieve final paramountcy over the subcontinent, with the company state increasingly engaged in mustering the "symbols and practices of sovereignty" that would come to undergird the imperial Raj.[57] If Rammohun held any claim to paternity, it was only to be granted to him posthumously and from within another era and episteme, which I refer to as the empire of reform.

India before India

It seems indisputable that in their youth both Sahajanand and Rammohun would have formed fairly concrete ideas about the places they lived, not to mention more inchoate but nonetheless compelling images of far-off places and foreign customs. Bayly's work suggests how vibrant were the networks of communication spread like skeins across regions like Awadh (Sahajanand's birthplace) and Bengal. Surely, as children born into literate communities, both young boys would have learned the names of sacred places and even far-off countries, not least those lands that were said to constitute the Bharatvarsha of the Sanskritic cosmopolis. We can imagine that both boys learned to associate distant places

with various myths and legends they had heard recounted from the
Epics, Puranas, and other vernacular traditions popular in their homes.
Beyond this it is difficult to be more specific, especially in Sahajanand's
case, for which we are largely dependent on hagiography.

In Rammohun's case we have more concrete, if not always consistent,
evidence regarding his early experience of Bengal and the subcontinent.
Records from his public life allow us to see how he responded to early
colonial transformations, to consider how his travels affected the trajectory of his career, and to appreciate the nature of his own creative responses to changes occurring in northern and eastern India. Furthermore, whereas Sahajanand hailed from a modest background,
Rammohun's family demonstrated a measure of economic and political
influence over successive generations, even if their fortunes had begun
to shift noticeably during the course of the eighteenth century. Finally,
while both Sahajanand and Rammohun benefited from contact with
early colonial actors in Gujarat and Bengal, the evidence for Rammohun's engagement is far more extensive and often forthright. For instance, late in life, while looking back on the time he spent traveling
throughout different "countries," he famously commented on feeling a
"great aversion" toward "the establishment of the British power in
India."[58]

Rammohun's use of the word "countries" in this passage is worth
noting, especially as juxtaposed with his reference to British power in
"India." What is the relationship between those countries he visited and
the India he comments on here? For one thing, it seems clear that Rammohun uses the word "country" to translate the Indic concept of *desh*
(Sanskrit, *desha*), which in either Sanskrit or Bengali might connote a
territory, a cultural region, or even a country. Thus Bengal would constitute a *desh*, just as would Gujarat—two regions Rammohun would
have situated within the "bounds of Hindoostan."[59] At the same time, a
term like *desh* could be applied to regions generally understood (even
by Rammohun) to lie outside the bounds of Hindoostan proper, regions
such as Nepal, Bhutan, or Tibet. And bear in mind that it seems as if
Rammohun traveled through portions of each of those Himalayan regions. Whether he ever reached Assam we cannot say, but in Rammo-

hun's day Assam would also have been considered external to Hindoostan, even if today it names a state within the Indian national republic. Put simply, Rammohun's India was conceptually both larger and smaller than what we think of as India today.

The feats of imperial and nationalist cartographic imagination that supported the construction first of British India and, later, of the independent Indian nation-state were of course many and contested; the imagining of modern India has involved (and continues to involve) the recognition and the suppression of other "countries" within its own borders: witness the different status within the Indian Union accorded to regionally situated ethnic groups like the Nagas and the Gorkhas. Scholarship since the 1990s has helped open up the processes of imagination, contestation, celebration, and denial that have attended the ongoing mapping of modern India.[60]

Much of this work is oriented in relation to developments during the late colonial period, when the likes of Lord Curzon, Swadeshi agitators, and revolutionaries, not to mention newly proclaimed devotees of Mother India (Bharat-Mata) helped consolidate the spatial articulation of modern India.[61] But by dropping back to the era of Sahajanand and Rammohun we have an opportunity to consider chronoscapes less oriented in relation to the Indian nation; this is our chance to allow Sahajanand and Rammohun to be homeless, untethered to history with borders.[62]

Among the most generative of premodern sources behind early colonial understandings of India would be the classical idea of Bharat-varsha. Both Sahajanand and Rammohun drew on the idea of Bharat-varsha to think about their worlds (sometimes invoking cognate terms such as Bharata-khanda or Bharata-Bhumi). As noted already, both men were Brahmins who had been schooled in the literature and myths of the Sanskrit *shastras*; and seemingly both found the concept of Bharat-varsha a natural one to employ. But what did it connote for them? With roots in the Epics and Puranas, the category speaks to an overarching, if nonempirical, cosmography, advanced in terms of a vast chronotope of worlds, continents, and eons (in Sanskrit, *lokas*, *dvipas*, and *yugas*, respectively).[63] We can see how useful such categories proved to be for

Sahajanand when it came time to establish the Puranic bona fides of his own new polity; likewise Rammohun could invoke them when making sense of the countries and regions of Hindoostan.[64]

It seems safe to say that when Sahajanand (then known by his boyhood name of Ghanashyam) left his family home near Ayodhya to take up a life of wandering, he did not set off in search of "India." For him, to be born a human being in Bharatvarsha would have constituted a precious blessing; moving through this quasi-mythic realm offered Nilakantha (the renunciant name taken by Ghanashyam after leaving home) the opportunity to seek out and learn from a variety of holy people (*sants*) at celebrated sacred sites, be they temples, ashrams, mountains, rivers, or hot springs. And if Nilakantha was not in search of India, it seems safe to say he was not motivated by the desire to commune with other "Hindus." His early colonial world would not have been parsed in this fashion. What, then, did it mean to take up a life of wandering across Bharatvarsha before the crystallization of such categories?[65]

Many of the sites to which Nilakantha is said to have traveled can certainly be located on maps of the "real world"; we can pinpoint places like Badrinath in the Himalayas, Ganga Sagar on the Bay of Bengal, or Rameshvaram at the southernmost tip of the South Asian peninsula.[66] In order to visit these sacred sites, Nilakantha would have had to wend his way through the very same "countries" mentioned by Rammohun, regions that lay both within and beyond the boundaries of Hindoostan. In his travels, no less than those of Rammohun, Nilakantha crisscrossed a landscape structured and complicated by overlapping and shifting ecological, linguistic, ethnic, political, and religious frontiers. In the text we examine in Chapter 4, the *Satsangi Jivanam,* this world manifests itself as a kind of kaleidoscopic pluriverse—a space more mythologically dense but just as elusive as Derozio's native India.

When we turn to Rammohun's life story, we can see how circumstance caused him to bring the chronoscape of Bharatvarsha into a more direct relationship with modern cartographic knowledge. This is nowhere more evident than in testimony from the final year of his life, when he communicated his understanding of India to an eager British public:

India, anciently called the "Bharata Varsha" after the name
of a monarch called "Bharata" is bounded on its south by the
sea; on the east partly by this sea, and partly by ranges of
mountains separating it from the ancient China, or rather
the countries now called Assam, Cassay and Arracan; on
the north by a lofty and extensive chain of mountains which
divides it from Tibet; and on the west partly by ranges of
mountains, separating India from the ancient Persia, and
extending towards the Western Sea, above the mouth of the
Indus, and partly by this sea itself. It lies between the 8th and
35th degrees of north latitude, and the 67th and 93rd degrees
of east longitude.[67]

What strikes one is the ease with which Rammohun adopts the conven-
tions of modern geography. He not only positions Bharatvarsha in relation to contemporary polities such as China, Persia, and Arracan (today's
northern Burma), but he even employs modern coordinates to map
Bharatvarsha against the imperial meridian. It bears noting that, by this
point in time, the study of modern geography was just beginning to establish a foothold in India, fueled by Enlightenment faith in scientific
observation and Christian zeal to "enlarge the mind" of the Hindu.[68] In
fact, one of the earliest and most influential maps of Bengal—by Major
James Rennell—had only just been published in Rammohun's own day,
the very moment when modern cartography was coming to the aid of
expanding empires.[69]

   Even so, during Rammohun's lifetime South Asia's mythic chronoscapes had not been fully displaced by cartographic knowledge, a fact
confirmed by Thomas Babington Macaulay's disparaging comments on
Puranic geography and their "seas of treacle."[70] For Macaulay, Puranic geography constituted a field for improvement, while for Rammohun the
name of Bharatvarsha still conjured memories of the legendary king
Bharata. Likewise, Rammohun found other Indic concepts like the ancient realm of Aryavarta still relevant for mapping his world. Rammohun
knew Aryavarta as a "civilized and sacred land," widely attested in the
ancient legal literature; he situated it in space as the area that extended

from the Indus River in the northwest to Allahabad in the southeast and that stretched between the foothills of Nepal and the Vindhya mountains to the south. Most importantly, Rammohun knew that the sanctity of Aryavarta was set apart from the lands of the so-called barbarian (*mleccha*). And it no doubt bears noting that Rammohun knew the realm of the barbarian might itself happen to be "included within the Bharata Varsha."[71]

In fact, Rammohun employed the distinction between Aryavarta and the land of the barbarians (Mleccha Desha) as a way to remind his readers that, for ancient geographers, knowledge of Bharatvarsha required comprehending a wide range of "divisions and subdivisions," not to mention "separate and independent kingdoms." Once again we are reminded of a kaleidoscope, even if Rammohun also periodically shifts to modern cartographic terminology to make sense of Bharatvarsha's internal disunity. At one point, speaking more as modern cartographer than Puranic sage, he attributes the cause of Bharatvarsha's repeated conquest to the fundamental fact that "parts of it" were "contiguous to foreign lands." These parts thus regularly came under the authority of other powers.[72]

In Rammohun's comments on Bharatvarsha, we get the first inkling of how Puranic notions of history and space could be factored into the articulation of a new imperial formation under the British. For Rammohun, the frontiers of Bharatvarsha mark those points in time and space when the land fell victim to conquest. He thus points first to the rise of the Mughal Empire; next he turns to the advent along the northwest frontier of the Sikh polity of Ranjit Singh in the Punjab; and finally he turns to the rise of the British East India Company. In so doing, Rammohun begins to imagine the space of Bharatvarsha in terms of the history of modern India. But for him the evidence of Puranic cosmology does not serve as a marker of primordial national unity; as we have seen, he presumes Bharatvarsha to be a complex set of kingdoms and polities extending through space and subject to repeated change.[73] Indeed, at one point he remarks that India was a country that had never been touched by "the notion of patriotism." He therefore concedes that for India to be born as a nation, it would require the consolidating force of British imperial rule, a force he notices is itself something new. As he put it, only very recently had Britain managed to cement its own "divided resources" into the new and "subsisting union" known as Great Britain.[74]

Do such passages reveal Rammohun to be India's "first and . . . greatest nation-builder"?[75] Or do we not also detect in them the passing of a kind of kaleidoscopic South Asian space? Here it is worth calling attention to a gloss Rammohun employs at one point, referring to "India, anciently called Bharata Varsha." In this bipartite phrase we have an eloquent witness to the transitional character of the early colonial moment. Hovering between Bharatvarsha and India, Rammohun and Sahajanand lived at a time when their worlds formed the backdrop for the emergence of a wide range of new political formations and religious polities; their deaths came just at the moment when the British began to more comprehensively subsume such changes under the empire of reform. Knowing this should be enough to cause us to slow down. Before slotting the accomplishments of Sahajanand and Rammohun into narratives of empire, reform, and nation-building, it is well worth pondering what they were able to accomplish as the articulators of two innovative early colonial religious polities.

2

Fluid Landscapes

I F THERE IS A kaleidoscopic quality to the space of early colonial South Asia, the same might be said about the identities of Sahajanand Swami and Rammohun Roy. They both defy easy categorization. We might of course identify them as Brahmins, but this would actually tell us very little about the varied careers, communities, and locales they inhabited. The case of Sahajanand is particularly instructive, since he acquired that particular title only after transiting through a number of other names. Beginning life as the Vaishnava boy Ghanashyam, he went on to spend years as a wandering ascetic with the Shaiva name of Nilakantha; only after settling in the community of Ramanand Swami was he initiated as Sahajanand. But even that did not completely settle his identity, since after Ramanand's death Sahajanand would be recognized as Lord Swaminarayan, the divine name by which he is worshipped today.

Each of these names encodes not just a personal history but also a set of values and practices, from bhakti religiosity to ascetic wandering, yogic training, and the promulgation of an innovative new theological outlook. Rammohun's case is scarcely more straightforward, as is made evident when one attempts to epitomize the man: Brahmin, Islamicate intellectual, polymath linguist, religious polemicist, global republican theorist, East India Company servant, friend of Unitarians, defender of Hindu theism, scriptural interpreter and translator, envoy for the emperor in Delhi, and promulgator of the Brahmo code and morality. As with Sahajanand, these identities fluctuate, morphing gradually in relation to Rammohun's movement through time and space. And as with Sahajanand, only after finally settling down does Rammohun emerge as the creative force behind a transformative new religious polity.

The discussion in this chapter responds to the importance of the dialectic of movement and settlement for understanding these men and the polities they created, the Swaminarayan Sampraday and the Brahmo Samaj. In both cases, the constitution of these new polities—articulated through the promulgation of new rules and organizational structures—followed on the establishment of significant ties within local communities and in relation to other existing forms of authority. Our thinking about these religious polities will benefit from an attempt to situate the early careers of both Sahajanand and Rammohun within the dynamic physical and discursive landscapes through which they moved as "homeless" spiritual aspirants and intellectuals. Only after moving through and learning from the early colonial landscape of South Asia would these two settle down and bring forth distinctive new religious polities. I believe the way we speak of their work should therefore reflect both dimensions of their homeless histories—that is, the time they spent as wanderers and the fact that, even after settling down, the polities they brought forth were not predicated on a bordered awareness of India as nation.

In this spirit I hope to raise a number of questions: What is the best way to understand the kinds of changes occurring in the early colonial period? What can we say, more specifically, about changes taking place in Gujarat and Bengal between roughly 1780 and 1830? And how can an appreciation of those local contexts help us rethink what Sahajanand and Rammohun each accomplished? And, most importantly, can we frame useful judgments about the sorts of developments taking place in these two regions without falling back on depictions of Bengal as the bridgehead of progressive reform and Gujarat as a wild and distant frontier? Can we, in a word, tell their stories without relying on familiar tropes of reform, awakening, and national aspiration?

Here we must remember that both Gujarat and Bengal have been freighted with their fair share of historical typologies rooted in assumptions about the dwindling power of the late Mughal Empire, not least as one moved from the imperial center in Delhi to the frontiers of Mughal rule.[1] As we have seen, such typologies used to go hand in hand with the presumption that imperial unity was achieved by overcoming pre-modern anarchy.[2] By now it should clear that we must be careful to avoid both sets of presuppositions.[3] In the discussion that follows, I avoid the binary language of center and periphery, preferring to think instead of fluid landscapes marked by multiple, fluctuating regional borders and varying types of geological, political, and cultural frontiers against which change may be charted.[4] The key question is, when we position ourselves in Gujarat or Bengal, what features of the early colonial landscape are relevant for thinking about the work accomplished by Sahajanand and Rammohun?

Ascetics, Warriors, Traders, and Pilgrims

Both Sahajanand and Rammohun were able to draw on categories of South Asian space-time to make sense of change; they would have also been attuned to a range of political and cultural boundaries; but it is not clear that they viewed their worlds or approached such frontiers with preconceptions about backwardness, decay, or anarchy. These values were the particular legacy of a kind of British imperial discourse that was only beginning to emerge in their lifetimes. And far from registering the facts on the ground, such imperial discourse grew out of British anxieties surrounding their own intervention in the economy and cultural life of South Asia. Some of these anxieties were to become full-blown imperial obsessions, as we know. Among the most relevant of such obsessions for colonial policy makers and agents of revenue extraction was the troubling figure of the rootless wanderer, the unsettled and therefore seemingly uncontrollable mendicant, trader, pilgrim, or herdsman.

For the British, one particularly troubling manifestation of such pre-colonial mobility fell under the category of "warrior ascetic."[5] Anxieties here may have been rooted in certain ground-level realities (there clearly were armed mendicants who participated in all manner of skirmishes and political battles), but the British anxieties were also to a large extent self-inflicted. These armed ascetics came to be figured as a kind of unrestrained force inimical to the interests of the East India Company. This despite the fact that armed ascetics were often recruited to fight the company's battles with local rulers. Then again, in some contexts, such as late colonial Punjab and Sind, the British actually managed to set aside their deep-seated disdain for South Asia's holy mendicants long enough to take advantage of one particular type of Muslim holy man. This was the local Pir, more especially the Pir as hereditary custodian (*sajjada nishin*) of a local shrine. As the British sought to extend their hegemony in such regions, they discovered that, with the bestowal of official recognition, the authority attached to the figure of such Pirs could be yoked to the purpose of ensuring local stability.[6] But as Katherine Ewing has shown, even when the British took advantage of figures like the Pirs, when the latter were figured as valued loyal chieftains, it necessarily furthered the kind of mind-set in which other forms of religious mendicancy were viewed as suspect and deviant.[7]

We can actually take advantage of the anxieties swirling around the figure of the religious wanderer to shed some light on the character of religious life in early colonial South Asia, provided we work carefully to interrogate key tropes by which the British sought to control such mobility. In the present context, such an exercise is especially important because the early careers of both Sahajanand and Rammohun were structured in terms of extensive movement. If we are to situate them in their lived worlds and the discursive landscapes through which they moved, we must try to un-think some of the discursive figurations that eventually came to structure reflection on modern Hinduism. Here, the Indian ascetic wanderer comes to our aid by providing a frame of reference against which to challenge standard interpretations of Sahajanand and Rammohun. We can take what we know about the fluid world of renouncers, warriors, and other itinerant actors to plant both Sahajanand and Rammohun in somewhat less familiar backdrops. We can ask, what looks different about their careers if we focus on such themes as asceticism, pilgrimage, and the fluidity of premodern religious boundaries?

We know that as young men both Sahajanand and Rammohun pressed well beyond the frontiers of their home environments, each of them apparently traversing large swaths of the Gangetic valley and the Himalayas and even venturing (if we are to believe Sahajanand's biographers) as far as Rameshvaram in South India. Instead of reading such movement as evidence of sui generis spiritual heroism—as is especially customary in contemporary biographies within the Swaminarayan community—we might instead view such travels as a kind of unscripted and even inadvertent training program for prospective religious leaders. I say this because it would seem that by virtue of their travels, both Sahajanand and Rammohun came to learn new spiritual techniques and doctrines, to hone considerable skills at debate, and to solidify modes of spiritual mastery that would allow them to step forward as lords among their peers. In Chapter 3 I consider the importance of such lordship for the articulation of authority within a new religious polity, but for now it is enough to note that renunciant gurus and ascetics are even today often addressed using titles that bespeak royalty, not least that of Maharaj, or Great Ruler. What is more, the parallel between spiritual and worldly rule is deeply rooted in Indic traditions, as biographies of great figures like the Buddha and Mahavira confirm. Even if it is true that Rammohun was never explicitly revered as a guru, it is worth noting that he has long gone by the title Raja, which is to say, king.[8] A key point in the argument of Chapter 3 and the book as a whole is that both Sahajanand and Rammohun can be viewed as lords over new religious polities, polities that were themselves articulated in relation to the lordship these two men had come to acquire through their considerable wanderings.[9]

The goal of this chapter is to explore the kinds of background conditions during the early colonial era that would have supported the emergence of Sahajanand and Rammohun as new lords and masters. Theirs were times of extensive disruption, times that witnessed the rise of new modes of individual behavior, community formation, and political agency. Wars and famine, often triggered by East India Company intervention, led to the dislocation of farming families even as it opened up new avenues for others who were able to move: traders, pastoralists, caravan drivers, and religious leaders. And, much to the chagrin of the British, the early colonial moment saw the efflorescence of religious wandering, as bands of renouncers, yogis, and warrior ascetics sought to exercise and contest power—economic, political, and religious. All this disruption, mobility, and conflict created the conditions for discovery and innovation, for learning new truths about the world, and for articulating new values, rituals, and modes of social organization that held the promise of both spiritual solace and worldly success. From the peregrinations of Sahajanand and Rammohun through the early colonial world would come the articulation of two of the most innovative and durable religious polities in modern India.

Unsettling Mobility

It served the British well to think of both Gujarat and Bengal as frontiers because, when envisioned in this way, both regions could be deployed as spatiotemporal markers of the progress of empire. British rule was registered as the outward expansion of an ordered, disciplined, and benevolent government, and temporal schemes served spatial desires.[10] Central to the growing discourse of rule was the idea of the collapse or "twilight" of the Mughal Empire.[11] When paired with rhetoric around the evils of "Asiatic despotism," the idea of Mughal decline allowed the new imperial power to boast a benevolent mode of stabilizing authority.[12] Stability was the goal, and in its way stood the figure of the bandit, criminal, or warrior ascetic.

British concerns surrounding such figures began to spike in the late eighteenth century, as the first efforts were launched at land settlement and revenue collection. Official records attest to increasing anxiety over a range of purportedly destabilizing actors, from itinerant peddlers and long-distance traders to all manner of well-established religious orders and mendicant groups, these last registered under such names as Fakir, Sunnasee, or Gosain (from the vernacular terms *faqir, sannyasi,* and *gosain*). In the interests of security and ease of revenue extraction, the British goal became to settle—if not outright suppress—such mobile groups.[13] Official rhetoric played on a variety of fears useful for stigmatizing religious itinerants, beginning with the obvious fact of the nakedness of groups like the Naga Sannyasis (the term *naga* indicating their lack of clothing).

What is often obscured by the rhetorical fog around such groups is the fact that the British often owed their success to a canny manipulation of renunciant orders like the Nagas, Dasnamis, and Gosains. Groups like these were useful for consolidating British power because, on the one hand, far from being lawless brigands, they often were skilled and fearless fighters. The British were thus not averse to engaging them to fight their battles. On the other hand, far from being navel-gazing yogis, many of the early colonial renunciant orders were deeply invested in such occupations as trade, moneylending, and banking.[14] It was in the British interests to disempower such actors, profiting by their own intrusion into local economies. Overall one might say that the key to British figurings of the mendicant was to make a Protestant virtue out of economic necessity—they framed the Fakir as evidence of the errors of "self-justifying pride" even as they slaked their own thirst for profit.[15]

What the British could not afford to acknowledge was that the world of renunciation in South Asia was never one of anarchy and antisocial behavior; rather, it encoded and promulgated widely shared values about social life, ritual, and religious community. As the recent ethnographic work of Sondra Hausner has demonstrated, religious wandering is very much an organized, social behavior.[16] Indeed, the same Naga and Dasnami ascetic armies that so unnerved early British administrators could be taken as the very ideal-type of a premodern religious polity. Such groups would be known locally as *sampraday*, a widespread word connoting an organization recruiting followers into an initiatory community framed in terms of particular doctrines, ritual practices, and social norms. Even though leadership by a guru and modes of asceticism were distinctive to such *sampraday*, collective life and individual behavior nonetheless often involved the pursuit of wealth and patronage, not to mention the devoted service of vast communities of lay supporters. The figure of the lone renouncer is thus more often than not a bit of Orientalist fiction; even the most isolated of such figures remained linked by initiation and guru reverence to larger institutional and social structures.

The institutional and sectarian diversity among the many renunciant and monastic orders encountered by the British is suggested by the range of terminology in use in early colonial South Asia: Gosains, Bairagis, Naths, Udasins, Nagas, Fakirs, Dasnamis—not to mention other assorted yogis, babas, Kaulas, and Tantrikas. It is actually rather difficult to provide an overarching characterization that does justice to the spectrum of ideologies and practices encoded in names like these. Some groups, such as the Dasnami Sampraday ("the Order of the Ten Names"), moved regularly among widely scattered but settled monastic sites, or *mathas*; each of these groups boasted its own structures of authority, monastic regulations, and spiritual practice. While groups like the Dasnamis promoted the philosophy of Advaita Vedanta associated with the teachings of Shankaracharya, orders like the Nath Sampraday fostered more esoteric practices of yoga, which they traced to founding figures like Gorakhnath. Meanwhile, if many renouncers chose to adopt Shaiva or Vaishnava sectarian identities, others eschewed such markers of group affiliation, sometimes showing greatest allegiance to the unique teachings of a single guru or Pir. In the end, even if the boundaries of renunciant institutions were often carefully defined and monitored (particularly in early colonial texts like the *mathamnayas* of the Dasnamis), at the level of practice, things remained fluid, if not kaleidoscopic.[17] For instance, although the term Udasin often denoted a Sikh renouncer in particular, it could just as easily refer to any renouncer who was indifferent (*udasin*) to "worldly vicissitudes."[18]

Among renouncers, indifference to worldly life often ran parallel to the maintenance of worldly relationships. Some renouncers married, while others had children, both natural and adopted. Even those who remained celibate were nonetheless enmeshed in social fabrics; they took initiation into orders with long-standing rules for handling such issues as initiation, postmortem rites, and the transmission of monastic wealth and authority.[19] Meanwhile, as already suggested, many ascetic communities engaged in long-distance trade and moneylending, not to mention the arts of warfare and soldiering. Even when an individual renouncer's life was oriented around spiritual wandering and pilgrimage to holy sites, this did not necessarily entail living aloof from the world. No less than pilgrims and traders, holy men traveled the roadways, gathered at the bathing places, and rested in the shelters constructed by benevolent rulers. Frequently they traveled in groups, both for security and for the pleasures of shared experience. And as they traveled they carried news and information, sharing stories about holy sites, praising local patrons, trading spiritual genealogies, and exchanging songs. In a word, these early colonial renouncers were active and knowing agents fully vested in the economic, social, and political transformations of the worlds through which they moved.[20]

As they traversed the countryside, renouncers and their corporate bodies established enduring relationships with local rulers and communities. Beyond initiating new disciples or teaching lay followers, these relationships might involve handling bills of exchange, extracting tithes, trading with local merchants, or establishing new monasteries, temples, and schools. The obvious corollary was that renunciants could scarcely remain aloof from the demands of the communities they served, let alone the rulers who patronized them. They were thus often drawn into military campaigns on behalf of a local ruling family or into tax-collection for a powerful landlord. Villagers and poor peasants often looked to the renunciant orders for physical protection along with relief from periodic financial stress. It would have been incumbent on religious leaders to cultivate some kind of fruitful symbiosis with the local communities in which they lived or to which they returned on a seasonal basis. Those communities were likely to be most welcoming when the same renunciant polities were seen to bring real benefits. Conversely, by integrating themselves within the spiritual and economic worlds of local communities, renunciant orders hoped to realize the fruition of their own goals.[21]

Sahajanand's success on arriving in Gujarat after many years of wandering almost certainly derived from his ability to recognize and respond to such expectations. In Kathiawar he found a landscape structured in relation to different religious communities such as the Vallabha Sampraday and of course Ramanand Swami's Uddhava Sampraday. In fact, we are told that when Nilakantha initially encountered the group of renouncers belonging to Ramanand's *sampraday*, they informed him that their guru was currently away on business in another town. This may have been meant to indicate nothing more than the business of maintaining the security and integrity of the *sampraday*, but even that sort of work was what the leader of a religious polity would be expected to perform by advancing productive relationships with local patrons and communities. It is a useful reminder that the world of renunciation required work of all kinds to succeed and necessitated the maintenance of a range of relationships.

As the East India Company began to penetrate local markets in places like Gujarat and Bengal, it necessarily came into competition with the interests and investments of these same ascetic orders, their patrons, and their clients. This is one way to understand the reports of conflicts that had already begun to figure in the records as early as the 1770s in places like Bihar and northern Bengal.[22] As a result of such conflict, local economies were increasingly destabilized and poor peasants were often the first to suffer. Some of the wealthier monastic groups responded by fortifying their holdings and expanding their armies. The result was that during the last quarter of the eighteenth century the overall incidence of itinerancy was amplified. And as increasingly large groups of warrior-ascetics pledged their services to the defense of particular ruling polities, the company fought back, often through open warfare. Such a heated political landscape helped fuel violent succession struggles in regional kingdoms such as Koch Bihar in northern Bengal, where the British and other ascetic warriors found themselves embroiled in conflict.

Thus, far from engaging a moribund or decaying socioeconomic world, the British came face-to-face with long-established and still vital patterns of statecraft, trade, and religion. Their recourse—to tropes of decay and narratives of reform—speaks to their attempt to gain the upper hand in a dynamic and conflict-ridden world. Indeed, colonial-era accounts often breathe an air of jealousy; local company agents reported being outwitted by groups of sannyasis who knew better how to negotiate the local terrain and who proved skilled at eluding official tariffs, fees, and transport costs. Angry officials took umbrage at the tactics of these "sturdy beggars" who challenged them along their trading frontiers.[23] Over time the ascetic came to be represented as no better than a plunderer and extortionist, someone who preyed on an ignorant and helpless population.

Indrani Chatterjee has registered the cost of such colonial misreading of the landscape and the suppression of a vital monastic political economy that went with it.[24] Her work reveals what happened when cultures of religious itinerancy, monastic organization, and domestic life came into conflict with imperial notions of monotheistic religious truth and claims for secular government. That we struggle today to recover the early colonial worlds of "monastic governmentality" is one reminder of the

disciplined forgetting at the core of a ruling epistemology.[25] Here Chatterjee confirms a point stressed earlier when discussing the work of Michael Shapiro: powerful "structures of nonrecognition" are built into
modernity's "moral geography."[26] It is as if the mental maps bequeathed
to us by the imperial British have no spaces to accommodate the lived
worlds of early colonial actors, from householders and ascetics to women,
traders, and vernacular religious specialists. Only by reminding ourselves of the creative and deeply political activities of renunciants in early
colonial South Asia can we begin to rethink the history of South Asian
religion outside the frameworks of imperial reform.

It is worth noting that Chatterjee suggestively (if briefly) introduces
Rammohun Roy into this landscape. While he was never a renouncer,
his early career was shaped by interaction with the world of renunciant
religion, learning, and monastic life. His first spiritual teacher was a holy
man known as Hariharananda Nath Tirthaswami.[27] Hariharananda
had been born into a family of Sanskrit scholars in rural Bengal in 1752.[28]
While the title Tirtha suggests he had taken initiation into the Dasnami Sampraday, Hariharananda later took ordination as an Avadhuta
ascetic; one of his other designations was Kulavadhuta, which is to say
a practitioner of Tantrism. Later on I will have more to say about Hariharananda, especially since he was most likely the one who initiated
Rammohun into Tantrism. For now it is worth noting that, like so
many other renouncers, Hariharananda maintained ties to his family;
his younger brother Ramchandra Vidyavagish would also become one
of Rammohun's close colleagues. From the records we catch only a
glimpse of the monastic governmentality structuring the lives of men
like Hariharananda and Ramchandra, but their intimate alliance
with Rammohun and the support it provided for the articulation of his
own claims of religious mastery cannot be stressed enough. We return
to this in Chapter 7.

For now it is enough to emphasize that these are just the sorts of patterns we should keep in mind when thinking about the transformation
of religion in early colonial Gujarat and Bengal. British approaches to
law, property, revenue collection, and administration may have diverged
in these two regions, but renunciant communities—and the larger economies within which they flourished—were an important dimension of

religious life in both regions.[29] In the case of Sahajanand and Rammohun, we encounter individuals whose lives were shaped by dominant patterns of religious itinerancy, initiatory movements, and the social networks they sustained. In Chapters 4 and 5 we explore how both
men drew on their experience moving around the subcontinent to accrue valuable—if divergent—sorts of religious mastery; we shall come
to appreciate the contribution of their years of wandering to the constitution of new religious polities under their lordships. We shall also come
to see, in Chapters 6 and 7, what transpired when these two wanderers
each made a choice to settle down in one place and begin building something new. However, before we come to that, we should ask, what can
be said about the worlds of Gujarat and Bengal in which they eventually settled?

Rethinking Decay

Assumptions about precolonial social chaos in Gujarat are central in
standard accounts of the Swaminarayan Sampraday.[30] Invariably, the advent of Sahajanand is understood in terms of the providential appearance of a benevolent social reformer at a time when Gujarat was at the
nadir of moral decay, religious superstition, and peasant criminality. In
such narratives, the promulgation of Swaminarayan teachings is thought
to have set in motion the region's transition to peace and prosperity.
There is no need to begrudge Swaminarayanis their pride in Sahajanand,
but as scholars it behooves us to think through the wider implications
of such accounts. Obviously we can begin by calling attention to the
work done by colonial-era frameworks, in which progress associated
with religious reform necessarily depends on a priori evidence of decay.

For the British, standard scenarios of precolonial anarchy bolstered
claims for imposing rational and benevolent rule and for ushering in
what came to be celebrated in Gujarat as Pax Britannica.[31] For nationalist historians inspired by dreams of social progress, enlightenment,
and national awakening, it was equally handy to associate colonial-era
reforms by figures like Sahajanand with the defeat of superstition, social evils, and all manner of religious oppression that went by the name

of priestcraft.[32] But as I have argued elsewhere, what works well to support nationalist aspiration tends to work less well as historical analysis.[33] It takes nothing away from Swaminarayani admiration for Sahajanand if we pause to reconsider some of these narrative constructions.

The British were not wrong in finding evidence of political contestation and even warfare in Gujarat; but they clearly also appreciated the advantages that came from highlighting signs of pervasive chaos and conflict. If influential British images of social decay in places like Gujarat were produced out of an imperial positionality that favored their own self-presentation as emerging frontier masters and the bestowers of peace and order, they were also predicated on evidence that the British themselves may have misunderstood. As Muzaffar Alam has observed, the Mughal chronicles to which the British turned for help in understanding local affairs may have often seemed, on the face of things, to support perceptions of anarchy and decline. However, what the British failed to appreciate was that the goal of such texts was not to provide objective historical data; rather, they reflected the anxieties of certain landed gentry who had thrived under Mughal rule but who were beginning to see their monopoly over resources challenged by new political actors.[34] Thus when the chroniclers spoke of "upheaval" (*inqilab*) in a region, what they gestured to was not an economy in collapse but, if anything, the rise of influential new culture brokers who threatened the once-comfortable status quo. What the British failed to appreciate was that money was flowing and artists were innovating, even if such creativity was being channeled along new pathways. Thus by drawing selectively on such sources to confirm their predetermined assumptions about the need for change, the British queered the pitch. Generations have followed the same misdirection.

Gujarat

We thus need to be both cautious and also somewhat creative in how we go about framing the emergence of groups like the Swaminarayan Sampraday in the context of early colonial Gujarat. Attention to the discursive work done by colonial-era sources (not to mention the chronicles they often uncritically relied on) requires thinking anew about the positionality and interests of the various authors of such sources. An exemplary effort has been made in this direction by Harald Tambs-Lyche, who has questioned standard accounts of lawlessness, violence, and criminality in precolonial Gujarat. As he notes, a great deal depends on the angle from which one views the scene.

Take the case of the so-called criminal castes and tribes of early modern Gujarat, groups like the Kathis, Kolis, and Dangs. Viewed through the lens of imperial law and order, the British framed the behavior of such groups as criminal and deviant. Viewed in terms of indigenous norms of warrior culture, however, the wildness of such groups is no objective marker of deviance; rather wildness could be said to constitute an "integral part of the political order."[35] As Tambs-Lyche argues, warriors are not wild because they are criminal; they are wild because wildness frightens the enemy and occasions awe. There is thus no need to inscribe wildness into the nature of the "tribal."[36] Tambs-Lyche crucially stresses that, while warrior wildness is often associated with so-called tribal groups like the Dangs, it was just as common among other groups, including Rajputs, Marathas, and Muslim mercenaries.[37] In all these cases, cultures of masculine warrior prowess represented a way to articulate political power. The behavior of such actors may seem "unruly" from the vantage point of settled interests, but this does not make them "uncivilized."[38]

As in the case of British recourse to Mughal chronicles, we must reckon with the interests that tended to shape dominant historical narratives. Tambs-Lyche notes that groups like Brahmins or Banias (merchants) in Gujarat were invested in exercising control over actors they saw gaining new footing in the local political economy. There is no need to presume the moral superiority of the Brahmin or Bania groups; like the category of civilized behavior, such terms are relative. If anything, we should think in terms of expediency. For Brahmins there were benefits to be had by casting their rivals—like Rajput chieftains—in the guise of socially pernicious actors. Looking at Saurashtra, Tambs-Lyche suggests it was the settled merchant communities in the region who began to prosper with the advent of new economic possibilities; not coincidentally, these merchant groups also helped perpetuate now-familiar narratives about premodern Gujarat as "torn apart" by feudal warfare and in need of a reformer's message.[39]

The trope of progressive reform, as found in accounts of Sahajanand's advent, papers over these realities, preventing us from developing more reliable models to explain how a new polity like the Swaminarayan Sampraday was able to insert itself into the landscape. In Sahajanand's case we need to set aside presuppositions about decay and think instead about his astute negotiation of local possibilities. We know that by the late eighteenth century the Vallabhites (followers of the devotional leader Vallabhacharya) had acquired a significant presence within Gujarati merchant communities. If we want to know how Sahajanand was able to succeed in Gujarat, it makes sense to consider how he worked to position his new Sampraday in relation to prominent groups like the Vallabhites. This he did in part by reaching out to new constituencies, not least the same supposedly unruly and criminal Kathis of Saurashtra (or Kathiawar) and the Koli and Kanbi peasants of central Gujarat.[40] Conversely, by affiliating themselves to Sahajanand's new Sampraday, groups like these found valuable resources for advancing their own efforts at improved social status and increased political influence.

Attention to the dynamic political space of Saurashtra is thus more illuminating than is recourse to blanket narratives of reform. If Sahajanand entered the larger Gujarati region as an unknown wandering renunciant named Nilakantha, his efforts to advance a new polity in western India would have required him to adopt a conscious strategy of emplacement. Like the sacred, a religious polity is not something given but made; it needs to be situated and placed in the world.[41] Hagiography may attribute the origin and success of the Swaminarayan Sampraday to Sahajanand's transcendent powers as guru and deity, but the historian should look instead to the landscape of Gujarat and to the work Sahajanand accomplished in parlaying subregional loyalties and caste dynamics into a base for his new polity. If the Vallabhites had already established themselves in central Gujarat, Sahajanand must have realized he would need to focus on the peripheral region of Saurashtra to gain a foothold for his polity.[42] This helps explain the nature and purpose of his work there with Kathi chieftains such as Dada Khachar of Gadhada.

In the relationship between Sahajanand and Dada Khachar we can gain some insight into the process through which an aspiring religious lord could align himself with—and draw on the authority of—a local ruling figure. It is worth noting that 70 percent of the discourses recorded in the *Vachanamrut* were preached by Sahajanand in the courtyard of Dada Khachar's residence in Saurashtra.[43] The significance of the setting is evident, as the chieftain welcomes the guru into his *darbar*, or court, and provides him with an occasion to display his glory, his wisdom, and his grace. Notably, every discourse commences with a description that highlights Sahajanand's self-presentation as a kind of ruling lord. Thus, the earliest recorded discourse in the *Vachanamrut* depicts Sahajanand (or Shriji Maharaj, as he is called in the text) seated in the residential hall that Dada Khachar has provided for Sahajanand and his sadhus. Notice how the depiction of Sahajanand emphasizes the symbolism of ruling authority:

> On the morning of Maha *sudi* 8, Samvat 1876 [23 Jan-
> uary 1820], Shriji Maharaj was sitting facing west on a large,
> decorated cot on the platform under the neem tree in front of
> the mandir of Shri Vasudev-Narayan in Dada Khachar's
> *darbar* in Gadhada. He was wearing a white *khes* and had
> covered Himself with a white cotton cloth. Also, He had tied a
> white *pagh* around his head and had tied a *bokani* with one
> end of the *pagh*. A garland of white flowers decorated the *pagh*
> as well.[44]

One cannot help but be struck by the way Sahajanand is decked out in all the paraphernalia of ruling authority—from a throne established on the temple veranda to a royal turban (*pagh*) and garland of flowers.[45]

Sahajanand's lordship was thus not merely a matter of devotional theology; it spoke to a kind of emerging mastery over a local polity, itself akin to a royal court. That respect for his mastery would eventually extend to claims about his ability to pacify even the wild tribes of Saurashtra surely helped amplify local admiration for the new guru and his Sampraday; this in fact became one dimension of his reputation that caught the attention of British actors in Gujarat, as we shall see. The point is, there is no need to invoke the discourse of reform to make sense of the advent of Sahajanand or the early success of his efforts. If anything, it makes more sense to consider the canny way Sahajanand translated an aura of personal charisma and a regimen of disciplined leadership over the Uddhava Sampraday into the articulation of an entirely new polity by the name of the Swaminarayan Sampraday. Reform-based discourse would have us focus on the theological content of his message or the purity of his moral life, but attention to conditions on the ground in Gujarat leads us to ponder the significance of his lordly performances in contexts like Dada Khachar's *darbar*. Ultimately, then, if one were to ask why his efforts first gained momentum in Kathiawar, the answer is clear: because it was a political space within which his mastery could be articulated.[46]

Standard accounts tend to place a great deal of emphasis on Sahajanand's apparent success at persuading the British to provide aid to suffering chieftains in Saurashtra.[47] Typically this is adduced as evidence of a fundamental congruency between the British desire to advance peace and improve affairs in the region and Sahajanand's own moral mission. That is, we are asked to ponder the confluence of two reformist programs. However, in light of the foregoing it is reasonable to ask whether another narrative could be framed around the consolidation and projection of power in Gujarat by two up-and-coming polities—the East India Company and the Swaminarayan Sampraday. We do not have to endorse the story of a unified campaign of reform to be able to appreciate that it was by cultivating useful relationships with the British in Gujarat that Sahajanand was able to advance his work. Once the parvenu holy man began to consolidate his religious authority, would it not have made good political sense to seek accommodation with the rapidly expanding polity of the East India Company?

None of this is meant to undercut the fact that western India had seen its fair share of political instability and had witnessed shifting lines of political power since the death of Aurangzeb in 1707. Instead, it is to recognize that, amid the inevitable sparring among Rajput chieftaincies and Kathi chieftains in the region, the arrival of Dutch and English traders, and the repeated and disruptive incursions of the Marathas during the first half of the century, conditions had been created that tended to promote new developments in the areas of trade, commerce, and communications. If the stability of coastal centers had been somewhat diminished during the early decades of the eighteenth century because of shifting trade patterns throughout the Arabian Sea, conditions were to change once again after the British gained control of coastal Surat in 1759. In any case, overland routes back to heartland cities like Agra remained vital for the health of trade in the region. And so, by the latter half of the eighteenth century, as Ghulam Nadri has noted, the center of gravity for transport and trade had gradually shifted inland from Surat to cities like Ahmedabad.[48]

During Sahajanand's day the religious economy of Gujarat was flush with different "religious franchises," all benefiting from the dynamism of a coastal trading environment.[49] The expanded role of merchant groups in cities like Surat and Ahmedabad, along with the creation of what are sometimes termed Anglo-Bania alliances, also had a transformative impact in this regard.[50] Many low-caste peasant groups had begun to improve their economic conditions, and women were beginning to gain greater access to religious life in the process.[51] At the same time, the non-sacrificial, Vaishnava devotional (*bhakti*) ethos of merchant communities like the Vallabhites began to call into question the practices of local goddess cults (not least blood sacrifice) and the ritual polities around them that tended to be grounded in the norms of Rajput ruling culture.[52] Of particular importance was the Vallabhite ethos of self-surrender and inner-worldly asceticism, which famously found an affinity with the lifestyles of emerging mercantile groups in urban centers like Ahmedabad. This was the overall environment within which Sahajanand needed to situate his new polity, one in which bhakti-inflected religiosity rubbed shoulders with the religious worlds of a range of other groups including Rajputs, Jains, and Muslims.[53]

The prominence of Vallabhite concerns over Rajput sacrificial religion should further remind us that Sahajanand's oft-touted rejection of goddess worship and sacrifice was nothing particularly unique or visionary. And, in any case, once one chooses to exit from the self-congratulatory narrative of Swaminarayan reform as the progressive rejection of cruder forms of religion, there is no reason to presume that sacrificial religion was necessarily always destined to be reformed. In contrast to such teleological thinking (with its debt to deep-seated Protestant values), we might just as easily think of two structuring frameworks that helped make sense of local religious life at the time: mercantilist-Vaishnavism and Rajput-Shaktism.[54] Only after—and precisely because of—economic gains made by merchant groups in the early colonial period could groups like the Vallabhas (and latterly the Swaminarayanis) begin to advance their attacks on goddess worship and Rajput theology. Once again the historian might wish to be cautious about valorizing such developments as reforms in the name of Brahmanic purity or true Vaishnavism.

The point is, it makes very good sense to argue that the Sampraday's eventual success in Gujarat depended on taking advantage of emerging colonial opportunities. Rather than thinking of Sahajanand and his new followers as radical change agents, we might actually invoke the idea of "avoidance protest," as developed by Douglas Haynes. As Haynes demonstrates, merchant groups in early colonial Surat were historically and professionally risk-averse; they preferred to pursue social gains using low-profile methods that took advantage of, but did not visibly contest, the changing political economy of the region.[55] To what degree might we say Sahajanand's success was predicated on similar strategies of cautious change rather than unflinching reformist zeal?

Consider the notoriously ambiguous position adopted by Sahajanand on the issues of caste and equality. On one level, as a proponent of bhakti religion, one expects to find in Sahajanand's teaching a measure of social leveling. He tended to employ the dichotomy between body and soul as a way to dismiss caste as simply a matter of embodiment; he urged his followers to adopt a transcendent perspective of spiritual equality. And yet on another level, he endorsed conformity to existing social norms and counseled respect for caste distinctions. In this way he could avoid a measure of conflict, successfully accommodating Vaishya / Bania merchant egalitarianism without challenging conservative Brahmanic values. As Bayly put it, this is precisely how Sahajanand made his peace with Gujarati society.[56] If anything, then, Swaminarayan religion is less a reform of traditional Hinduism and more a "powerful and partially modernized organizational expression" of it.[57]

Finally, when thinking of Sahajanand in Gujarat, emphasis should be on the plural nature of the landscape and less on anodyne invocations of religious pluralism; our goal should be to understand how actors and institutions worked to address particular needs, articulate particular ideologies, and frame particular codes of conduct for living within a multiscalar, early colonial world. Such plurality may have occasioned competition among religious franchises, but this need not be construed as communal conflict. We might better think of a scalar array of polities that existed in overlapping, sometimes congruent, sometimes competing modalities. A local ruler or chieftain was free to endow a Hindu temple and a Muslim madrasa; both forms of largesse represented viable means for articulating sovereignty. Likewise, deity temples or the tombs of local saints (*dargahs*) existed within a single landscape and served multiple community, caste, class, and devotional identities. It is precisely the discursive legacy of the empire of reform that has caused us to forget this pluriform, fluid, and non-identitarian world of early colonial religion.[58]

Bengal

Scholarship on religious change in colonial Bengal has tended to focus largely on the world of urban reform in the metropolis of Calcutta. There are obviously good reasons for this, beginning with the centrality of Calcutta in narratives about the progressive spread of reform from this vaunted epicenter of imperial rule; and certainly the city was an important locus for major developments, including the promulgation of new systems of law, education, and governance; the advent and rapid spread of print-based media and public debate; and the concomitant rise of an influential class of new culture brokers, known as the *bhadralok*. This class took a leading role in translating colonial epistemologies and technologies into new forms of cultural life while eventually contesting egregious forms of British chauvinism, racism, and Christian missionary proselytizing.[59] This constellation of concerns has historically constituted something like the sweet spot for scholarship on reform in colonial India. What I hope to suggest, however, is that something is lost if we focus too closely on the metropolis and its culture brokers without attending to the broader regional context. As a colonial city from its very inception, Calcutta was also cosmopolitan, polyglot, polyethnic, and polyreligious; it was far from unified as an urban or cultural space. When thinking of the early colonial period in particular, we do well to remember the city first coalesced out of an agglomeration of three riverside villages—Sutanuti, Kalikata, and Govindapur—each indebted to the authority of local ruling families and supported by vital markets and busy riverside landing stages. Under the British, these villages were reoriented to a rapidly growing military, trade, and administrative settlement first localized at Fort William on the eastern shore of the Hooghly River.

By the late eighteenth century, Calcutta was already developing into a major port for ocean trade even as it became the launching point for military incursions and inland river trade into the Gangetic heartlands. Iconic images of the early waterfront wharfs, as depicted in the paintings of Charles D'Oyly from the 1840s, attest to the flourishing of the early port with its bustling wharfs and new government buildings. But D'Oyly's paintings also reveal the persistent traces of rural Bengal that served to inflect the cityscape well into the nineteenth century. From his paintings, we come to appreciate how the fabled City of Palaces was in fact an organic synthesis of dirt roads, rural bungalows, localized bazaars, newly built temples, and the majestic homes not only of the colonial elite, but also of a new class of wealthy Bengal nouveaux riches, many of whom went in for Palladian structures with ornate decoration and ample spaces for public entertainment.[60]

D'Oyly's depiction of the persistence of the Bengal village within the colonial city once again serves to remind us of what we so often fail to recognize when we embrace linear and triumphal narratives of modernity. Lost in narratives of East India Company progress and the rise of the colonial metropolis are a host of messier and less linear historical tangents that, once recognized, allow us to appreciate early colonial Calcutta as a variegated and lively chronoscape not yet (if ever fully) imprisoned by the flattened grid of colonial order. Maps, censuses, and municipal plans would all come with time, but in the early decades of the nineteenth century the cityscape remained dynamic. Even the familiar distinction between the so-called White Town and Black Town fails to capture the city as a space growing along diverse pathways.

D'Oyly's paintings remind us that terracotta temples in the distinctive Bengali architectural idiom and European-style garden houses often occupied the same street; and along those same streets one can spot the movement of various caste groups, tradespeople, holy men, civic functionaries, and company officials. Furthermore, those who called the city home—Bengalis, Hindustanis, Armenians, Chinese, and many others—were not mere victims of an urban world changing willy-nilly around them; they were themselves active agents in the construction and articulation of new urban worlds; they had trades and industries to promote, identities to celebrate, reputations to protect, and a range of political interests to advance and grow. They grouped and defined themselves in relation to mercantile concerns, occupational groups, ruling families, religious establishments, and increasingly, after the 1830s, various quasi-political associations. When Rammohun chose to make Calcutta his home after 1814, he did not descend like a meteor or even stand out as an anomaly; rather, his family (though based in rural Bengal) had well-established ties to the city, which Rammohun had begun to build on already by the end of the eighteenth century. Thus when he finally chose to settle in Calcutta, he was immediately able to draw on a range of family, professional, and political assets; he knew what it required to form allegiances and contest power within an dynamic urban public. The question I invite readers to ponder is, what would it have meant for Rammohun to project his own particular brand of religious mastery in such a context? Put differently, how was he able to muster the resources and attract the kind of following necessary to ensure the success of his new religious polity?

One might begin by noting that Rammohun was not the only raja in town. Early colonial Calcutta boasted a number of prominent and newly wealthy zamindar families who thrived in the wake of the Permanent Settlement of 1793; these zamindar families had already learned to use the city as a base for consolidating their own power and social influence. One important way for them to advance their political and cultural ends was by assuming the posture and accouterments of the royal court, the *darbar* or the *sabha*. Stepping forth as minor kings ensconced in courtly settings allowed new zamindar leaders to articulate a kind of majesty through the promotion of public works, patronage of learning, and endowment of religious institutions. Temple building was one mode of cultural practice that experienced something of a boom around this time. Prominent ruling families in different parts of the city—from Shobhabajar in the north to Bhukailash in the south—set about the construction of sometimes elaborate religious complexes featuring distinctive terracotta temples, large tanks, and public worship halls in which to celebrate seasonal festivals like Durga Puja. Along the way, a variety of religious orientations—Shaiva, Vaishnava, Shakta—found material expression as newfound wealth proclaimed its ability to shape the cultural world of the city.[61]

One could usefully map the cultural space of early colonial Calcutta in terms of the lavish new royal houses (raj baris) built by these zamindars to demonstrate their power and influence. The display of local mastery by Calcutta's new lords extended even to acts of largesse directed toward the British. For instance, the Raja of Shobhabajar, Nabakrishna Deb—whose palatial home still stands today—donated a large parcel of land for the construction of St. John's Church, while another "very eminent" Brahmin from Kidderpore donated land for a church to be built in the south of the city.[62] Such patronage should not surprise us, since the gifting of charitable lands to religious organizations was just one of many ways a king might establish a reputation; if a zamindar wished to articulate authority within the early colonial moment, it made sense for him to adopt the role of beneficent patron and to incorporate under his aegis a wide range of beneficiaries. Inclusivity had less to do with doctrine or religious affiliation than with fulfilling the role of early colonial lord. In this way Calcutta, no less than Saurashtra, may be thought of as a dynamic scale of forms.

Beyond Calcutta, the late eighteenth and early nineteenth centuries in Bengal witnessed something like a boom in the construction of terracotta temples. This too can be put in relation to attempts at the time by zamindars and wealthy merchant patrons to use temple patronage as a way to advance their own political and economic interests.[63] Even today the traces of such temple building can be found well beyond the borders of the colonial city. For instance, if one heads west across the Hooghly River, one finds that rural western Bengal was anything but a stagnant backwater. The landscape, folkways, river routes, and roadways of the *mofussil* were at this time undergoing profound transformations, akin to the changes shaping early colonial Calcutta. Small zamindari "kingdoms" in places like Bansberia and Sheoraphuli (both situated along the banks of the Hooghly River) rose to prominence during this transitional era. Like their urban contemporaries, the rulers of such realms promoted Sanskrit scholarship, temple architecture, and other plastic arts as a way to burnish their royal luster. Along the way they contributed greatly to the vitality of early colonial artistic and cultural production. At this time, too, characteristic Bengali festivals like the autumnal Durga Puja began to find their first articulation under the support of rulers in regional centers like Krishnanagar. The role of Bengal's many small zamindars beyond Calcutta in promoting new forms of ritual and devotion around deities like Durga, Kali, and Shiva is not often adequately recognized.[64]

One of the largest and most influential of such zamindaris was the Burdwan Raj, which rose to prominence along with the East India Company's expanding fortunes. I will have more to say about Burdwan when we discuss the early career of Rammohun Roy, but for now we may note its role in supporting modes of devotional life and in patronizing massive building projects like the stunning temple complex at Kalna on the west bank of the Hooghly River north of Calcutta.[65] The influence of the Burdwan Raj can also be felt in the expansion of an important regional pilgrimage center like Tarakeshwar in nearby Hooghly District. With hazy origins in the early eighteenth century, Tarakeshwar would develop over the ensuing century and a half into a regional center for devotion to Shiva and a popular pilgrimage destination. Its role as the site of annual festivals like Gajan proved central for the development of vernacular religion in colonial Bengal.[66] Tarakeshwar's success was also tied to the presence of monastic movements like the Dasnami Sampraday, which adopted the site as the principal seat of authority for what was once a vital network of monastic sites throughout the region.[67] Benefiting from the support of local landholding families, the Dasnamis became influential regional actors, from Burdwan south to the Bay of Bengal.[68]

The siting, designing, and networking of these small monastic sites— minor though they were in comparison to great Hindu temple complexes like Khajuraho or Kancipuram—attests nonetheless to the construction of religious polities supported by regional trade in commodities like cotton, silk, and salt. These physical sites also map closely onto the emergence of vernacular Bengali Hinduism from the sixteenth century onward, whether one thinks of the emotional and exoteric practices of Chaitan-yite Vaishnavism, the esoteric rituals of Bengali Tantrism, or the almost autochthonous Bengali affection for Shiva. Each of these modes of religion would find textual expression in Bengali poetry, song, and mythic narratives like the Mangal-kabyas, and each would support the rhythms of festival life associated with seasonal celebrations like Dol-Yatra, Gajan, or Durga Puja.[69] When one thinks about how sites like Tarakeshwar were scripted into vernacular narratives and then given temporal expression through calendrical festivals and fairs, one begins to get a sense for the vibrant world of lived Hinduism throughout western Bengal.

This is the world into which Rammohun Roy was born. If we shift our gaze from Calcutta as epicenter we thus come to appreciate the extent to which his world was pluriform and polycentric, energized by a host of new initiatives in religion, politics, and the arts. As we shall see, Rammohun's family hailed from Radhanagar, a small town situated within the thriving polity of the Burdwan Raj but that also had its ties to the Nawabi court at Murshidabad. Indeed, the Roy surname points to an honor bestowed on Rammohun's great-grandfather by the Nawab of Bengal in recognition of the role his family had once played in the Nawabi court.[70] We shall return in due course to the remarkable career of Rammohun—a Brahmin from rural Bengal who mastered both Sanskritic and Indo-Islamic knowledge systems before commencing a brief career under various company officials in different upcountry locations. And in a way that parallels what Sahajanand would accomplish after settling in Gujarat, we shall see that Rammohun was able to draw directly on both his impressive cultural repertoire and material assets when it came time to articulate the religious polity known as the Brahmo Samaj.

3

POLITIES
BEFORE PUBLICS

T HE TIME HAS COME TO introduce the concept of religious polity, around which I propose to advance an alternate history of the emergence of the Swaminarayan Sampraday and the Brahmo Samaj. As noted at the outset, I propose we speak of religious polities in preference to religious reform movements (or the like) as one way to disentangle the specifics of early colonial origins from subsequent interpretive frameworks developed under the conditions of late colonialism and often adopted with too little reflection by nationalist thinkers and even by scholars of religion in South Asia working in the present. I contend that in the concept of religious polity we have a tool not merely for escaping the clutches of reform-based discourse but also for generating new sorts of comparison between the work of two figures who shared a singular moment in South Asian history. Additionally, by reframing developments in early colonial religion in terms of polities promulgated by sovereign religious lords, I hope to briefly reconsider the relationship of these original polities to the forms of public Hinduism that would begin to flourish in the late colonial period. These later Hindu publics arose within and took expression against the backdrop of late colonial bordered histories and as such represent significant transformations of earlier polities such as we find in the case of the Swaminarayanis and the Brahmos.

I do not wish to propound an ironclad theory about how polities become publics, but I do think it is important to explore what differentiates the two, especially since considerable effort has been made recently by scholars to press our understanding of religious publics backward into the early modern era in South Asia. As I hope to show, even when such efforts are framed as exercises in conscious anachronism aimed at opening up new interpretive avenues, they nonetheless run the risk of projecting a modern category onto eras and epistemes in which the category seems out of place; in so doing they short-circuit more fruitful ways to analyze the articulation of new religious associations and communities in the early modern as well as the early colonial era.[1] As we have seen, in their late colonial and postcolonial histories both the Brahmos and Swaminarayanis have experienced moments of visibility and influence when either might rightly have been dubbed the "public face of Hinduism."[2] I would argue that the very publicness of those moments has everything to do with the rise of particular modes of urban, bourgeois, print-based culture and the concomitant rise of more identitarian expressions of religion and national belonging. Such public articulations of Hinduism are thus informed by—and inscribed within—bordered histories in ways that the two early polities under examination here were not.[3]

To demonstrate what I mean by this and to open up a pathway for understanding the distinctiveness of the religious work accomplished by Sahajanand and Rammohun in the early colonial period, I want to spend some time thinking about the concept of religious polities, especially as it has been employed by scholars like Ronald Inden and Amrita Shodhan. My contention is that when we attend more closely to the process of polity formation as treated by Inden—not least his emphasis on the role of ruling lords who articulate a kind of sovereign mastery within an existing scale of forms—we have an opportunity not just to reevaluate conditions shaping the first emergence of groups like the Swaminarayan Sampraday and the Brahmo Samaj; we also have a chance to ponder the subsequent transformation of these original polities in the late colonial moment. The question to which the present chapter, and ultimately this book, leads is this one: Would the legacies of Swaminarayan and Brahmo sovereignty in the modern public sphere appear any different to us if we were to differentiate their late colonial discursive framing from the early colonial conditions shaping their first emergence?

A Poet and His Rules

Since my goal is to disentangle the early emergence of these two religious polities from the entanglements and transformations occasioned by imperial discourse and nationalist aspiration, it is useful to begin in the late colonial moment, using a sermon by Rabindranath Tagore from 1901 to illustrate key elements of the late colonial Brahmo-bordered history and new national sense of the public.[4] I have in mind remarks delivered by Tagore at the ashram school he had only just founded at Shantiniketan, in Bolpur, Bengal. In turning to Rabindranath, it is important to remember that he occupied a prominent place within an already long-storied lineage of Brahmos who had championed Rammohun's ideals across the nineteenth century. And in his Shantiniketan address he speaks at just the moment when the Indian nation was becoming the focus of intense reflection and aspiration among his fellow Indians.

The Bengali date for Rabindranath's remarks was 7 Poush, a date hallowed among Brahmos as the day his father Debendranath had officially embraced the Brahmo faith. That was in 1843, a decade after Rammohun's death. Debendranath's initiation into what he would come to call Brahmo Dharma marked a significant moment of recovery for the Brahmo Samaj, which had nearly passed into oblivion after Rammohun's departure from India and death in Britain—a fact that should remind us not merely of the unique charisma of Rammohun but also of the unifying force of his rulership over the Brahmo polity. With the loss of the Raja, the sovereign authority behind the polity was lost. It was only with the advent of a new spiritual master that the Brahmo Samaj regained its cohesion and its purchase in colonial life. That spiritual master was Debendranath, on whom followers bestowed the title of Maharshi, or "great sage."[5]

For Brahmos, the affective associations surrounding the life and work of the Maharshi were powerful and enduring. This is no less true for his own son, Rabindranath, who inherited both wisdom and property from Debendranath. The two were symbolically united in Rabindranath's creation of Shantiniketan—an ashram school rooted in Upanishadic values established on lands originally acquired by Debendranath to serve as a place of personal spiritual retreat. The memorial date of 7 Poush is a condensation of the Brahmo story to that point. By selecting that memorial date in 1901 as the occasion for his remarks, Rabindranath linked his own attempt to inspire his students to the earlier revivification of the Brahmo community accomplished under Debendranath. In his sermon, Rabindranath honored his father's original acquisition of the Bolpur property while announcing a new sense of purpose for his ashram school. He would put Brahmo conviction in the service of Indian national aspiration. His was a pedagogy rich with national purpose.

Rabindranath's sense of connection to the work of his forebears helps us appreciate what it had meant to create and sustain the Brahmo religious polity over the course of the nineteenth century. But his remarks also provide a point of entry for thinking about how the Brahmo narrative came to be told in relation to the ideals of reform as well. In his remarks, Rabindranath outlines just the kind of "moral geography" identified by Michael Shapiro, which is to say a geography that serves to map the nation of India as an affective chronoscape.[6] In this moral geography, Rabindranath subtly attenuates any overtly Brahmo theological content in order to make more room for a vision of community that would expand beyond the locus of Shantiniketan to encompass the entire nation. The moment is less a further step in the articulation of the original Brahmo polity than it is a remapping of Brahmo sentiment in relation to a sense of public identity, one suitable for a new age (nava-yug) in India's history.

By 1901 Indian national aspiration had begun to coalesce around a range of mythic, historical, and spatial imaginings. All of these inform Rabindranath's remarks. We hear him ask his young Bengali charges to look upon their country as their mother and father (pitamata).[7] He hopes to yoke such affective commitment to a particular historical awareness, asking his students to ponder how much India had deviated from its ancient glories. Pointing to the selfishness of his own contemporaries, whom he accused of chasing single-mindedly after wealth, Rabindranath claimed that if there were to be a national awakening, it would have to begin with a recommitment to past ideals.[8] This kind of appeal to India's past had of course become increasingly common by this time; Rabindranath merely joined the ranks of other modern Indians motivated by a sense of the degeneration of their tradition.[9] Like Radhakrishnan a half century later, Rabindranath spoke in the first person plural of a new Indian public; his story would be "our" (*amader*) story.[10]

Our story was the Brahmo story, and so Rabindranath opened his address with a summary of some of the theological essentials of the Brahmo path. He stressed the need for his students to embrace belief in the one true god of the Brahmos as taught in "our Veda."[11] For Rabindranath, the Brahmo story is true Hinduism as Rammohun had first taught and as his own father had attempted to carry forward. He thus reminded his students that they were sitting in the "guru's house." There, on ground first hallowed by Debendranath, the students were asked to adopt a solemn and collective vow (*vrata*) to remain true to the course charted by Rammohun. A life of meaningful study in Rabindranath's ashram school required not merely a life of Vedic chastity (*brahmacharya*), but a deeper commitment to goodness, fearlessness, and truth.

Commitment was essential, and so Rabindranath laid out a set of rules (*karya-pranali*) for student conduct. The rules were to some degree spiritual or ritualistic in nature, including a requirement to recite the Gayatri Mantra as a part of daily ritual practice.[12] But in other ways, the rules were down-to-earth, including advice on how to manage budgets. This appeal to the need for careful accounting might seem prosaic, not least given the sacred setting of the guru's house. However, we need to appreciate that inherent in Rabindranath's delineation of rules was the attempt to both reanimate and regulate the vitality of what remained for him a meaningful Brahmo habitus. In his rules—spiritual as well as prosaic—Rabindranath hoped to link ashram life to the beliefs and norms originally promulgated by his father and his father's guru, Rammohun.[13] Crucially, however, Rabindranath also hoped to kindle a spirit of patriotic devotion (*desh-bhakti*).

Approaching his remarks in terms of structure and process, we might follow the lead of Marshall Hodgson and think of the long course of Brahmo history to that point as comprising three moments of creativity.[14] To begin with, there was a moment of creative action that set something new in motion; this moment may be understood in terms of a miraculous event, the advent of a charismatic prophet or teacher, or the assertion of a new revelation. This creative moment was followed, secondly, by the crystallization of what Hodgson called an "immediate public."[15] For Hodgson, the emergence of such a public depended on the fostering of new patterns of group commitment, which would be expressed in relation to the defining creative moment. Group commitment could then be operationalized around beliefs and practices that would be carried forward through time; this supported further patterns of institutionalization. The ongoing need for these institutionalized expressions of commitment directs us to a third and final moment that involved the generation of new currents of vitality. This moment was defined especially by efforts to establish regular, patterned interactions "among those sharing the commitment." Here we might think of such things as formalized systems of discourse, debate, or dialogue in relation to the community's values and the larger world around it.

What is attractive about Hodgson's model is that, quite apart from its explanatory economy, it manages to balance the force of the original creative moment against subsequent acts of recommitment and the many ongoing opportunities for innovation and change that constitute an institutional history. Thinking of the Brahmo polity in these terms honors the creative event under Rammohun, the efforts of later religious masters like Debendranath, and the eventual manifestation during Rabindranath's day of new features of national affect and aspiration that had not originally been associated with the meaning or purpose of the polity. This model can thus help us think about how a polity that had come into being in the borderless realm of the early colonial could over time attain a more bordered character, especially as the solidification of imperial rule in the last half of the nineteenth century had engendered among later generations of Indians powerful forms of anticolonial aspiration.

This model allows us to recognize Rammohun as the founder of an early colonial polity, even if we need not retroject onto him the notions of reform or national awakening that were to become dominant only during Rabindranath's day. To place Rammohun within such a historical perspective is to envision the Brahmo tradition as a "chain of memory" that required ongoing acts of re-remembering in order to revitalize commitment to past ideals and to garner new kinds of commitment in the present.[16] This chain of memory is not merely an intellectual tradition, nor is it a matter of theology alone. It is also an institutional chain composed of linkages forged anew and transformed in each iteration by developments taking place at the material, technological, legal, social, and political levels. The Brahmo polity in this sense was ever-renewing, self-sustaining, and yet never self-same. Most importantly, if we keep in mind the third moment identified by Hodgson, we have to recognize how an original courtly polity such as was first articulated under and around the authority of Rammohun, could—through the ongoing interaction of Brahmos among themselves and in relation to their colonial environment—acquire new meaning and new force as a modality of Indian public life.

Compared to this model, standard discourse around reform movements is not only more nebulous but significantly blind to the way later colonialist notions of progress, purification, and improvement have worked to obscure or redefine the initial work and purpose of polity articulators such as Rammohun. Indeed, the ubiquity of reform as a presumed motif of colonial religious life threatens to plunge us into a proverbial night in which all cats are gray. What does it mean to say that Rammohun was a reformer, Debendranath was a reformer, his protégée Keshub Chunder Sen was a reformer, his Brahmo contemporary Shibnath Shastri was a reformer, Rabindranath was a reformer? It means they all favored change of a progressive sort and tells us little else besides. By contrast, the gain we make in thinking of the Shantiniketan address along the lines of Hodgson's model is twofold: On the one hand, we come to appreciate how symbolic "links" located within the chain of memory are invented anew to reinforce the impression of an enduring tradition. On the other hand, by recognizing the moment of Rabindranath's speech as one of national public aspiration, we are reminded how distorting it would be to project his bordered history onto the original creative moment under Rammohun, for whom neither Shantiniketan nor India were meaningful sites of public commitment.[17]

Early Modern Religious Polities

As we go about rethinking colonial religious history, it proves useful to retain an awareness of what distinguishes a polity from a public, especially since the latter term is finding new traction within the study of early modern religion. Here it may be à propos to say something more about Hodgson's terminology, since he invokes the creation of an "immediate public" in his three-part scheme discussed above.[18] I believe he uses the term in a rather under-determined sense, which is suggested by the fact that he employs "public" variously when describing each of the three moments in his model of change. He begins by saying that, in the original creative event, there must be a "receptive public" eager to take up the creative event and "assign it value."[19] This is just to say there must be an audience to whom the original event speaks; otherwise, the event would simply pass into oblivion. By saying this public is immediate, he appears to mean no more than that it shares proximity in space and time with the original event. In the second moment of institutionalization, this audience or public, having found the original event to be "normative for them," seeks to constitute itself as a "continuing body" of people who share a "common awareness."[20] Here he appears to use public to suggest the quality of shared commitment among a group that has an awareness of itself in relation to the original normative vision. This would be congruent, as we shall see, with the kind of choice that characterizes membership within a polity, whether Swaminarayani or Brahmo. The emphasis here is on the adoption of a kind of discipline in relation to a group—about which I will have more to say later.[21] Finally, in Hodgson's third moment, this enduring commitment must be "confronted ever afresh" from the vantage point of "cumulative interaction" from within a life of shared purpose. Here he speaks of tensions that can arise between the public (that is, open and shared) embrace of a path like Islam and private efforts to make sense of that path, whether in circumstantial or logical terms.[22] If anywhere, it might be in this third moment that we could accommodate the gradual shift from polity membership into modes of public or national confession such as we find expressed in Rabindranath's 1901 address. And this would be the very marker of having shifted from polity to public.

For now, what seems evident is that Hodgson is not arguing for the immediate creation of a reified public in a Habermasian sense; rather his goal is to provide a kind of structural typology for the dynamics of a long-term cultural process wherein "at any given juncture"—and in relation to varying kinds of "circumstances, commitments, and problems"— different forms of institutionalized expression and commitment may arise.[23] I would argue that this is what makes his model so appealing, not least because it holds original vision, institutionalization, and ongoing change in a kind of productive tension. I therefore propose we use Hodgson's model heuristically to think about how polities can yield publics. In this way I believe it becomes possible to situate late colonial Swaminarayani and Brahmo publics on a critical horizon of community formation without projecting familiar aspects of their modern publicness onto their early colonial origins.

On Religious Polities

When it comes to the nature of religious polities, my understanding owes much to the work of two scholars who have developed the insights of R. G. Collingwood in order to analyze different dimensions of South Asian social and religious change. Ronald Inden is the more widely recognized of the two scholars, thanks in part to the influence of the trenchant post-Saidian analysis he offered in his *Imagining India*. That work is ostensibly a critique of European Orientalist constructions of India, but it also provides a valuable point of entry into Inden's other contributions around the history of premodern South Asia.[24] Both in contesting the essentializing epistemologies of Orientalism and in attempting to make sense of medieval kingship, Inden turned to R. G. Collingwood's concept of polity.

What Inden found useful in Collingwood was not merely the idea that polities are historically conditioned but, further, the claim that polities exist along a scale of forms. When applied to South Asia, this suggested that, rather than essentializing Hindu society and then looking for variations in relation to a presumed generic original, it made more sense for historians to look for evidence of the coming into being of a variety of religio-political formations; these might range from village caste councils or urban assemblies to trans-regional guru movements or royal courts. None of these formations represent naturally existing entities; they are constituted and maintained over time through the articulation of power or authority through what Inden refers to as "complex agency"— which is to say the phenomenon whereby any institution is constituted both by itself and by others.[25]

In fact, to properly qualify as polities, each of these formations—no matter how localized or expansive—requires what Collingwood construed as the combination of a community and a ruling power. In his *New Leviathan*, Collingwood had stipulated that polities emerge out of what he called nonsocial communities. For a community to qualify as a community, it has to maintain that which makes it distinct (its *suum cuique*). This is accomplished by the establishment of ruling power: "A society is a *self-ruling* community."[26] And this work, a kind of joint willing of the members of the society, is also never completed; it must be maintained over time.[27] As Inden rephrased this point, "Because it is continually changing its composition and because its members differ in their interests and purposes, the 'constitution' of a polity is, thus not a settled thing. It is something that its members continually alter and renew, decentring and recentring it."[28] As one example of a South Asian polity, Inden points to a religious order like the Dasnami Sampraday: it represents what he calls a particular society with a "limited writ."[29]

Building on Inden's work and bringing its analytical insights to bear on the modern moment, Amrita Shodhan takes up Collingwood in order to explain how premodern religious polities came to be transformed under the conditions of colonial bureaucracy, legal procedure, and Orientalist enunciative authority. Commencing with an awareness of how the contemporary world of South Asian religion is framed around the existence of discrete and homogeneous religious communities, Shodhan asks how this came to be the case. Like Inden, she is troubled by tacit reliance on essentialist paradigms, which encourages scholars and politicians to retroject the idea of primordial Hindu communities into the past. In response she looks to Collingwood, who reminds us that we live "in a world where nothing stays put, but everything moves." This being the case, then "the things we say must move too, in the same rhythm as the things we are talking about."[30]

For Shodhan this means questioning the presumed naturalness of the premodern Hindu community, not least because such a concept blinds us to the play of power and decision making in history.[31] Her goal is to capture this dynamism; toward this end she asks us to think about early modern polities like the Vallabhites as "contractual / associational, partially self-governing groups that had jurisdiction over their members." Even if polities like these did not grant equal participation in governance to all their members, they nonetheless did operate by including their male members in the settlement of disputes. For Shodhan this suggests that such polities were premised on the principle that they could "change their actual practices and religious beliefs."[32]

What I find especially useful in Shodhan's approach is that her understanding of colonial history mirrors that of Partha Chatterjee. Like him, she stresses how important it is to distinguish the early colonial moment from both the premodern and the late colonial eras. When we do this, Shodhan suggests, we come to appreciate that answers to the present-day "question of community" (i.e., the problem of communalism) will best be found not by projecting the bounded communities of the late colonial era into the past but by asking two other kinds of questions: First, what distinguishes the early colonial as a brief but consequential transitional moment? Second, what sort of developments had to take place in the shift from the early colonial episteme to the late in order to witness the rise of bordered refiguring of what had once been more malleable communities? In other words, like Chatterjee, she cautions us that when we allow ourselves to distinguish only broadly between the premodern and the modern, we open the door to all sorts of egregious essentialisms about religions like Hinduism; we fail to register how such essentialisms rest on questionable dichotomies about tradition and freedom, community and the individual, that are scripted into one particular late colonial narrative of modernity. To correct for this sort of error, she proposes we focus not on the transition from premodern to modern but on what changes between the early colonial and the late colonial eras.

Contrasting the early and the late colonial periods, Shodhan argues that we discover at least three things. First, the earlier period was characterized by a certain fluidity within political and religious formations; there were no primordial allegiances or eternal communities. Second, awareness of the fluidity of the early moment serves to invalidate the kinds of teleology that purport to explain South Asia's modern predicaments around communalism and religious violence.[33] There are no primordial or essential communities. Third, and perhaps most centrally, we come to see that our task ought to be to historicize developments taking place between the late eighteenth and late nineteenth centuries so that we can appreciate how it came to be that polities like the Vallabhacharyas or the Khoja Ismailis in western India came to be enshrined in British law and colonial sociology as homogeneous communities. In other words, we are led to ask, how did these polities succumb to the empire of reform?

Religious Polities and Colonial Law

Shodhan's work turns on a comparison of court cases and public controversies around religion in the nineteenth century, most notably the Aga Khan case and the Maharaja libel case. Both of these are well known, and I will not recapitulate their histories here.[34] Suffice it to say that Shodhan's analysis reveals how the increasing hegemony of European Orientalism and the power of colonial legal courts operated in tandem to alter, if not suppress, earlier modes of governance within religious polities like the Khoja Ismailis and Vallabhites, respectively. As the early colonial moment gave way to late colonial patterns of enumeration and codification, these polities were likewise disciplined to conform to textualist depictions of Islam and Hinduism that embraced originalism to rule out the manifestation of later modes of religious life and practice. Within the emerging empire of reform after the 1850s, this is the kind of thinking—one that prioritized original purity and stasis over histor-ical change and the governing agency of communities—that bolstered the rise of reform-based discourse.

Shodhan calls particular attention to British Protestant conceptions of religion, church, and sect.[35] She also highlights an important incon-sistency in attitudes toward sects in Britain and in India. In Britain, she notes, the nonconformists were understood to stand in a "contrapuntal" relationship to the established church; most importantly, they were pre-sumed to be capable of legislating for themselves in matters pertaining to their doctrines and rituals. However, in India, when the British ob-served polities like the Khojas or Vallabhites, they failed to recognize any evidence of what they could understand as ecclesial governance. Their failure was translated into legal and administrative fiat. Presuming the lack of self-governing capability among Indic communities, they ar-rogated to themselves the role of adjudicating what constituted true doctrine or right practice within such communities. And to do this, they fell back on Orientalist assumptions about the relationship between scripture and religious authority. Furthermore, the kind of textualist hermeneutics that were preferred by the courts operated in concert with the efforts of late colonial reformers like the journalist Karsandas Mulji, who advocated in the name of progressive, enlightened change and the limiting of religious authority. This led in time to two eventualities. First, overreliance on the idea of primordial scriptural truth led to the discur-sive consolidation of religions like Hinduism; in time this would help define the lineaments of "syndicated" Hinduism.[36] Second, as the law courts took over the adjudication of religious authority, the internal gov-erning structures of Hindu polities were gradually disestablished. Drawing on Collingwood and Inden, Shodhan shows how the pluralist governing logics and complex agency of early colonial forms came to be essentialized through the imposition of unified textual enunciations.[37]

One of the more striking ways Shodhan gestures toward this change is by demonstrating that during the early colonial period the East India Company in Bombay was in fact ready and willing to deal with reli-gious polities as internally governed contractual bodies (e.g., the *sabha* or *panchayat*).[38] Company servants vested with framing policies for western India recognized that local polities were governed by various agents, including judges (*nyayadhisha*), headmen (*patel*), accountants (*kulkarni*), revenue superintendents (*deshmukh, deshpande*), and religious scholars (*shastri*).[39] The official regulations compiled under Duncan and Elphinstone in Bombay responded to this fact of ruling authority within polities. As a result, these more pluralist regulations differed significantly from the work of Jones, Colebrooke, and Hastings in Bengal, who were fixated on creating a single code of Hindoo Law.[40] This leads Shodhan to conclude that there is no need to assume that the colonial syndication of Hinduism was something foreordained by the logics of Hinduism. Quite the contrary. As she puts it, the evidence from early colonial Bombay suggests that things might have gone differently. As evidence of this claim, she calls attention to an early court decision involving the Khojas from 1847. In this case, the judge demonstrated his respect for the ongoing operation of customary practices within the Khoja polity instead of bringing to bear on the community his own essentialized notion of scriptural truth. Of course, as Shodan goes on to reveal, over time and with the consolidation of what I am calling the empire of reform, the more open pluralism of the early Bombay Regulations yielded to the uniformity of the Bengal Code.[41]

I find this analysis highly useful for revising our standard views of the Swaminarayan Sampraday and the Brahmo Samaj. Most importantly, by returning to the early colonial moment we have the opportunity to observe how a polity like the Swaminarayan Sampraday was originally articulated in relation to fluid conditions on the ground and was also responsive to diverse forms of authority, from Kathi chieftains to British administrators. In this sense it is not even proper to ground the relative modernity of a polity like this in the biography of its founder Sahajanand. His rulership is better understood in terms of the complex agency behind a self-constituting, malleable polity. Likewise, whereas a late colonial writer like Monier-Williams was inclined to view the Swaminarayan Sampraday as medieval because of its apparent reliance on tradition, and the Brahmo Samaj as modern for its presumed openness to the West, Shodhan's approach allows us to opt out of this imperial binary. We can say instead that both polities were articulated as open and responsive to local communities and contexts, as we will explore in coming chapters.

There is no denying that the two polities were distinct in many fascinating ways, but we can now dispense with the idea that their differences reflect their relative embrace of modernity. Rather, these differences can be interpreted in relation to the creative response of figures like Sahajanand and Rammohun to the other authorities, actors, and opportunities they encountered in places like Gujarat and Bengal. There is no need to make pronouncements about which polity broke more effectively with the past, which challenged tradition, or which embraced modernity more fully. What I hope to demonstrate in the chapters that follow is that for all their distinctiveness, when we compare the Swaminarayan Sampraday and the Brahmo Samaj as early colonial religious polities, we position ourselves to think anew about how modern Hinduism first began to take shape in an era before the hegemony of reform, a time that was still largely untouched by late colonial teleologies of the Indian nation.

As we have seen, a central feature of a polity is that membership to some degree involves choice—the choice to follow a certain rule and live in relation to a disciplinary habitus. For this reason we should bear in mind the persistent tension between structure and choice within associational bodies like the Indic *samaj* / *sabha* or *sampraday*; as polities, such associations are rule-bound, but in view of the ever-present fact of choice they remain malleable. In Hodgson's terms, an association remains oriented to an original creative moment but is also shaped by decisions made as its members respond to their environment. Recent work on early modern polities in South India provides a useful illustration. Valerie Stoker has examined the role of Shaiva monastic polities in the consolidation and expansion of the Vijayanagara Empire during the sixteenth century. Stoker suggests that we think of the Indic concept of *matha,* typically translated as monastery, as something more like a sect, or small-scale polity. She gives us a way to think about the premodern *matha* along the lines of a *sampraday,* an association with disciplinary boundaries that is also always borrowing from its environment.[42] As with the early colonial Vallabhites, the range of actors in the life of a Shaiva monastic polity were many, including rulers, courtiers, ascetics, merchants, military leaders, and agriculturalists.[43]

Stoker's approach thus supports a contention found in Inden and Shodhan, both of whom ask us to stop thinking of Hindu sects (the word most often used to translate *sampraday*) as radically bounded or self-existent. The legacy of Christian, not to say post-Reformation, understandings of the church-sect relationship on modern constructions of Hinduism is too well known to merit belaboring.[44] When we render *sampraday* as sect, we are prone to figure it as a social group established "in opposition to some other church."[45] One hopes the foregoing exploration of early colonial polities will be enough to show how problematic such a usage is for capturing what we might better think of as polities. Furthermore, once we recognize how terms like church, sect, and schism operate within the late colonial empire of reform, we appreciate just how a reformer like Mulji was able to excoriate the Vallabhites for their purported deviations from primordial truth.[46]

From Sects to Publics

It is understandable that such reflections would prompt a desire to rethink our conception of religion in South Asia even before European intervention. Might we be able to go back to the premodern past of South Asia and frame alternate portraits of the religious landscape? Shodhan is certainly not alone in her conviction that the premodern world of religion was more pluralist than either the colonial archive or contemporary politics suggests; some even make a distinction between the "fuzzy" religious boundaries of premodern South Asia and today's world of "enumerated" religion.[47] Eager to make sense of this open and fluid premodern scene, other scholars have turned to the concept of religious publics as a tool that might be useful for making sense of devotional, theological, or ritual life prior to colonial rule. Admittedly, if one were to relinquish the presumption that religious publics are somehow uniquely modern in their origin and expression, then this critical move would seem to offer an attractive way to bridge the worlds of the premodern and the modern. But is this the case? Or does the search for such a bridging concept inadvertently cause us to forget what is in fact different, not to mention to overlook the singular sorts of developments taking place between the early colonial and the late colonial eras?

Elaine Fisher employs the concept of religious publics to examine what she calls the prehistory of pluralism in South Asia.[48] She adduces evidence of intellectual debate and the "theologization" of public discourse in seventeenth-century South India as a way to controvert the logic of sectarianism as applied to Hinduism.[49] She would highlight instead the plurality of religion in the premodern world, while construing it as a form of publicly performed but noncompetitive sectarianism; she does not deny the reality of religious conflict, but believes plural sectarianism thrived through recognized processes of resolution rather than outright conflict.[50] Her other goal is to highlight premodern sectarianism as a way to query standard narratives about secularization and civil society in the modern era. Contrary to the standard logic of secularity, she argues that the movement of religion outside the "walls of the monastery" ironically made religion more rather than less salient for the framing of public life.[51] As such, she argues that in the premodern era religion served as a vibrant component of public engagement; liberal secularist anxieties about religion in public life and calls for its privatization are thus rendered suspect. Fisher disavows a prescriptive agenda, but she nonetheless makes it clear that she is uncomfortable with the modern liberal framing of religion—which she also associates with the work of Martha Nussbaum. Hers is thus a "political agenda" to make visible a South Asian past invigorated by "religious pluralism."[52]

The backstory here, as always, involves engagement with the work of Jürgen Habermas on the public sphere. Today there is a robust literature seeking either to provincialize Habermas's critical apparatus or to find ways to translate it into non-European contexts.[53] With the critical upsurge of interest in empire, colonialism, and the problem of the Indian nation after the 1980s, this literature has taken off considerably.[54] Initially much of this work was concerned with the modern era in South Asia, looking to apply the concept of the public sphere to developments during the late colonial period.[55] Following on these efforts, scholars have been emboldened to ask if there is any utility in extending such analysis into the early modern or precolonial eras. Do such phenomena as devotional religious movements, monastic institutions, vernacular literary cultures, or subcontinental informational networks lend themselves to being studied as what can be called South Asian publics?[56]

As Farhat Hasan has asked, "Can we . . . use Habermas's insights on the emergence of bourgeois public sphere for a better understanding of the relationship between culture and power, and the processes of inter-subjective communication and identity-formation in medieval India?"[57] Hasan answers with a qualified yes, advancing a number of examples that seem to offer parallels between premodern South Asian life and the associational behavior and economic relations Habermas took to be characteristic of the modern public sphere. Thus, looking at Mughal-era cities like Delhi or Faizabad, Hasan finds evidence of public poetry sessions (*musha'ira*), public markets (*chawk*), and even coffeehouses (*qahwa khana*) that offer spaces for public gathering. While each of these examples speaks to the interaction of diverse social groups in "inclusive sites of public deliberation," Hasan is aware that the Mughal state and other post-Mughal polities typically sought to control the production and circulation of authorized knowledge.[58] Was free and public association really possible? Hasan concedes that although these examples are no evidence for a bourgeois public sphere, they are nonetheless evidence of certain kinds of premodern publics.

Others have pursued a similar tack, seeking to carry Habermas beyond Europe and to search for evidence of his public sphere before modernity.[59] Relevant here would the work of Christian Novetzke on the worlds of Maharashtrian devotionalism and Marathi vernacular culture. Novetzke develops his understanding of premodern bhakti publics in a contrapuntal fashion; he credits Habermas with raising the problem, but distances himself from the particulars of Habermas's model. He is less interested in searching for Habermasian indicators like the coffeehouse (à la Hasan) and more concerned in asking how publics are produced and sustained through performance, memory, and social engagement. Perhaps even more than that of Habermas, the work of Michael Warner provides Novetzke with a way to conceptualize the public: "A public enables a reflexivity in the circulation of texts among strangers who become, by virtue of their reflexively circulating discourse, a social entity."[60]

One of Warner's most productive ideas is that of the counterpublic, a term he coined to examine the case of queer social groups looking to arrive at new modes of public sociality in opposition to dominant bourgeois culture.[61] In the concept of counterpublics we have a tool to crack open the apparent solidity of bourgeois cultural production and to begin thinking more broadly of public culture. In the process we make room for other and wider streams of what might be called public culture. Fisher herself has gestured approvingly at Novetzke's use of public culture as a way to gather under the notion of the public wider processes taking place at the vernacular level.[62] She thus shares Novetzke's desire to escape the gravitational pull of Habermas while retaining the option to theorize popular culture as a space in which actors carry on public conversations about such issues as devotion, gender, or caste.[63]

The work of Fisher and Novetzke represents a valuable contribution to attempts to rethink premodern religion. Notwithstanding my respect for what they have accomplished, I harbor one concern, which has to do with what we might call the translational residue that carries over into premodern contexts when we frame them as publics. That residue can be detected in the undeniable anxiety manifested by scholars seeking to employ the public as a tool for thinking about premodern South Asia: is it possible to distinguish any premodern example of a public from Habermas's robust (and seemingly determinative) ideas about modern communicative action and the bourgeois sphere? In face of this anxiety, Novetzke's solution is to engage in what he calls deliberate "anachronism."[64] We shall see in a moment where this leads.

Polities before Publics

In the wake of Said's *Orientalism*, Inden famously called for the Western academy to come to terms with some of the lingering essentialisms and disciplinary cages that he felt had constrained the ability of scholars to make sense of medieval and modern India. Inden had argued that the state itself comes to play the role of a kind of transcendent essence—what Daud Ali has referred to as a kind of bureaucratic entity "suspended above" Indian society.[65] To redress the hypostasization of the state, Inden and, later, Daud Ali both propose thinking of the state as constituted by individuals acting in contexts like royal courts. The difference in critical posture here may seem subtle, but it is crucial. Instead of the royal court being taken to symbolize the workings of a preexisting state—that may, for instance, seek to legitimize its authority via certain ritual forms or material artifacts—the activities of the court in fact *are* the state, as Ali puts it.[66]

The significance of this critical shift in perspective for the current project becomes evident if we link the critique of state-based thinking to Inden's adoption of Collingwood's work on polities. Among the elements of Collingwood's work that Inden found valuable was the idea that we could investigate a range of polities as existing along what the former called a "scale of forms." The utility of this idea was that it would allow the scholar to tackle the great essentialisms of South Asian studies, not only caste and Hinduism but also such widely embraced dichotomies as that between householder and renouncer.[67] Following Collingwood, the idea would be to consider the work of particular actors who come together in varied kinds of associations—from caste councils to religious *sampradays* to royal courts—arranged along something like a continuum of what Inden called lordships. The question then becomes, how is lordship articulated and rearticulated through the complex agency of texts and actors operating within overlapping realms of power?[68]

At the apex of the medieval ideal stood the royal court, whose lordship was assented to and addressed by a variety of actors, right down to those with the lowest level of mastery (agriculturalists, for instance).[69] However, since the court is not the concretization of some ideal state, the entire sociopolitical field may be rendered as fluid and open to constant refashioning. Furthermore, since the scale of forms does not oppose a single state to a mass of society, but figures society in terms of a range of divergent, multiscalar polities, this model allows room for understanding how certain kinds of power could be both articulated and assented to by different actors. This is what had led Inden to think of the religious *sampraday* as a kind of polity—not something opposed to the state (as it might be in the church-sect paradigm), but situated along a scale of power relations and within a range of governing norms. Rather than construing certain cultural practices around ritual, display, or aesthetics as taking place apart from the political, they are instead understood to be key factors in the articulation of political spaces.[70]

This is what makes recourse to the idea of polities so compelling and suggests it might deliver greater critical rewards than analytical models based on the idea of publics. Put simply, I fear scholars like Fisher and Novetzke are ultimately unable to answer a query posed long ago by Pamela Price: What is the difference between acting in public and constituting a public?[71] If the former is taken simply to mean behaving in a manner that is visible and / or accessible to a range of actors, it yields little analytical value for thinking about the work accomplished by forms of religious display or debate. What do we gain, by defining a bhakti public as "a social sense of general devotion shared by many people in a region yet not confined to any given sect, religious order or explicit community"?[72] By contrast, if Daud Ali admits we could label some aspects of the premodern royal court "public," this should not be taken to mean these were open or accessible to all. Instead, it would be to say that everything about the behavior of a royal household signified in publicly meaningful ways within the polity.[73] Following this, it seems wiser to contend that it is only with the rise of a recognizable bourgeois public sphere during the late colonial era that one can begin to meaningfully distinguish private from public life. As such, the concept of a premodern bhakti public seems to identify little more than a shared "culture of worship."[74]

It seems to me that Fisher's work also risks reinscribing the public-private distinction within premodern religious life in problematic ways. Her portrait of the scholar Nilakantha Dikshita seems to endorse modern liberal notions of bifurcated religious identity, whereby someone might act like a Vaishnava in public but a Shaiva at home (let alone a Shakta in private, as she puts it).[75] By contrast, if we were to think in terms of religious polities, we might escape the aporia of apparently conflicting devotional habits; we would inquire instead about the polities within which such habits were articulated and maintained. Instead of situating a private Shaiva within a shared Vaishnava public sphere, we might— thinking of Stoker's work on Vyasatirtha—ask about the work accomplished by the overlapping practices of religious actors who sought to negotiate differing polities like the monastery, royal court, or frontier garrison.[76] By contrast, Fisher runs the risk of appearing to be in the position to call out inconsistent behavior when she chooses to judge the viability of premodern religious forms against contemporary notions of public behavior.[77]

With this we come, at last, to the problem of anachronism that I highlighted earlier in this chapter. As I indicated then, the scholar whose work raises this problem is Christian Novetzke, who, in his recent attempt to define a premodern vernacular public in western India, professes to indulge in an exercise of deliberate anachronism.[78] A fascinating scene in Novetzke's *The Quotidian Revolution* centers on the occasion when Chakradhar, the founder of the Mahanubhav devotional community, is brought to trial by the Yadava polity in the late twelfth century. Novetzke uses the trial of Chakradhar to conjure what he calls the world of a vernacular devotional public, but I believe if we read Novetzke's account against the grain we encounter some of the pitfalls of his anachronism.

The Mahanubhavs were a society of renunciants in Maharashtra that came into being under the leadership of Chakradhar, a figure whose life and teachings are the focus of a Marathi text known as the *Lilacharitra*. Though a Brahmin, Chakradhar taught an egalitarian path open to both men and women; many of his followers were widows. Novetzke suggests that one of the reasons Chakradhar adopted Marathi as his preferred language instead of Sanskrit was so that he would be able to speak directly to audiences of women devotees.[79] His innovative effort at opening up the path of salvation to a wider premodern public is one of the key elements in what Novetzke dubs the "quotidian revolution."

To appreciate the force of such innovation, Novetzke situates the work of Chakradhar in relation to the constitutive role played by Brahmanic discourse—especially around dharma—within the Yadava ruling polity. Committed to upholding the prerogatives of the Brahmanic order, the Yadavas were lavish patrons of monasteries, educational centers, charitable endeavors, and elite literary activity. And among the literary projects they endorsed, pride of place was given to the study of *dharmashastra*, those classical authoritative treatises on duty and the socio-cosmic order that are synonymous with Brahmanic authority. Literary explication of dharma under the Yadavas took place through Sanskrit, and the overall effect was to create a cultural environment in which the ideal of "Brahminness" (*brahmanatva*) reigned supreme.[80] As a Brahmin scholar himself, Chakradhar was a master of such literature and the ethics it enshrined. Many of his followers were also Brahmins and, as such, accustomed to the support given by the Yadava state to the maintenance of the Brahmanic order.

Despite his bona fides as a Brahmin, Chakradhar's teachings and his appeal among women followers seems to have gone beyond what the Yadava court was willing to countenance. In the hagiographic narrative of the *Lilacharitra* are found several episodes prior to the trial in which Brahmin agents of the status quo attempt to hinder Chakradhar in his work, which they construe as an assault on Brahminness. Naturally the saint is too clever and too good to be brought down; rather, he delivers sharp rebuffs to the pretensions of Brahmanic culture. The fact that Chakradhar at one point even appears to win over the wife of the greatest Sanskrit scholar at the Yadava court brings the story to its boiling point. This poor scholar, Hemadri, is completely flummoxed by Chakradhar; he is so thrown off his game that he even begins to wonder whether his attraction to his own wife is due to the fact that she had been blessed by Chakradhar![81] It therefore isn't long before soldiers under orders from Hemadri come to take Chakradhar to a temple in Paithan, where a trial is to be held. Novetzke offers a veritable transcript of a "thirteenth-century courtroom drama," revealing his narrative flair but also painting himself into an analytical corner with respect to the trial's significance.[82]

To begin with, Novetzke construes the trial as a public event, since it was held at the Paithan temple and not at the Yadava capital at Devgiri. However, it is difficult to discern what public would mean in this case; there is little that conforms to our notions of a public—let alone publicized—trial. Furthermore, this way of construing the public character of the trial against the ostensive privacy of the royal court misconstrues key elements of royal polities as understood by Ali. According to Ali's analysis we would expect that every gesture and act of the Yadava court constituted some kind of affirmation of the hierarchies and differentiations that served to articulate their royal polity. As such, it seems rash to translate the trial scene into terms more appropriate within the modern civil sphere.[83]

The problem becomes particularly acute when Novetzke turns to a decisive moment in the trial when two of Chakradhar's followers forcefully object to the court's charge that women seem to be inordinately attracted to their guru. These two devoted followers rise to their feet and accuse the tribunal of conspiring against Chakradhar; then, expressing outrage at the conduct of the accusers, they depart. Analyzing this dramatic moment, Novetzke finds in it signs of an incipient "legal public," one that has become informed about the ideal of a fair and speedy trial "by one's peers."[84] Viewed from this perspective, he takes Chakradhar's followers to be "men of integrity" who mount a "protest" at the "prejudice" of Chakradhar's accusers.

I take all of this to be a vigorous exercise in anachronism: here Novetzke clearly errs on the side of translating Chakradhar's trial into terms familiar to his readers, who will of course cheer in support of Chakradhar's two faithful devotees and their commitment to the cause of justice; readers today may even be expected to chafe at what appears to be the abuse of due process and an infringement of Chakradhar's rights. But one has to ask, is this the best way to read the trial?[85] If nothing else, as reference to the work of Ali suggests, this way of understanding the proceedings in Paithan fails to register the way the scene of the trial might in fact be used to illustrate how power comes to be articulated within a premodern polity.

To read Novetzke against the grain, we might begin with an operative term like *sabha*, which Novetzke translates as "tribunal." In the context as sketched, this seems a reasonable choice for translating *sabha*; we are clearly dealing with a formal meeting of official figures appointed to make a decision on a topic of concern to the Yadava polity. Furthermore, we know that the convening of *sabha*s like this is a topic treated by the major *dharmashastras* that were so in favor in the Yadava polity. And yet if we were to look at the *dharmashastra* of Manu (*Manava-dharmashastra*), it might be argued that the rules he frames for the proper convening of a *sabha* constitute something better understood as the enunciation of a polity. Manu requires three Brahmins, learned in the Vedas, and an officer of the king; this, he says, constitutes the "court of Brahman."[86]

Within the Yadava polity, to convene the "court of Brahman" would have been to bring to bear on local concerns the full authority of Brahminness as articulated and sanctioned by texts like Manu. The goal of the Paithan *sabha*, then, would be not merely to assert the power of the Yadava polity, but to rearticulate its overall contours—to enact it. In this regard, it helps to think of the *sabha* not merely as tribunal or trial, but as itself a kind of royal court (also *sabha*). From the account found in the *Lilacharitra*, it seems clear the *sabha* convened at Paithan consisted not merely of Brahmins bent on asserting their privileges; the court appears to have comprised a far more diverse set of actors. The *Lilacharitra* tells us that among those present at the *sabha* were not merely key actors like Chakradhar, Hemadri, another pandit, and Chakradhar's two Brahmin followers; in attendance were also (in Novetzke's translation) "the major leaders of the village, the Brahmin elites [*mahajan*], scholars, historians, holy men, celibates, Jain ascetics, members of the Natha sect—they all assembled."[87]

This capacious list of attendees certainly suggests a gathering of more complexity than Manu's *sabha*, but it is appears to be something quite different from a modern courtroom. What the *Lilacharitra* describes might better be likened to a royal court, which is to say a ruling polity standing at the head of a number of lesser polities, all aligned with it along a "scale of forms." As a ruling polity, the Yadava court (itself non-Brahmin by lineage) articulated its mastery not merely in terms of the ideals of Brahminness, but in relation to a range of other polities it sought to encompass, including Jains, Nathas, and other unnamed celibates and holy men. In this respect it is worth noting that Chakradhar, when asked about his own identity, responded by mirroring the articulation of the polity within which he found himself: "You who have assembled are the leaders of all eighteen families [of Paithan], Jain ascetics, Natha yogis." And he later adds, speaking to members of the tribunal, "Each of you holds a position of political importance."[88]

Are we really witnessing a sham trial, as Novetzke's reading seems to suggest? Or does the *Lilacharitra* allow us to witness the ritualized enactment of a premodern polity, made manifest in terms of complex agency along a scale of forms? Surely his hagiographers hoped to valorize Chakradhar's resistance in the name of his spiritual authority. But rather than being a public display of what we would today call personal integrity, what we seem to be witnessing is a religious leader questioning the authority of the Yadava polity to intervene in his own religious polity. In other words, Chakradhar is less a heroic bhakti reformer and more the author of a new devotional polity. For that matter, what Novetzke construes as the Yadava state is better read as a polity: an association with ruling power, which it articulates both internally along Brahmanic lines and externally by forging ties with other groups like the Jains and the Nathas. These other groups, in turn, are polities that follow their own rules for behavior and endorse their own particular theologies; and they recognize other kinds of masters, whether it be Jain tirthankaras and sage-kings like Bahubali or great yogis like Goraksha. Even so, within the context of premodern Maharashtra, these groups recognize the lordship of the Yadava polity. What the *sabha* at Paithan thus makes manifest is the moment when Chakradhar sought to forge an appropriate relationship with the principle governing authority in his world.[89]

If my reading of Chakradhar's trial may be admitted, I believe it directs us toward an alternate way to frame the emergence of new religious polities like the Swaminarayan Sampraday and the Brahmo Samaj. What we should attempt to consider are the ways in which what Sahajanand articulated through his charismatic mastery, delivery of community rules, and construction of new temple centers was a religious polity claiming its own internal mode of governance while nonetheless orienting itself in relation to other governing polities present in Gujarat. These polities would have included local landlords and petty rulers as well as mercantile guilds, not to mention the newest player on the scene, the East India Company. Viewed in this light, the much-touted close relationship between Sahajanand and the British need be read neither as evidence of the broad-minded tolerance of a pluralist genius nor as the unfortunate capitulation of a failed Indian patriot. Instead, it may be understood as Sahajanand's attempt—akin to that made by Chakradhar— to situate his new *sampraday* within an existing field of overlapping spiritual and temporal masteries.

Likewise, turning to Bengal, the early life and work of Rammohun lends itself to a similar interpretation, even if the conditions on the ground and the intellectual and theological resources at his disposal necessarily led him to convene an assembly (initially a *sabha,* latterly a *samaj*) that was articulated in relation to a differing vision of theology and ethics. Rammohun oriented his new polity in relation to Upanishadic, Islamic, and post-Enlightenment intellectual and political traditions; he worked to give it meaning in relation to what were already rapidly evolving Western construals of "Hindooism" by British actors in Calcutta. Rammohun also found ways to inculcate associational norms for corporate and individual self-governance that drew on developments in his urban environment and that proved useful for the expansion of new relationships with the emerging British imperial polity.

Yes, Rammohun was more attuned to Europe and more engaged with Europeans and Americans than was Sahajanand; but in Chapter 6 we shall see that Sahajanand was by no means unaware of or unconcerned with the British presence in Gujarat. We do well, then, not to pin these men's historical legacy on simplistic conceptions of Western influence. For the early colonial period, at least, it makes better sense not to speak generically of Western influence but to think more deliberately about the presence on the scene of the East India Company as yet another ruling polity that had inserted itself within an already rich, scalar world of South Asian polities. Viewed in this way, British rule in India looks akin to an imperial formation as defined by Inden, which is to say an empire along with its "allies and foes."[90] From there we may go on to consider how its project to articulate British mastery and ruling prerogatives factored in to the complex agency surrounding the emergence of other associational polities such as the Swaminarayan Sampraday and the Brahmo Samaj.[91] It is the simultaneous emergence of these two polities during the early colonial moment—and not their relative embrace of progress—that should lead us to recognize the Swaminarayan Sampraday and the Brahmo Samaj as among South Asia's first modern Hindu polities.

Reading the life and work of Sahajanand and Rammohun against such a backdrop, there is no need to invoke the idea of an anachronistic public sphere, just as there is no real reason to celebrate the work of these men as evidence of premodern Indic religious pluralism, at least not as that concept is understood and employed irenically today. Likewise, if in the following chapters I turn to a closer review of the lives and achievements of Sahajanand and Rammohun, it is not to reinstate a Great Man theory of religious reform, but to ponder how two contemporary religious lords emerged from the fluid landscape of eighteenth-century South Asia to articulate two new polities that took expression within a complex and dynamic scale of religious forms. Only later, over the course of the following century, would the Swaminarayan and Brahmo polities come to be defined in relation to new notions of progress, reform, and improvement. It would be in those terms that they would take on transformed roles within the Indian public sphere. But what I hope to suggest is that, in the moment of their first emergence, they were neither communal nor nationalist, revivalist nor reformist. Those categories are artifacts of the empire of religion, as we shall see.

4

ON THE ROAD
WITH NILAKANTHA

HAGIOGRAPHIC TEXTS PRODUCED WITHIN THE early Swaminarayan community purport to recount the life of Sahajanand, including his journey across South Asia as the young renouncer, Nilakantha Varni. In recent years Nilakantha's story has been brought to life in a dramatic IMAX movie, *Mystic India*. The fact that this movie is shown during guided tours at the major BAPS Swaminarayan complexes known as Akshardham suggests the central role Nilakantha's story plays within the movement.[1] As one late twentieth-century appreciation of Sahajanand puts it, "He roamed about in the company of holy ascetics (*sadhus*) or alone, over the whole length and breadth of India . . . finally reaching Gujarat and Kathiawar which had the privilege of becoming the land of his action and contribution for the rest of his life."[2] In both text and film, Sahajanand's advent as a religious leader in Gujarat is seen as the culmination of a long history of mobility during which he visited holy sites, studied yoga with different teachers, challenged erroneous doctrines, and fashioned himself as a living exemplar of devotion to God.

I propose to read one particular hagiographical account of Sahajanand against the backdrop of religious change in early colonial South Asia, key elements of which I have already attempted to delineate. My focus is on the earliest and most copious of hagiographies, the *Satsangi*

Jivanam. As the title suggests, this text purports to recount the life (*jivanam*) of a member of the fellowship, or *satsang*. It may seem curious that the transcendent figure whose story is told in the text would be identified by such a humble epithet. One might have expected the protagonist to be given a more elevated title, like Guru, Acharya, or even Bhagavan.[3] But as a paradigmatic account, the text is not merely interested in demonstrating the manifest spiritual authority of Sahajanand; it also offers a model of "personality, behavior, spiritual qualification and scholarship" for others to emulate.[4] In other words, the *Satsangi Jivanam* speaks of the life of the miraculous Lord Swaminarayan and of the life to which his followers are called.

Peter Schreiner has observed that the *Satsangi Jivanam* is somewhat unique insofar as the impetus to provide an account of Sahajanand's charisma does not come from his followers; it comes from Sahajanand himself, who is said to have instructed one of his closest disciples, Shatanand Muni, to craft the hagiography.[5] As I see it, such a self-conscious hagiographical strategy is congruent with Sahajanand's efforts at the time to articulate his authority and solidify the commitments of Satsangis within the new polity.[6] He is greatly assisted in this regard by Shatanand's decision to adopt a recognizably Puranic mode of storytelling that situates Sahajanand's life within a vast mythic chronoscape and charts his work as the fulfillment of a divine mission to restore proper Vaishnava devotion. At the same time, as we shall see, it seems possible that Shatanand was also able to incorporate information he had learned directly from Sahajanand or that reflected knowledge current in Gujarat at the time. As I hope to show, it may even be the case that there is a measure of historical veracity to some of what we learn about Sahajanand's youth and early travels. Between Shatanand's creative hand and Sahajanand's guiding voice, the *Satsangi Jivanam* reads rather like a hybrid auto-hagiography.

Even after discounting for the mythic backdrop and Shatanand's robust attempt at theological system-building, one thing the *Satsangi Jivanam* allows us to appreciate is the pattern of peregrination and settling down that I began to highlight already when speaking about the early colonial moment.[7] On the one hand, Sahajanand seems perennially in motion—both as a young renouncer traversing the subcontinent and after finally arriving in Gujarat in 1800. Once there, he continued to move, ever in pursuit of new followers, new alliances, and the bolstering of new institutions. But amid all the movement, certain places do tend to matter. Thus, from his earliest career, the *Satsangi Jivanam* pictures Sahajanand gravitating to sacred locales to advance his own yogic mastery or to catalyze spiritual transformations in those he encountered. Overall, whether challenging misguided spiritual practitioners (notably Tantrikas and Shaktas) in northern India or seeking the support of Kathi rulers in Saurashtra, Sahajanand remained on the move, apparently committed to reconstituting the habits of all he encountered. His articulation of the early *sampraday* depends on this very twofold dynamic; it is a polity that draws on the authority of a wandering master to foster and maintain local communities through a process that Peter Schreiner calls "ritualization." Schreiner has in mind certain specific textual strategies found in the *Satsangi Jivanam*, but we can expand the idea of ritualization to include Sahajanand's articulation of new rituals and practices around morality, communal life, personal vows (*vrata*), and temple worship.[8]

For now I want to focus on the period of Sahajanand's life prior to his reaching Gujarat. In doing so, my goal is to illustrate the role spiritual wandering played in his accrual of various forms of spiritual mastery on which he would subsequently call when establishing his new polity (a process I turn to in Chapter 6). For now I draw heavily on the account of Sahajanand's early travels as found in the *Satsangi Jivanam,* doing my best to suggest some ways in which the mythic account created by Shatanand may actually dovetail with available historical evidence. Even if the veracity of many dramatic scenes remains open to question, I hope to demonstrate that the *Satsangi Jivanam* can be used to illuminate key elements of early colonial religious life that help us understand the resources Sahajanand drew on when advancing his new polity.

Ghanashyam Comes of Age

Sahajanand's story begins in 1781, far from Gujarat, in the Gangetic heartland of present-day Uttar Pradesh. There, in the small town of Chapaiya near Ayodhya, a boy was born into a Savariya Brahmin family with the surname Pande. The boy was named Ghanashyam by his parents, Hariprasad and Bala, upon whom the *Satsangi Jivanam* bestows the identities of Dharma and Bhakti (that is, Duty and Devotion).[9] Members of his particular lineage were said to be masters of the Sama Veda, and Ghanashyam was raised to carry on that special heritage.[10] At the age of eight he went through the life-cycle rite of *upanayana*, which marked his investiture with the sacred thread (*janeu*). Henceforth he was eligible for the ritual life of the twice-born Vedic student.[11]

A curious account of the *upanayana* ceremony is embedded in one of the earliest English-language accounts of the Swaminarayan movement, written by James Burgess and published in 1872. Burgess, who drew on an even earlier source, tells us that for the ceremony Ghanashyam was joined by his older brother, Rampratap. As part of the ceremony, the two boys were asked to do a bit of playacting, whereby they would give performative expression to the rejection of worldly life. The boys were told to run off in mock horror at the perils of embodied existence. Everyone on hand would surely have understood that this was no more than a performance intended to give symbolic weight to the ideals of renunciation and holiness. Those in attendance fully expected the two boys to sprint off and then just as quickly double back, their brief symbolic gesture at renunciation completed. Following that, they could be invested with the thread and assume their responsibilities as Brahmanic householders. And so the boys took off on their ritualized sprint, with a maternal uncle running behind to eventually guide them on to the remaining rites. Burgess tells us that Rampratap quickly ran out of gas and willingly surrendered to his uncle's embrace. Not Ghanashyam— he kept running until he had covered an astounding distance of six miles! The poor uncle kept up his pursuit, even if he had long since lost all patience with this tomfoolery. Eventually, Ghanashyam turned on his uncle and called out, "Are you so stupid as not to understand that it is not my fate to return to the world?"[12]

Despite this stunning declaration, tradition tells us Ghanashyam eventually did complete his initiation. He returned to his home and took up the next phase of his education, but in Burgess's telling he remained a precocious child who seemed destined for another path. We are meant to see this in his response to his initiation, a rite that is supposed to honor the ancient ideal of the chaste Brahmanic student (*naishthika brahmacharin*). No matter how his brother responded to the rite, for Ghanashyam it announced a meaningful goal. Thenceforth he began studying under a guru, who introduced him to Vedic knowledge and the *shastras*. His early education also seems to have focused on texts in the Ramayana tradition alongside the study of the other Vaishnava texts like the Bhagavad Gita and Bhagavata Purana. The importance of the latter scripture is evident throughout the *Satsangi Jivanam*. In fact, we are told that it was through intensive reading of the Bhagavata Purana that Shatananda Muni (himself originally from Mithila in north India) had a vision of Sahajanand, who instructed him to write his life story.[13]

Three years after his initiation, Ghanashyam lost both his parents. Sources describe the punctiliousness with which his elder brother Rampratap undertook the requisite postmortem rites; they also suggest that at this time Ghanashyam's mind began to turn toward the idea of renouncing worldly life. If he did not immediately take that step, we are told, it was only because of the love and affection he felt for his extended family. His sense of commitment to them stood in the way of realizing true *vairagya* or dispassion. If he were ever to succeed in going forth as a renouncer, he would need to cultivate a higher kind of renunciation.

Needless to say, the moment eventually arrived when Ghanashyam could no longer put off this step. We are told he said a special prayer to Ganesha, asking the deity to remove the last obstacles standing in his path toward renunciation. Shortly after muttering his silent prayer, he set off from home. It was early morning, and those around him suspected nothing; they presumed the boy had simply gone off to perform his daily ritual bath. However, he was never to return. He had finally renounced the world; ideologically and literally he had become "homeless" (*ageha*).[14] The date is remembered as a Friday, the eleventh day of the bright fortnight of Ashadh. For devotees of Swami Narayan, it was the beginning of a new era. The *Satsangi Jivanam* is remarkably laconic: "On the eleventh day, having become detached from home life, he went forth."[15]

Ghanashyam began his new life by heading directly away from town. His path brought him in due course to the banks of the Sarayu River. Only a short time before he had stood on these banks as his father's ashes were immersed in the water. Now he lingered in solitude before eventually crossing the river and setting off on a journey to the north. On the way he cast off his clothes and replaced them with the humble loincloth and deerskin upper garment of a wandering holy man. The only vestige of worldly life he retained was his sacred thread. In his hands he carried the traditional emblems of a holy wanderer: a wooden staff, rosary, and water pot. Around his neck he hung a small casket in which he deposited a Shaligram stone (a non-iconic form of Vishnu) and a small image of the child Krishna. He was entirely alone now, his old identity cast off; though still only a boy, he had become a new man, a renouncer focused on the highest truth.[16]

Nilakantha on the Move

The name taken by Ghanashyam after becoming a homeless wanderer was Nilakantha Varni. The epithet Nilakantha belongs paradigmatically to Lord Shiva the supreme yogi, who became the "one with the blue throat" (*nila-kantha*) after saving the cosmos by drinking the world-destroying poison during the churning of the milk ocean. The term Varni is used to refer to high-caste religious students, someone from a twice-born class (*varna*) who has renounced the world. Taken together, the two names capture central symbolic associations relevant at this stage of the young boy's life. Ghanashyam had now become a high-caste religious seeker on the path of ascetic denial. The *Satsangi Jivanam* understandably stresses the uniqueness of Nilakantha's spiritual journey, but what needs to be recognized is how closely his experiences are mapped onto long-standing South Asian patterns of asceticism and renunciation. Here there is something utterly stereotypical in Nilakantha's story: the sudden and unannounced departure from home, the shedding of worldly belongings, the adoption of the markers of ascetic life, and even the Himalayan routes along which the boy first traveled— all represent paradigmatic elements within South Asian narratives of renunciation.

I say this because placing too much emphasis on the heroic dimensions of Nilakantha's renunciation threatens to blind us to something we have noted already: his world was populated by countless individuals engaged in the same kind of pursuit, from solitary babas and fakirs to initiated members of mendicant orders, like the Dasnamis, Nath-Yogis, or Sufis. The activities of all these figures were structured in relation to general patterns of South Asian religious life and oriented toward a range of shared destinations: pilgrimage centers, monastic complexes, sacred sites, seasonal fairs, and trans-regional gatherings like the bathing festivals at Allahabad, Haridwar, or Nasik. Therefore, instead of construing Nilakantha as a unique specimen of the solitary spiritual hero, it proves far more useful to insert him into this active religious landscape and consider how he might have been nurtured, mentored, hosted, challenged, inspired, or rebuffed by any number of other such figures throughout seven years of extensive wandering.

Seven years is a long time, and the *Satsangi Jivanam* tells us that during this period the boy journeyed across the entire length and breadth of the subcontinent, beginning with lengthy pilgrimages to major sacred sites in north India, not least the Himalayan sites of Badrinath, sacred to Vishnu, and the city of Varanasi on the Ganga, sacred to Shiva. Leaving as he did from Ayodhya, it comes as little surprise that Nilakantha first oriented himself to the religious and political region of the Gangetic valley and Himalayas. He would have easily found his way along an existing network of Mughal-era roads, pilgrim pathways, and trans-Himalayan trade routes; along such routes countless sannyasis, fakirs, and Gosains wandered in search of wisdom. However, as we have seen, they also traveled these same routes on business, for instance carrying pearls and coral from the seacoasts that could be bartered for diamonds, musk, or textiles in any number of Himalayan trading centers.[17] Imagine what a young boy new to the road might learn from the traveling bands of ascetics, pilgrims, and traders he encountered on his travels. This gives us another way to appreciate the remark of one later commentator, who noted that Nilakantha had been trained in the "school of spiritual vagrancy."[18] That school would have taught much more than spirituality, we can be sure.

As we have seen, according to the *Satsangi Jivanam*, Nilakantha first set off to the north, a decision that makes sense in view of the long-standing association of the Himalayas with ascetic practice. Even as a young boy, he surely had come to possess more than a passing under-standing of the sanctity of the Himalayan landscape; he must have known the names of major pilgrimage sites and might well have felt a desire to visit the legendary ashrams of great sages associated with the mythic history of Bharatvarsha as found in the Epics and Puranas. Needless to say, once on the road, those mythic perspectives would have been augmented by a new understanding of geography, landscape, and people; he would have developed a new sense for time, as well, shaped by the experience of traversing long routes and spending extended pe-riods of time in various locales. Remarkably, neither the scope nor the duration of his undertaking seems to have deterred him. Rather, the *Sat-sangi Jivanam* gives us the impression that Nilakantha used his exten-sive time in the Himalayas to seek out religious teachers and to engage in a wide array of challenging austerities.

A key moment came early on, when Nilakantha had wandered as far north as the Gandaki River and the shrine of Muktinath, situated along the present international border between India and Nepal. This region holds profound resonances for Vaishnavas; the nearby riverbed is an important source for the sacred Shaligram stones worshipped by devotees as Vishnu's naturally occurring form, one of which Nilakantha carried in the casket hung around his neck.[19] True to the auto-hagiographical intention of the *Satsangi Jivanam*, the voice of Nilakantha occasionally inserts itself in the text by way of narrating ele-ments of his spiritual quest. At one point he meets the representative of a local ruler who has become curious about his antecedents. Nilakantha tells the king's emissary that he had learned devotion to Krishna by reading the Bhagavata Purana as a boy; from that text he came to know about the ashram of Pulaha; he had come in hopes of seeing Krishna in that same place. In the *Satsangi Jivanam*, such information is delivered as the *ipsissima verba* of Sahajanand and, as Peter Schreiner has argued, this technique represents one of the self-certifying mechanisms em-ployed by the text to bolster the charisma of its subject.[20] Obviously for Nilakantha to express the desire to deepen his devotion by visiting sites sacred to Krishna would prove useful for Sahajanand's larger goal of articulating the Vaishnava bona fides of his new polity. As for estab-lishing the spiritual powers of the young ascetic, readers of the *Satsangi*

Jivanam learn that, after arriving at the Gandaki River, Nilakantha bathed three times in its icy waters, standing for a time on one leg, with both arms over his head. Needless to say, onlookers were amazed. They asked themselves, could this be Shiva's own child?[21]

After departing from the region around Muktinath, Nilakantha chose to spend several months on his own deep in the valleys of the Himalayas. During this time he came upon a figure seated on a deerskin mat, wearing the matted locks and loincloth of a renouncer. Nilakantha watched as this yogi first worshipped the Shaligram stone and then recited the Bhagavad Gita. He came to know this was the sage Gopala.[22] Impressed by Gopala's practice, Nilakantha chose him as his spiritual preceptor and learned from him the practice of eightfold yoga. He is said to have amazed the teacher by the speed with which he gained yogic mastery.[23] This is another paradigmatic moment in the text, serving to ratify both Nilakantha's intellect and his yogic powers. Both would equip him to engage with the other teachers he was to meet along his travels, all of whom claimed forms of spiritual mastery and yet all of whom were also in danger of leading followers astray with the dark arts of Tantra or other un-Vaishnava practices.

After three years together, Gopala died, and so Nilakantha set off again on his travels. He supposedly carried with him a small manuscript copy of teachings bequeathed to him by Gopala.[24] Notwithstanding the fabulous character of Nilakantha's experiences, the narrative retains a ring of truth; after all, even mythic journeys bear the traces of real-world pathways. Thus we are told that, after heading south and east, Nilakantha came down from the mountains and entered the plains of north India. Then he wended his way eastward toward Bengal. Such a route is entirely plausible, since Bengal figured prominently in the itineraries of early colonial pilgrims and holy men, who traveled annually to a number of religious fairs and pilgrimage sites throughout the region.

By Nilakantha's day, many long-standing routes linked major *tirtha*s like Varanasi and Gaya in the Gangetic north with local temples and *mela*s scattered to the east across upper and lower Bengal.[25] In this region the sacred landscape was inscribed with the practice of both Shaktism and Shaivism; and since the death of Chaitanya Mahaprabhu in the early sixteenth century, Bengal had been the locus of Vaishnava theological innovation and institution-building. Countless Vaishnava devotees, both lay and initiated, passed back and forth through Bengal, moving among sacred sites around Mathura on the Yamuna River and Puri on the seacoast, not to mention lesser-known places farther east such as Kheturi in what is now northern Bangladesh. What is more, the main route leading south through Bengal to the great temple of Jagannath in Puri was by no means reserved for pilgrims; it also served as a major conduit for trade, state-building, and war-craft. It would have been dotted with caravanserais, market towns, and rural military garrisons. By Nilakantha's day, the old Puri road was a vital artery bustling with local commerce, European traders, and bands of ascetics, pilgrims, and other officials and functionaries.[26] Along such routes the school of spiritual vagrancy would have offered a rich and compelling curriculum!

Nilakantha in Bengal

Our bordered histories often cause us to overlook the role that such routes played in fostering trans-regional and long-range communication across South Asia and beyond.[27] The annual migratory routes followed by Gosains, fakirs, and pilgrims are just one case in point, stretching as they did from important Himalayan sites like Badrinath and Haridwar to destinations along the coast of the Bay of Bengal like Puri, Sagar Island, and Chandranath near the boundary of present-day Bangladesh and Myanmar. One especially common pilgrimage route cut across the Himalayan foothills of the Nepal *terai*, crossed the Mahananda River, and continued on into northern Bengal.[28] From there travelers could either continue on to the northeast to visit sacred sites in present-day Assam, or turn south through Rangpur and Bogra (both today in Bangladesh). Throughout the region, renunciant orders and Sufi lineages all had local patrons and followers, often clustered around monastic sites or the burial shrines (*dargahs*) of holy men. And we should bear in mind that the regular visits to Bengal of all these travelers had not merely spiritual but also economic motivations. The early colonial cartographer

James Rennell served in this area under the East India Company and reported that, annually, itinerant religious orders raised as much as £5000–£6000 from local donors.[29]

To mention Rennell is to remember that during the decades running up to Sahajanand's birth, one particular region—between Rangpur and Bogra—had become the site of frequent skirmishes between the expanding forces of the East India Company and roving bands of ascetics who often traveled in armed units, replete with horses, elephants, and arms. Rennell himself was once seriously wounded in an armed engagement with a group he described as a "Tribe of Facquirs (a kind of sturdy beggars)."[30] It was on the basis of reports like Rennell's that early British officials were able to fashion the stereotype of the warrior ascetic that we have already discussed—that figure so closely tied to colonial anxieties surrounding extortion, banditry, and sedition.[31]

The view from the other side of such skirmishes was of course rather different. One well-known fakir leader by the name of Majnu Shah actually drafted a letter to Rani Bhabani, the influential ruler of Natore, south of Bogra, complaining about the restrictions being imposed on his followers by the British. Majnu Shah pointed out that ascetic groups like his had "for a long time . . . been entertained" in the region, which they visited to worship at "several shrines and altars."[32] What the British framed as seditious resistance and economic plundering was in Manju Shah's eyes part of a robust political economy linking the trading and warrior talents of ascetic orders to the needs of local communities and the political projects of small polities like the Natore Raj.

Both Rennell and Majnu Shah were active in northern Bengal during the peak of a decades-long struggle over revenue, landholding, and political control that would come to be known as the Sannyasi Rebellion.[33] The aggressive policies of the British and the resistance of various Sannyasi leaders during the 1760s and 1770s have come in for considerable study, and we cannot afford to linger on the details here. But such studies prove useful for further contextualizing Nilakantha's travels. They help us appreciate the vital economic tendrils and tangled motives that supported trade, travel, and statecraft in the region and also allow us to register the disruptions wrought by the incursion of a new imperial polity.

It is important to have all this in mind when we picture young Nilakantha on the road. The *Satsangi Jivanam* may not be an entirely reliable record of Nilakantha's travels, but the routes it maps and the engagements it highlights seem to be rooted in the memories of a man who actually walked these roads. Those memories were brought to life again by his amanuensis, Shatanand Muni. Nor does it seem Shatanand was a stranger to the disruptions of the era, having also relocated to Gujarat from northern India during this same moment. While there is no reason to expect the *Satsangi Jivanam* to examine the turbulent political, economic, and social contexts in which Nilakantha found himself, that should not prevent us from reading the text in light of these developments.

When we layer this sort of historical awareness onto the mythic paradigm of Nilakantha's journey, we become attuned to the significance of Bengal within the South Asian religious imagination, both as a frontier zone lying to the east of the Gangetic heartland and as a sacred realm in its own right, dotted with centers of great antiquity. For instance, immediately adjacent to Majnu Shah's fort at Bogra stands the far older complex of Mahasthan; the very name, "great place," gives an indication of the site's importance. Thanks to modern excavations, one can see today at Mahasthan the remains of a major Buddhist complex that once marked the periphery of ancient Mauryan imperial expansion.[34] Later this region came to be known as Pundravardhana, one of the major political divisions of ancient Bengal. With the arrival of Islam in South Asia, the area experienced new political and religious expansion. Legends speak of the defeat of the last Hindu ruler, Parsuram, by Muhammad Shah Sultan, who came to be recognized as a great spiritual teacher, or Pir. The tomb of Muhammad Shah Sultan, which is attested in a seventeenth-century land grant, sits adjacent to Mahasthan, constituting one of several Muslim shrines in the area. In the late nineteenth century the site remained in good repair, and one observer reported the Pir's *dargah* was visited annually by "thousands of pilgrims."[35]

Part of what made this region so attractive to rulers, traders, and pilgrims was the presence of the Karatoya River, which used to flow south past Mahasthan in greater force than it does today.[36] The Karatoya represents an ecological boundary in the region, dividing the hard red clay of its western shores from richer alluvial soil to the east. In ancient times this ecological boundary also constituted a political frontier, setting Pundravardhana apart from the region to the east known as Kamarupa. These two were among the many countries or *desh* within the Bharat-varsha imagined by early colonial leaders like Sahajanand and Ram-mohun. In mythic terms, the Karatoya was endowed with particular sanctity, its name referring to the pouring of water (*toya*) into Shiva's hands (*kara*) on the occasion of his marriage to Parvati.[37] This in turn reminds us of the prevalence of worship to Shiva and the goddess in the Bengali cultural region. On the banks of the river just south of present-day Bogra, at Bhabanipur, is an important Hindu temple to the goddess Kali. The site is revered as a *pitha sthan*, marking the spot where a portion of the goddess (or in this case a piece of her clothing) fell to earth during Shiva's mythic dismembering of her body after her self-immolation at Daksha's sacrifice.

The temple to Bhabani Kali benefited greatly from the patronage of the same Rani Bhabani to whom Majnu Shah had directed his appeal. Rani Bhabani (1716–1795) holds a special place in the Bengali—and the Indian—imagination for her many achievements as a woman ruler during the early colonial period. She was, in particular, a great patron of Hindu institutions from Bogra all the way to Varanasi.[38] She played a particularly important role in the promulgation of goddess worship, helping advance the popularity of annual rituals such as the autumn festival of Durga Puja.[39] Her support for the temple at Bogra is indicated in the name of the goddess, Bhabani Kali.[40] Since she financed the construction of a large embankment allowing devotees and pilgrims to reach the temple even during the heaviest monsoon flooding, we are again encouraged to think about how such local patronage left its mark on the very landscape traversed by renouncers like young Nilakantha.[41]

I mention all these details because, if we follow the narrative in the *Satsangi Jivanam*, it seems as if the area around Bogra was the first important stopping point on Nilakantha's itinerary after coming down out of the Himalayas. Arriving there, the text tells us, he made his way to a city called Sirpur, which is likely present-day Sherpur, a town located about fifteen miles south of Bogra. Sherpur sits along the road that follows the Karatoya River south to the Rani's Bhabani Kali temple. According to the *Satsangi Jivanam*, the ruler of Sirpur (Sherpur) was a righteous man named Siddhavallabha. His name, "Beloved of the Spiritual Adepts," alerts us to the fact that the ruler was an enthusiastic patron of various practitioners known generically as adepts or "perfected" beings (*siddhas*). Given the Vaishnava mission of Nilakantha, the ruler's name is intended to conjure the image of a suspect milieu dominated by ascetics, Tantrikas, yogis, and yoginis.[42] Although the goal of the *Satsangi Jivanam* is to undercut the validity of such religious paths, we must remind ourselves that this list identifies a range of figures who would certainly have gravitated to the court of a real-world ruler like Rani Bhabani. We only have to recall her support for goddess worship, blood sacrifice, and Tantra.[43] It is not hard to imagine the young Nilakantha being drawn to such a court, buoyed along by the flow of other ascetics and pilgrims. Needless to say, within the narrative of the *Satsangi Jivanam*, the goal is to demonstrate how Nilakantha deployed his devotional charisma and yogic skills to vanquish these practitioners of the "black arts." It thus clearly makes hagiographic sense for Nilakantha to visit a site like Sherpur / Bogra.[44] What one has to wonder is whether later in life Sahajanand might have told his disciple Shatanand about what he had seen when traveling through Bengal.

The *Satsangi Jivanam* tells us that when Siddhavallabha invited Nilakantha to stay in his capital, the latter agreed, spending the four-month rainy season there. During his sojourn in at Siddhavallabha's court, the devout young Vaishnava set out to overcome all the adepts and wonder workers who enjoyed the ruler's largess. Predictably, the yogis and Tantrikas responded by attempting to defeat the upstart ascetic using their own sinister wiles. They chanted awesome mantras and tossed around black gram infused with deadly charms. Details of the lifeworlds of Sirpur's tantric practitioners are obviously not provided in the *Satsangi Jivanam*; it deals only in familiar tropes and caricatures of the tantric dark arts. Overall the text adopts a moralizing tone, taking aim at the sinful pride (*darpa*) afflicting the Siddhas.[45] Their spiritual arrogance is opposed by Nilakantha's saintliness, self-control, and humility. Of course, thanks to his training, Nilakantha is able to best them all in yogic attainments. But in the end it is his love for God that determines ultimate victory; through the love of Hari he is able to cure victims of tantric spells and ultimately to win over the ruler to Krishna devotion. Needless to say, throughout it all Nilakantha never boasts for his own sake; he serves only God.[46]

The narration of events in Sirpur allows us to appreciate that while the *Satsangi Jivanam* trades on the generic trope of the black arts to announce the moral and spiritual supremacy of devotion, the agenda of the text does not prevent us from reading the account of Siddhavallabha's court in relation to the historical context of early colonial Bengal.[47] In this religious landscape, local rulers patronized a wide variety of religious practices and ritual styles, sometimes Shakta / Shaiva and sometimes Vaishnava. Alongside the Kali temple at Bhabanipur, we could point to another site about seven miles west of Bogra known locally as Jogir Bhaban, or "The Yogi's Home." Dating from the era of Rani Bhabani's rule, this monastic establishment was created for the use of the Dasnami Sampraday, which had begun to establish its presence in Bengal during the eighteenth century. Inscriptions at Jogir Bhaban indicate there was new construction at the site at precisely the time when Nilakantha would have come through the area (provided we grant at least some historicity to the narrative of the *Satsangi Jivanam*).[48]

The *Satsangi Jivanam* thus brings into view the dynamic religious world of early colonial Bengal and allows us to draw a connection between hagiography and history. Stepping back and thinking in more general terms, it is worth noting how well the goals of a text like the *Satsangi Jivanam* harmonize with early modern bhakti-informed narratives the purpose of which is to celebrate the victory of nonviolent and morally restrained devotion over the practice of magical and sacrificial modes of religion as found in goddess cults and Tantra. There is much in the story of Nilakantha's mission to spread the religion of Hari that meshes with vernacular hagiographies from north India, such as the *Bhaktamala* of Nabhadas. In such texts we find narratives promoting the superiority of devotional service (*seva*) over ritual sacrifice and of the primacy of reciting God's name instead of engaging in esoteric practices of mantra recitation and visualization.

Turning the table around again on history and hagiography, it is worth noting that hitherto scholars have not been averse to taking such early modern bhakti narratives as historically accurate; they have found it convenient to treat such hagiographical literature as direct evidence of the growing superiority of devotional religion in the early modern era. What they have sometimes lost sight of is the fact that texts like the *Bhaktamal*, no less than the *Satsangi Jivanam*, are highly normative and fictive accounts committed to endorsing one kind of religious habitus. They celebrate the superiority of self-effacing, nonviolent, bhajan-inflected bhakti over all modes of embodied and ritualized practice, not least the death-defying wisdom associated with a wide range of ascetic, yogic, and tantric communities. Having just made the case for grounding the *Satsangi Jivanam* in history, I now register this cautionary remark because it is important to appreciate how easy it would be for late-colonial, Protestant-inspired understandings of spiritual reform to find proof of a certain kind of religion by selectively approving one genre of religious texts without considering their own intentionality. Just as Muzaffar Alam demonstrated how colonial authors tended to be led astray by taking Mughal-era chronicles at face value, scholars like William Pinch have reminded us that colonial-era authors likewise tended to codify their own preference for a spiritually sanitized religion of faith (i.e., bhakti) over equally prevalent forms of warrior asceticism and tantric corporal technologies. Pinch reminds us that bhakti has been given a special place in what I am calling the empire of reform.[49]

All of this is to say we should be careful when reading texts like the *Satsangi Jivanam*. Its celebration of the superiority (morally or demographically) of a privatized, devotional, and depoliticized religion does not necessarily accord with the kinds of evidence we can gather about religious life during Rani Bhabani's day. In fact, the eagerness of later colonial commentators and present-day scholars to slot Sahajanand's new polity into the rubric of beneficial reforms has led many to accept simplistic, prima facie readings of the text. In so doing, they not only tend to misrepresent the religious landscape of places like Bengal and Gujarat (as we have seen in Chapter 2) but they also miss an opportunity to consider with more nuance the world through which a figure like young Nilakantha would have moved—a world of diverse ritual practices, competing ascetic disciplines, and the material endorsements and political agendas of various regional lords and rulers.

Overall it helps to think of Nilakantha not as a lone spiritual pilgrim, but as one of countless religious itinerants, enacting long-established patterns of behavior around sacred space and buffeted by a range of impersonal factors including trade, warfare, commerce, and politics. Here the Dasnamis of Jogir Bhaban can be of some help. Although we have no evidence that Nilakantha traveled with Dasnami sannyasis or resided at any of their monastic settlements, it seems incontrovertible that he walked along paths and visited sites that owed more than a little to the work of the Dasnamis and their local patrons like Rani Bhabani.[50] It was precisely during Nilakantha's lifetime that the Dasnami Sampraday was spreading into lower Bengal and establishing a network of monastic sites.[51] If Nilakantha arrived in Sirpur via the well-trodden pilgrim path leading south from Rangpur, he had to have shared the road with Dasnamis, not to mention Nath Yogis and others. Put differently, even if Raja Siddhavallabha is a hagiographic fiction, Rani Bhabani is not.[52]

Angry Siddhas and Hot Springs

Let us follow Nilakantha even farther east in order to develop this point in more detail. After passing four months in Sirpur, Nilakantha followed a group of Siddhas who set off toward the region of present-day Assam, in the ancient region of Kamarupa. There his destination was an even more renowned goddess shrine, that of Kamakhya Devi. Predictably, Kamakhya figures in the *Satsangi Jivanam* as an ideal place for a virtuous bhakta to prove the superiority of Krishna devotion. Here the story turns on the figure of a drunken Brahmin. Though he had once been dedicated to his prescribed duties (*svadharma*), a good husband, and a man of virtue, this poor soul had been led astray by association with Shaktas (*shaktasanga*); and so his downfall began.[53] He turned from the Vedas and began reading certain non-Vedic tantric Agamas like the *Kularnava Tantra*; he also took to drinking alcohol and eating meat and was known to drink the ritual fluids used in the secret Kaula worship of young girls.[54] With bloodshot eyes and reeking of raw fish, he brandished his iron trident and taunted the other Siddhas, proclaiming himself the only true Siddha.[55] His is a clear case of what the *Satsangi Jivanam* disparages as spiritual pride (*abhimana*), made worse by being combined with loss of Vedic propriety and a turning away from God.

At this moment we are geographically almost as far as possible from the land in which Sahajanand would ultimately spread his teachings. But it would not be lost on early Satsangi audiences that Nilakantha was destined to reach Gujarat and undertake the conversion of very similar goddess worshipping groups there. In this way, his visit to Kamakhya serves to prefigure future spiritual battles and to demonstrate beyond doubt the depth of Nilakantha's antagonism to non-Vedic religious life. The central trope is one of spiritual conquest. However, although the evil Brahmin manifests all manner of magical spells and incantations, and summons the darkest agents of destruction, his defeat comes with no violence on the part of Nilakantha. Confronted by outraged black magicians, Nilakantha asks them to do their worst, all the while remaining calmly seated in the hero's pose (*virasana*). The scene is reminiscent of Mara's troops assailing Siddhartha but finding no way to deter his transit to Buddhahood. In the *Satsangi Jivanam*, the story ends with the evil Brahmin being returned to his Vedic ways, instructed in the Bhagavata Purana and Bhagavad Gita, and learning devotion to Krishna. And in fact, here the text does call to mind the teachings of Krishna in the Gita, since we learn that the Lord has taken human form as Nilakantha in order to uproot evil (*adharma*) and to preach "the highest devotion to Krishna."[56]

Having traveled to Kamakhya in the company of the Siddhas, Nilakantha then parts ways with them. He sets off for what sounds like an entirely mythic locale known as Mount Navalaksha.[57] The location of Mount Navalaksha is not specified. What the *Satsangi Jivanam* does stress is that the site had been overrun by Siddhas, who were spreading their false religion in the usual ways. To underscore the threat, the name Navalaksha is supposed to conjure up the specter of nine hundred thousand (*nava-laksha*) Siddhas all practicing dark and deviant religion in that place. It certainly makes for an intriguing venue in which Nilakantha will be able display his religious virtues and promote devotion. Even before having a chance to take on the Siddhas, he must ascend the mountain, a feat that confirms Nilakantha's boundless physical vigor— something his later disciples would be keen to praise.[58]

Surprisingly, the hagiography once again includes the traces of some telling geological and historical details that allow us to map the place of Navalaksha against the known world of eastern Bengal. One detail in particular fairly leaps from the text: the *Satsangi Jivanam* describes the landscape in this region as punctuated by fires that appear to "burn without fuel" (*agnijvala api nirindhana*). A second interesting detail soon follows: the area is also said to feature a number of hot and cold springs (*kund*). Both details are so vivid and so specific that one has to ask whether the *Satsangi Jivanam* has in mind an actual mountain locale characterized by the presence of flaming geysers and scattered natural springs. Geologically, the setting sounds plausible.

It turns out there is just such a place, situated to the south and east of Kamakhya and lying along what might be thought of as the frontier between South and Southeast Asia; indeed, this is a region so far removed from Manu's Gangetic heartland of Aryavarta that, in classical Hindu texts, it qualifies as *mleccha* or barbarian country.[59] Although peripheral, the region is nonetheless not entirely removed from the Hindu universe; in fact it has its own Puranic associations. This is the area of the Sitakund Range, lying just north of the present-day port city of Chittagong on the coast of Bangladesh. Most remarkably, when one looks at the Sitakund region, one finds that it constitutes an active geological zone featuring volcanic eruptions, hot springs, and occasional seismic activity.[60] And here one also finds important Hindu pilgrimage sites like Chandranath and Sitakund itself.[61] The temple to Chandranath remains even today an important hilltop shrine visited by Shaiva pilgrims, while Sitakund has long been famous for its hot springs. According to legend, Sita bathed in the waters of this tank while in exile with her husband, Lord Rama.[62]

What is most intriguing for anyone interested in siting Nilakantha's journey in time and space is that just north of Sitakund we find another pilgrimage site known as Lavanaksha (or Lavanakhya). This site is famed for its saltwater spring (hence, *lavana*).[63] It takes only a bit of reflection to appreciate how the name Lavanaksha could be transformed into Navalaksha. Either through deliberate or accidental transposition of a mere two letters, the salt spring became the spiritual haunt of nine hundred thousand Siddhas. And if the *Satsangi Jivanam* calls the place a mountain, this too makes sense, since Lavanaksha is situated within the Chandranath range of hills, whose peaks—if hardly Himalayan in scale—rise to a height of several hundred feet above the surrounding plains.

Could this really be the place visited by Nilakantha? The *Satsangi Jivanam* gives us one more piece of concrete evidence to bolster this assumption; the text mentions that, while staying at Mount Navalaksha, Nilakantha took time to visit a spring called Barava Kund. As it turns out, a hot spring by that same name exists just a stone's throw from Sitakund. A Shiva temple there purports to be centuries old.[64] While residing at Barava Kund for three days, Nilakantha was captivated by the eruptions of wind, fire, and water (*vayvagnipathas*).[65]

If the sites mentioned in the *Satsangi Jivanam* do correspond to Lavanaksha, Sitakund, and Barava Kund—and the correspondence among the story, the natural phenomena, and the toponyms is hard to deny—then it is reasonable to ask whether this might be one point where the *Satsangi Jivanam* actually preserves something like Sahajanand's own memories of his travels, even if now mediated by Shatanand. That is, one could imagine a context in which Sahajanand himself regaled his followers with stories of his travels in far-off lands and dramatic locales. Even if that is going too far, we might nonetheless ask how an author like Shatanand (a Maithili relocated to Gujarat) would have come to know enough about such site-specific details to include them in his text.

Perhaps by the early nineteenth century, when Shatanand wrote, places like the hot springs and temples of Lavanaksha had gained some notoriety across South Asia. If our cartographic imagination of South Asia tends to orient us to the core Gangetic valley, the Himalayan north, or the prominent temple towns of the south, Nilakantha's story reminds us that premodern narrative traditions mapped the space of South Asia in different ways. It is worth noting that the regions of Chandranath, Sitakund, and Lavanaksha do figure in some postclassical Puranas and Tantras. They are particularly prominent in texts that promote the virtues of Shaiva and Shakta practice; in such texts, these sites are narrativized in relation to stories of Sati's dismemberment, the exile of Rama and Sita, and the manifestation of Shiva's flaming linga (*jyotirlinga*).[66] This may be precisely why Nilakantha chose to visit the area around Chandranath and Sitakund; by his day this was a renowned and sacred precinct.

Chandranath in particular had by the late eighteenth century developed into an important trans-regional pilgrimage destination. Both the Ramanandi Sampraday and the Dasnami Sampraday established themselves in the area around this time.[67] Their presence around Sitakund alerts us to other kinds of changes that were taking place during Nilakantha's day; most notably, these two renunciant polities—one Vaishnava and the other Shaiva—had begun to contest claims regarding their roles and entitlements within this locale. Records reveal that during the 1780s and 1790s the hot spring and tank at Sitakund had in fact become the focal point for a minor dispute between the Ramanandis and Dasnamis.[68] The immediate trigger for the dispute seems to have been the construction of a Kali temple at the site by the Dasnamis, who would have tolerated the routine sacrifice of animals to the goddess. But that practice elicited "aversion" among the vegetarian Vaishnavas, and therefore the Ramanandis sought to challenge the legitimacy of the Dasnami claim to the site.[69] The dispute appears to have simmered at a low boil for several years before finally bubbling up at the colonial court in Calcutta in 1791.

Two fascinating possibilities present themselves at this point: First, could it be that Nilakantha was drawn to the Sitakund region by word of this dispute, the repercussions of which must have rippled through the communication networks linking ascetics throughout eastern India? It certainly fits with the hagiographic image of Nilakantha as the charismatic defender of Krishna devotion to picture him marching off to Sitakund to aid in the defeat of Shaivas and Shaktas. Second, even if the story was invented by Shatanand, is it possible that he drew on some knowledge of the dispute, information that had perhaps reached colonial Gujarat by word of mouth or through early print media? If so, is it not possible that Shatanand drew on the dispute at Sitakund as a backstory to foretell the kind of victories Sahajanand was to have in Kathiawar? The entanglement of history and hagiography around the events at Sitakund, no matter how it came about, speaks volumes to the contested world of religion in early colonial South Asia.

From Journey to Path

Given what we know about the level of Ramanandi and Dasnami activity in eastern Bengal at the time, it should come as no surprise to learn that, when Nilakantha departed from Sitakund, he set his sights on visiting the ashram of the legendary sage Kapila Muni on Sagar Island, situated at the confluence of the Hooghly River and the Bay of Bengal.[70] Known more generally as Ganga Sagar and celebrated as the confluence (*sangam*) of the Ganga and the ocean (*sagar*), this is one of South Asia's major *tirthas*. It is amply attested in both mythic narratives and historical documents. Annually it attracts thousands of pilgrims for its bathing festival (*snan-yatra*) in the cold winter month of Magh.[71] It is no exaggeration to say that all of South Asia's renunciant groups made Ganga Sagar their regular destination. And for this reason, the site was to become another scene of contestation. In fact, over time the Dasnamis, who had early on established a monastic residence (*matha*) on the island, appear to have been ousted from their position of control by the Ramanandis, whose presence is notable at the site even today.

As to mythic scenarios, when Nilakantha reached the ashram at Ganga Sagar, the *Satsangi Jivanam* tells us he was greeted by none other than Kapila himself. Since Kapila is the legendary founder of the Samkhya system and one of South Asia's greatest yogis, the significance of his appearance needs little discussion. Suffice it to say that, while Nilakantha is pleased to encounter in Kapila the very embodiment of duty, restraint, knowledge, and yoga, what really matters is that when Kapila enters into a meditative trance, he recognizes Nilakantha as Lord Krishna himself.[72] Here devotion encompasses and thereby surpasses yoga. Nilakantha remains a master yogi, but his restraint and his meditative powers are deployed in devotion to Krishna and oriented toward the restoration of true bhakti religion on earth. The grand narrative of bhakti that harmonized so well with later Protestant valorizations of a higher, reformed vision of Hinduism is once again evident.

There is little history to recount from Nilakantha's visit to Ganga Sagar, and after spending a month in Kapila's ashram, he chose to cross back to the mainland. Then he proceeded south to the Vaishnava pilgrimage town of Puri, revered as the sacred realm of the Ultimate Lord (*purushottama kshetra*). This leg of his journey will surprise no one familiar with either Vaishnava bhakti traditions or the well-worn routes of renouncers during the early colonial period. As noted earlier, the road leading south through Bengal to Puri was another of those major arteries plied by traders, troops, pilgrims, and ascetic wanderers. And of course, by making Puri his goal, the *Satsangi Jivanam* ensures that all due emphasis is placed on Nilakantha's ability to fulfil his mission by conquering the enemies of religion and establishing duty and devotion to Krishna. Borrowing from the Mahabharata, one could say that, as far as the *Satsangi Jivanam* is concerned, where there is Nilakantha there is victory (*jaya*).[73]

From Puri, Nilakantha was to head even farther into the south, addressing his vision of true religion to Vaishnavas and Shaivas at numerous sacred sites such as Rameshvaram, Kanchipuram, and Srirangam. Later in life, after he had begun articulating his new religious polity in Gujarat, Sahajanand would draw on these experiences to prove his claims of spiritual mastery and to illustrate the true meaning of devotion to the members of the fledgling *satsang*. For instance, some two decades after his travels, he told a gathering of holy men and disciples about his journey to Rameshvaram. He said that, while visiting that sacred town, he came across another sadhu named Sevakram. As it happened, Sevakram was carrying one thousand rupees worth of gold coins—yet another reminder of the complicated economic lives of early colonial holy men! For whatever reason, Nilakantha chose to fall in with Sevakram and accompany him on the road.

At some point Sevakram became gravely ill. Nilakantha stayed with him, promising to serve and care for him. He faithfully tended to Sevakram, even cleaning up after Sevakram's bouts of bloody dysentery. All the while, Sevakram guarded his gold coins carefully; whenever Nilakantha left him to procure food, Sevakram would give him just enough money to cover the costs. Eventually Sevakram recovered and the two men continued on their journey. Now the elder Sevakram began to make Nilakantha carry his large bundle of belongings. And so Sevakram strolled merrily along chanting his rosary while Nilakantha struggled with the heavy load. To make matters worse, Sevakram never offered his companion any food, despite the tremendous exertions Nilakantha was making on Sevakram's behalf. From this Sahajanand drew a simple lesson:

> Although I served that sadhu and helped him recover, he did
> not offer me even a single paisa worth of food. Therefore,
> realizing him to be ungrateful, I abandoned his company. In

this way, a person who does not appreciate favours done by
others should be known as an ungrateful person.[74]

This short sermon illustrates one way Nilakantha's journeys were linked
to Sahajanand's eventual promulgation of the Swaminarayan path. It
also intimates how Sahajanand's memories of travel proved useful for
illustrating important aspects of the path. This suggests that his eventual request to Shatanand that he write a full hagiography may have reflected his desire to see the dharma of his new polity directly anchored
in his own experiences. Shatanand's great accomplishment was to craft
a kind of modern Purana in which movement, space, conflict, and devotion become the thematic backdrop for the articulation of a new religious polity. This hagiography maps the origin story of the Swaminarayan Sampraday onto the sacred landscape of South Asia, using
Nilakantha's journeys through that landscape to demonstrate the spiritual mastery and moral supremacy of the new guru, Sahajanand.[75] Stepping back, we can also see how the *Satsangi Jivanam* employs the structuring trope of a grand circumambulatory pilgrimage (*digvijaya*) around
the subcontinent to ground Sahajanand's authority in the values of an
ancient religio-political concept. This too is important to stress.

In Chapter 6 I turn to a more detailed explication of how Sahajanand
went about advancing the values and institutional structures of the
Swaminarayan Sampraday after settling in Gujarat. For now it is enough
to recall what Ronald Inden once pointed out about the relationship between the act of circumambulating Bharatvarsha and the enunciation
of authority by a religious king in medieval South Asia. As Inden noted,
the ideal way for an aspiring "king of kings" to announce his service to
the highest gods was through the establishment of a temple. Ideally, this
"crowning" achievement was something that could be undertaken only
after the would-be ruler had completed a successful "conquest of the
quarters," or *digvijaya*.[76] Understanding that Sahajanand was no king,
recourse to Inden's reflection on the *digvijaya* should nonetheless remind
us that religious and political ideologies were both encompassed within
the premodern conception of a great "chain of being." As such, rather
than thinking of Sahajanand as guru in the narrow sense of religious
teacher, it helps to also picture him as a kind of ruling lord, the figure

Inden calls a master. As a ruling lord, Sahajanand used the mastery made evident through his circumambulation of the subcontinent to support the projection of his lordship over the Swaminarayan Sampraday. In other words, the ascetic pilgrim Nilakantha went on to become the religious master Sahajanand, who would in time present himself to the world as none other than Lord Swaminarayan.[77]

Bearing in mind this model for understanding the articulation of lordship in a religious context, it is worth considering how much emphasis is placed in the earliest Swaminarayan literature—the *Vachanamrut* especially—on depicting Sahajanand in the fashion of a royal lord. I had occasion to highlight this issue in Chapter 2 when discussing Sahajanand's appearance in the *darbar* of Dada Khachar. The textual accounts of his holding court, as it were, remind us that the work he did after coming to Gujarat required the conscious effort to manifest himself not merely as teacher, but as powerful master and lord. This helps explain the amount of moving he continued to do even after leaving behind his ascetic identity of Nilakantha. His peregrinations around the region of Gujarat were punctuated by the attempt to articulate his own growing authority in relation to existing modes of religious and political power on the ground. He thus accepted invitations to stay with local chieftains, in whose courts he could manifest and amplify his mastery. He had temples built in selected locations to proclaim his authority. And he was not shy about cultivating connections to the East India Company. We shall turn to some of these issues in Chapter 6. For now it is enough to emphasize that Sahajanand's recourse to local courts and his outreach to British administrators should not be interpreted as evidence of capitulation to foreign rule, nor as cynical politicking. If anything, his relationship to British authority is the very proof of his attempt to introduce a new polity within the early colonial scale of forms in the region. And, as the *Satsangi Jivanam* puts it, wherever there was Sahajanand, there would be victory for the new polity.

5

UPCOUNTRY
WITH RAMMOHUN

I T IS IRONIC THAT during his lifetime Sahajanand Swami remained
largely off the colonial radar, and yet we possess a lengthy (if hagiographic) account of his early life, whereas in the case of Rammohun Roy,
who was at the forefront of global conversations about India during his
day, we have no comprehensive narrative of his career generated from
within the early Samaj. Just as remarkable is the fact that although our
models of modern reform tend to presume the naturalness of the process whereby a guru like Sahajanand is scripted into myth, we rarely acknowledge how much our celebration of Rammohun depends on near-
mythic tropes. We like to say Rammohun was born at the *dawn* of India's
awakening, the herald of an Indian *renaissance*. In prose bordering on
the hagiographic, Rabindranath Tagore went so far as to describe Rammohun descending godlike into the blind darkness that was India, on a
mission to revivify a country that was as good as dead.[1] This is not so
far removed from themes sounded in a text like the *Satsangi Jivanam*.
And then there is the central myth of national paternity—Rammohun
Roy, the Father of Modern India.[2]

   All of this is to say that when we read a text like the *Satsangi Jivanam*,
we are alive with skepticism about its hagiographical intent, but when
we read about a so-called great man like Rammohun, we pay little

attention to the tropes and conceits through which his legacy has been transmitted.³ But if we are to reconsider the role of reform-based narratives in shaping attitudes toward modern Hinduism, empire, and the Indian nation, we must address the work done by such tropes. One might even say there is as much need to demythologize Rammohun as there is in the case of Sahajanand. In the case of Sahajanand, we instantly recognize traces of the medieval; in Rammohun's case, we are habituated to see only the modern—the triumph of rational monotheism over the corrupted imagination of the Hindus.

I therefore propose to do something akin to what I attempted with respect to Sahajanand's early career as Nilakantha. I want to examine Rammohun's early life in relation to the physical and discursive landscapes through which he traveled before settling down in Calcutta. Just as with Sahajanand, my goal is to reflect on how Rammohun came to acquire the kind of spiritual mastery that equipped him to become the successful author of a new religious polity. The comparison with Sahajanand is not incidental here; the young Rammohun also traversed a number of northern and eastern routes that provided him with an education in religion, ethics, and new possibilities emerging in the early colonial moment. Following Rammohun along these routes allows us to appreciate three things: First, there was nothing unusual about being on the move in this way; his reasons for traveling were consistent with the broader habits of his day. Second, by traveling and studying in a range of distinctive cultural environments, Rammohun accrued a diverse set of tools for rethinking the meaning of religion. And third, the mastery he displayed in this regard would be crucial for the work he would undertake after settling in Calcutta.

Traces of the Young Rammohun

It is not difficult to picture Rammohun in motion; we know he traveled in his youth because he tells us so in two important autobiographical passages. However, beyond this, the task of garnering further details to situate him within his early world proves rather more difficult. We are told that he published some articles about his early travels in the Bengali journal *Sambad Kaumudi*, but sadly such evidence has not been found.[4] As a result, the editors of one exhaustive compilation of official documents relating to Rammohun's life conclude that there are no extant records to inform us about the bulk of his activities before he reached the age of twenty-five.[5] Were it not for scattered reports made about him by various friends and acquaintances, we would have very little to work with; and much of this material constitutes something more like hearsay than history, when it does not veer into outright legend.[6]

We must therefore fall back on those two extant autobiographical statements. And here it is important to note that the two pieces of autobiography were composed on either side, as it were, of his emergence into public life and rise to prominence in Calcutta and beyond. Put differently, these two documents are separated in time by three decades, three consequential decades in which much would change in Rammohun's life and world. The first piece of autobiography is found in Rammohun's earliest extant work, the Persian *Tuhfat-ul-muwahhidin*, a remarkable text he published even before he had settled in Calcutta. I discuss this work at length later, but for now it is enough to note that in the preface to *Tuhfat* he tells his readers he had spent several years after his sixteenth birthday (ca. 1788) traveling "in the remotest parts of the world, in plains as well as in hilly lands."[7] This geographical gloss is as tantalizing as it is brief; it hints at—but does not further specify—vast spatial distances, not to mention significant cultural variations between the regions of the Himalayas and the Gangetic valley.

So far as his age is concerned, the account in *Tuhfat* is consistent with Rammohun's second autobiographical statement, which was composed in 1833. There too he gives age sixteen as the year he left home.[8] In Chapter 1 we had occasion to examine this text as a means for exploring Rammohun's conception of the chronoscape of Bharatvarsha. There we saw that Rammohun compiled his remarks in connection with testimony delivered while in Britain during what was to be the final year of his life. Even though the authenticity of this document has been debated, I follow Dermot Killingley and take it at its word.[9] Not only is the overall tone consistent with Rammohun's usage, but the way the author of these remarks frames his travels is clearly meant to situate an earlier period of his life in relation to what he later went on to achieve during his public career in Calcutta.

This text offers a clear rationale for Rammohun's departure from home, one that is every bit as dramatic as was the case with young Ghanashyam. Rammohun tells his readers that at the age of sixteen he "composed a manuscript" in which he questioned the "validity of the idolatrous system of the Hindoos." He states rather delicately that this produced a "coolness" between him and his family. This is what seems to have led to his decision to travel. One British contemporary and friend, William Adam, actually reported that Rammohun was "religiously disposed" as a fourteen-year-old to adopt the life of the sannyasi, and was dissuaded only through his mother's tearful entreaties.[10] Such a remark is enough to place both Ghanashyam and Rammohun, if only briefly, on shared emotional and spiritual ground.

It is only fair to ask what might have imbued Rammohun not merely with an instinct for renunciation but also, more importantly, with the requisite skills as a teenager to craft a work attacking Hindu patterns of worship. Here his autobiographical remarks actually work to simultaneously conceal and reveal one important piece of information: at one point he comments that, following a practice common on his father's side of the family, he had studied Persian and Arabic. He tells us nothing further; we are thrilled to learn of this early educational exercise and also left to wonder where it might have led. One thing seems all but certain: this must have happened when he was as young as eight years old.[11] At that time he was sent away from home to study, first in Patna and later in Varanasi. Early biographical accounts are quick to suggest that it was the combined influence of his exposure to Islamic theology in Patna and the doctrines of Vedanta in Varanasi that set the young boy's mind firmly against all forms of so-called idolatry and polytheism.[12]

For his part, Rammohun does not go into such details, and sadly the infamous manuscript he says he composed has never been found. If it had been as forthright in its critique as his later reputation might lead us to suppose, it is easy to believe his family would have destroyed it. It seems we cannot know any more than this. However, if we accept the story of time spent in places like Patna and Varanasi, it does help us imagine how young Rammohun might have come upon the idea for his first assault on Hinduism as he knew it.[13] We have only to wonder why, in 1833, he felt no desire to provide such background. We might well ask if, by this point, the world-renowned reformer was content for his followers to focus on his expertise in Hindu scripture. But for a figure who is also celebrated as a comparativist, it is surprising that, alongside his travels, he did not choose to make more of the nature and scope of the education he received as a boy.

In the 1833 autobiographical account, Rammohun moves quickly from the fact of having caused a "coolness" within his family to the decisive act of leaving home, which follows as if it needs no justification. He simply states,

> I proceeded on my travels, and passed through different countries, chiefly within, but some beyond, the bounds of Hindoostan, with a feeling of great aversion to the establishment of the British power in India. When I had reached the age of twenty, my father recalled me, and restored me to his favour; after which I first saw and began to associate with Europeans, and soon after made myself tolerably acquainted with their laws and form of government. Finding them generally more intelligent, more steady and moderate in their conduct, I gave up my prejudice against them, and became inclined in their favour, feeling persuaded that their rule, though a foreign yoke, would lead more speedily and surely to the amelioration of the native inhabitants; and I enjoyed the confidence of several of them even in their public capacity. My continued controversies with the Brahmins on the subject of their idolatry and superstition, and my interference with their custom of burning widows, and other pernicious practices, revived and increased their animosity against me; and through their influence with my family, my father was again obliged to withdraw his countenance openly, though his limited pecuniary support was still continued to me.[14]

Considering that he had just testified before Parliament about the impact of British rule and was savoring the victory he and Governor-General William Bentinck had won in outlawing the custom of widow immolation, we can appreciate why he may have wished to record his eventual conviction as to the beneficial character of British rule in India. In this respect, we might read the second autobiographical statement as a celebration of the spirit of reform in India written for the benefit of his host nation, which was at that very time gripped by the craze for reform in law, social custom, and government. And if we recall Partha Chatterjee's reflection on what died after 1830 (as opposed to what was born), we might even read Rammohun's remarks as an unintended epitaph for the unique world of the early colonial modern. Rammohun even gestures toward the first glimmer of the late colonial, which after Bentinck became increasingly shaped by what I am calling the empire of reform. We can hardly forget that Rammohun was in London in part to provide evidence in relation to debates over the renewal of the East India Company charter and the future course of improvement in India. Just as he went about his work in London, the Scottish Presbyterian missionary, Reverend Alexander Duff, was getting busy in Calcutta with a concerted program to evangelize, educate, and convert the so-called heathen. Feeling the flush of reform, a writer in the *India Gazette* felt sanguine enough to report that the "brutal tyranny" of "priestcraft" in India would soon be overthrown.[15]

This is why I mentioned the need to bear in mind the time lag between the 1833 autobiographical statement and the account Rammohun provided in his *Tuhfat* some three decades earlier. If we are to use the later statement to think about Rammohun's early years, we have to postpone envisioning him as triumphant modern reformer. What we want to envision instead is the world of a sixteen-year-old Brahmin boy from rural western Bengal, who set off to traverse the landscape of north India. Thankfully, Rammohun gives us something to work with—even if again we must fill in important elements of context. He provides, for instance, a rather detailed sketch of the cultural and economic forces affecting his family during the 1780s. Here we get some valuable clues as to the nature of local ruling polities in Bengal as well as to the ongoing hold of

Brahmanic authority. Both were of great importance in shaping opportunities within his family and its world. He writes,

> My ancestors were Brahmins of a high order, and, from time
> immemorial, were devoted to the religious duties of their race,
> down to my fifth progenitor, who about one hundred and
> forty years ago gave up spiritual exercises for worldly pursuits
> and aggrandisement. His descendants ever since have fol-
> lowed his example, and, according to the usual fate of court-
> iers, with various success, sometimes rising to honour and
> sometimes falling; sometimes rich and sometimes poor;
> sometimes excelling in success, sometimes miserable through
> disappointment. But my maternal ancestors, being of the
> sacerdotal order by profession as well as by birth, and of a
> family than which none holds a higher rank in that profes-
> sion, have up to the present day uniformly adhered to a life of
> religious observances and devotion, preferring peace and
> tranquility of mind to the excitements of ambition, and all the
> allurements of worldly grandeur.[16]

Rammohun famously depicts a family divided between paternal and maternal patterns of professional and cultural identity. On his mother's side, the family expected to benefit from the customary religious prerogatives that accrued to Brahmin "sacerdotal" families in early colonial Bengal. His mother's people thus expected him to study Sanskrit and the works of "Hindoo literature, law and religion."[17] Hence, one presumes, his early sojourn in Varanasi. If a boy like Rammohun could master Hindu scripture, law, and ritual, he would have open to him a range of opportunities for earning a living, perhaps by becoming a ritual specialist or legal adviser to a local ruler. Not that those sorts of opportunities were free of all risk. A family like Rammohun's might be able to gain financially by providing ritual services or legal counsel to a zamindar—types of services that tended to bring a range of perquisites like grants of land and other kinds of entitlements. But a family in this position also ran the risk of falling foul of an unstable ruler or being too closely yoked to the changing fortunes of the local economy. After all, the late eighteenth century was an era just beginning to experience the effects of new opportunities and challenges associated with the activities of the East India Company in Bengal.[18]

The ability to be of service and to carve out small domains of mastery within the political economy of rural Bengal required a family like Rammohun's to maintain a diverse intellectual and professional portfolio. Here the maternal-paternal bifurcation highlighted by Rammohun suggests some of the advantages that might come to a family that possessed not merely mastery in Sanskrit and Hindu law, but also could pursue "aggrandisement" by drawing on skills in Persian and Arabic. These latter languages were central to the customs, modes of conduct, and moral values shaping zamindari court polities, which was the world of Rammohun's paternal forebears. He tells us, for instance, that his father understood that the study of Arabic and Persian were "indispensable to those who attached themselves to the courts of the Mahommedan princes."[19] This helps explain why the young boy had already been sent to Patna; by studying there he had some hope of internalizing the kind of professional habitus associated with premodern scribal elites trained in Persian and Arabic. Such training was common among Bengalis of the Kayastha or "writer" caste, but it was not unusual for Brahmin families like Rammohun's to acquire and deploy similar kinds of mastery.[20]

Although much has been made of the maternal-paternal dichotomy in shaping Rammohun's worldview and even psyche as a reformer, there is no need to delve into psychology here.[21] We may simply pause to appreciate how much Rammohun himself assists us by bringing into view the range of intellectual, cultural, and practical factors that would have been in play during his formative years. Since one of our goals is to move away from viewing Rammohun as sui generis reformer in order to situate him within the multiscalar polities of his day, it is especially important to register how much we learn from his own writings about overlapping systems of authority and power as these came to bear on a service-oriented Brahmin family in late eighteenth-century Bengal.

We are alerted, first of all, to village- and caste-level polities that articulated Brahmanic authority, not least the ritual and social engagements around Rammohun's home in Radhanagar; from there our attention shifts to the court of the Maharaja of Burdwan, who exerted tremendous authority over the regions of Bengal west of the Hooghly at that time; the Maharaja of Burdwan was himself situated in relation to the ruling authority of the Nawabi court at Murshidabad, which in turn was oriented toward a horizon bounded by the Mughal court in Delhi. It had been the Mughal imperial court that had bestowed on one of Rammohun's forebears the honorific title of Raya, or King—whence the Roy in Rammohun's name.[22] The title of Raya (or Roy) was gifted by the emperor through the Nawab in recognition of services rendered to the court; but it was also for that same reason a powerful symbolic means for securing the loyalty of Rammohun's family. Recognizing this, we can appreciate how an otherwise inconsequential Bengali family could become enmeshed in a range of symbolic and economic relationships during this period.

In fact, when we refer to Rammohun's home as the village of Radhanagar, this too obscures some of the political-economic realities that shaped rural life in Bengal at that time. Radhanagar was indeed the site of Rammohun's birth, but his family lived at and either owned or managed several other properties throughout that portion of western Bengal. As it turns out, the bulk of the official records we have for the family consists of various deeds, testimonies, reports, affidavits, and court records associated with landholding and property disputes.[23] These records attest to common practices of gifting, regifting, buying, and selling of property among members of an extended family. Following the trail of these deeds, one is led to estates managed by Rammohun's father as far south as present-day Medinipur District.

Reading between the lines of such records affords us a glimpse at how a local ruling polity like the Burdwan zamindari—one of a group of Mughal-era landholders whose power expanded significantly in the early eighteenth century—could effectively acquire vast holdings in land, whether through conflict, purchase, or diplomacy. Like the well-known *matsya nyaya*, when it came to zamindaris, the big fish often consumed the holdings of other smaller ruling polities, as the Burdwan Raj did with the lands associated with the once powerful Bhurshut Raj.[24] Reading Rammohun's family records in terms of the ups and downs of property acquisition and legal disputes, one gains an even better sense for the forces of opportunity and necessity that eventually led a young Brahmin to travel in search of education and employment. To survive in such a competitive environment—an environment just beginning to feel many of its customary patterns coming under strain—would require not just innate skill but considerable preparation. Did Rammohun really leave home because he had offended his family's religious opinions? It scarcely matters; by leaving home he increased the range of opportunities open to him.

Rammohun on the Move

The evidence we have suggests that Rammohun traveled and lived not only locally around the immediate region of southwestern Bengal, but also far more widely across the Gangetic valley, Himalayan hills, and parts of northern and eastern Bengal. During this period he also paid occasional visits to Calcutta. That city would not become his home, how-ever, until 1814, by which point he was already in his forties. That leaves many decades of youth and early adulthood, during which time his life revolved more meaningfully around upcountry towns as far afield as Varanasi, Patna, Murshidabad, and Rangpur. These place-names alone are suggestive of rich intellectual traditions and cultural resources; they represent a constellation of expertise and modes of authority having to do with Indic and Indo-Islamic learning, Hindu and Muslim religious life, north Indian political regimes, and older and newer networks of trade and commerce throughout the Gangetic north. As such, if we are to be attentive to the pluriform world of early colonial India, it is impor-tant not to dissociate a purportedly Hindu Varanasi from Muslim cen-ters of culture like Patna or Murshidabad.[25] In the Indo-Islamic *ecumene* of the late eighteenth century, it can be difficult to disentangle the roles of Hindu and Muslim cultures in articulating norms of cultural and po-litical conduct.

We may also need to re-center some of our familiar maps; well be-fore the rise of colonial Calcutta, cities like Patna and Murshidabad were major epicenters for trade, power, and learning. Although we think of places like Murshidabad as provincial cities, in the early colonial era they were anything but backwaters. As David Boyk has pointed out, in the eighteenth century, to be urban and therefore cultivated in a certain way meant living in one of a "galaxy" of such regional towns and cities. In Rammohun's day the decline of such centers was still at least a century away.[26] And so while Rammohun had begun the study of Persian at home under his father's tutelage, clear benefits were to be found by sending the boy to a city like Patna. Although we have records demonstrating the existence in rural Bengal of schools offering instruction in Bengali, Sanskrit, and even some Persian, such schools fostered little more than basic skills at numeracy and accounting. If a parent hoped to provide their child with a robust education in the court language of Persian and related cultural forms, something more was required.[27]

Rammohun arrived in Patna in 1780 and remained there for three or four years. At that time the city was very much a "living center" within north India's still vital landscape of Indo-Persian learning and urbanity.[28] The precise nature of the curriculum he studied is unknown, but it has been suggested that while in Patna he received a standard madrasa education that focused on study of the Qur'an, jurisprudence, theology, and philosophy; he was also led to appreciate Islamic approaches to reason and science through reading Arabic translations of Aristotle and Euclid.[29] It is likely, too, that his abiding admiration for such poets as Hafiz and Rumi dates from this period.[30] Almost certainly Rammohun also imbibed a great deal of Sufi learning, both through formal curricula and as a dimension of the larger intellectual and cultural climate at this moment in north India. As Muzaffar Alam has noted, the Sufis of eastern north India had developed a kind of pragmatic approach to reconciling faith claims, political realities, and the need to live alongside their Hindu neighbors. The ability of the learned Sufi to chart a life course that preserved spiritual identity while embodying integration in a larger community is an ethic that rings true to Rammohun's own subsequent career as theist, political theorist, and exponent of the rights of Indians within an emerging imperial regime.[31]

Of course there is nothing particularly new about calling attention to Rammohun's background in Islamic thought and culture; attempts to trace the roots of his monotheism or his rationalism to his study of Persian and Arabic date back nearly a century.[32] However, my goal here is to reframe this issue away from the thorny (and perhaps irresolvable) question of influence and toward a simple appreciation for the intellectual life of what we might call a provincial frontier—wherein provincial suggests not backwardness but another kind of early modernity as yet unrelated to developments in a place like Calcutta. I do not hope to quantify the degree of Muslim influence on a major Hindu reformer, as much as to rethink the genesis of a religious leader like Rammohun outside the urban milieu and standard narrative model of reform. The long-familiar model requires that we focus on the uniqueness of the reforming genius and encourages us to find a singular point of origin for their reforming work; it could be Vedanta or it could be Mutazalite theology, but it should be some discrete teaching that the reforming prophet can reveal and claim to return to purity. To circumvent those kinds of assumptions, I would like to emphasize the plurality of intellectual options that were in play during Rammohun's youth and to suggest that, as a savvy thinker, he sought to capitalize on a range of opportunities presented to him within the multiscalar world of early colonial religion. To do this, I may at times have to question certain elements of the reformer's own self-presentation, since these often—as with the 1833 statement—bear the traces of the emergent discourse of reform.[33] After all, we may well believe that by 1833 the celebrated "reformer" would have found it useful to give the impression that his career in reform had commenced at an early age. What I hope to suggest, by contrast, is that if Rammohun is exemplary, it is not so much that he entered the world uniquely equipped to undertake reform. Rather, attention to the specific contours of life in early colonial South Asia can help us appreciate the range of religious possibilities he responded to and eventually built on in constructing his new polity.

Reading the "Gift"

To pursue Rammohun upcountry and along the provincial frontier is another way of working against the grain of the kinds of "history with borders" alluded to in the Introduction—those modern, nation-centered, and fundamentally Eurocentric histories that have supported the kinds of attitudes about Hinduism and India I hope to challenge.[34] Such histories, Tavakoli-Targhi suggests, are epistemologically and politically unable to appreciate the fact that someone like Rammohun is not really even reducible to the "Indian" context. After all, he would go on to become the editor of one of the world's first Persian newspapers, the *Mirat-al-Akbar*. In reminding us of Rammohun's border-crossing commitments to Persian, Tavakoli-Targhi provocatively speaks of elements of Rammohun's work being "homeless"—that is, his intellectual contributions resist being pigeonholed historically or ethno-politically.[35]

This is a wonderful way to think not merely of a journal like *Mirat-al-Akbar* but, more importantly, of the earliest extant published work we have from Rammohun—one that has always proven somewhat hard to reconcile with the larger corpus of his other work. I refer, of course, to his *Tuhfat-ul-muwahhidin* (Gift to Monotheists), a work he composed in Persian, along with an Arabic preface, that was published from Murshidabad in 1803–1804.[36] The work is always included in editions of Rammohun's collected works but sits somewhat to the side, as it were, like a homeless visitor amid the other well-known works on Vedanta, Hindu theism, Christian doctrine, and writings on the colonial administration.

Persian intellectual norms, debating styles, and quotations from his beloved Persian poets give *Tuhfat* its distinctive structure and tone.[37] It is a work that offers what one scholar has recently described as a "strong critique" of the "irrationalities and superstitions" of the religions of his day.[38] Rammohun opens the Persian body of the text by announcing that "happy is the time" dedicated to a search for truth amid the "different principles of religion held by different people."[39] As he proceeds from there he seems to take delight in exposing evident contradictions among religious claims and to find a kind of pleasure in pointing to the folly of religious credulity. In terms of logic, Rammohun employs the antinomies of Hindu polytheism and Muslim monotheism to pull the rug out from under all theological posturing. In terms of morality, he skewers people who place their faith in particular religious teachers even when those same teachers clearly do not merit their trust. Rammohun associates such blind devotion with both the more "heinous crimes" that can be laid at religion's door and the general mischief it tends to engender for society as a whole.[40] The book concludes with a terse summary of the world of religion as far as Rammohun sees it. He parses this world in terms of four categories of people: those who deceive, those who are deceived, those who both deceive and are deceived, and those who are neither.[41] As for the author of this confident critique, he betrays little anxiety about causing offense and seems undeterred by fears of reprisal. Bowing to no authority, he writes chiefly out of a desire for justice.

When read retrospectively, with a mind to celebrating Rammohun's career as a reformer, it is all too easy to view *Tuhfat* as the opening salvo in a campaign of enlightened reform. This is how it was understood by Sophia Dobson Collet in her influential early account of Rammohun. Collet took *Tuhfat* as proof that young Rammohun was constitutionally unable to put up with "priestly impositions" in religion.[42] Collet of course knew no Persian, and her celebration of the reformer's critique of "priestcraft" depended on a late-nineteenth-century English translation of the text, a translation situated within what J. Barton Scott has dubbed the "reform assemblage," a globally circulating discursive field that relied heavily on tropes of priestcraft and idolatry in order to promote more modern and rational views of religion.[43] In the spirit of postponement, I propose we need to resist reading *Tuhfat* in this way, if only because presuming it to be a work of modern reform eliminates at the outset other possible ways of reading the text. Marginally more helpful is an earlier epitome of the text that was framed by Rammohun's own British secretary, Sanford Arnot. Arnot saw in *Tuhfat* a clear critique of idolatry, but rather than locating the author in some reformed space outside his own cultural context, Arnot viewed the text as necessarily composed for a "higher class of Hindus and Musulmans."[44] His comment shifts our attention from author to audience, reminding us to first consider the world of Indo-Islamic learning and culture out of which it emerged.[45]

And when we think of audiences, we can immediately call attention to the fact that *Tuhfat* did provoke a reaction among some readers. However, the audience he upset is not one we typically include in our narratives of religious reform in early colonial Bengal. Rammohun's arguments in *Tuhfat* seem to have been received with considerable concern by Zoroastrian intellectuals, who began to attack the work.[46] This too is an important fact to highlight, allowing us to further contextualize Rammohun's early thought within a broad Persianate intellectual world, a world whose community boundaries were porous enough that Muslims, Zoroastrians (or Parsis), and Brahmins found ways to learn from and argue with one another.[47]

One gains a further appreciation of this open and expansive intellectual space when one considers that—prompted by the objections raised by Zoroastrian critics—someone composed an anonymous defense of the *Tuhfat*. The work is titled *Jawab-i Tuhfat ul Muwahhidin*, or Answer to the Gift to Monotheists, and has in the past been ascribed to Rammohun himself. However, although it makes sense to imagine the author of *Tuhfat* drafting his own defense, stylistic analysis appears to rule this out.[48] Instead, it is most likely that the *Jawab* was written by one of Rammohun's Muslim admirers—although the identity and location of the author remains unknown. For our purposes it is most important to emphasize that here we have the case of a Muslim author defending the work of a Brahmin intellectual whose book in Persian appears to have upset a section of the Zoroastrian community in eastern India.[49] And, since *Jawab* was not published until some two decades after the publication of *Tuhfat*, we have to be impressed not merely by the plurality of intellectual currents in play but also by the vitality and durability of such debates at the time.

The linear teleology of modern Hindu reform has trouble accommodating facts like these. And yet, what does the foregoing provide if not a kind of thumbnail sketch of the intellectual and religious worlds of provincial north India during the early modern era?[50] What the *Jawab* reveals, if only obliquely, is that young Rammohun clearly felt at home, and sought to accrue to himself a kind of power, within just such a plural environment. This is further confirmed by the fact that, according to his own admission, *Tuhfat* was not the first book he had composed in Persian. In the final paragraph of *Tuhfat*, after delivering his summary conclusion about the four types of religious people (mentioned above), Rammohun directs his readers to another of his works in which he claims to have provided a more detailed examination of such matters. The title he gives is *Munazarat ul Adyan*, or Debates on Various Religions. It is a revealing title, slotting it into the large genre of *munazarat* or debate literature. Sadly, the text is not extant. But in referring to it as one of his works, Rammohun gives further indication of how he saw himself actively participating in the universe of Indo-Persian religious disputation.[51]

It turns out that the genre of the debate text, or *munazarat,* played a prominent role in the north Indian world of Persian letters and religious doxography. The best-known example of such a text is the *Dabistan-i Mazahib,* the School of Religions, a voluminous seventeenth-century work that sets out to survey the diverse field of religious doctrine and practice in early modern South Asia. More than one scholar has suggested that the neo-Zoroastrian synthetic vision of the *Dabistan* provides a kind of mirror in which to understand the concerns of Rammohun's *Tuhfat.*[52] Apart from the *Dabistan's* evident interest in comparing religious systems—something so central to Rammohun's own later project—it is worth noting that the theme of travel serves as a central trope in the *Dabistan.* Travel and comparison go together, as it were, since movement through the world offers one of the most valuable ways to experience religious difference. As we have already seen, the theme of travel is announced right away in the Arabic preface to *Tuhfat,* when Rammohun commences by speaking of his travels throughout the "remotest parts of the world."[53]

If it is fair to include Rammohun's other missing Persian work and *Tuhfat* alongside the *Dabistan* in the genre of *munazarat* literature, this should alert us to the vital role played in South Asia by the discourses of xenology, doxography, and even what we might call skepticism or freethinking. Within this genre, Islam and other traditions are laid open to critical scrutiny, even as the overall project tends to support the validity and implementation of Islamic methods of textual analysis and argumentation. Orthodoxy, in these texts, often comes under scrutiny from higher or more esoteric mystical perspectives, and the theologies that emerge often seem more eclectic than systematic. Notably, these are some of the very tendencies in Rammohun's *Tuhfat* that interpreters have tended to judge negatively.[54] And yet, when viewed against the backdrop of the larger genre of *munazarat* literature, *Tuhfat* seems to be a rather predictable specimen of critical intervention around questions of religious difference and theological critique. To borrow an idea from Rebecca Gould, we could even say that in *Tuhfat* Rammohun aimed to provide his educated readers with a way to go about managing religious difference from within the Muslim tradition.[55]

Managing difference is at the heart of *Tuhfat*, and it bears noting that Rammohun concludes the work by appealing to a sense of justice. This points to the overriding moral force of the work, which seeks to steer readers away from the contradictory and often violent externalities of scripture and dogma toward a single moral truth that lies at the heart of all religion. The way in which Rammohun advocates a process of inquiry based on impartiality and a "sense of justice" should thus clue us in to one final framework that can help situate the work in its Indo-Islamic context.[56] I refer here to the discourse and culture of ethical formation that is known in Persian as *akhlaq*. Recently Shomik Dasgupta has convincingly argued that greater attention needs to be paid to the role of *akhlaq* in giving form and significance to Rammohun's thought. Dasgupta actually offers a highly compelling interpretation of Muslim thematics within Rammohun's entire corpus; he encourages us to ponder how concern for the norms of *akhlaq* might have guided Rammohun's interrogation not merely of Islam, but of Sanskrit scriptures and British legal norms as well. If we are to follow Dasgupta's lead, we obviously have to broaden our horizons of interpretation to include the universe of Persianate literature and the moral curricula associated with *akhlaq*. Not least we should recognize the appeal, during Rammohun's day, of the immensely influential *Akhlaq-i Nasiri* of Nasir al-Din Tusi (1201–1274). Dasgupta convincingly shows that Rammohun's exposure to Nasirean ethics fostered in him the advancement of a consistent hermeneutical strategy premised on the idea of ethical readership.[57]

By calling attention to the landscape of ethical formation around *akhlaq*, Dasgupta shifts our focus from narrow questions of influence to the more important task of situating Rammohun within the larger world of eighteenth-century Persianate education. Historically speaking, this was a multicultural world; texts like the *Akhlaq-i Nasiri* were profoundly indebted to Greek, Arabic, and Persian thought-worlds. What is more, it was during the rule of the Mughal emperor Akbar that Tusi's Nasirean ethics became a central component within a madrasa curriculum that found room for both Muslim and Hindu intellectual production. This was certainly a pattern replicated in the kinds of study Rammohun completed in Patna.

To illustrate the sort of thought-worlds produced by such an education, Dasgupta directs our attention to an early modern figure like Chandra Bhan, a Brahmin bureaucrat of the late seventeenth century. Chandra Bhan's work may be said to have been both administrative and poetic, and this was by no means an odd combination.[58] The merger of aesthetics and administrative capabilities would come to be styled as impractical—if not effete—during the era of high colonial rule, but this was not yet true in Chandra Bhan's day, nor in young Rammohun's. We should not make the mistake of inserting such late colonial judgments into our understanding of the creative life and practical careers of men reared under the discipline of *akhlaq*. Put differently, we should not construe Rammohun's early immersion in the world of Persianate ethical culture as marginal to his overall project. His embrace of such thought and values constituted much more than a passing intellectual fad.

To appreciate this fact, Dasgupta chooses to speak of the "ethical poetry" of late Mughal Persianate culture.[59] One enduring and productive element of this premodern ethical world was the ideal of living respectfully with members of other religious communities. For his part, Muzaffar Alam has pointed to the connection between the general Mughal endorsement of Nasirean ethics and their "extraordinary interest" in promoting an appreciation for other religions. He quotes a passage from Abu Fazl's introduction to a Persian translation of the Mahabharata that seems in some respects to prefigure Rammohun's concerns in *Tuhfat*. In this passage, Abu Fazl not only calls attention to the wisdom and beneficence of rulers who seek to overcome religious discord; he also marks for censure those figures within any religious community who pretend to lead when what they are really doing is misguiding people through "fraud and fallacies" (*tazwirat-o talbisat*).[60]

This is highly reminiscent of Rammohun's fourfold classification of believers in *Tuhfat* mentioned above, not least the distinction he draws between those who deceive and those who are deceived.[61] Bringing such deceptive practice to light and countering it with fairness and clarity seem to be goals shared by both Abu Fazl and Rammohun. When Abu

Fazl expresses his desire to see a book like the Sanskrit Mahabharata rendered in "simple, clear and pleasant style," this likewise seems to harmonize—or perhaps better, to contextualize—Rammohun's later quest in *Tuhfat* to understand the truth of religion "without partiality and with a sense of justice."[62] In this regard, whereas earlier commentators on Rammohun have emphasized his appeal to reason—choosing that element of his work as being most in harmony with the spirit of modernity—when we situate his project within the ethical universe of *akhlaq*, we have to appreciate that reason shares critical ground with a sense of justice; both have a role to play in the formation of the early modern religious self.

By considering the training young Rammohun received in Patna, and by considering an early and seemingly singular work like *Tuhfat*, we can do much to re-center our understanding of the genesis and context of his work, both spatially and discursively. Rather than leaping to consider him as the quintessential Calcutta reformer, we might even prefer to call him an early colonial Nasirean reformer. Without falling back on imperial constructions of reform, we might then be able to think about Rammohun's work in terms of the quest to benefit the world around him through the promotion of norms of personal morality and public justice associated with the traditions of *akhlaq*. Within such a moral project, the goal is to refine what is presumed to be an already noble human person. In this respect, Tusi considered *akhlaq* to be like medicine insofar as it aimed to promote the natural healthy state of a person. Ethics, however, is even nobler, since it operates on the highest human faculties.[63] Whether we choose to style Nasirean ethics as a kind of reform, it is clearly a very different project from the Protestant-inflected reform-based discourse of religious progress promoted under the British empire of reform.

Upcountry with Rammohun

Following young Rammohun to provincial cities like Patna and Murshidabad, and thinking about the importance of travel for his early ethical and intellectual formation, is useful preparation for considering the twelve years he ended up working in various *mofussil* or upcountry locations in eastern India. These appointments, too, must not be relegated to the status of mere stages on the way to later glory; in these places, and in a variety of roles, Rammohun flourished in keeping with the values, aesthetics, and prerogatives of any number of late-Mughal administrator-intellectuals. It was precisely Rammohun's ability to serve in such official roles as *amal, sheristadar, munshi,* and *dewan* that eventually brought him to the attention of East India Company officials.[64] This was neither a period of youthful distraction nor even a mere prelude to a later career; this upcountry life of professional service was both in keeping with the ethical culture Rammohun had embraced and congruent with the ends to which he would later direct his energies.

Initially Rammohun's training and skills qualified him for a position in Faridpur, in what is now Bangladesh. After a short time there, he then shifted to Varanasi in the Gangetic north before returning once again to Bengal, where he accepted service in the East India Company at the old Nawabi capital of Murshidabad. It was while living in Murshidabad around 1803–1804 that he was able to publish his *Tuhfat.* This was also the time and place when his path crossed that of a British civil servant by the name of John Digby, whom Rammohun had first come to know during a short stint in Calcutta. Back then Digby had been studying at the College of Fort William in Calcutta, and Rammohun had tutored him in Persian.

It seems that Digby's grasp of Persian was never very firm, so that when he once again encountered Rammohun in Murshidabad, he hired him to serve as his personal *munshi,* or teacher. It is likely the two dropped easily into this relationship; not only were they already acquainted, but by this time Rammohun had already served as *munshi* for other British civilians in Bengal.[65] The relationship proved to be a success; Rammohun would serve Digby for nearly a decade and would travel with him to several other upcountry towns in Bengal and Bihar. They lived briefly in places like Ramgarh, Jessore, and Bhagalpur before settling for several years in Rangpur in what is now northern Bangladesh. Digby served as collector in Rangpur, and Rammohun proved to be a great asset to him. At one point, in 1814, Rammohun was even asked to serve on a minor diplomatic mission to the ruler of the Himalayan kingdom of Bhutan.[66]

The Bhutan trip is another reminder of the varied and far-flung world through which Rammohun moved before settling down in Calcutta. The East India Company had been advancing along the Himalayan frontier since the last quarter of the eighteenth century, eager to foster political conditions conducive to the opening up of lucrative trade relationships. At this time much of the northeast could be thought of as constituting one of those many "countries" Rammohun had referred to when thinking about Bharatvarsha. Not least, this region was dotted with many important political entities such as the kingdoms of Cooch Behar, Bhutan, and Assam. At this time much of the northeast still remained something like terra incognita for the British, into which they gradually pressed, through a combination of diplomatic and military means.[67] It was only around the time of Rammohun's birth that the East India Company had managed to conclude a treaty with the rulers of Cooch Behar, having heeded that ruler's pleas for help in dealing with predatory incursions from his neighbors, the Bhutanese. Records from the period reveal a multiscalar dispersion of varying polities spread across the Gangetic and Brahmaputra valleys, across the Himalayan *terai* and on northward all the way to the court of the Tashi Lama in Lhasa.[68]

As we noticed when discussing the travels of Nilakantha, the region of northern Bengal was a dynamic crossroads for all kinds of religious, political, and economic actors—traders, sannyasis, fakirs, diplomats, and military contingents moved continually throughout the region. As the British sought to extend their control, bands of armed ascetics made their way along annual pilgrimage routes, not least the very one that (as we saw) ran south from Rangpur toward Bogra.[69] Indeed, Rangpur sat at the crossroads of traffic coming from the northwest and heading off either to Assam or the lower Bengali delta. This made Rangpur an important frontier outpost for the British. Sitting in his residence in Rangpur, the British collector regularly received visitors and petitions from a range of regional courtly representatives and less-official religious advisers associated with smaller courts and polities. These advisers were sometimes themselves religious leaders such as the heads (or *mahants*) of monastic organizations. One of the more well-attested among such figures was Sarbananda Gosain, the family preceptor and confidential adviser to the Queen Mother of Cooch Behar. Sarbananda, whose title Gosain alerts us to his status as a Shaiva ascetic, looms large in colonial records as a figure with immense power; he owned vast amounts of property and had access to important official channels.[70] As the British were drawn into the internal disputes of the Cooch Behar court, they reported finding "mercenary Sannyasis" like Sarbananda ranged on both sides. In a pattern we have already observed, the British could be at once troubled by sannyasi interventions in politics and also willing to employ individual sannyasis to advance their own ends.[71]

By coming to Rangpur with Digby, Rammohun entered directly into this fluid world of political contestation. In addition to the courtiers, sadhus, zamindars, and British company officials he interacted with in northern Bengal, Rammohun also came to know the local community of Marwari traders who had settled in Rangpur, many of them Jains originally from western India.[72] And when he was recruited for the diplomatic mission to Bhutan, he came into direct contact with representatives of various Himalayan Buddhist communities. All these associations make up the kind of multireligious universe Rammohun referenced only obliquely when he spoke in 1833 of having spent considerable time in "hilly lands." It scarcely matters whether he actually made it as far as Tibet; between Rangpur and Bhutan he had ample occasion to investigate the worlds of Buddhism, Jainism, Hinduism, and Islam as practiced cross-regionally.[73] Just as we saw in the case for Nilakantha, Rammohun's time on the road would have offered a broad and compelling learning experience. He surely came to appreciate the important role played by vast trans-Himalayan networks stretching from Kashmir to Assam. And he may have been among only a few South Asian intellectuals during this period with a keen awareness of how long-standing patterns of trans-regional monastic life, gender norms, and property relations were succumbing to colonial interventions in land settlement and legislation.[74]

Rangpur thus adds another page to Rammohun's early curriculum vitae and allows us to further complicate what can be known about his ethical-professional formation. When we practice "history with borders," we tend to think of places like Patna and Rangpur as marginal to the expanding British epicenter at Calcutta. However, when we remap history and attend to other circuits of migration, education, and employment in the early colonial era, such provincial cities register as more than merely peripheral. The very patterns of travel, cultural contact, and economic interdependency we note in Rammohun's early career were in fact constituted in and by the norms and opportunities he encountered in precolonial centers like Patna, Murshidabad, Varanasi, or Rangpur. Stretched across the Gangetic basin and Himalayan foothills, these were "confluent territories," and if we are to appreciate Rammohun's eventual role in shaping new expressions of religion, it helps to view his own intellectual and moral formation as equally confluent.[75]

Experience Lost and Found

One reason I was keen to follow Nilakantha in his travels through Bengal was to place him, if only briefly, within the same religio-cultural landscape as was traversed by young Rammohun. Both of these figures experienced the confluent cultural worlds of northern and eastern India at the end of the eighteenth century, just as British imperial intervention was beginning to make its presence felt in so many ways. And it is interesting that, in the moral geography of the late-colonial empire of reform, both the messiness of the worlds through which they moved and the diversity of rules and styles for living they would have observed were actively forgotten. Instead, if these two men were to live up their reputation as reformers, it was imperative that they embody—from the very outset—a kind of purity of identity and message; their reforming projects had to be traced to one particular source and had to be seen to point toward a goal congruent with the ratification and preservation of a single fundamental truth.

In this regard, we might say that Nilakantha's experiences in Bengal, as I have tried to recover them, have little to do with the present-day work of the Sampraday, which is oriented toward fostering true devotion to Lord Swaminarayan. What matters to the Sampraday today is that Sahajanand's hagiography ratifies the valiant work of young Nilakantha in mastering a set of Vedic, Brahmanic, and yogic regimens and subsequently using that same mastery to overcome religious error as found in the straw-man enemies he meets in places like Sirpur, Kamakhya, and

Sitakund. Put bluntly, we can say that for all intents and purposes, Sahajanand learns nothing from his environment; it serves as only the backdrop to his cosmic mission. Oddly, the more positivist narratives of Rammohun are not all that different. They are more historical in tenor, to be sure, but the narratives of Rammohun's early career are hardly more interested in pausing to reflect on the curriculum he learned—and came to embody—as a result of transiting through major life experiences in places like Patna and Rangpur. At best, seeking the roots of the reformer's message, these narratives may give a nod to Islamic monotheism or Mutazalite rationalism as possible influences on Rammohun's theology. But in such accounts, Rammohun tends to move across northern and eastern India without really picking up much baggage. Needless to say, this lends only greater force to narrative celebrations of Rammohun's advent in Calcutta, ex nihilo as it were.

What is missing in both cases is not just historical detail but the quest to interrogate the travels of both men for what they can tell us about the kinds of masteries that would equip each of them to go on to establish new religious polities. In this regard, the fact that Swaminarayan hagiographies make a distinction between Nilakantha and Sahajanand is actually something of a blessing. While there is a teleology to his life narrative, at least we are encouraged to isolate the experiences of young Nilakantha and to think about how the neophyte renouncer managed to negotiate the religio-political terrain as he did. For Rammohun, the challenge is not so easily addressed; his departure from home is premised on his own precocious critique of existing religious forms; as such his is every bit as teleological a life-narrative as Sahajanand's. We recognize the reformer right from the beginning, and for that reason we tend to ask questions like, What did the reformer learn in Patna? How did the reformer make use of his time with Digby?[76] We scarcely notice that Rammohun's early teachers go unnamed, and we find it unsurprising that he experienced neither a remarkable conversion nor any kind of initiation into a recognizable form of life or school of thought. His is the quintessential story of a self-made modern man.

In this chapter, and in Chapter 4, I have had to work against such narratological instincts. My decision to follow Nilakantha into lower Bengal and to go upcountry with Rammohun is based on my conviction that we must work hard at the task of un-thinking the way reform narratives have been told. This involves a refusal to use the early textualization of these men's careers as the tacit support for a single foregone conclusion: Sahajanand is a medieval reformer whose life is characteristically available only in a compendious, quasi-scriptural hagiography, whereas the modern reformer Rammohun not only left us an autobiographical essay (what could be more modern?) but also attracted the respect of his liberal and progressive contemporaries. When we postpone the application of such critical frames, we equip ourselves to discover parallels and elements of shared experience. We come to find that both men left home at an early age, traveled far, met countless teachers, encountered new theologies and modes of religious practice, and over the course of many years accrued considerable religious authority of their own. Next, in Chapters 6 and 7, my goal is to carry such elements of commonality forward to think about how these two figures came to deploy their newfound authority in projects to articulate new religious polities.

6

THE GURU'S RULES

H OW DID SAHAJANAND GO ABOUT articulating and solidifying a new polity governed by his ruling authority as guru in the first decades of the nineteenth century? To answer this question I once again plan to draw on the *Satsangi Jivanam*, since for all that it purports to tell the story of a divine incarnation sent to spread the truth of devotion to the supreme Lord, the text also conveys valuable information about Sahajanand's efforts to codify and regulate Swaminarayan conduct. The *Satsangi Jivanam* reveals how, toward the end of legitimizing the Sampraday and his authority over it, Sahajanand drew on important textual exemplars like the Bhagavata Purana, a work of central importance for early modern Vaishnava movements generally.[1] However, beyond legitimization, the *Satsangi Jivanam* also speaks to the discursive task of articulating a new disciplinary order for the Swaminarayan polity. Thus while the text seems akin to a Purana, the *Satsangi Jivanam* is also a kind of Dharmashastra, a code of ethics and conduct for members of the Swaminarayan Sampraday.[2] The enunciation of parameters for Vaishnava devotion and duty are both central to the work accomplished under Sahajanand's leadership.

The project to orient the Sampraday in relation to the specific ideals and practices of Bhagavata Vaishnavism is particularly apparent when one considers that the *Satsangi Jivanam* comes equipped with its own "glorification" (*mahatmya*), a paratextual addendum that celebrates, sanctifies, and serves to operationalize the benefits of the text. The creation of such a glorification was nothing new to Sahajanand. Sacred texts in South Asia are often armored with layers of preliminary and concluding material intended to ensure the sanctity of the text and to produce the optimal conditions for audiences to profit from hearing or reading them. The most ubiquitous and most modest of such paratextual devices are the opening benediction verses (*mangalacharana*) honoring deities and gurus that precede the body of most sacred texts. The provision of such paratextual elements supports the articulation of a group's identity, values, and prerogatives, acting not so much as supplement to the text as celebration of the habitus it promotes.[3]

The *Satsangi Jivanam Mahatmya* consists of nine chapters appended to the front of the *Satsangi Jivanam*. The text is framed as a dialogue between Shatanand Muni, composer of the main text, and a ruler identified variously as Hemanta Singh or King Uttam. The time is said to be a few months after the death of Sahajanand. The setting is Gadhada, home of the Kathi chieftain Dada Khachar—who is in fact one and the same as King Uttam. We are told that when Shatanand learned there was to be a gathering at Dada Khachar's court, he made his way there. Upon his arrival, the acharyas present for the occasion ask him to recite his composition, employing the first-person plural as if to include all who have gathered there: "You are the author of the *Satsangi Jivanam*, a work that leads to liberation. We long to hear this from you, O revered one of enormous intellect."[4] This is the setting in which the *Mahatmya* was recited as well; it celebrates not merely the text of the *Satsangi Jivanam* but also the community's new sense of corporate identity more generally.

One might say that while the ostensible goal of the *Mahatmya* is to eulogize the text, it also does significant work by way of shaping Satsangi conduct and forestalling the possibility of error.[5] Enjoining all future reciters of the text and their audiences to give the *Satsangi Jivanam* the respect it is due, the *Mahatmya* lays out what constitutes the correct behavior and comportment of a Satsangi: calmness, restraint, equanimity, devotion.[6] In this way, the *Satsangi Jivanam Mahatmya* embodies the early community's attempt to display, inculcate, and propagate a unique devotional habitus—a form of life that is recognizably Vaishnava but distinctly Swaminarayan. Furthermore, certain traditionalizing gestures facilitate the integration of Sahajanand's new polity into the existing religious ecology of early colonial Gujarat.[7] All of this, as we shall see, is entirely consistent with the ambitious project begun during Sahajanand's own lifetime to articulate his new polity through acts of textual production, ethical guidance, institutional innovation, and the creation of new material sites for worship.

Sahajanand's Rules

Fourteen days after the death of his guru Ramanand, the leader of the Uddhava Sampraday, Sahajanand was approached by a group of monks, laymen, and laywomen from the community. They expressed their conviction that he was the one true path to salvation and embraced him as their new guru and lord. And they beseeched him to instruct them in the rules by which they should henceforth live.[8] Acquiescing, Sahajanand is said to have replied, "Listen to me, all of you, men and women alike. I will tell you the rules that accord with the true scriptures and are appropriate to worshippers of the blessed Lord."[9] And so he began to instruct his new community, beginning with an injunction to rise early in the morning and greet the day with devotional songs directed to him and with the recitation of the names of God. According to the *Satsangi Jivanam,* there then flowed from Sahajanand's lips a comprehensive list of obligations. This list occupies nearly one hundred verses.

These instructions are followed by injunctions to avoid alcohol and food not properly offered. Strict warnings are given about forming proper associations (*sanga*) with others. Satsangis should never associate with those who do not love the Lord, or with those who have fallen from their religious vows. As for those who might take up the dharma only to fall away—one should avoid them as if they were dog-cookers. By contrast, those who have attained the strictest levels of dispassion, who are righteous and fully devoted to Krishna, should be viewed as teachers in their own right. Every effort must be made to avoid atheists, and Satsangis are advised not to converse with teachers from other *sampradays* or even listen to their books. These make up some of the general observances (*sadharan dharm*) for sadhus and householders alike.

Following these general rules come a set of special observances, first for sadhus and then for householders. Over another fifty verses the text lays out prescriptions for the maintenance of celibacy and dispassion among sadhus while enjoining chastity and devotion among householders. The avoidance of women by sadhus and the restraint of women's conduct within household life are prominent themes.[10] The substance of this chapter—known as the "song of Narayan" (*Narayan-gita*)—is reminiscent of a classical *dharmashastra*. In fact, early in the text we are told that Sahajanand had enjoined Shatanand to compose his work as if it were a *dharmashastra*.[11] Not surprisingly, then, the classical Brahmanic ideal of *varnashrama dharma* is promoted; Brahmins are given special reverence; and considerable concern is generated with respect to the conduct of women. These concerns regarding women's conduct echo rules promulgated by Manu, not least the words, "women must not be independent" (*striyah svatantra naiva*).[12] As with Manu and the Bhagavad Gita, the emphasis here is on faithful observance of one's "own duties" (*svadharma*). At one point Sahajanand tells his followers, "Here is my instruction to all of you: never abandon the particular duties I have assigned to you (*svasvadharmani*) as long as your body and your memory persist."[13]

Among the tens of thousands of verses that constitute the complete *Satsangi Jivanam*, the Narayan Gita tends to receive special attention in the community. It is said to be not merely the core of the text, but the "weightiest" of all the *shastras*—precisely because it issued from the very mouth of Sahajanand, channeled through Shatanand, and thereafter shared for the benefit of all. To put its observances into practice is to bring one's life to complete fruition.[14] Such claims about the weightiness of the Narayan Gita are reflected in the fact that it is placed near the beginning of the *Satsangi Jivanam*. Itself a kind of paratext, the Narayan Gita provides a preliminary frame according to which the life and teachings of Sahajanand should be approached and put into practice. The very image of a frame is apt, since it suggests the role of the Narayan Gita in establishing boundaries for conduct. In fact, one word Sahajanand uses frequently—both in the *Satsangi Jivanam* and in other texts—is *maryada*. To invoke *maryada* is to speak of boundaries, since a *maryada* is both a rule and a kind of limit.

Another significant element of Sahajanand's usage is his invocation of a communal "us," which mirrors the first-person plural employed by those followers who asked Shatanand to recite the *Satsangi Jivanam*. These pronouns suggest an answer to the pressing question, who are we in relation to other associations and polities? Thus, shortly after the delivery of the Narayan Gita, Sahajanand was called upon to say whether his followers should engage with popular festivals like Navaratri that honor deities such as Shiva or Durga. It was a fair question, given what we know of Nilakantha's earlier efforts to defeat followers of cults associated with blood sacrifice or the consumption of forbidden substances. Are Brahmins in the Sampraday allowed to officiate at such ceremonies? It is not just a question of ritual, but of economics; such service could form an important part of a Brahmin's livelihood.

Sahajanand's response to this question reveals his skill at positioning his new polity in the local religious landscape. When a question was raised about Navaratri, he referred to Shiva's consort Parvati and claimed her as the embodiment of the very virtues that were central to the *satsang*, not least dharma, *jnana*, *tapas*, yoga, and *vairagya*. Then he reminded his followers that Parvati is important "for us" (*asmakam*).[15] The modest Sanskrit pronoun encodes a savvy act of boundary-making. On the one hand, Satsangis are told there is no need to shy away from rituals like Navaratri, since Parvati is a deity "we" recognize as good (*sattvika*). Thus a Brahmin priest may perform the relevant rites. On the other hand, "we" are a distinct polity, and followers should take care to avoid demonic (*asura*) deities that violate "our" norms. As such, even in the case of Navaratri, the Brahmin priest is told to follow any rites he performs for the occasion with an act of penance (*prayaschitta*).[16]

A Code for a Polity

The boundary-defining significance of the Narayan Gita is echoed in what is perhaps one of the most central texts of the Swaminarayan Sampraday, the *Shikshapatri*, or "Letter of Instruction."[17] Comprising 212

Sanskrit verses, the *Shikshapatri* was completed in 1826.[18] It is a remarkable work for more than one reason, not least because in the second verse Sahajanand reveals himself as its author and declares his desire to write for the benefit of his followers.[19] One dimension of Sahajanand's project in formulating the *Shikshapatri* seems to have been to establish his new polity as a legitimate Vaishnava *sampraday*. Arun Brahmbhatt has recently called attention to a passage in the Gujarati *Harililamrita* in which Sahajanand comments on how crucial it is for a new *sampraday* to demonstrate its mastery of, and conformity to, *shastra*. Brahmbhatt concludes that Sahajanand was thus concerned that his *sampraday* be reckoned a full-blown initiatory community under his leadership and not just another devotional path, or *panth*.[20] The *Shikshapatri* fosters this goal by situating the Sampraday in relation to authoritative sources on Hindu dharma, the truth of which Sahajanand has himself distilled.[21]

A second important dimension of Sahajanand's boundary-making endeavor in the *Shikshapatri* was to formulate a disciplinary code that would further regulate behavior of Satsangis within his new polity. As he put it toward the end of the text, "It is incumbent upon my followers, having their minds well controlled, to conduct themselves in conformity with its precepts, and not according to their own wills."[22] In this respect the text offers a straightforward code of personal ethics and is once again explicitly framed in relation to the textual traditions of *dharmashastra*.[23] However, Sahajanand seems to have intended that the text also have a life beyond the exegetical concerns of legal specialists and pandits. No mere legal code, the *Shikshapatri* was to have a place in devotional life.

As a way to underwrite daily recitation of the text, Sahajanand declares that the *Shikshapatri* is not merely his word (*vani*) but his "personified form" (*rupa*).[24] As a kind of image of God, it thus merits reverence in its own right. Anyone unable to read the text is told to have it recited for them, while those who could manage neither were instructed to simply worship the text as God's form.[25] Here we might think of the *Shikshapatri* as both an index and an icon of Sahajanand's own spiritual power (to borrow from the semiology of C. S. Peirce). Having been written by Sahajanand himself, the text was a direct index of his presence, like an inscription visible to the eye.[26] But as his very image, the text may be thought of as an icon, fit for worship just as one might worship the physical form (*murti*) of God. Like any sanctified object, the text was meant for the hands and affection of only those who had made themselves "heavenly."[27]

Not surprisingly, the *Shikshapatri* has garnered considerable attention from scholars. An English translation appeared as early as 1849 in a book by H. G. Briggs, whose significance I discuss in Chapter 8. Several decades later, in 1882, the Oxford Sanskritist, Monier Monier-Williams published the Sanskrit text along with his own English translation, working from a lithograph copy of the text presented to him by the Maharaja of Vartal.[28] Since that time, the text has assumed a place of prominence in modern discussions of the Sampraday, due in no small part to the possibly apocryphal story of Sahajanand himself presenting a manuscript copy of the text to the then governor of Bombay Presidency, John Malcolm, in 1830.[29] Whether or not that story is accurate, it speaks to a perceived need on Sahajanand's part to strategically situate the Sampraday in relation to British ruling authority (a topic I return to below).[30]

For now, thinking of the *Shikshapatri* as enjoining commitment helps us appreciate its importance for the polity-in-construction. We have already seen how its legislative project gained traction by invoking and mirroring the classical *dharmashastras*. We might further consider how the community's reverential ritual deployment of the text serves to ratify and perpetuate Sahajanand's ruling authority. Finally, in terms of boundary construction, the text reminds us of Sahajanand's attempt to situate his new polity in relation to the authority of other groups like the Vallabhas. In all these respects, the *Shikshapatri* served as a powerful tool for advancing Sahajanand's articulation of spiritual mastery. That Sahajanand was well aware of the question of power is suggested by a vignette cited by one modern author, who reports a scene in which a certain Rajput was reluctant to follow Sahajanand's new rules. To him Sahajanand supposedly said, "If you don't obey me, you will have to obey per force a power that will soon come."[31]

In terms of power relations, the *Shikshapatri* recognizes the challenge faced by the new polity in inserting itself into the scale of forms that constituted the early colonial world of Gujarat. Not only does Sahajanand begin and end the text by contemplating Lord Krishna and beseeching his blessings for the spiritual welfare of his community; he also repeatedly advises Satsangis—as he had in relation to Navaratri—to honor the other deities inhabiting the world around them. Though clearly Vaishnava in orientation, the *Shikshapatri* contains a number of verses that recommend honoring Shiva; there is even a command to stop, salute, and take *darshan* of Shiva if one should happen to pass by one of his temples.[32] At one point Sahajanand even gives instructions for conducting proper worship of Shiva.[33] Perhaps just as remarkably, he allows followers born into Shaiva families to carry on wearing their customary *rudraksha* beads and sectarian marks.[34]

In light of such evidence, the objective of the *Shikshapatri* is clearly not the simple purification of behavior.[35] Rather, it seeks to establish for devotees a distinctive niche within a plural world of scaled religious polities. This scale of forms begins with family and caste traditions, village festivals and temple traditions, and extends to other formal initiatory polities, or *sampradays*. As Sahajanand tells his followers, "Men should adapt their conduct, business, and penances, to their country, time, age, means, class, and ability."[36] In a commentary he composed for the *Shikshapatri*, Shatanand indicates that what Sahajanand means is that Satsangis should follow existing norms around daily bathing, the payment of debts, the performance of caste-based practices, and the earning of wealth.[37] In this regard, Sahajanand did not seek to utterly replace old customs or modes of religious life; to the contrary, he enjoined Satsangis to conform themselves to the worship practices (*seva-riti*) promulgated by the other prominent Vaishnava *sampraday* in the region, the Vallabhites.[38] Such deference to the mastery of another polity seems remarkable if we cling to notions of sectarian exclusivism. But we have to recognize that the gesture here is one of fitting into an existing religious landscape.[39] Toward this end, Sahajanand is not averse to referring to the leader Vallabhacharya as the king of all Vaishnavas; he even replicates Vallabhite traditions around the transmission of authority within that community (recognizing the claim of Vallabha's son Vittalanatha) as a way to validate his advice that Satsangis should emulate Vallabhite practices overall.[40] Meanwhile, on the theological level, he identifies his teaching with the doctrines of Vishishtadvaita Vedanta as found in the works of the Indian philosopher Ramanuja.[41]

In light of such evidence, it is fair to say that what we see enacted in the *Shikshapatri* is more an exercise of placing than of replacing.[42] This is not a zero-sum game. Sahajanand is prepared to acknowledge a range of masteries in the universe—what Inden calls the great chain of being—from the highest God down through his worldly representatives and all the way down to local rulers, caste councils, and parents. The cosmos of the *Shikshapatri* therefore includes not just heavenly lords but also worldly masters. These gradations of power are the stuff of Sahajanand's social vision: the master of a house should provide for his servants; officers should have qualifications commensurate with their rank; and conversation with others should always heed their station in life. Above all, respect (*sammana*) must always be shown to any recognized master, whether guru, king, elder, renouncer, or those who can fly in the air like birds (due to their yogic prowess).[43]

Guru and Governor

What about those new masters in the region, the British? They were clearly to be included in the scale of forms recognized by Sahajanand. We can see this if we attend to some of his discourses. For instance, one evening during the winter of 1821 he was seated on a cot in the assembly hall of Sura Khachar, a local chieftain.[44] At his feet were gathered a number of disciples and sadhus. He was in a pleasant mood, and he invited the sadhus to ask him questions. On the previous evening he had spoken about the need to eradicate pride while appreciating the greatness of God and the qualities of a true sadhu. On this occasion, he addressed the possibility of a virtuous person suddenly turning evil. This seemed to surprise the sadhus, because one of them asked how such a thing could happen. Sahajanand framed his reply in terms of the need to understand the true self (*atman*), to maintain faith in the Lord, and to restrain the senses. A person who lived this way could never falter from the truth. On the other hand, not even faith in the Lord would be enough to save someone who remained wedded to the senses. This was how virtuous people turned evil. Someone who gave in to the senses would not even be above criticizing true sadhus.

Upon hearing this, another sadhu asked why it was that sometimes one noticed people who did well in the community of *satsang* even though they still made the mistake of identifying the self with the body and carried on indulging their senses. How could one explain this? Sahajanand's reply was simple. Such people do well only until something unpleasant happens, at which point they reveal their true colors. Consider the case of a sadhu who faulted someone for harboring traces of pride or anger. Since the person so criticized was indeed still wedded to the passions, he would surely come to disdain the sadhu and thus in time would become alienated from the *satsang*.[45] But someone who loved God, knew the self, and controlled their senses would be safe from such error.

Now suppose someone entered into an assembly but was not shown respect by the sadhus gathered there. If he were to conceive hatred for the sadhus, that would prove he had not developed a true respect for the holiness of others. To illustrate this point, Sahajanand drew an analogy from contemporary experience:

> If the British Governor of Mumbai were seated in an assembly, and if at that time a poor man were to enter that assembly but was not given a seat or welcomed in any way, would the poor man become angry with the Governor? Would he feel like swearing at the Governor? Not at all. Why? Because the poor man has realized the eminence of the British official; that is, "He is the ruler of the land, and I am a mere pauper." Hence he does not become upset.[46]

This is a telling passage, and not just because it mentions the British governor.[47] What is intriguing is the way Sahajanand uses the authority of the colonial ruler to think about how deference should operate within the *satsang*. If we think of the new Sampraday as a polity subject to a range of governing powers, this passage gives us an indirect glimpse of how Sahajanand recognized the operation of different kinds of sovereignty in the region. Sahajanand embodies the sovereign power of the guru-as-Lord. He manifests this authority while seated in the court of a local ruling lord, namely Sura Khachar. And in his comments he also demonstrates his recognition of the ruling authority of the new British governor.

Though far from prominent in texts produced within the Sampraday during the early period, the figure of the British governor (*gavendra* or *gavendar*)—and sometimes that of the king (*raja*)—plays a significant role in Sahajanand's teachings. There are actually two occasions in the *Satsangi Jivanam* when Sahajanand speaks of a savior figure from the West who will come to the aid of his ascetics when they face persecution from local forces in Gujarat. This savior is even identified as a Christian king, white-faced, and carrying weapons; he will oversee the dispensation of justice.[48]

We know that in the mythic terms of the *Satsangi Jivanam*, the forces opposing Nilakantha's teachings are depicted as demonic followers of dark gods like Kali or Bhairava; sometimes they are likened to demons (*asuras*) bent on upsetting Nilakantha's dharmic work. But the battle to establish the new Sampraday was apparently never really quite so Manichean; the success of Sahajanand's work required the support of other worldly powers and other agents of the good. Among these we can include even the white-faced Christian king. At one point the *Satsangi Jivanam* goes so far as to reproduce a version of the Ten Commandments by way of affirming a kind of basic congruency between this Christian king's dharma and that of Sahajanand.[49]

The timing of Sahajanand's remarkable prediction about the white-faced king seems to have coincided with a moment when the leader had to address a situation in which his fledgling ascetics were facing considerable resistance within local communities. Recognizing that the move to insert his polity into the existing landscape had generated the ire or jealousy of other actors, Sahajanand made the rather drastic move of telling his sadhus to shed their sectarian marks so that they might wander incognito, just as the Pandavas were compelled to do in the final year of their exile.[50] Interestingly, after this reference to the Mahabharata story, the *Satsangi Jivanam* becomes curiously specific about historical details: it informs us that Sahajanand is residing in Gadhada. At that time a messenger arrives, dispatched by an unnamed governor (*gavendra*). This governor—some British agent or other—was passing through Rajkot on his way to Mumbai. He wished to meet Sahajanand. The latter agreed to rendezvous with the governor in Rajkot.[51]

Upon Sahajanand's arrival, the governor is said to have bowed respectfully. He then expressed a desire to learn about the path to salvation. When informed about the challenges faced by Sahajanand, the governor committed himself to protecting Sahajanand's sadhus from further persecution. He even invited the guru to stay with him in Rajkot. Sahajanand expressed his desire to return to Gadhada, but nonetheless thanked the governor for his offer of protection. In doing so he managed to offer some praise of the latter's knowledge of politics (*nitishastra*). When Sahajanand returned to Gadhada, he had good news for his sadhus: there was no more need for secrecy—they could roam safely, secure in the governor's protection.[52]

The *Satsangi Jivanam* reports that these events occurred in the year 1808 (that is, Vikram 1864), but it is hard not to hear in them a clear echo of the much-discussed later encounter between Sahajanand and Governor Malcolm, which took place in Ahmedabad in 1830, just a few months before Sahajanand's death. On this occasion, Sahajanand is supposed to have presented Malcolm with a manuscript copy of the *Shikshapatri*.[53] Whether or not this actually happened, the meeting was of enormous import. Sahajanand was in fact meeting with the highest representative of British power in the region. Whatever claims the Swaminarayan community have since built around this event, there is no doubt it represents a crucial moment in the ratification of the new religious polity: it suggests precisely how a polity seeking to insert itself within an existing scale of forms might secure its future welfare by cultivating useful relationships with other external ruling powers.[54] This cooperation between guru and governor seems to be encapsulated in Malcolm's receipt of Sahajanand's book of dharma. That Malcolm may have had his own reasons for cultivating relations with the Sampraday is of course not insignificant, but takes nothing away from the importance of this conjunction of Sahajanand's regulatory program and the British colonial project.[55]

This encounter is often mentioned in the literature on the early Sampraday; typically it is taken as evidence that in Sahajanand the British had found a local religious leader who "shared a common interest in social order and harmony."[56] In an era and a region framed as rife with crime and barbarism, the meeting between Sahajanand and Malcolm is supposed to mark a providential moment for the advance of religious reform. We are told that by working alongside the Sampraday, the British were able to oversee the eradication of such backward practices as female infanticide while promoting more progressive notions of ritual and caste status. It is just this sort of interpretation that helped ratify the place of Sahajanand within the ranks of modern Hindu reformers. Even so, proponents of this view have had to reckon with the fact that Sahajanand actually held rather rigid and nonprogressive views about patriarchy, gender segregation, and even caste hierarchy.[57] Squaring this circle has not been easy. The thesis advanced by Raymond B. Williams has won the widest support: in Sahajanand we have to reckon with someone who has one foot in the Middle Ages and the other in the modern era. What cannot be explained from one vantage point makes sense from the other.

I propose we forgo such dichotomizing around the medieval and the modern in favor of thinking of the historical constitution of a religious polity in the early colonial moment. This is not to leave moral questions to the side, but to view them in relation to a pair of contemporaneous projects at articulating ruling authority—by the British and Sahajanand alike. Compelling research by Shruti Patel supports this effort to rethink the standard narrative around Sahajanand and social reform. Patel asks why it was that Sahajanand preferred to present new British acquaintances with a work like the *Shikshapatri* instead of other devotional works that might better highlight his transcendent identity and doctrinal uniqueness. Why offer a "manual of behavior" and not the more lively *lila-charita*s, with their compelling vignettes of devotional life? If the distinctiveness of the new path lay in Sahajanand's theological vision, why did he not offer the British texts that foregrounded his understanding of God, the self and bhakti? Patel's answer is that Sahajanand must have determined that he could best advance his status with the British by offering them something like a "template" of Satsangi comportment.[58] She further suggests it is plausible that Sahajanand deliberately directed attention away from the *lila* texts—rich with mythology and cosmic narratives—because they would have posed challenges for his British contemporaries. This makes good sense.

Later we will have occasion to consider an even earlier meeting between Sahajanand and a representative of British power in the region, Bishop Reginald Heber. Like the encounter with Malcolm, the meeting with Heber is widely cited in histories of the Sampraday, not least because it constitutes one of the earliest published European accounts of Sahajanand. Heber had gotten word of a so-called reformer in Gujarat and was curious to learn more. But when his new acquaintance began to speak of Krishna, *avatars,* and other sorts of "Magic," Heber was "alarmed."[59] What did Sahajanand take away from his meeting with Heber? Perhaps he learned that if he sought to cultivate useful relationships with local British authorities, he would do well to keep things on a disciplinary rather than theological level.

In any case, it is unlikely that Sahajanand met Heber out of an interest in finding theological common ground. It makes more sense to think of him seeking alliances with the governing power of the British in order to solidify his regulatory authority as guru. Heber may have been interested in meeting a reformer, but Shruti Patel is surely right to suggest that the formation of the Swaminarayan Sampraday in this early period looks more like a "process of creation" than one of "reform."[60] Such creative work required building new relationships, both within the community and in relation to external ruling powers. Chief among the latter were the British, but we must not lose sight of Sahajanand's newfound relationships with local chieftains such as Sura Khachar and Dada Khachar; conversely, we should be careful not to miss the significance of the serious competition Sahajanand faced from other Rajput leaders in the area, rulers made anxious by his bid for ruling authority. Rajput resistance was significant enough to be incorporated into the mythic scenario of the *Satsangi Jivanam,* framing the reason for the Lord's arrival on earth. As Lord Swaminarayan, Sahajanand had come to do battle with demonic temporal and spiritual leaders like the Rajputs who corrupted true religion.[61]

Stepping back and looking at the process of Sampraday creation in this way, we can see how well it conforms to Hodgson's model, as introduced in Chapter 3. Here we have the advent of a charismatic leader with an innovative doctrine. That leader establishes an "immediate" connection with an audience. As that audience feels the force of Sahajanand's message, they respond to his efforts to institutionalize a community by generating hagiographies, crafting rules for communal discipline, and solidifying the status of the new polity in relation to existing powers. If Patel's focus tends to be on the presentation of new ideas in this context, it is worth stressing that we are also looking at the emergence of a new the regulatory habitus.[62] And whereas Hodgson emphasized the role of charisma in attracting the attention of an "immediate public," we should not take this to mean the Sampraday arose in an unmediated fashion. As the work of both Habermas and Warner suggests, there is no way to imagine such an unmediated social phenomenon. The preceding review of Sahajanand's early efforts should suggest how much was owed to the mediating structures of language, textual traditions, ritual norms, and religio-political regimes. The original articulation of the Swaminarayan Sampraday occurred precisely through the promulgation of a range of texts, rituals, paratextual strategies, and local contacts with representatives of other polities, religious and otherwise—including the governor, in whose hands rested new responsibilities for ensuring justice and order in the region.

Satsang as Rule of Life

The confluence in Sahajanand's teaching of internal and external strategies of governance conforms to the logic of what we might call the Swaminarayan *regula fidei*, or rules of faith. We can say that such rules are less about regulation in a narrow sense than they are about the cultivation of new ways of living. In this regard, the rules propounded by Sahajanand stress that the embodiment of proper living is *satsang*. To realize *satsang* is to realize a "form of life"; it is to establish life in common.[63] The goal is to become a Satsangi, and the centrality of that ideal is enshrined in the title of the great hagiography, the *Satsangi Jivanam*. This is why so many of Sahajanand's conversations in Gujarati circle back to the need to maintain good company (*sadhuno sanga*) and avoid bad company (*kusangano tyaga*). As he put it, the creation and maintenance of *satsang*—theological assertions aside—depends on the observation of rules (or limits) laid down in the scriptures (*shastrani maryada*).[64]

Central to the fulfillment of a rule-based form of life is restraint of the mind and senses. Sahajanand sometimes employed the image of the British ruler to make this very point. On one occasion in 1827, while sitting on the veranda of Dada Khachar's house in Gadhada listening to the sadhus sing devotional songs, Sahajanand interrupted and said, "Let us talk about God." He began to speak of how a person's life is contingent on karma: that is, on one occasion a person may be healthy and on another he may be ill; one may find oneself alone or in the company of others. All this is due to karma. So the question becomes, how well does one maintain the rules of life (*niyam*) when faced with change? Sahajanand gave a concrete example. Suppose a ruler "like the British" were to detain a person; that person's ability to act would be curtailed. Well, the mind and the sense organs are "also like the British"; they can keep a person under their control. When that happens, it becomes a question whether such a person will be able to remain in *satsang*. Why? Because to be in *satsang* is to observe the discipline (*niyam*) and rules (*maryada*).[65] As Gunatitanand Swami, one of Ramanand's original disciples, put it, observation of the rules is a weighty matter (*bahu moti vat*).[66]

On the one hand, there is the external law of the land; on the other hand, there are the rules found in the scriptures and endorsed by the Sampraday. You might find yourself arrested by the British and put on trial, the subject of suspicion and questioning. On the other hand, any one of us is also liable to incarceration and punishment by our own desires and ego. As such, what one ought to do for oneself is just what the British threatened to do to those who violated their laws: put shackles on our senses and drag them into "the witness box"! And the best shackles are the five religious vows (*panch-vartaman*).[67] If such carceral imagery seems dramatic, it comes from Sahajanand himself, a graphic reminder of how much emphasis he placed on the steadfast regulation of behavior. For the well-being of *satsang* and Satsangi alike, there could be no leniency. The senses are enemies; show them mercy and they will lead you down the path of sensory pleasure. Before you know it, you will be drawn to "women and other objects."[68]

If we focus too much on what appear to be the doctrinal dimensions of a text like the *Shikshapatri,* we risk losing sight of the fact that, for this emerging polity, it was crucial that the rules of behavior and liturgy could be successfully mapped onto a form of life. One might even say that life within the *satsang* is liturgy.[69] The *Shikshapatri* is a call to adopt a particular *forma vivendi,* understood not in terms of this or that act, but as "the entire existence of an individual."[70] In this respect, the ideal listener should be like the king at the beginning of the second section of the *Satsangi Jivanam Mahatmya,* who, after hearing scores of verses on rules for performance, says to Shatanand, "I am eager to know more about the scriptural rules found in this treatise!"[71] His request is not for wisdom, but for the kinds of injunctions (*vidhi*) that would make him a better Satsangi. As Shruti Patel suggests, Swaminarayan subjectivity is premised on following rules as a way to "exercise anticipatory behavior," which is to say, to become a better Satsangi.[72]

I have drawn on the work of Giorgio Agamben to emphasize that we should think of religion not as an exit from the world, but as the constitution of a world. No less than in the traditions of Western monasticism studied by Agamben, this renouncer-centered Sampraday, with its large and active householder community, is a political entity. In texts like the *Satsangi Jivanam Mahatmya,* the *Satsangi Jivanam,* and the *Shikshapatri* we are dealing with conscious political gestures as much as with the promulgation of theological doctrines. Agamben refers to Wittgenstein's observation that one cannot follow a rule privately; to follow a rule is to inhabit a community and embrace a "set of habits."[73] This is *satsang.* As Sahajanand taught, no one ever develops dispassion by thinking only of themselves; a devotee serves others.[74] This is why, among the six required duties as enjoined by Sahajanand in the Narayana Gita, the sixth and last is to remain in *satsang.*[75]

A Charter for a Rule of Life

The decade of the 1820s was a momentous one for the articulation of the new Swaminarayan polity, witnessing the establishment of patterns for its transmission over time and its successful emplacement within the

Gujarati religious landscape. In terms of promoting a distinctive *forma vivendi*, both the *Satsangi Jivanam* and *Shikshapatri* were composed (or, in the former case, initiated) during this period; likewise it was during this period that the discourses forming the *Vachanamrut* were delivered. Taken together, these texts serve to articulate a coherent model of "personality, behavior, spiritual qualification and scholarship" centered on and dedicated to the life and teachings of Sahajanand.[76] While the *Shikshapatri* represents Sahajanand's particular vision of his polity, the other texts—not to mention commentaries on these works produced by the likes of Shatanand—were composed or compiled by his most dedicated bhaktas. Their work underwrites Sahajanand's mastery and speaks to his followers' commitment to the promotion of the new Sampraday in relation to the Vaishnava textual canon.[77]

Alongside such doctrinal and scriptural work, Sahajanand explicitly articulated injunctions to establish the proper institutional organization of the Sampraday and to ensure the transmission of authority over time. Texts like the *Shikshapatri* and *Vachanamrut* provide rulings around issues like ritual entitlement for initiation and respect for the true gurus within Sahajanand's dharmic family (*dharma-kula*). Sahajanand was explicit about the transmission of authority. In the *Vachanamrut* he tells his follows that "our" gurus all follow a particular line of succession from Sahajanand's own guru, Ramanand Swami; importantly, the latter had been initiated by the recognized South Indian authority, Ramanuja Acharya.[78] And while the supreme chosen deity of the community may be Lord Krishna, Sahajanand stressed that he himself was the spiritual master, guru, and preceptor of the Sampraday. "All of you should behave according to my words in the form of the respective injunctions which I have prescribed."[79]

Among these injunctions, some of the most consequential are those from 1826, recorded in an important text known as the *Desh-Vibhag-no Lekh*, or the "Document pertaining to the division of the country" (hereafter, simply, *Lekh*).[80] This is a text Sahajanand dictated to his disciple Shukamuni; in it he enunciated key organizational features of the Sampraday, not least rules for the recognition and transmission of authority within his dharmic family.[81] Sahajanand named two figures who were to act as the first hereditary acharyas, or preceptors, of the Sampraday: Ayodhyaprasad and Raghuvir, the sons, respectively, of Sahajanand's older and younger brothers. Sahajanand took the additional step of adopting these two as his own sons. It was to be through them, and them alone, that future initiations would occur; and it would be under only their authority that new images could be installed in Swaminarayan temples; finally, to each would fall as jurisdiction one half of the entire realm (*sarva desh*) of India, divided by a line running east to west from Calcutta in Bengal to Navnagar, near the Vaishnava sacred town of Dwarka, on the Gulf of Kutch in Gujarat.[82]

Overall the *Lekh* gives the impression of Sahajanand creating a new kind of charter intended to articulate and foster the interests of the Sampraday. The Sampraday begins to manifest itself in terms of what Inden has called complex agency. And as we have seen, the new polity is placed within, rather than set in contrast to, a larger scale of regional polities. In the *Lekh* we witness Sahajanand working to secure the perpetuation of his own lordship by constituting a perduring model of rule that assigned roles to his regents and to what we might call, also after Inden, the subject-citizens of his new polity.[83] Overall we can say that one measure of Sahajanand's genius was his ability to bring into being a highly detailed yet supple organization by drawing on existing models and sources, not least those found in the established Vallabhite tradition.[84]

As a kind of charter, the *Lekh* had several intended audiences. The chief audience comprised the "ruling" authorities named therein, that is, the acharyas. A second audience would have been the larger body of the Sampraday, who would look to the document as an expression of their organizational identity. Finally, the document would have spoken to local audiences outside the Sampraday, not least those communities among which Sahajanand hoped to insert his new polity, especially the Vallabhites. As Françoise Mallison has pointed out, in developing his organizational structure, Sahajanand directly followed the example of the Vallabhites, whose hereditary leaders (descended from Vallabha via his son Vitthal, as we have seen), had each been assigned authority over a particular jurisdictional *gadi* (or religious "throne"). Mallison says that once we acknowledge this fact, we are able to dismiss one of the most stable myths about Sahajanand, namely that he was out to reform the errors of the Vallabhites. If anything, we see how respectful he was of that community and how creatively he drew on their example. Furthermore, Sahajanand knew how much the support of Vaishnava communities like the Vallabhites would assist him in his efforts to establish a new Sampraday.[85] Far from being a target of reforming animus or puritanical zeal, the Vallabhites offered an audience, a template, and even a religious space in relation to which the Swaminarayan polity could take form.[86]

This is not to say that Sahajanand did not also take pains to impress on his followers the exclusive honor due to him, his acharyas, and the structures of authority within his *satsang*. At certain points in the *Lekh*, Sahajanand explicitly closes the door on the expression of competing claims for leadership. To begin with, only the acharyas were allowed to establish temples; likewise, no sadhu within the Sampraday would ever be allowed to take control of a temple.[87] Furthermore, Sahajanand stipulated that no one—no matter their knowledge or attainments—should ever be granted greater respect and authority than the acharyas.[88] Finally, Sahajanand used the *Lekh* to remind sadhus and householders of the rules he had laid out in the *Shikshapatri*.[89] For all these reasons, it makes sense to think of the *Lekh* as the charter document of a self-governing association of subject-citizens who had a "partial capacity . . . to combine within and among themselves and order their own affairs" even while recognizing that the success of the collective endeavor required finding their "proper relationship" to other powers and polities in the region.[90]

Finally, the *Lekh* reminds us of another dimension of Sahajanand's efforts to articulate and ensure the future of his polity, which had to do with the construction of new temples. Some time ago Raymond B. Williams pointed out how the success of the Sampraday was made concrete in the built landscape of Gujarat, Kathiawar, and Kutch.[91] Already by the time Sahajanand came to dictate the *Lekh*, he had established new temples in places like Ahmedabad and Vartal.[92] In fact, his decision in the *Lekh* to apportion the space of the Swaminarayan polity between the two new acharyas was done with an eye to linking their respective authority to these two new temples.[93] Once again we have occasion to appreciate how astutely Sahajanand negotiated—and transformed—the religious and political terrain of early colonial Gujarat.[94]

The first of the temples created under Sahajanand's leadership was the Nara-Narayana temple in Ahmedabad, which was consecrated in February of 1822, some four years before he had completed the *Shikshapatri*.[95] By this time the British had assumed control of Ahmedabad. Given Sahajanand's ability to read the prevailing political winds and his canny awareness of how his authority could benefit by being expressed in relation to that of the new rulers, it comes as little surprise that he approached the British collector in Ahmedabad for assistance in establishing the new temple. Naturally, in a hagiography like the *Satsangi Jivanam*, we are given the impression that Sahajanand's desire to establish the temple was sparked by appeals from his devotees, who are the ones who encouraged him to approach the governor's local representative for a donation of land.[96] One suspects this is not quite how things played out. Given what we know of other meetings between Sahajanand and British officials, it seems more likely that Sahajanand worked knowingly to cultivate a relationship with the collector in order to earn his trust.[97] Either way, land was eventually gifted to the community and the temple was built, following the appropriate Sanskrit shastric requirements. Some accounts say that many as fifty thousand Satsangis turned out for its consecration.[98]

Other temples were constructed on lands donated by wealthy and influential devotees. The *Satsangi Jivanam* follows the account of the building of the Ahmedabad temple with chapters on the construction of the next two temples, in Bhuj (1823) and Vartal (1824) respectively. In both cases these temples were established on lands dedicated to Sahajanand by his bhaktas.[99] Notice that here we have clear evidence of Sahajanand's ascent to a position of respect among local populations, not least among local rulers.[100] It was in Bhuj that he had intervened in the performance of animal sacrifices at a local ruling court; and in Saurashtra he had made great inroads among the Kathi chieftains.[101] Sahajanand's successful establishment of temples in places like Bhuj (1823), Vartal (1824), Junagadh (1827), and Gadhada (1828) thus speaks to the expansion of his mastery across the larger Gujarati cultural region. The founding of the Gadhada temple may be thought of as the capstone to a period of successful temple-building that helped secure his claim to the territory. When he died in 1830, he was indeed a *puissant chef religieux*.[102]

Sahajanand's efforts to promulgate scriptural knowledge, disciplinary norms, organizational rules, and material structures for the new Sampraday can be understood as the articulation of a new devotional polity centered on a guru, framed by rites of initiation, governed by layers of authority, and made visible in the local landscape. What is more, his clear respect for other communities like the Vallabhas and his dependence on figures like the British governor enhance the impression that this polity was both self-governing internally and responsive to governance from without.[103] This was also a form of life framed in relation to Sahajanand's teachings about lay and renunciant life, his rules for regulating moral and religious behavior, his delineation of authority, and his support for recognizable forms of devotional practice and temple worship. All these elements worked in tandem to support the integration of this new polity within a regional landscape marked by what Inden might call "plural rulerships."[104]

The point is that the Sampraday was not some relic of a fast-dwindling premodern past. Rather, given the enormous changes taking place in Gujarat at this time, we have to think of the Swaminarayan Sampraday as a polity very much shaped by—and expressive of—the moment of the early colonial modern. Sahajanand's engagement with the British is but the most obvious reminder of this fact. Even if during his lifetime the Sampraday had yet to adopt the printing press or other markers of modern public life, we have clear evidence of new textual production and the guru's own awareness of how colonial administrative and judicial systems were beginning to define a new kind of imperial formation. Thinking of Sahajanand's work to articulate his polity in relation (rather than opposition) to British power shifts our attention from the question of his relative allegiance to some retrojected idea of India and onto the exploration of complex agency working to foster and sustain a new religious polity in the early colonial moment. Likewise, rethinking his debt to the Vallabhites allows an important opportunity to put to rest the tired conceit of Sahajanand as a modern reformer bent on correcting the errors of Vallabhite deviancy. From the vantage point of a late-colonial reformer like Karsandas Mulji (whom we encountered in Chapter 3), it might have made sense to conjure Hindu reform as the progressive purification of religion, but the interpretation offered here suggests no such agenda was at work. That agenda and its attendant tropes would be bestowed on the Sampraday only from within the later empire of reform.

7

THE RAJA'S *DARBAR*

W HEN RAMMOHUN SAILED FOR Britain in 1830, he did so with a new title, bestowed on him by the Mughal Emperor Akbar Shah II. Henceforth he would be known as Raja Rammohun Roy. In a sense this new title only reduplicated the status he had inherited from his father's side of the family, who as we have seen had been granted the honorific Ray (whence Roy) by the Nawab in Murshidabad. Perhaps what makes the title of Raja so significant is that it was bestowed on Rammohun directly by the emperor. Is there anything odd about the fact that the so-called Father of Modern India was given the title of Raja and thus symbolically incorporated into the imperial formation known as the Mughal Empire? From the vantage point of nationalist historiography the fact is certainly awkward, but is less so when we approach this investiture in terms of the imperial scale of forms within which the East India Company itself continued to operate at the time. The company still served under the auspices of, and was at least formally beholden to, the emperor in Delhi. In this respect, the title of Raja, which prima facie suggests august authority and a kind of supremacy, actually reminds us of Rammohun's newfound status within a hierarchical scale of forms that commenced with Akbar II, descended through regional rulers like the Nawab of Murshidabad and the East India Company, down to various zamindars like the Raja of Burdwan, until finding a place at last for the emperor's envoy to the Court of St James's in London.

I emphasize this scale of lordships because in this chapter I attempt to approach Rammohun in the same way we approached Sahajanand in Chapter 6, which is to say as a kind of early colonial lord or master. Is there a way to think of Rammohun's role in establishing the Brahmo Samaj in terms that are analogous to Sahajanand's articulation of his new Sampraday in Gujarat? The challenges here are great, not least because it will seem to many a distortion—if not denigration—of Rammohun's status as a reformer to approach him in terms of the acquisition and extension of religious and political mastery. However, my goal is not to denigrate Rammohun, nor to question the fact that he would in time come to be seen as India's first great reformer. My goal is rather to postpone advancing this latter sort of assessment long enough to see whether there is another way to conceptualize what he accomplished with the founding of the Brahmo Samaj. If so, would we then be able not only to think anew about his accomplishments, but also to view them as in some respects analogous to those of Sahajanand? And in thinking through what both men achieved, might we arrive at a new way to think about the emergence of modern Hinduism in the early colonial moment?

Fürst among Equals

Needless to say, the standard approach within narratives of modern Hinduism and the Indian nation is to take the honorific Raja as a signifier of Rammohun's greatness; though curiously medieval, the title of Raja somehow highlight's the enormity of Rammohun's newness, crowning him as a forerunner of modernity. He is *primus inter pares* among those "eminent Indians" whose life stories would come to fuel nationalist aspiration in the late nineteenth and early twentieth centuries.[1] By that time it had become axiomatic that character was destiny and that history was made through the vital agency of noble characters. Rammohun's death centenary in 1933 marked the final crystallization of his status as father of the nation, and yet this kind of thinking has its roots in the first flowering of the empire of reform after the 1830s. A fine example may be found in a notice published in the *Bengal Herald* in January of 1841:

> The character of a nation is always in a great degree dependent upon the character of individuals. Names of men like Shakespeare and Milton and Bacon and Newton, give a more distinct idea of England's mental greatness than could be produced by an elaborate essay on the subject. . . . The single name of Rammohun Roy is cherished by the more enlightened of his countrymen with a gratitude and veneration because they feel how much the owe him.[2]

That this kind of rhetoric could be quoted without an ounce of irony by a scholar writing in the late twentieth century as proof of Rammohun's greatness speaks to the power—and persistence—of such reformist logic.

Though there are reams of such rhetoric to plow through, one can occasionally find small points of access that lead to alternate paths of interpretation. One excellent example can be found in the words chosen by the Oxford Sanskritist F. Max Müller to laud Rammohun's greatness. Drawing on his fluency in German, Müller wrote,

> The German name for prince is Fürst, in English *first*, he who is always to the fore, he who courts the place of danger, the first place in fight, the last in flight. Such a Fürst was Rammohun Roy, a true prince, a real Rajah, if *Rajah* also, like *Rex*, meant originally the steersman, the man at the helm.[3]

Müller used this rhetorical flourish as a takeoff point for exploring Rammohun's status as a Great Man, someone who could tower over the likes of even Napoleon. Advancing his argument, Müller identified three "essential elements" in Rammohun's greatness—his unselfishness, honesty, and boldness. At first glance Müller's remarks sound like a modern manual on leadership skills, something like the three essential keys to success. But on further reflection, one comes to appreciate that these otherwise anodyne virtues harbor profound resonances that guide us back to older ideas of princely nobility. To appreciate this point, we need to postpone implementing the logic of modern reform and notice that what Müller hints at is as much the medieval prince as the modern prince of progress. Wittingly or not, he suggests that, as with the German term Fürst, the honorific Raja communicates a certain conception of lordship; it is less about a character trait than about a premodern respect for sovereign power. By postponing the translation of raja into the characterology of modernity, we are thus able to situate Rammohun within another world—the courtly world of what Daud Ali has called the "dynastic polity."[4]

Ali's work on dynastic polity, like Inden's, calls our attention to the operation of early modern notions of mastery and lordship in South Asia.[5] In this respect, the honorific bestowed by Akbar II on Rammohun secures for the latter a place within the scale of polities that constituted the moral and political landscape of early colonial Bengal. In this landscape, the qualities of "service, devotion and favor" were central to the articulation of ruling protocols.[6] Long before he earned his own royal honorific, Rammohun watched as his father Ramakanta attempted the delicate and fraught task of navigating court protocols while serving both the Burdwan ruler and the East India Company.[7] By virtue of the codes that operated within these courtly, or at least court-like, settings, Ramakanta had profited materially and symbolically—even if his royal entanglements also led him to run aground on the shifting sands of power in the company's fiscal relations with the Burdwan polity. The high stakes of gaining recognition and mastery within this context are illustrated by the case of Ramakanta's eldest son, who was imprisoned in Medinipur District after he defaulted on payments due to the Raja of Burdwan.[8]

One thing is certain: Ramakanta's years of service—even if not unblemished—had allowed him to amass esteem and wealth, the latter in fixed property and revenue estates in and around present-day Hooghly and Medinipur Districts. Some of this wealth would in time accrue to Rammohun. But Ramakanta's career also carved useful political channels down which Rammohun would be able to move, especially after separating from his family and taking up life on his own. As early as the 1790s, Rammohun had begun to manage his father's properties, and during those years he moved frequently between the family home and places like Calcutta and Burdwan; he also maintained Ramakanta's properties farther south in Chetua and Bhurshut Parganas.[9] During this same period, Ramakanta parceled his holdings among his three sons. By the age of twenty-seven, because of this settlement, Rammohun had come into considerable wealth, including a house in the Jorasanko area of north Calcutta and two parcels of land near Burdwan.[10] By 1801, he had drawn on his financial status to begin working for different British agents in the city; here he was able to trade on his skills in Persian, accounting, and trade. This was when he first met John Digby, under whom he would later serve as Dewan in Rangpur as we have seen.

I will return below to Rammohun's eventual decision to settle in Calcutta in 1814, but for now it is worth noting that by the time he made that decision, he was already well acquainted with—and well connected in—Calcutta. His negotiation of that environment, whether in 1797, 1801, or 1814, never seems to have been tenuous or overly fraught with challenges. He did not come to Calcutta as a country bumpkin or struggling economic migrant. There is no need for us to impose on him the kind of Horatio Alger stories that cluster around someone like his younger contemporary Ishvarchandra Vidyasagar, who arrived in the city as a poor student and struggled to survive with a father who was then earning a mere pittance.[11] Instead of picturing Rammohun just getting by in the city, I prefer to think of him bringing it under his mastery. It is telling, in this regard, that one Bengali commentator uses the word *aishvarya* when imagining Rammohun in Calcutta, especially in the years after 1814. That word expresses the idea of lordship or sovereignty associated with being a lord (*ishvara*).[12] This reminds us of Müller's recourse to the concept of Fürst: as early colonial lord, Rammohun was first not merely in terms of character, but also in terms of power. Far from being a nameless figure on Calcutta's streets, Rammohun was, from the beginning of his career, *ganamanya*, respected by those around him. He cut the figure of a lord in his lifestyle, habitation, dress, and friendships.[13]

A few reminiscences from Debendranath Tagore, who knew the Raja as a young boy, may help bring this into view. Debendranath recalled there was "no end of visitors" to Rammohun's house. Debendranath describes a situation that is a cross between the modern bourgeois salon and the premodern court. In Bengali, such a space is called (after the Persian) a *baithak-khana*, something like a "personalized darbar."[14] The *baithak-khana* was a formal space set aside for meeting guests and enacting the protocols associated with relationships of devotion and service. Debendranath tells us that some visitors to Rammohun's *darbar* came there to engage him in theological debate—something a ruler might encourage among his retinue of court scholars. But Debendranath also says visitors often simply bored Rammohun, not least "with their irregular and irreverent talk." Like a noble lord on his dais, Rammohun would patiently hear his visitors out, with attention to court etiquette preventing him from asking anyone to leave. Instead, "he would listen with all due courtesy."[15]

This is the Raja—the Fürst—enacting his lordship through the disciplined performance of hospitality, generosity, courtesy, and patience.[16] These are not just the good manners of a modern gentleman. Modern bourgeois norms of civility would eventually come to shape the elite world of native Calcuttans, but if we drop back to the first two decades of the nineteenth century, it is possible to detect the persistence of other modes of sociality and power.[17] These point to the kind of courtesy Daud Ali defines using the Sanskrit term *dakshinya*—a complex ethical category that captures a ruler's ability to be kind, but to do so in a way that is skillfully attuned to the importance of hierarchical protocols and the demands of balancing the display of affection and the bestowing of favors.[18] When paired with what we have learned about Rammohun's training in Nasirean ethics, we may appreciate how both Persianate and Sanskritic courtly norms converged in his lordly demeanor as generous and high-minded. Like a chivalric lord of old, he resided atop a "vast hierarchical order."[19]

In its earliest phase, the courtly world of Rammohun's *darbar* was structured by norms of civility that were enacted in displays of regal generosity, fostered by the cherishing of close relationships, and preserved from disorder by the maintenance of symbolic lines of respect and distance. If we fail to appreciate that Rammohun's *baithak-khana* was structured this way we miss an important chance to think about the conditions under which he soon would work to articulate his new religious polity. The wealth, power, and social relationships put on display in this fashion provided certain proof of the luster of Rammohun's court. Here too we should not think of luster only in terms of luxury or wealth; in the context of the Indic royal context it signifies a ruler's *tejas*, the "luminous energy" manifested by a sovereign lord.[20]

The connection between the splendor of court and the new religious polity is captured once again by Debendranath, who wrote with particular fondness of what he remembered about the weekly gathering of the group that made up the earliest cohort within the Brahmo Samaj. He observed these gatherings from a distance while still a young boy and in his reminiscences called particular attention to how Rammohun used to insist on convening something like a small processional in order to travel from his north Calcutta garden house in Maniktola—itself a marker of both prestige and power—to the Brahmo Samaj premises off Chitpore Road in Jorasanko.[21] The import of this kind of processional was not lost on Debendranath, who stressed that this was no mere whim of Rammohun's. "The Raja had peculiar feelings on the subject."[22] Those peculiar feelings were tied up with the importance of such a royal processional for manifesting to the people of Calcutta the mastery of this particular lord.

Feeling it inappropriate to ride to worship in a carriage, Rammohun would insist on walking to the meeting in a group. Nor would the ordinary *dhoti* and *chadar* suffice; he would put on "court dress on all such occasions." What is more, the mode of dress was invariably Islamic, since "his idea . . . was that God being man's King and Master in going to His court, one must dress oneself properly, and must appear before Him as one fit to be present at the court of the Prince of Princes."[23] As one source quoted him saying, "What is a worshipping congregation but a *durbar* of the King of kings. We should therefore dress in a way worthy of the solemnity of the occasion."[24] This gives a clear indication of how Rammohun himself understood his own place within a worldly and heavenly scale of forms. Donning the dress appropriate to a Persianate ruler and accompanied by his court, the Raja would formally process to the court of his highest Lord, the one true God of the Brahmo faith.[25]

The Raja of Rangpur

It would be fair to ask how Rammohun was able to attain such *aishvarya* and display such *tejas* within a relatively short period of time after settling in Calcutta. One way to answer that question would be to suggest that by the time he arrived in the city he had already acquired significant wealth and a dignified reputation. He had done well for himself within the upcountry orbits of his early career, having skillfully negotiated overlapping spheres of patronage: the Nawabi court, the Burdwan zamindari, and various East India Company postings in places like Calcutta, Faridpur, Murshidabad, and Rangpur. Thanks to opportunities developing in relation to such sites, Rammohun was well on his way to becoming a big man with wealth and influence even before he settled in Calcutta. The defining features of his career that we examined in Chapter 5 have tended to receive less attention from scholars, not least from scholars of religion, who often gravitate to issues of scriptural hermeneutics or theological doctrine associated with Rammohun's work in Calcutta. But if we are to understand how he came to advance his hermeneutical and theological program, we need to attend to the cultural and moral prehistory of his later public career. And sometimes it is not even just about religion, narrowly defined. We have to remind ourselves that, even before coming to Calcutta, Rammohun was not merely the recipient of a salary with access to British power; he was beginning to trade on his own wealth and authority to advance his interests. There is actually a minor disagreement in the literature around this topic.

Writing in the *Calcutta Review* in 1845, Rammohun's contemporary Kissory Chand Mitter shed some raking light on the circumstances under which Rammohun served John Digby while in Rangpur. Reading between the lines of Mitter's account, it seems Digby may have deliberately inflated Rammohun's status in his office by stipulating that his Bengali colleague not be treated like a mere *amla*, or native clerk. Although Mitter's stated purpose was to call attention to the otherwise abysmal "hauteur" of British civilians toward natives, one has to wonder to what degree Digby encouraged a kind of hauteur in his native assistant.[26] The question appears more than moot, since Mitter went on to cast some doubt on the means by which Rammohun acquired his wealth while working in a place like Rangpur. Not only had Digby singled out Rammohun for special respect, he also promoted him rapidly to the higher post of Dewan. Mitter seems to insinuate that Rammohun may have used the position of Dewan for personal gain—even perhaps by means of fraud or deception (Mitter uses the Bengali word *juyachuri,* or swindling). Mitter asked his readers if it was possible to square Rammohun's reputation as high-minded reformer with his role as powerful local agent, seated in the office of Dewan hearing pleas and drafting legal documents. Mitter cannot resist saying that, if Rammohun avoided abusing his authority, he must have been a "splendid exception" to the rule![27]

Other biographers have been quick to refute the "unworthy insinuation" that Rammohun would have sold favors while in service.[28] One scholar has even suggested that Rammohun's subsequent nomination to the Calcutta Municipal Board is clear enough proof of his "impeccable" business practices.[29] However, one could go too far in this direction. There is no need to overlook the way in which authority and influence operated in places like early colonial Bengal. As noted already, the *aishvarya* of a local lord was less about morality and more about the ability to exercise power within a particular political context. In this respect, Rammohun's early career allowed him an occasion to advance his lordship by amassing property, reputation, influence, and money. Serving as Dewan in Rangpur proved significant for just this reason. Furthermore, by this time, having amassed significant land holdings of his own, he himself became a zamindar.[30] As a petty landholding lord, he had his own retinue of servants, including an accountant (*hisabnavis*).

After all, a lord needs a court, and while serving in Rangpur, Rammohun built a home for himself where he began to hold evening gatherings to discuss religious topics.[31] This was the setting in which he entertained and came to know members of the local Marwari Jain community.[32] Not so much a modern salon, the setting is reminiscent of the *darbar* or *baithak-khana* discussed above. Like the famously curious and pluralistically minded Akbar, we can picture Rammohun convening his own regular assembly, or *sabha* as a site in which to patronize religious learning and exchange. It is what a lord might do—being gracious enough to entertain the opinions of those who did not necessarily share his views.[33] Beyond the convening of a *sabha*, the ancient texts on dharma tell us a king should also carry out works on behalf of the public good. And Rammohun did this as well, being credited with the excavation of a "big tank" near the courthouse.[34] Placement of the tank suggests that Rammohun was nothing if not strategic in the way he sought to establish his authority and reputation.

South Asian rulers typically have an inner circle that includes a number of trusted advisers, not least a chaplain (*purohit*) and a preceptor (*acharya*).[35] Rammohun was no different. It has long been noted that he maintained a close relationship throughout his life with one particular renouncer and tantric practitioner named Hariharananda Tirthaswami Kulavadhuta (1762–1832).[36] It makes sense to think of Hariharananda as Rammohun's *purohit*, a figure traditionally charged not just with mastery of scripture but with a kind magical prowess as well. Who better than a Shaiva-Avadhuta ascetic to fill such a role, since the *purohit*'s charge was to protect the king by using his secret attainments?[37] And Hariharananda was well positioned to serve as Rammohun's chaplain. Back when he was still known by his worldly name, Nandakumar Vidyalankar, Hariharananda had taught Sanskrit to the young Rammohun.[38] After renouncing the world and becoming an Avadhuta ascetic, Hariharananda may have initiated Rammohun into Tantra.[39] The theological significance of this fact has long been noted, but it bears noting that such an initiation also had a political dimension. Tantra and kingship have long been associated with each other, and tantric initiation may be thought to have conferred a kind of spiritual lordship on Rammohun.[40]

The exact nature of the relationship between these two is difficult to reconstruct, since there are no detailed records. It was certainly profound, lasting the entire course of Rammohun's life. It certainly seems significant that when Rammohun took up residence in Rangpur, Hariharananda followed him there and served him as what we might call both his *purohit* and acharya.[41] This is most likely the time during which Hariharananda educated Rammohun in Tantra. This makes all the more interesting Shibnath Shastri's passing comment that Hariharananda helped render Rammohun's time in Rangpur "fruitful."[42] The immediate fruit of their association was Rammohun's articulation of a courtly platform from which to accrue further mastery in economic, political, and religious matters. Connections fostered in that court helped him consolidate his economic and cultural capital, while strengthening his position at the nexus of British authority and local ruling polities. We do not know the precise constitution of Rammohun's Rangpur court, and I do not wish to stretch the available evidence too far, but simply bringing this courtly polity into view helps extricate Rammohun from the hold of reform-based discourse. It may be disorienting to think of Rammohun as Raja in this way, but a bit of critical vertigo may be a necessary side effect of rethinking his career.

In standard narratives, Rangpur is viewed as a period of important preparation for Rammohun. Yet in the same narratives it typically remains just that, preparation. For Rammohun to be appreciated as the great modern reformer, standard accounts need to emphasize what he accomplished after settling in Calcutta. Needless to say, this way of telling Rammohun's story tends to construe his advent in Calcutta as marking the dawn of modernity in India. This is when Rammohun is said to make his "break with the past."[43] To lend support to the idea of the sudden advent of modernity, two developments are often cited: Rammohun's founding of a new society for religious discussion, the Atmiya Sabha, and the publication of his first masterwork, the *Vedanta Grantha*, both of which took place in 1815.

And yet this way of construing things begs the question I posed at the beginning of this section: How was it possible for Rammohun to accomplish so much so quickly, if in 1815 he had still hardly unpacked his belongings?[44] Here is where some reflection on Rammohun's time in Rangpur proves important. If nothing else, it allows us to see that Rammohun came to Calcutta with immense capital to spend.[45] He had financial resources and valuable professional connections, the latter fostered over years of work in the city on behalf of his family's business interests, not to mention in his minor role at the College of Fort William. Furthermore, attending to what he had achieved in Rangpur allows us to appreciate that he came to the city not only with a plan, but also with the core of a courtly polity already in place.[46] Thus, rather than a radical break, we might think of the royal progress of the Raja of Rangpur from his base in the mofussil to the metropolis of colonial Calcutta. This is to put an entirely different spin on the progress of reform.

A Court of One's Own

The founding of the Atmiya Sabha in 1815 is typically taken to mark the birth of modern associational activity in colonial Calcutta.[47] Allied to the idea of Rammohun's sudden advent in the city, standard accounts suggest that his decision to create a voluntary association was the result of his being ostracized by urban Hindus because of his open contestation of traditional forms of religious life. Markers of his break with tradition included not merely his rejection of polytheism and image worship, but also his adoption of Persianate styles in dress, food, and comportment; all of these are said to have set the teeth of orthodox Hindus on edge. We are asked to imagine him somehow alone and at a loss; finding himself shunned by influential members of the Hindu community, he thus turned to his "friends," which is one meaning of the Bengali term *atmiya*. In his new "Society of Friends," we are told he created a space for "collective thinking, discussion, and reform."[48]

This is certainly a plausible narrative for the founding of the Atmiya Sabha, especially if one is oriented to the emergence of Calcutta's early colonial public sphere, within which associational activity played such an important role. Even so, I would like to explore the possibility of interpreting the constitution of the Atmiya Sabha a bit differently. If I choose not to focus on the novelty of the Atmiya Sabha as proof of Rammohun's status as the first modern Indian, it is because I want to explore what the creation of that association—or polity—reveals about the work of one early colonial lord in constituting a new community articulated in terms of his own distinctive vision of social, moral, and religious order.

We can begin by returning to the name of the society. By now enough has been said to appreciate the resonances of a term like *sabha*, which suggests a court formed under the authority of a ruler and articulated in several material and symbolic registers (space, dress, comportment, discourse). That we may take the risk of construing Rammohun as the lord of a *sabha* is suggested by Debendranath's memory of Rammohun's habit of processing to the meetings of the Brahmo Samaj (mentioned above). That leaves the other term, *atmiya*. As noted, in Bengali the term may be used to speak of "friends," but this is something of a derivative, second-order meaning. In a more literal sense, *atmiya* designates "one's own people," lending the term a set of associations around the logic of family, kinship, and caste. In English we might think of the term "relatives," which is to say, those who are bound to us by more than simply terms of familiarity or fondness. This would suggest that the Atmiya Sabha was less of a "friendly society" (as one finds it often translated) and more a court of Rammohun's own people.

What would that mean? Here we need to distinguish between the act of establishing a modern bourgeois voluntary association and constituting something on the model of a royal court. Given the early colonial context for the founding of the Atmiya Sabha, I do not rule out that there is a certain merger of both social ideals taking place, but by thinking further about Rammohun's *sabha* as a court, we call attention to his ruling authority in the sense made pertinent within Inden's framework. If there is a modern equivalent of such gatherings, it would not be the coffeehouse so central to critical accounts of the bourgeois public sphere but perhaps the aristocratic salon that was such an important space for the articulation of social and political power in places like eighteenth-century Paris. Any reader of Proust knows that admission to the salon was hardly open to all comers. And the salon was also a space where rank and reputation mattered; mild derision occasioned by the minor faux pas was certainly always possible but, more consequentially, expulsion or outright social ostracism were also always a possibility. In other words, power was in play in the salon, expressed in subtle codes of etiquette and conviviality.[49] By comparing the early colonial *sabha* to the salon, I mean to suggest that in the space of the early colonial assembly, one would have found a similar convergence of early modern and modern notions of sociality, no matter the vast cultural divide from Paris.

To develop this parallel, we might think of the concept of *goshthi*, or social circle, a term used in the Indian context to denote a select group of sophisticates entitled to gather in courtly or semi-courtly settings where wealth, comportment, and certain kinds of "connoisseurial knowledge" were the essential binding forces.[50] Among his social circle, Rammohun displayed and expanded his own *aishvarya*. Far from merely a cozy gathering where friends could escape the watchful eye of coreligionists, Rammohun's *sabha* was a space for more constructively enacting a polity; it announced his authority, yoked it to the support of "his own people," and put it in the service of his own ruling agenda.

Two of the most consequential of Rammohun's "own people" at this time were Hariharananda, on the one hand, and Dwarkanath Tagore, on the other. Hariharananda brought the authority and prestige of Brahmanic knowledge and tantric mastery (itself closely associated to the pursuit of royal power, as we have seen). Dwarkanath, the so-called Merchant Prince of early colonial Calcutta, would have brought material resources as well as political connections of his own on which Rammohun could draw to garner further prestige.[51] In addition to being one of the most successful native merchants at the time, Dwarkanath was himself a zamindar, head of the Jorasanko Tagore family. Representing a curious blend of free-trade liberalism and aristocratic prestige, Dwarkanath shared Rammohun's agenda and played an important role in the early articulation of his polity—materially but also symbolically.[52] To mention a zamindar like Dwarkanath is to remind ourselves that Calcutta at this time was flush with a set of nouveaux riches families, each with dedicated supporters and sycophants, and all wedded to the pursuit of power, wealth, and social advancement through creative relationships with the British and other actors. Into this scale of forms Rammohun sought to insert his new polity.[53]

This helps us appreciate why support for the *sabha* is said to have come from other members of the "richest and most influential" families of native Calcutta.[54] Among these figured men like Kalishankar Ghoshal of Bhukailash, whose zamindar family had profited from alliances with the East India Company, and Prasannakumar Tagore of the Pathuriaghata Tagores, another influential family in the city. These were "respectable" people, as long as we understand respectability as a measure of both political authority and elite comportment.[55] The leaders of such families had suffered ups and downs as a result of various engagements in moneylending, trade, and rent farming; they would have been looking to compensate for recent financial setbacks by linking their interests to up-and-coming patrons and promising new networks of power.

We should therefore be cautious about taking at face value the comments of a later Brahmo like Shibnath Shastri, who classed early members of the Atmiya Sabha into three groups: those who wanted to rub shoulders with someone great; those who sought the great man's assistance in a practical matter; and those who were motivated by "genuine sympathy."[56] Shastri preferred the last group overall, viewing the *sabha* as an expression of friendly association and not as an arena for expressing power. His preference for those members drawn by nothing more than sympathy smacks of a later bourgeois notion of sincerity that obscures (when it doesn't dismiss) the reality of politics and concerns with prestige. Even so, when read against the grain, Shastri's scheme manages to communicate the idea that Rammohun was the kind of ruling lord with the status and the power to get things done for his "own people." He constituted a court that helped express his lordship by incorporating lesser lords within his realm; and those other princes rendered him tribute and sought to benefit from association with him.[57]

Shastri's remarks also raise the question of what it meant to be a member of such a body. To speak of membership is once again to risk translating the Atmiya Sabha into the sociology of modern voluntary associations; it is to conjure bureaucratic systems framed by rules and maintained through processes of subscription, enrollment, dues collection, and elections to office. These are certainly features that would become central to the world of associational activity that was only just beginning to erupt in colonial Calcutta; but it has been noted that the Atmiya Sabha was actually idiosyncratic in this respect: it possessed "no formal organization, no constitution, and no program for action."[58]

What need for rules and membership rosters, when what is articulated is a set of relationships around a ruling figure? Rather than speaking of members, we might think instead of those who came to Rammohun's court as bhaktas.[59] I recognize that this may seem like an outrageous proposition to anyone acquainted with what would become Brahmo egalitarianism and rational worship of God. But I propose here not to direct attention to bhakti as emotional religion, but simply to bhakti as what Inden construes as the posture of the "devoted participant." Inden sought to stress that the root meaning of "participation," so central to treatments of bhakti religiosity, could also operate in a less emotional register. A person could thus become a "devoted participant" in the life of any sort of ruling lord, human or divine.[60] To attend upon and engage with a king in his court is to be a bhakta, a devoted participant seeking to be incorporated into the ruler's world.[61]

Initially the Atmiya Sabha met in Rammohun's impressive Maniktola garden house, where he reconstituted the kind of *darbar* he had presided over in Rangpur. Collet describes these meetings as "not quite public." Hers is a telling choice of words, confirming the impression that the Atmiya Sabha served as something like a privileged assembly, with certain parallels to an aristocratic salon, as suggested above.[62] Alongside his *purohit* Hariharananda, Rammohun now gained another important assistant, who we may think of as his acharya. This was Hariharananda's younger brother, Ramchandra Vidyavagish (1786–1845).[63] Rather quickly Ramchandra assumed a position of increasing visibility, while Hariharananda slipped into the background.[64] To use another telling expression found in Collet, Hariharananda became Rammohun's "shadow"— bound to him closely but also somehow indistinct, the precise nature of his role occluded.[65] It is of course possible that this development correlates with a shift in the focus of Rammohun's interest from Tantrism to the public promotion of Vedic scripture and the Upanishads in particular. In this dimension of the project, Ramchandra's role as acharya was central. He began addressing the other bhaktas on topics of scriptural import and the moral vision of Upanishadic theism.[66]

From Sabha to Samaj

What bears noting is that, in its early years, the Atmiya Sabha lacked a formal religious constitution, at least if we look for anything like a programmatic statement framing a set of theological views in relation to the responsibilities associated with institutionalized commitment or membership. Rammohun had his dedicated followers—his bhaktas, if you will—but their devotion seems originally to have been oriented toward him as their quasi-royal patron—the kind of patron who had not only capital to expend but new ideas to debate. To get to the point where we may speak of a more formalized religious polity, two further elements were needed: first, an act that would solemnize, or at least ratify, formalized commitment, and second, the designation of a particular space within which to meet as a society and enact a shared ritual life.

Here we may recall a point made by Inden, which is that the mere articulation of a theological vision—what Inden calls a "world account"— is not in itself sufficient to realize a religious polity.[67] Just as we noted in the case of Sahajanand, a polity requires a theology and a disciplinary habitus enshrined in a set of rules. Ramchandra seems to have appreciated this. One early account suggests that Ramchandra expressed concern that merely gathering together at Rammohun's home to discuss the Upanishads and argue over theological issues would not be enough to secure the stability of the group. He sought some way to garner greater commitment among participants, something like a rule-bound declaration of faith (*vidhivat pratijna*).[68] This concern over regulating Brahmo commitment was in fact to persist well after the founding of the Brahmo Samaj and the death of Rammohun. It would be an important factor in Ramchandra's later relationship with Debendranath Tagore, the figure credited with reviving the Brahmo Samaj after Rammohun's demise.[69]

Rammohun seems to have understood Ramchandra's concerns and to have made gestures toward addressing the lack of ritual forms. We notice that just a few years after forming the Atmiya Sabha he published his ideas for a liturgy based on the ancient Vedic Gayatri Mantra.[70] However, nothing took immediate hold. In fact, it would not be until the next generation of Brahmo leaders that new rituals of initiation were formalized. Even so, we can see the degree to which these new rituals hearkened back to Rammohun's original focus on the Gayatri Mantra. As Debendranath would later write,

> No undertaking succeeds without method. Therefore, in order
> that the conversion to the Brahma Dharma might be made in
> due form, in order that the worship of Brahma might be
> substituted for image-worship, I drew up a declaration of faith
> for initiation into the Brahma Dharma, which contained a
> clause to the effect that daily worship was to be performed by

means of the *Gayatri mantra*. This was suggested to me by
Rammohan Roy's injunction to adopt the *Gayatri* for the
purpose of worshipping Brahma.[71]

That the framing of rules would play a crucial role in transforming Rammohun's original "debating body" into a proper religious polity is something Collet seems to have recognized; at one point she comments on how important it was for the early Atmiya Sabha to reconstitute itself as a "distinctly religious fellowship."[72]

It is well known that during the years of less formalized gathering, Rammohun had begun attending services convened by the former Baptist missionary William Adam, who had become a Unitarian after working closely with Rammohun on a translation of the New Testament. During the 1820s, Rammohun joined Adam on the Calcutta Unitarian Committee, and this is when he began to attend services.[73] It was not long before some of his devoted participants asked him, why do you attend these Christian services when it would be better if we had our own place and pattern of worship?[74] Rammohun registered their disappointment. According to one early account, this marked the great eureka moment that catalyzed the eventual founding of the Brahmo Samaj. Rammohun is supposed to have responded to his bhaktas on the spot, promising them that he would immediately begin looking for a suitable parcel of property on which a worship space could be erected. Although he envisioned building a new structure, at the time no suitable property could be located. Thus, for the time being, arrangements were made to rent space in a house near Dwarkanath Tagore's home in Jorasanko. This would become the first Brahmo meeting hall.[75] No less than Sahajanand, Rammohun paired the promulgation of theology and the convening of a new association with the construction of a physical space in which to emplace his new polity. Just as we saw with Sahajanand, Rammohun appreciated how "our" commitment required being articulated not only liturgically, but spatially as well.

And so we arrive at the moment when the Atmiya Sabha took new shape as the Brahmo Samaj. What Collet calls the "great commencement" of the "native Theistic Church" of India took place on Wednesday, August 20, 1828. A fair amount of ink has been spilled over the years regarding whether the group was known initially as the Brahmo Sabha or Brahmo Samaj. On most levels this might be dismissed as of little significance, and much of the literature on the subject smacks of quibbles over irrelevant semantics.[76] And yet, in the context of the present discussion, there is a way in which the distinction can be shown to point toward a significant difference at the level of institutionalization. Put simply, the eventual adoption of the term *samaj* confirms the sense that the Brahmo polity coalescing under Rammohun's leadership was intended after 1828 to be more than just a temporary assembly (one sense of *sabha*) and something more like an enduring, rule-bound society—a *samaj*.

This distinction also provides an important way we might go about distinguishing the religious polity constituted by Rammohun from the one articulated by Sahajanand in Gujarat. Not only did Rammohun's polity assume the organizational identity of a *samaj*, it notably did not assume the identity of a *sampraday*. This point is not insignificant since, on the face of it, there is no reason why Rammohun might not have identified his group as a *sampraday*. In the early decades of the nineteenth century, the latter term was coming into use for a variety of new associational purposes. Some of these coinages even worked to translate the term away from the explicit realm of religion. For instance, one notices a passage from 1818 in which the Calcutta School Book Society is labeled a *sampraday* for the "preparation of books for local schools."[77] It may seem an odd usage to readers accustomed to references to devotional or other religious *sampraday*s, but this new application of the term reflects a moment in which the vocabulary of associational behavior was clearly still in flux.[78]

However, when we consider Rammohun's well-known animus toward the errors of Puranic Hinduism, it is not hard to imagine he would have kept his distance from a term like *sampraday*; to him it would have smacked too much of the world of guru-led Hindu polities, mythic narratives, and embodied deities with lavish material cults. What is more, he would have known very well that one target of missionary preaching at the time was the "sectarian" confusion of Hinduism.[79] He might well have been reluctant to suggest that his new Brahmo polity was in any way associated with Puranic, schismatic, or what are even today referred to as "sampradayik" modes of Hindu life and practice.

Interestingly, this may point to one major reason why Rammohun objected to the idea that he was a reformer. In his *Defense of Hindu Theism* from 1817 he took issue with an opponent who dared to suggest that Rammohun arrogated to himself too much credit by claiming to bring the truth of Vedanta to light. The opponent's point was that the teachings of Vedanta had long been known and celebrated, at least since the time of the Shankaracharya. And the great Shankaracharya never called himself a reformer![80] Rammohun was obviously troubled by this kind of criticism, and he used the occasion to think out loud about the meaning of his own work. In his reply he claimed he had never assumed the mantle of a reformer; he did not pretend to have discovered anything new. His was thus not merely some new *sampraday.* In fact, he taught only what had always been true of "real Hindooism." It is as if he appreciated that ready-built into the logic of reform were concerns over schism and sectarianism. And since he had been "stigmatized" by his coreligionists, he feared this would be taken as proof of his being a reformer—since what do reformers do if not promote schism? His response was unequivocal: just because he had been challenged for his views, it did not make him a reformer.[81] Whether or not his argument was entirely ingenuous, it demonstrates the degree to which he was reluctant to yoke his work to the discourse around reform that was beginning to shape religious debate in a place like Calcutta.[82]

We come to appreciate that, during Rammohun's early colonial moment, translational possibilities and pitfalls were everywhere. Even though he skillfully navigated his way around sticking points associated with terms like sect, schism, and reform, these terms would in time become central within standard accounts of the Brahmo Samaj. In late colonial histories, the Samaj was to become a "Theistic Church" (as we saw in Collet's words quoted above), and the story of that church would be translated into claims about the reform of narrow sectarian religion toward universal religious truth. Notably, in 1879, G. S. Leonard wrote of the Brahmo Samaj, "The history of the Brahma Samaj is not so much the narrative of any particular sect or religious order as it is that of a general reformation of the condition of the Hindus in all that relates to their spiritual, social, and moral concerns."[83] In support of this claim, Leonard referred to a tract titled "Brahmaism Is no Sectarianism," most likely written by Rajnarain Bose, a prominent later Brahmo.[84] Both Leonard and Bose wrote from within the empire of reform (which I return to in Chapters 8 and 9), during a moment when claims about the Brahmo Samaj as an Indian reformed church proved useful for a number of actors ranging from missionary propagandists to anti-imperialist Britons to early nationalist voices of resistance. Whether decrying the failure of the Brahmos to embrace the one true church of Christ or using Brahmo universalism to challenge European cultural arrogance or elevating Rammohun to the status of India's first great reformer, the rhetorical and political ends to which these actors put the Brahmo story fit poorly with what we know about the polity's first emergence in the early colonial moment.

The Trust Deed

Instead of invoking an ecclesiastical model or Reformation parallels for making sense of what Rammohun articulated by way of the Brahmo religious polity, I suggest we consider the significance of the Trust Deed of the Brahmo Samaj. Drafted in 1830, the Trust Deed marks a signal moment in the history of the Samaj. Leonard found in it clear proof that a momentous "epoch" had drawn to a close, its closure marked by the formal establishment of the Samaj and Rammohun's departure for England shortly afterward in 1830. We might pick up on his comments and ask, just what sort of end does the Trust Deed mark? As we have seen, Leonard was prone to emphasize Rammohun's role in India's "religious reformation"; with his departure and death, the glorious moment of origin reached its climax. Now charisma would become canon, and the reformer's vision would become a global movement. Stepping outside Leonard's interpretive frame, it helps here to recall Partha Chatterjee's reflection on the end of the early colonial modern. Following his lead, one might argue that what came to an end in that moment was a distinctive era whose political, economic, and epistemic contours had left an impress on Rammohun's efforts at polity formation. With the end of Rammohun's era came the closure of certain possibilities, as we saw when reviewing Chatterjee's discussion of the Calcutta Town Hall (in Chapter 1). Coming to an end were patterns of Indian-European cooperation and a basic optimism about shared economic opportunities, even if the scene was also set for the flourishing of a vibrant colonial public sphere and the emergence of new norms and practices around associational organization and behavior.

In this moment it appears, too, that what had begun as a quasi-courtly articulation of a religious polity under the mastery of Rammohun, began to take shape as a more recognizably modern religious association. The Brahmo Trust Deed is one clear instantiation of this moment. For one thing, the composition of the Deed coincided with the completion of a new, purpose-built structure on Chitpore Road in north Calcutta that would house the meetings of the Brahmo Samaj. For another thing, the creation of this new space happened just as the community had begun to articulate a set of binding rules to structure Brahmo life and worship. Most commentators take note of this, not least Collet, who long ago remarked on the linkage between the new "place of worship" and a "remarkable theological document."[85] While it is true that the Trust Deed encodes the principles of Brahmo theology, it is also a modern legal covenant. Its purpose is to articulate the meaning and centrality of non-idolatrous worship in relation to a set of rules around the Chitpore space and to codify issues of trusteeship and superintendence of the site.

In this respect, although we can say that both Sahajanand and Rammohun achieved a final articulation of their polities through acts of textualization, spatialization, and disciplinary organization, the polities they constituted would diverge in important ways. Sahajanand appointed acharyas, parceled out his spiritual kingdom, codified his dharma, and installed images in temples. Rammohun negotiated the purchase of property for a new space of communal, nontheistic worship, simultaneously enshrining his values in a set of guiding rules for the Samaj. The audience for his Trust Deed was clearly quite different from Sahajanand's intended audience. In the Trust Deed, Rammohun spoke to fellow subject-citizens no longer as a lord over a court, but as a fellow stakeholder in a voluntary association; he spoke not to sadhus and Satsangis but to trustees and members. His charter is no less religious than the *Shikshapatri* and no more political than the *Lekh*, but the religion and politics of the Trust Deed are more firmly imbricated within the logic of liberal discourse as it was beginning to take expression under colonial rule and among Indian actors at the time.

In the Trust Deed, we witness the familiar set of local zamindar lords—Rammohun, Prasannakumar, Dwarkanath—opting in to a new mode of public, associational commitment. They collectively agree to make over a parcel of land to be held in trust for the purposes of constructing thereon a "brick built messuage" to serve as a "place for religious worship."[86] The Deed stipulates that the building will be a place of "public meeting" to be used by "all sorts and descriptions of people without distinction," provided they "behave and conduct themselves in an orderly sober religious and devout manner" and dedicate themselves to "the worship and adoration of the Eternal Unsearchable and Immutable Being who is the Author and Preserver of the Universe." This Being will not be given a name "peculiarly used for and applied to any particular Being or Beings by any man or set of men whatsoever," and worship will never involve the adoration of any "graven image statue or sculpture carving painting picture portrait or the likeness of anything." There are to be no sacrifices, no offerings, no oblations; no animal will be "deprived of life" either in the building or on the premises generally. There will be no feasting or "rioting," nor will there be the reviling of other deities—animate or inanimate—as worshipped by others. No one is to be "slightingly or contemptuously spoken of," whether in "preaching praying or in the hymns or other mode of worship that may be delivered or used."

These restrictions on ritual behavior and public conduct are accompanied by stipulations making it clear that anyone who speaks—whether in a "sermon preaching discourse prayer or hymn"—should do so out of a desire to promote contemplation of "the Author and Preserver of the Universe" and to encourage the practice of "charity morality piety benevolence virtue and the strengthening the bonds of union between men of all religious persuasions and creeds." At the level of organization, the Deed provides for the naming of one individual of "Good repute" and recognized piety to serve as "resident Superintendent" of the space, charged with ensuring that the Deed is followed. Finally, worship is en-joined on a daily basis or, at the very least, "once in seven days." The Deed was duly signed by all trustees and witnessed by a British attorney-at-law and another Bengali gentleman. No less a guiding charter than the *Lekh*, the Trust Deed served to ratify and communicate publicly the place of the Brahmo Samaj within the social space of Calcutta and the rapidly consolidating imperial formation of British India.

Executed on January 8, 1830, the Trust Deed both marks a moment in time and represents a particular kind of legal artifact. Taken together, these demarcate a kind of epistemic boundary between the possibilities found in the formation of an early colonial religious polity and the kinds of expectations that cluster around a modern religious association—not least an association that would link older modes of ruling authority to new norms of public conduct and social responsibility. In the Trust Deed, it is not just that the will and authority of Rammohun are formally en-trusted to a larger governing body; it is also the case that the future struc-ture and purpose of the Brahmo Samaj are here expressed in relation to a bureaucratized and publicly certified understanding of religious commitment.

As a result of this transition, we might now say that those who had once formed the circle of Rammohun's "own people" (*atmiya*)—his bhaktas—began to reconstitute themselves as his "friends" (*atmiya*), which is to say as people who chose not merely to live according to his norms and regulations, but to work collectively according to new social patterns then taking shape in a city like Calcutta. In this moment, id-ioms such as *sabha*, *samaj*, and *sampraday* would begin to be translated anew so as to harmonize with emerging norms governing the constitu-tion of modern voluntary associations. The societies coming into being at this time sought to place their impress on urban public life. As the polity became a public society, the Brahmo religious life was reshaped, amplified, and disseminated in relation to a host of new projects around publishing, education, philanthropy, and social criticism.[87]

The transition was not necessarily smooth. Notwithstanding the legal clarity of the Trust Deed, the health and vitality of the Brahmo Samaj suffered greatly after the departure of Rammohun for England. This tes-tifies not merely to the loss of Rammohun's charisma; it reminds us

more concretely of the role played by his lordship and mastery in ce-
menting the constitution of the original polity. That the Samaj did not
entirely fade away has long been credited to the commitment and energy of the acharya, Ramchandra, who sustained the ongoing practice
of regular meetings. More than this would be needed, however, for the
Samaj to survive. As it turned out, new resources and opportunities for
sustaining the work of the Samaj were available. Aside from Ramchandra's indefatigable stewardship, the most important development in this
regard was a concerted effort to disseminate Brahmo teachings in public.
We thus notice that by the middle of the 1830s the early Bengali sermons
of Ramchandra had begun to circulate in book form.[88]

By the close of the decade, Ramchandra had met and allied himself
with Debendranath Tagore, Dwarkanath's son, who at this very moment
found himself drawn toward the vision of Upanishadic theism. Together
the two established a new society with a Brahmo-style commitment to
celebrate the profound truths of Vedanta. This was the Tattvabodhini
Sabha (The Society for the Propagation of Truth), established in 1839.
Under Debendranath's leadership, the Sabha immediately launched what
I have elsewhere referred to as a project of "direct marketing," the goal
being to attract a wider audience of educated Bengalis who might be
eager to join a group that was committed to exploring questions of morality and theology free from the pressures of Christian proselytizing.[89]
The approach succeeded. Thanks to Debendranath's organizational vision and Ramchandra's scriptural mastery, the two were able to reener-
gize the original purpose behind Rammohun's polity. The new society
began to publish Brahmo teachings in their new journal, *Tattvabodhini
Patrika*, and opened their own primary school as a new space within
which to ratify and promote Brahmo values.

In all these ways, the Tattvabodhini Sabha was initially responsible
for opening up opportunities to be "Brahmo without Rammohun."[90]
This is worth highlighting, since as a result, Brahmo values and lifestyle
came to find new outlets along numerous channels in the rapidly urban-
izing, bureaucratic, and bourgeois world of 1840s Calcutta. Even if, in
time, Debendranath would choose to take initiation into the Brahmo
Samaj, and the Tattvabodhini Sabha would eventually be folded into the
organization of the Samaj, it is worth pausing to think about what tran-

spired during the liminal period of the late 1830s and 1840s. It is during this moment—when Rammohun's vision was propagated widely without being directly yoked to his personal mastery—that we can mark the beginning of a transition from Rammohun's ruling polity toward what we might call the modern Brahmo public. It is in this moment that we begin to witness the kinds of developments that would eventually contribute to the merger of Brahmo ideals and Bengali identity that were to become a hallmark of modern Bengali society henceforth.[91] And as I have tried to argue elsewhere, it is really only in this moment that Rammohun is for the first time discursively framed as the founder of the reform movement.[92] The process of looking back and reassessing the early colonial moment had now begun.

8

THE EMPIRE
OF REFORM

I N THE FIRST QUARTER OF THE nineteenth century, European and American observers imbued with the spirit of progressive melioration in religion embraced Rammohun and the Brahmos as evidence of the advent of reform in Indian religion and the advance of Christian truth in the farthest corners of the globe. Foremost among these early admirers were Rammohun's Unitarian friends, not only in Calcutta but also in Britain and America, with whom he had begun correspondence well before setting sail for Britain in 1833. These Unitarian enthusiasts helped spread the word that Rammohun was a progressive thinker, a staunch monotheist, and a friend to Christian learning. Indeed, one of the goals of Rammohun's visit to Britain was to deepen his connections with his Unitarian friends. His untimely death came as a devastating blow in this regard, but it did not terminate the promise of Brahmo-Unitarian allegiances.[1] If anything, Rammohun's death provided the perfect occasion to cement his legacy as a reformer.

The British Unitarian Lant Carpenter, who had hosted Rammohun in Bristol, took an important step in this direction by promptly publishing a biographical memoir of Rammohun. In this work he described his friend as a "Hindoo reformer" and suggested that Rammohun's work had produced nothing short of a "reformation of the religious belief and practice of his countrymen."[2] His assessment of Rammohun's legacy highlights key elements within the discourse of reformed religion, not least the idea of reform as an expression of civilizational progress in line with the story of Western modernity: it is enlightened, not prejudiced; morally edifying, not debasing; monotheistic, not idolatrous; rational, not absurd.[3] A kind of rhetorical peak is reached in the series of five sonnets Carpenter appended to his memoir, occasioned by the interment of Rammohun in Bristol's Stapleton Grove. Here the tropes of reform overwrite the older idea of the ruler's *tejas*, with Rammohun's luminous energy becoming the "heavenly light" announcing his "ardent zeal" to awaken India from "pagan gloom" and direct her "fallen people" toward the "Sun of Righteousness." As a chosen son of empire, he was aided in his work by a "holy band" of Christian patriots from "our blest Isle," whose hearts were ever imbued with love of freedom.[4]

Here we have compelling evidence of the early and exuberant incorporation of Rammohun into the empire of reform. From Carpenter to F. Max Müller, the steady growth of the global discourse around reform, especially when paired with late colonial notions of Great Man history à la Emerson and Carlyle, would lead inexorably to the familiar paradigm of the reformer as a kind of hero at the head of a noble reform movement.[5] Furthermore, inserting these events into the spatiotemporal logic of imperial expansion, there had to be an epicenter from which reform could be propagated. Calcutta became the place and Rammohun became the Fürst, the Raja, the "man at the helm."[6] Needless to say, this worked to relegate his contemporary, Sahajanand, not only to the frontier, but also to the past. Even if Sahajanand had drawn support from members of the same holy band of Britons who brought the light of progress to India, within the empire of reform he was destined to remain in exile, barely peering over the horizon of premodernity.

There is thus good reason to think of the empire of reform as what Milinda Banerjee has called a "political metaphysics." In this discourse, modernity is pictured "as a force providentially and rationally reordering society from above."[7] It truly is a higher metaphysics, since to speak of the empire of reform is not merely to map the spatial diffusion of new modes of religion beyond Bengal, but is also to associate modernity in religion with a particular conception of higher truth—a conception promoted by the monotheistic rationalism of a Rammohun. And as a metaphysic, the empire of reform would become the unmarked truth that made sense of all other religious modernities in India, be they revivalist, vernacular, or sampradayik—all these are marked as lesser if not erroneous. Here was a new way to consider what Rammohun set in motion with his valorization of Vedanta as the ground of true Hinduism: he named the highest (shall we say, *nirguna*) truth against which all other manifestations of modern Hinduisms would be judged.

With the emergence of the empire of reform as a metaphysic of religious modernity, a paradigm was established for writing about modern Hinduism that has remained largely intact at least from Müller's day down to the present. In fact, we might well press the emergence of this paradigm back even further, to works like Horace Hayman Wilson's *Two Lectures on the Religious Practice and Opinions of the Hindus* (1840) or Frederick Denison Maurice's *The Religions of the World and Their Relation to Christianity*, first published in 1846.[8] Or, as we shall see later in this chapter, we could turn to a lesser-known work on Gujarat from 1849, *The Cities of Gujarashtra* by H. G. Briggs. Well known among aficionados of the Swaminarayan Sampraday, Briggs's book has much to say about the empire of reform. And in that connection, it even has a bit to say about Rammohun. But in Briggs, the whole story becomes just a bit more complicated.

Briggs can be situated toward the end of an early lineage of British observers on the ground in Gujarat in the first half of the nineteenth century who began to think comparatively about reform (we will meet some of the others below). For now, it is worth noting that some of the conclusions Briggs reached regarding religious reform in Gujarat may come as a surprise, since they reposition the significance of Sahajanand and Rammohun relative to each other. The goal of this chapter is to set Briggs in the context of a number of early conversations about reform in Gujarat precisely in order to trouble the familiar narrative of modern Hindu reform. I want to show how these early efforts to measure Sahajanand and Rammohun against the standard of reform were shot through with a measure of uncertainty and ambivalence. By illustrating that the discourse of reform has been from its beginning less stable than we assume, I hope to embolden us to ask how much longer we are prepared to reproduce it. At some point, one even feels a bit bemused by the whole business, just as Queen Victoria's ministers were rather confused by her response to a proposed reform in the treatment of facial hair in the Indian Navy. Her Majesty appreciated the need for change, but she also felt beards without mustaches were more "soldierlike." Yet she acknowledged that such a provision went against the goal of removing the need for sailors to shave daily. So she decreed: let them have full beards. But, she added, they must be kept "short and very clean." Ahem, would that not require a certain amount of trimming? Never mind. But one thing must be clear: "On no account should mustaches be allowed without beards." Looking at the developing discourse of reform in colonial India, one cannot help but sympathize with the Queen's ministers.

Comparing Reform across Two Frontiers

To appreciate the early reach of reform-based discourse and to overcome our habit of situating groups like the Swaminarayan Sampraday and Brahmo Samaj at opposite poles of the spatiotemporal diffusion of modernity in South Asia, it makes sense to bring together what our histories have torn asunder: Gujarat and Bengal. To do this, we need to question the problematic assumption that, whereas the modernity of the Brahmo Samaj is tied to its origin in progressive Calcutta, the presumed premodernity of the Swaminarayan Sampraday reflects its genesis in distant (and backward) Gujarat. Thus far, by drawing on new avenues in South Asian history and utilizing the concept of religious polities, I have tried to situate Sahajanand Swami and Rammohun Roy within a shared spatiotemporal context and to explore what they shared as articulators of two early colonial religious polities. Now the task is to consider how, with the passing of the early colonial era and the rise of the empire of reform, these two figures and their polities came to be plotted in contrastive ways within the study of modern Hinduism.

We can begin by calling attention to something rarely noted, which is that Sahajanand and Rammohun were the subject of active comparative reflection during their own lifetimes; and such reflection did not originate in Calcutta, but in Gujarat. We know this because recent scholarship has brought to light a number of resources on the early Swaminarayan Sampraday that allow us to push back the dates for some of the earliest encounters between the followers of Sahajanand and the British in Gujarat.[9] Such contact offered the earliest occasions to think about Sahajanand as a kind of Hindu reformer and to compare him to another reformer who was then garnering attention in Bengal, namely Rammohun. At least two influential British travelers—both Anglican clergymen, as it happens—passed through Gujarat in the 1820s, and each of them left an account of Sahajanand, or Lord Swaminarayan, as he was becoming known at the time. Each of these travelers benefited from the local knowledge of British officials who had taken up posts in the region after 1818 and the defeat of the Marathas.

The first of these travelers was the Reverend William Hodge Mill, then principal of Bishop's College in Calcutta, who visited in the early summer of 1822.[10] Mill was on the return leg of a journey to South India and chose to stop in Baroda. There he dined with Resident James Williams. Mill engaged Williams in discussion of Rammohun Roy, whom Mill had come to know from his time serving in Bengal. By this time Rammohun had gained notoriety for challenging both Hindu and Christian doctrine, and Williams knew of him. In fact, he confided to Mill that it boded ill for the British if people were allowed to upset Brahmanic opinion or challenge religious authority the way Rammohun did.[11]

Shortly after meeting Williams, Mill traveled to Ahmedabad where he met with Collector John Andrew Dunlop.[12] Dunlop was familiar with Sahajanand and his community and had even written down some observations in a short memoir titled "New Sect of the Hindus," which he shared with Mill.[13] Mill was so struck by this text that he transcribed portions of it verbatim in his own diary. His diary contains the following comment:

> Extraordinary Guzerattee reformer Swami Narayana lately at
> this (his native) place—who preaches of caste & several
> Hindoo superstitions [though he says, for *civil* custom's sake
> he will not himself violate the rule of caste] having several
> proselytes—among them several young men, learned in the

Shastras—to whom he refers disputers, as not worthy to
contend with himself, till after beating these young cham-
pions (which none of them can do). Attended in his marches
from place to place by several Hindoos of distinction.[14]

What bears noting is that in transcribing this passage Mill took the liberty of introducing the term "reformer" to describe Sahajanand. Dunlop
had not used the term in his own manuscript. Mill's insertion is a significant editorial addendum, not least since it was made by a Protestant
clergyman. Equally interesting is the fact that Dunlop had likened
Sahajanand to a "Roman Pontiff" who claimed to absolve his followers
of sin and to "grant indulgences." Although Mill would have shared
Dunlop's dim view of the Catholic Church, he omitted Dunlop's reference
to the pontiff—though he did retain another detail about Sahajanand
granting absolution and indulgences.[15]

What is going on here? I believe in Mill's editorial choices we can detect a certain ambivalence about Sahajanand, an ambivalence that
would persist within future depictions of Lord Swaminarayan. Although
Mill would have been troubled by parallels to papal authority, his omis-
sion of the reference to the "Roman Pontiff" suggests he hoped to ward
off what we might call today knee-jerk assumptions about Sahajanand,
not least those that would tarnish his otherwise laudable career as a reformer. His focus was on Sahajanand as a leader committed to promoting monotheism and battling superstition. In these tendencies Mill
saw signs of "favorable change," noting that Sahajanand might in time
become a "clear & useful handmaid to Christianity."[16] This was reason
enough to downplay the theme of papal authority.

It is worth noting that, as Richard Fox Young has pointed out, Mill
never engaged in the kind of pointed criticism of Hinduism one associates with his Baptist contemporaries in Bengal, such as Marshman and
Carey; his High Church commitments seem to have tempered his views
in this regard.[17] But Mill was also clearly keen to portray Sahajanand as
someone "extraordinary" in the field of religious reform. And so we detect one of the early manifestations of what I have elsewhere called the
Janus face of reform, as Mill tempers his anti-Catholic sentiments in
order to stress Sahajanand's progressive values.[18]

Personal contacts with Swaminarayanis may have helped modulate Mill's response, since while staying in Ahmedabad he was able to meet some members of the Sampraday, both sadhus and householders. One sadhu by the name of Bhajananda hailed from as far away as the Punjab. He too chose to talk with Mill at length about Rammohun Roy, at one point even requesting that Mill send him copies of Roy's published works.[19] During this same period, Mill also dined at the home of Thomas Williamson, an assistant to Dunlop, who had invited Dunlop and another gentleman as well. Conversation again turned to Rammohun Roy.[20] These conversations with Williams, Dunlop, Bhajananda, and Williamson provide striking evidence of the degree to which Rammohun's name had already gained currency across India.[21] And not only Rammohun, but reform itself was up for debate, discussion, and comparison. At one point Mill adds a cryptic parenthetical comment in which he appears to list other reformers who might compare with Sahajanand and Rammohun, including Guru Nanak and a certain S. A., which most likely refers to Shankar Acharya.[22]

Thomas Williamson, who hosted Mill, was instrumental in introducing another Anglican clergyman to Sahajanand. This was Reginald Heber, who passed through Ahmedabad in 1825 while serving as bishop of Calcutta. Heber kept a detailed journal of his travels.[23] While passing through Baroda he had heard talk of Sahajanand and his Sampraday. From Baroda he traveled on to Kheda District (central Gujarat), where he met Williamson. Williamson pointed out to him the good work being done by a "Hindoo reformer, Swaamee Narain." It is unclear from Heber's journal whether the designation of reformer originated with Heber or Williamson.[24] Regardless, Williamson had stressed Sahajanand's efforts to promote a better standard of morality and to advocate the virtues of lawfulness and good conduct. Williamson further emphasized Sahajanand's monotheism.[25]

In what is now a well-known passage, Heber recorded going out on tour with Williamson. While they were out, they were approached by a handful of Sahajanand's followers, who indicated that their teacher wished to meet with Heber. A rendezvous was arranged for the following day. Heber's account of the meeting is frequently used as evidence of the unstable and lawless terrain of early colonial Gujarat, since when Heber and Sahajanand met they were each accompanied by a small force of armed men. Heber found it almost humiliating that they had to travel with their "little armies," even if he was certain his men could carry the day if necessary. If we think of the Sampraday as an early colonial religious polity, Heber's comments on Sahajanand's camp followers, his "moral grandeur," and the utter devotion of his devotees to their guru all speak to the idea of a powerful religious lord processing at the head of a complex religious polity.[26]

As with that of Mill, Heber's report cuts two ways. On the one hand, Heber came to see in Sahajanand someone committed to the moral uplift of his people and the propagation of an ennobling theology. But on the other hand, Sahajanand's evident charisma and his unapologetic support for image worship were troubling to Heber. The worship of images in his mind represented "no more than some Christians of the Romish Church express." After learning this about Sahajanand's convictions, he came to think "less favourably of his simplicity and honesty of character."[27] Like Mill, Heber struggled to come to terms with—when he did not openly reject—the "Romish" quality of Sahajanand's religion. He had hoped their meeting might portend a grand alliance and the eventual victory of Protestant Christianity in India, but what was he to think when the handmaid of Protestant conversion bore a likeness to the pope?[28]

It is worth noting that although the question of reform comes to the fore in Heber's account of Sahajanand, he does not record any explicit comparison with Rammohun Roy, despite the fact that his contemporaries in Gujarat seem to have circled around to this topic regularly.[29] That said, elsewhere in his travelogue Heber does offer some remarks on the work and character of Rammohun.[30] This may be more than happenstance. Heber's remarks about Rammohun clearly show he admired elements of the latter's work for social change, not least his role in opposing the custom of *sati* and promoting English-language learning in India. But when it came to Rammohun's religious vision, Heber was reluctant to bestow on him the title of reformer. By contrast, he was willing to apply the term to Sahajanand. Why this discrepancy? Here I believe we are brought face-to-face with a root ambivalence around use of the term reform at the very moment when that category began to prove useful for British observers.

The root cause for such ambivalence was empire. The earliest British accounts of Sahajanand's work, recorded in the wake of Pax Britannica in Gujarat, would become something like imperial *doxa*: Sahajanand was a useful reformer whom the British could count on to promote moral uplift without threatening the stability of Brahmanic society.[31] Put simply, he was a reformer the empire could get behind, even if that meant glossing over his Romish qualities. One might have imagined that, by virtue of his own moral program and monotheistic theology, Rammohun would also be greeted as a valuable reformer. However, his copybook had one serious blot: he was too radical.[32]

Imagining an Empire

The idea that Sahajanand represented the best path for reform in colonial South Asia found its quintessential expression in a work that has found a prominent place in the literature on Swaminarayan Hinduism but that has otherwise had no appreciable role in shaping scholarly views of modern Hinduism. I refer to *The Cities of Gujarashtra*, published in 1849 by Henry George Briggs. Briggs wrote the book after touring western India between 1842 and 1847.[33] Although Briggs had no immediate interest in Bengal, he knew about the life and activities of Rammohun Roy, and this knowledge is what makes the book so important in the present context, because like Mill and Heber before him, Briggs felt compelled to comment on the relative merits of Sahajanand and Rammohun as reformers. I turn to his conclusions in a moment, but first a bit about the book.

The Cities of Gujarashtra is a curious—but hardly atypical—specimen of nineteenth-century imperial writing, combining elements of journal, travelogue, romantic history, ethnography, geography, and encomia on the emerging British Empire in South Asia. Briggs wrote the book as both a personal narrative and an authoritative account of history and current events. In the opening "Advertisement," he apologized for the delay in the publication of the book, explaining that it was due to a prolonged illness and also to the "infant condition of typography in this Presidency." This conjunction of the personal and the world historical is characteristic of the book. When we are first introduced to Gujarat, Briggs tells us it lies "between Lat. 21° 30′ and 25° N. and Long. 71° to 74° 30′ E," but adds that it is a country of "warriors and judges and bards" where princes "showered their gifts as munificently as princes only can."[34]

Briggs begins his journey with little fanfare: "Embarked on board the Bombay Steam Navigation Company's Steamer *Surat*, at 5 P.M., on Tuesday, the 26th October 1847." However, no sooner is he underway than he is confronted by a stunning sunset that kindles the flames of his imagination. Soon he is conjuring the Adriatic coastline near the island of Patmos, famous for its association with John the Baptist and the Book of Revelation. The quotidian becomes the sublime, and Briggs finds himself in thrall to the "power of association." Bombay makes him think of Catherine of Braganza's dowry to Charles the Second; this puts him in mind of George Canning's trade negotiations with the Brazilian empire. Pondering the etymology of Bombay, he turns to the goddess, Mumba Devi, which leads him on to antiquarian findings about ancient "monachism" and eventually deposits the reader in an "Augustinian repository of letters." At last a new diary entry returns us to the present moment: "9 P.M.—A steady breeze from northward." Sadly, this comes as little relief; annoyed by a gust of windborne soot, Briggs laments that, what with "the stifling odour produced by the mass of natives on board," it was going to be "an uncomfortable night."[35]

We have scarcely left port and Briggs has managed to combine some of the quintessential features of imperial travel writing: classification, aestheticization, appropriation, negation, debasement, nostalgia, and surveillance.[36] Personal space becomes historical time, such that sailing offshore from the ruins of the fort at Bassein, Briggs recalls a bygone era when Portuguese traders fended off the "annoyance" of Muslim power. Returning to the present he notes that the cathedrals and convents of Bassein are now in ruin, a reminder of the passing of an earlier empire—not to mention an empire based on the errors of the "Papistical creed."[37]

If Bassein registers the passing of Portuguese hegemony in South Asia, Briggs reads its monuments as a testimony to the rise of British supremacy. He jumps from the sixteenth century to the dawn of the nineteenth, remarking that it was by virtue of the 1802 Treaty of Bassein that the East India Company had come to subdue the Maratha Confederacy. The success of the company along the coast was to lay the groundwork for the flourishing of its subsequent maritime empire: here at Bassein, he informs his readers, two of the first four pinnaces of the future British Indian Navy were built.[38]

Briggs's need to celebrate the emergence of Britain's new empire should remind us that by 1849 the early colonial moment was rapidly giving way to the era of full-blown imperial rule in South Asia. In fact, one purpose of *The Cities of Gujarashtra* appears to be to provide evidence for bolstering British imperial confidence. The book attests to the spread of East India Company rule across the subcontinent, to the increasing importance of the Indian economy within global trade and industry (not least the cotton market), and to manifold British projects to discipline the peoples and cultures of South Asia. When the amassing of evidence is complete, Briggs asks his readers to consider what it reveals: the "strength" and "spirit" of Muslim rule has been shattered; the "arbitrary feudalism" of the Marathas has been annihilated; and the mighty Sikh empire of Ranjit Singh has come and gone. Alluding to a practice common to the world of joint stock companies, Briggs imagines calculating the "erudition, the labor and the care" of the British government in India and presenting this data to the public in the form of an annual report. What satisfied stockholders the British public would be to see that everything is ruled "so adroitly, so pacifically, and yet so vigorously!"[39]

The character, force, and purpose of such imperial discourse needs little further amplification. Instead I want to call attention to the way in which this calculation of the benefits of imperial rule depends on the projection of a particular view of religion structured by the logic of reform. Reform represents progress, and Briggs gives us a "Blue Book" of results to prove the case. This fits well with what Amy Allen has written about progress. Allen argues that claims about progress typically tend to be grounded in two presumptions: First, there is the "fact" of progress, which one proves by adducing evidence of all the past errors that have been overcome. Second, there is a presumption that progress represents a goal itself, what Allen calls progress *überhaupt*.[40] In other words, proponents of reform are always looking for evidence of errors rectified and abuses curtailed, while simultaneously gazing ardently into the future, inspired by the utopian prospect of reform. As Asa Briggs put it in his classic study of improvement, for nineteenth-century reformers the facts of progress caused people to "dream dreams."[41]

When it came to religion, to speak of progress was to speak of reform. To see this, we might turn to Peter Auber's 1837 work, *The Rise and Progress of British Power in India*. His account of the rise of British power begins with a central moment in modern parliamentary reform, namely Pitt's India Bill of 1784. From there the narration consists of a litany of reforms undertaken in India to address issues around land tenure, revenue policy, military policy, religious patronage, currency, civil and criminal justice, and on and on—right up to the age of Lord William Bentinck, governor-general of Bengal and a name synonymous with the "Age of Reform" in India.[42] It was under Bentinck that British India's first major religious reform was enacted with the promulgation of Regulation XVII of 1829, abolishing the rite of suttee (*sati*). That Rammohun's name became synonymous with this moment scarcely needs mentioning.[43] Auber has little interest in religious reform per se, but he does take the joint success of Bentinck and Rammohun in overcoming this "horrible rite" as sure promise of the eventual abolition of other "absurd" and "false" religious rites.[44]

To notice that Rammohun figures (if only briefly) in a work like this is to appreciate something of the rapid rescripting of his significance within the empire of reform. Notwithstanding Auber's obvious vision of imperial progress, we find hints of the transitional moment in which he writes; we sense the passing of the early colonial. Thus when discussing Rammohun's mission to Britain on behalf of the Mughal emperor in 1830, we catch a glimpse of the complex agency of a precolonial court. Auber describes the emperor's deputation of Rammohun as an attempt to "gain the mastery over" the governor-general in Bengal, who to him represented merely a "naib or vakeel."[45] The emperor, the governor-general, and the Court of St James's were thus integrated within a larger scale of polities that spanned Delhi, Calcutta, and London and one in which, prior to 1858, the company operated under the de jure authority of the Delhi court.

In a manner similar to Auber, Briggs brought forward evidence of past errors to demonstrate not just progress achieved but also the promise of future progress. Recall the pride with which he recounted the overcoming of both Muslim rule and the "Romish" errors of the Portuguese. And, even more than Auber, Briggs was keenly interested in the religious transformations wrought by British rule. *The Cities of Gujarashtra* reveals the degree to which its author had critically weighed a range of early British writing on religion in India: John Wilson and John Malcolm on the Parsis, William Jones and Henry Thomas Colebrooke on the ancient Brahmins, and William Ward, H. H. Wilson, and Edward Moor on the varieties of Hindu belief, ritual, and iconography. Looking at the Jains, Briggs noticed changes taking place in the areas of diet and ritual. He spoke of a "sweeping religious revolution" as the Jains began distinguishing their practices from those of non-Jain communities like the Vallabhites. This was not only a sign of progress-as-reform, but also demonstrated how British rule created the conditions necessary for positive religious change.[46]

Within Briggs's account, religious reform is closely associated with the critique of "works righteousness" or Pelagianism—the presumption that moral striving can play a beneficial role in securing salvation. The errors associated with works righteousness were that it promoted vanity, spiritual pride, and a corruption of the pure faith that should spring "from an humble and contrite heart."[47] Briggs advanced what might be called an anti-Pelagian imperialism that viewed India as hopelessly mired in works righteousness. It mattered not whether one looked at Jains, Buddhists, Muslims, or Hindus; they all nourished the misguided hope that salvation could be won by "human labor" and sheer "*works.*"[48] Thus, upon arriving in Broach on February 6, 1848, Briggs paused to marvel at the many wonders wrought by generations of "pagan monarchs" who had placed their trust in the works of their own hands rather than in the grace of God.[49] Briggs was not unwilling to acknowledge their accomplishments in art and architecture, but nonetheless saw in Broach's mosques and temples the evidence of "Samaritan charity and

Pelagian philanthropy."[50] Broach was a metonym for India: its ruins confirmed that the sun had set on its former rulers, but a new dawn was breaking.

The Empire of Reform

The epigraph to *The Cities of Gujarashtra* is the short phrase, "The graves of vanished empires." Briggs ascribes these words to Aaron Hill, a name that likely means little to twenty-first-century readers. However, Briggs's original audience would have recognized Hill as a contemporary of Pope and Richardson and a Deist poet of some note. They might also have known that one of the hallmarks of Hill's writing was its advocacy of rational inquiry and religious liberty. That such a strident voice of reason and liberty would be called on to celebrate the expansion of British power across the globe might seem odd, were it not that today we recognize how liberalism and empire tended to work hand in hand.[51] Even so, it bears asking why an author committed to an anti-Pelagian, Protestant empire in India would choose the words of a radical Deist poet for an epigraph.

To answer this question, it helps to look at the poem from which Briggs chose his epigraph, "Free thoughts upon Faith: or the Religion of Reason." This lengthy poem represents something like a Deist cri de coeur, in which Hill situates a "listless wanderer" in the "warring wild" of religion.[52] The world conjured by Hill is overrun by the enemies of reason and liberty, who sell credulity at the expense of genuine faith.[53] Hill has in mind not merely the usual list of priests, pontiffs, and schismatics who darken Protestant Reformation discourse; he takes in a wider world comprising Jews, Tartars, and Brahmins, not to mention "Arabia's swarthy sons" and "far China's dateless race." All pretend to be brokers of religious authority and lay claim to being "heav'ns choice."[54] They trade in revelations and miracles and dangle juicy morsels of tradition before unwitting souls. Each sworn to the supremacy of their own creed, they are enemies of religious liberty; they twist religion into "canton'd snarls" and happily commit murder in the name of mercy.[55] In their wake they leave truth a tattered and tangled mess.

As Hill's references to India, China, and Arabia illustrate, the horizon of his world was shaped by the expansion of European power. He cherishes Britain's paramount role in the extension of maritime trade and conquest and celebrates the nexus between European expansion and the achievement of Christian supremacy. In this respect, he takes his place among an early generation of those who celebrated what David Chidester has called the "empire of religion."[56] Incipient imperial taxonomies are evident as he follows religion among the "white-fac'd, olive-hued and sably jet."[57] All the same, he is alert to the dangerous ambiguities of empire, taking aim at "missionary rapine's holy ken" and pondering the complicity of European trade in the promotion of religious zealotry. Thus in Hill we find Eurocentrism wrestling with critical Deism.

It is this tension that prompts the poet to ask himself whether religious might makes religious right. Pondering this, he considers the fate of earlier empires such as the Babylonians, Greeks, and Romans. Where are their deities today?

> Turn thy sight *Eastward*, o'er the time-hush'd
>   plains,
> Now *graves* of vanish'd empire—*once*, gleam'd,
>   o'er,
> From flames on *hallow'd altar's*, hail'd by hymns
> Of seers . . .[58]

The words of Briggs's epigraph are thus set within a verse that appears to offer anything but a celebration of empire. In these lines Hill is more cautionary than celebratory; he warns readers against making facile associations between imperial mastery and claims about religious truth. The sheer roster of fallen empires should remind us how dangerous it is to strike a posture of "imperious, positive, disdain" predicated on nothing but global dominance in maritime trade. Does history not suggest the need for humility? Is there not room for some "modest doubt"?[59]

Ah, but the Christian will claim to possess superior virtue. To this Hill replies, if virtue were enough, then wherever we saw humankind committed to the denunciation of immorality we should be prepared to acknowledge the operation of truth. But this would mean we would need to open our church to Africa's "Wood-men," India's "mopes," and the denizens of Columbia's "bow'ry groves," not to mention all manner of Turk, Jew, and Australian. If mere virtue were enough to count as faith, then:

> All among these, who love not vice, draw claim,
> from lives, of simplest sanctity—to heaven.[60]

What drew Briggs to such an expansive Deist worldview would seem to have been Hill's steadfast opposition to presumption in religion. For Hill, what mattered most was a sense of humility and a spirit of constant self-correction. Even error deserves respect, "if it's end is grace / and aims at reformation."[61] If we have a duty, it is to find freedom in the variety of creation, lest we unwittingly fall victim to the "pomp of positive presumption" and yield to the temptation of "self-preferring scorn."[62] These are words consistent with strands we associate with the Radical Enlightenment, yet churning beneath them are also the currents we associate with the Protestant Reformation.[63] This seems to be where Briggs felt a kinship with Hill. For if Martin Luther had urged the primacy of faith by encouraging Christians to "sin boldly," Hill asked his readers to doubt boldly, even while trusting God. Hill's was something like a priesthood of Deist believers that drew its energy from an unnamed Pauline conviction that spirit triumphs over law, reason over ritual.

This helps us appreciate Briggs's comments on the "Samaritan charity" of Broach's pagan monarchs. He recognizes such work as charity; but by calling it Samaritan he reminds his readers of the presumption of those pagan rulers who placed too much confidence in their own virtue. The problem with Samaritan charity is thus not that it is *charity* but that it is *Samaritan*. It is too enamored by the pomp of its own presumption. No less than Hill, Briggs fears what follows, and his disdain for the Portuguese empire fits neatly with Hill's characterization of the Pope as the "heretic presumer."[64] As Briggs saw it, Britain's emergent Protestant empire promised to renounce all unholy alliance with pride, ritual, and tradition. The Portuguese had come to India as fishers of men, compelled by their mistaken reverence for the pope in Rome. As fishers of men they were eager to cast "tradition's line" on the water in order "to hook mankind."[65] This would not be Britain's course; she would pursue India's reformation on sound principles and out of respect for reason informed by grace.

Of course, Hill had also warned his readers to be most cautious "where most thou trust'st."[66] For him reformation took the form of a rigorous intellectual and moral practice, a posture of constant self-scrutiny against the dangers of presumption. However, for Briggs, reformation was less a process of self-discipline than it was an accomplished fact, expressed through Britain's embrace of Protestant truth. Whereas in the "graves of vanished empires" Hill pointed to the folly of virtuous Pelagianism, Briggs saw only the graves of earlier Pelagians. The ruins around him were, as Amy Allen's work suggests, evidence of the truth of a higher reform. The demise of the Portuguese thus offered no cautionary tale, but proof of progress. Gaze on the graves of vanished pagan monarchies! Behold the empire of reform!

Two Reformers Compared

The tensions inherent in the close coupling of liberalism, reform, and empire help make sense of one important passage in Briggs, in which he compares Sahajanand Swami and Rammohun Roy.[67] The passage is well known to all historians of the Swaminarayan Sampraday. But what has not hitherto been appreciated is what this passage says about emerging notions of reform at the dawn of the late colonial era.[68] What Briggs offers here are two possible routes that reform might take in imperial India. And only one earns his endorsement. It is with this passage from Briggs—far more than with the earlier comments of either Mill or Heber—that the act of comparison finally brings the category of reform out into the open; here we see for the first time what is at stake. Until now I have emphasized Briggs's disparate references to Pelagianism and his odd kinship with Aaron Hill. Keeping all this in view, when we turn to his comparison of Sahajanand Swami and Rammohun Roy, we come to see just what he thinks about the nature and validity of reform.

Bear in mind that when Briggs arrived in the city of Ahmedabad in December of 1847, it had been some twenty years since Bishop Heber's visit. By this time, Ahmedabad had become what Briggs calls the "glory of the Gujarat province." He makes it clear how delighted he is to tour the city's many tombs and ruins, which (true to his form) conjure both the Samaritan charity of prior rulers and the imminent onset of the new anti-Pelagian empire.[69] In his tour of the city he visited many of the major monuments and mausolea dating from pre-British times; and he also paid a visit to one more recent edifice—the Nara-Narayana temple constructed under Sahajanand's leadership in the Kalupur section of the city.[70]

Briggs was apparently so impressed by his interaction with Satsangis that he felt the need to provide an account of Sahajanand. Throughout the relevant passage he refers to Sahajanand as "the Reformer," at one point confessing that his account owed a good deal to "Bishop Heber's graphic pen."[71] Even so, Briggs offers a new and distinctive depiction of Sahajanand, whom he calls "the Swami Narayen." His portrait is generous and detailed, providing information on Sahajanand's origins in north India and presenting him as a figure of great learning, rectitude, asceticism, and philanthropy. At one point he tells his readers that "the Hindu world is indebted" to this singular individual for having delivered the first "violent shock" to the persistent patterns of "mimicry" that are the very stuff of Hindu doctrine and practice.[72] His use of the concept of mimicry—or "medieval mummery"—to describe Hindu life, when coupled with a reference to the pernicious forces of Hindu priestcraft aligned against Sahajanand, situate his account squarely in the discursive field of reform polemics.[73]

How are we to make sense of the level of charity Briggs—as imperial apologist and something of a Protestant chauvinist—musters in his account of Sahajanand? Here it is precisely his agenda as a defender of empire that is of utmost importance. Briggs had no particular interest in promoting a Hindu religious teacher per se; rather, he sought to indicate the proper course for reform to take in India. Here Sahajanand suited his purpose well, serving as a handy foil against which Briggs could call into question the work of another reformer, namely

Rammohun Roy. Bear in mind that it is the 1840s, and Rammohun was by this time widely celebrated not only in Calcutta, but also in Paris, London, and Cambridge, Massachusetts.

On December 27, 1847, Briggs paid a visit to a Jain temple and met with members of a wealthy banking family in Ahmedabad. During the day he had been graciously welcomed at the temple and allowed to enter its sanctum. While at the temple he was entertained by a lively debate over the pros and cons of requesting British aid for Sanskrit instruction in local schools. Ever on the lookout for evidence of ways to improve the lives and beliefs of those he met, Briggs felt "mingled courtesy and esteem" for his industrious Jain hosts.[74] Once again Hill seems to have been his muse, leading him to recognize accomplishment, progress, and improvement when and where he found it. Such was the case when he took up the case of Sahajanand as well.

The entry for the next day begins with Briggs bemoaning the "solemn stillness" wrought by generations of Hindu ignorance and religious "mimicry." The horizon of the future would appear dark to him, were it not for the advent of an "extraordinary" Brahmin by the name of Sahajanand. Briggs remarks that it would be thanks to the "ability and energy" of this Brahmin that the mimicry and morbidity of established Hindu custom and belief would be shocked into life. This is a man fully deserving the title of "Hindu reformer."[75] As if to justify bestowing such a significant title, Briggs launches into a short biography of Sahajanand. We might almost call it an imperial hagiography, since the saint portrayed by Briggs represents great hopes for Britain's new empire. Born in humble circumstances, inquisitive by nature, prone to scorn the pride of his own Brahmin caste, given to asceticism, and driven by a sense of "rectitude," Sahajanand was destined to cultivate and embody the virtues most desperately wanting in the India of his day. Skipping over the years of Sahajanand's extensive travels, Briggs leads him quickly from Ayodhya to Gujarat. For it was there that Sahajanand would begin to exercise his "extraordinary influence."[76]

Briggs lauds the influence wielded by Sahajanand even as he hints that it depended on a measure of Hindu priestcraft, not least the powers of "mesmerism." With his ability to put people in "trance," Sahajanand

drew the multitudes to him. His powers and his influence were significant, and this meant that he found arrayed against him a cast of local
rulers who, as feudal barons, were naturally prone to "petty jealousies and
vexatious feuds."[77] This framing helped Briggs ensure his readers would
appreciate Sahajanand's arrival as a blow to the tottering fortress of
medievalism in Gujarat. When Sahajanand threatened to manifest his
spiritual powers at a major festival, one local ruler sounded his "superstitious alarm," which triggered the arrival of horsemen who took the
reformer away and threw him in a dungeon. Needless to say, the ruler's
"tyrannical behavior" only served to engender further sympathy for the
reformer's cause. Sahajanand is soon set free, and the number of his
"proselytes" begins to grow exponentially. He had shown he would not
cower before threats and intimidation; the heroic work of reform had
begun in earnest.[78]

What did Sahajanand teach? Briggs accepted Heber's description of
Sahajanand's "strange mixture of pure Theism and Hinduism," adding
that it owed much to a kind of "eccentric asceticism."[79] Sahajanand's was
a stern morality, tinged with celibacy, and made honorable by a respect
for learning. Yet Sahajanand had not come to earth merely to reinstate
the "virgin integrity" of Hinduism; his larger goal was to confront the
"irregularities" of his age and to reassert the priority of law and order
in a region given over to chaos, disruption, and predatory violence.
Thanks to Sahajanand, Gujarat became "undisturbed." And for this he
deserved the mantle of reformer.[80]

Briggs ends his account of Sahajanand by noting how, shortly after
the latter's demise, all sorts of "innovations" came to be introduced by
his followers; this reflected both their respect for the lord and their desire to ensure the longevity of their new "creed." Some of these innovations Briggs traces to hagiographies like the *Satsangi Jivanam*, though
he does not mention that text by name. The key point for Briggs was
that texts like this had worked in pernicious ways to invest Sahajanand
with miraculous powers and gifts of prophecy, not to mention to grant
him a seat in the "awful conclave" of heaven itself.[81] Briggs wondered
whether in time Sahajanand would not find a "niche" in the great
shrine of Krishna himself. Notwithstanding these anxieties about the

apotheosis of Sahajanand, Briggs was keen that the reformer be given his due, adding that it was a pity Sahajanand's name was not more "extensively known."[82]

With this remark Briggs turned his attention to the other reformer on his mind, Rammohun. Unlike Sahajanand, Briggs saw in Rammohun a figure of global renown. His intellectual accomplishments alone, as Briggs put it, had been "wonderful and varied"; they had caused Rammohun's name to be trumpeted across all of British India and onward to "Europe even." No less than Jeremy Bentham had found in Rammohun a "devoted collaborateur in the service of mankind."[83] And Rammohun's renown rested in part on his keen instinct for truth; Briggs pointed in particular to Rammohun's efforts at weighing the merits of various religions, from Judaism, Islam, and Vedanta right down to "Church-of-Englandism." No devotee at a "particular altar," Rammohun represented the quest for a morality common to all. As a reformer, his name would always be associated with the official abolition of suttee. Pausing for a moment, Briggs has to admit that it was hard to know whom to admire more, Sahajanand or Rammohun. To be sure, "both were reformers"—equally "assailed by calumny" and equally unflinching in their work.[84]

We might understand it if Briggs had chosen to leave matters there, but he did not. Scarcely had he expressed his admiration for both Sahajanand and Rammohun than he pronounced a singular distinction between the two:

> Both were reformers; the one an equivocal theorist whose brilliant coruscations have misled, and will continue to mislead many of his gifted countrymen . . . the other a practical philanthropist, who, without like position or like wealth, has rescued hundreds from destruction, and thousands from wanton pursuits. The merits of men of this latter class are only discovered long after their generation has passed; the splendid career of the former leaves too indelible an impression grateful to the vanity of our race—'to be erased so speedily: and while Rammohan's name is about being forgotten, Sahajanand's will wax brighter by that waning influence.[85]

This is an important passage for two reasons: First, Briggs establishes what would become the standard view of Sahajanand in relation to British power in Gujarat. According to this view, Sahajanand was of great political utility to the East India Company insofar as his practical philanthropy supported British efforts to establish a reign of peace and prosperity in the region—Pax Britannica.[86] As we know, this view of Sahajanand is celebrated even today among Satsangis. Second, Briggs advanced a compelling argument for dismissing Rammohun as an agent of mischief and a threat to imperial peace and stability. Notwithstanding his professed admiration for Rammohun, Briggs let loose with a host of negative claims about him. He was a freethinker. He was a political radical. His kind of brilliance was likely to blind more than enlighten. He was someone whose theoretical "coruscations" were destined only to provoke political mischief among Indians. Finally, were Indians to follow Rammohun's example, they would soon embrace free thought and liberal politics.[87]

Here we might recall Sahajanand's famous meeting with Governor John Malcolm. Whereas Malcolm respected Sahajanand as an example of moderate change within the bounds of existing custom, Rammohun represented the kind of radical change Malcolm hoped to avoid. We know for certain that Malcolm feared sudden change; he preferred to see Britain "march slow time" toward progress, content for the time being to leave customs and hierarchies in place.[88] Briggs was of the same mind. Rammohun may have won "satellites" in India and abroad, he may even have been a great political thinker; but when it came to religion, with Rammohun all was "void." Ominously, Briggs added that Rammohun had died "without a religion."[89]

And so we come at last to the crucial point behind Briggs's comparison of Sahajanand and Rammohun. What Briggs offers is an argument about the proper course of religious reform in British India. Never mind that Rammohun's free thought and monotheism sounded like a clear echo of Hill himself; never mind that Sahajanand's success traded on a species of mesmerism and even priestcraft. Those were not the operative issues for Briggs. As far as he was concerned, the last thing the hoi polloi needed was freedom of thought; let them have a bit of mesmerism if it would ensure their compliance with foreign rule![90]

For an empire builder like Briggs, the autonomy of a Rammohun was unthinkable; far better the benign heteronomy of a charismatic leader. Briggs's syntax is awkward but his message is clear:

> Sahajanand was loved beyond belief by his disciples—
> comprising men of talent, of station, and of wealth; the poor,
> the ignorant, the rude—and who would have sacrificed life
> itself for their preceptor: his profound acquaintance with the
> Veds, earned him the meed due to a man of ability, and his
> modesty barbed many a venomous thought with the het-
> erodox Hindu wedded to the absurdities of his faith—and to
> this day he will be found to name Sahajanand with respect,
> whatever the differences in their observances of the like
> parent faith.[91]

What the British needed were more men "of the mould of the Gujarat reformer." Sahajanand was the best tool for eradicating error and abolishing evil; his work supported the "gradual yet sensible" path preferred by the likes of Malcolm.[92] In words that have continued to shape the Sampraday's understanding of its origins, Briggs extoled Sahajanand's reforming project while dismissing the alienating and "exotic" approach of a Rammohun:

> Sahajanand Swami had met the evil where most needed, and
> persuaded numbers of a province of nomadic tribes to
> peaceful and honorable occupations, and with the absence of
> any extensive educational measures upon sound principles
> among Hindus, their amelioration will for long be indebted,
> rather to practical example among their own kind, simply and
> lucidly conveyed, than to the most honest views at variance
> with their paternal creed propounded by exotic elements.[93]

If reform in India deserved a name, it should be Sahajanand, not Rammohun!

I need scarcely add that this is not the way the story of religious reform in India has typically been framed. After all, wasn't Rammohun

India's first modern religious thinker? Is Rammohun not the Father of Modern India? When have such things ever been said of Sahajanand? Can one point to a pathway leading from Sahajanand to the values of religious pluralism, liberal rights, and Indian patriotism that are so closely associated with Rammohun and the Brahmos? Would it not become a truism within the empire of reform, as voiced by the likes of F. Max Müller, that what happened in India during the nineteenth century was akin to the reformation within "our own church"—when the authority of "Pope and Councils" was set aside for biblical truth? Was not Rammohun therefore a kind of Indian Erasmus?[94]

The sheer fact that Briggs could arrive at a conclusion so greatly at odds with these hegemonic views should be enough to make us hit the "pause" button and look around for alternate critical frameworks to make sense of these two innovators. If nothing else, one begins to sense that neither Briggs nor Müller can help us situate the accomplishments of Sahajanand and Rammohun in their historical moment, or provide us with a useful analytic for thinking about how religious modernity has taken shape in India. Briggs may have sought to follow Hill's admonition to honor truth wherever it appeared, but in *The Cities of Gujarashtra* he demonstrates that the empire of reform often struggled to master its own logic.[95] Let the sailors have beards, or beards with mustaches, but let there never be mustaches alone!

9

OLD COMPARISONS
AND NEW

REFORM IS typically understood to be progressive, educative, and liberative. And yet as we learned in Chapter 8, the vaunted liberative force of reform can be construed in different ways. For Briggs, Sahajanand's teachings represented a viable mode of reform precisely because they appeared to pose no threat to the British imperial project. Sahajanand would liberate the people of western India from moral errors while educating his followers to adopt patterns of life and thought that remained congruent with the rise of British authority. We can be sure Briggs had little interest in fathoming—let alone promoting—the disciplined life of *satsang*. His Protestant theological leanings were pressed far enough by his own effort to make peace with those elements of "Romish" religion he detected in Sahajanand's community. The point is, Sahajanand had to emerge as the true reformer in order for Briggs to be able to assuage his anxieties surrounding the kinds of reforms represented by Rammohun. In Rammohun, the East India Company faced a dangerous rival. Despite his apparent fondness for the Deism of Aaron Hill, Briggs had no patience with Rammohun's understanding of reason and religion. Any embrace of radical reform could only lead to a future in which Indians would feel free and emboldened to question authority, to chafe under heteronomous rule, and to reject what Hill himself might have called the sheer presumption of empire. The irony of an apologist for a Protestant empire rejecting Rammohun in favor of a charismatic and deified guru who seemed to gain proselytes through mesmerism need detain us no longer. We understand the exigencies of empire all too well.

But the ironies of reform do not end there since, throughout the nineteenth century, even the progressive and educative promise of Rammohun's reforms would become closely linked to the project of empire. We may chalk some of this up to the inconsistencies of Rammohun's own vision when it came to its radical project. After all, Rammohun's recovery of Vedanta managed to marry his spirited iconoclasm to a species of scripturalism; his affirmation of a Hindu theology of "the Vedant" was tempered and tested by his vision of global religious harmony and universal truth; and his love of liberty and improvement led him to embrace some of the causes that—had they been fully implemented—might have spelled even greater doom for India, causes like English-language education, free trade, support for European settlers, and the promotion of a plantation economy. Milinda Banerjee puts his finger on some of these paradoxes when he writes that

> Rammohun . . . was not successful because he liberated
> Reason. He was successful because he knew when to gag it,
> substituting the endless chain of logical rationality with a
> mixture of scripture and common sense. He is great not
> because he had destroyed blind faith, but because right after
> he had shown the falsehood of all faiths, he took a leap into
> the faith of faiths and declared that it is the will of God to love
> one's fellow beings without distinction.[1]

Banerjee's analysis of the competing strands in Rammohun's thought and pragmatics is refreshing precisely because we simply aren't accustomed to talking about the Father of Modern India in this fashion. The one problem is that Banerjee himself remains a bit too dependent on the discourse of reform. That is, the irony as developed by Banerjee only works because we begin from the presumption that Rammohun was a reformer. Beginning there, what else can we feel but dismay when we are told that the radical reformer invented the Brahmo God in order to support his own vision of a rule-bound cosmos? And yet if we step outside the discourse of reform, some of these apparent inconsistencies disappear. We might thus understand many of Rammohun's choices as the strategic moves of a canny religious master working to articulate his own Brahmo polity amid an emergent imperial formation. As such, there is no more need to question Rammohun's commitment to reform than there is to register disappointment at Sahajanand's supposed failure to embrace modernity to the same degree. The paradoxes have everything to do with our own capitulation to the empire of reform.

This is where attention to the work of both Rammohun and Sahajanand as lords of early colonial polities may offer an altogether different and perhaps more productive starting point for thinking through the early history of modern Hinduism. This may not be the only way—or even the best way—to develop fresh perspectives on these remarkable contemporary figures, but it at least represents one step toward decoupling our understanding of their accomplishments and legacies from the teleologies of reform, empire, and nation. How much might it help to advance new conceptualizations of modern Hinduism if we could dispense with persistent and yet fundamentally ambiguous comparisons predicated on notions of reform? My contention is that by looking squarely at the terms of the old comparisons between Rammohun and Sahajanand we may move toward framing new comparisons for reckoning with persistent concerns around the nature of modern Hinduism.

Such a new comparative endeavor must begin by acknowledging that it was only thanks to the spatiotemporal logic of reform-based thought that the Calcutta Brahmos were discursively anointed to deliver the introductory curriculum in India's education in bourgeois nationalism. In this older comparative chronoscape, Sahajanand's community remained, by definition, isolated and irrelevant, trapped on the fringes of both empire and nation. In a spatiotemporal imaginary predicated on the gradual diffusion of bourgeois public culture, the Swaminarayan Sampraday necessarily betokens a kind of failure—a mode of religion that only partially made its way into modernity. It is almost as if the wave of reform had lost momentum by the time it reached distant Gujarat, so that Sahajanand's successors were never able to effectively insert themselves into the radiant new world of late colonial religion.

In this way the discourse of reform fails to make sense of a polity that was in fact neither reformist in the mode of late-nineteenth-century Brahmoism nor even strictly revivalist, if we adopt the term typically applied to other late colonial organizations like the Arya Samaj or the various Sanatana dharma *sabhas*. Swaminarayanis remain forever poised on the cusp of reform—neither here nor there. As a result, the solid and reliable Hindu reformer so admired by Briggs was all but forgotten, consigned to the footnotes of colonial histories and granted only a bit part in the nascent literature on comparative religion as it would be framed by the likes of Monier-Williams and Müller. When observed from London or Oxford, Sahajanand seemed little more than the founder of a quasi-medieval, parochial, and guru-based movement.

It is worth following up on some of these more consequential late colonial comparisons in order to appreciate just how firmly the empire of reform consolidated its verdict on modern Hinduism. After this, we might simply ask whether there are other ways to go about framing new comparisons of the Swaminarayan Sampraday and the Brahmo Samaj—comparisons that both acknowledge difference and point toward ways to address the challenges India faces today around religion and public life.

The Freshness of Reform

Beginning with Monier-Williams's early publications on Hinduism from the 1870s and 1880s and carrying down to the work of John Nicol Farquhar in the early twentieth century, it came to be accepted wisdom that while Rammohun had benefited from extensive contacts with Western Christian civilization in Calcutta, Sahajanand represented something like an untainted version of premodern Hinduism. Even when given credit as a reformer, Sahajanand would typically be styled only as a particular kind of reformer, one more familiar from India's past than her imperial present. Thus Sahajanand could be likened to Shankara Acharya or Guru Nanak—both labeled reformers by virtue of their emphasis on scripture and piety over empty ritualism—but he could not be comfortably accommodated within the framework of truly modern reform. As improbable as it must seem to us today, this failure could often be summed up by pointing to Sahajanand's ignorance of, or failure to engage with, the Gospel of Jesus Christ.[2]

It seems as if there was reform, and then there was reform. Put differently, reform wears a Janus face in the literature on modern Hinduism. Briggs was only one of those who could recognize reform and deny it at the same time; that his calculus tended to value Sahajanand more greatly than Rammohun is a reminder, as we have seen, that the faces of reform could be turned this way and that almost at will. We are given ample reminder of this when we look at the literature on religious reform as it developed in the latter quarter of the nineteenth century. What had been a robust and rather well-informed set of British conversations around the advent and significance of Sahajanand among early nineteenth-century observers scarcely lasted beyond the middle of the century. By the time of Monier-Williams and his ilk, the Swaminarayan community had all but vanished from the literature on religion in modern India. Readers will be forgiven if they find it hard to believe that it would not be until the publication of Raymond Brady Williams's first monograph on the "new face of Hinduism" in 1984 that the Swaminarayan Sampraday found its way back into scholarly literature on modern Indian religion.[3]

And yet even as the Swaminarayanis faded into the background, the category of reform itself went from strength to strength, gathering into its fold a vast range of developments taking place around the subcontinent. Reform became the master word for identifying modernity in religion and for understanding the dynamics of religious change in colonial India.[4] The paradigmatic quality of Rammohun comes to the fore here once again, since his example fostered a kind of mania for identifying reformers and their movements, and because he could be shown to have benefited from exposure to the salutary teachings of Christianity.[5] One century after Rammohun's creation of the Atmiya Sabha, the idea of the modern religious reform movement had so taken hold that it became the defining analytic for Farquhar's seminal—and still widely read—*Modern Religious Movements in India*. Not only does the Swaminarayan Sampraday find no place in Farquhar's book but, just as importantly, while reviewing the period from 1800 to 1828, Farquhar confidently asserted that no "fresh religious movement worthy of notice" had appeared during this same period.[6] So much for Sahajanand. That left Farquhar plenty of room to conclude that the fresh winds of reform only began to blow in 1828 with the founding of the Brahmo Samaj. Since we have every reason to suspect that Farquhar knew of the Swaminarayan Sampraday when he wrote these words, we must conclude that, for him, the Sampraday constituted nothing like a reform movement.[7]

One way to correct histories like this is of course to supplement them, to bring them up to date in terms of new information. This seems to partially capture the intention behind the efforts of those such as Williams, who are today committed to giving the Swaminarayanis a second look within the scholarly literature. That said, the result in Williams's case has been largely to reinscribe the Sampraday within existing histories of reform. On one level, this makes perfect sense; even if we grant Farquhar some leeway in preferring "fresh" movements over those he viewed as wedded to the past, it seems patently untrue that something new and exciting did not take place under Sahajanand's leadership. The solution looks straightforward: simply find a way to secure a place for Sahajanand and the Swaminarayanis within the master narratives of modern reform.

The problem is, of course, that to reinscribe the Sampraday within reform-based narratives, one must agree to the terms of the narrative. We saw this problem briefly in considering the comments of Milinda Banerjee above. This illustrates the subtle persistence of reform-based logics, which exert their influence even on objects that seem beyond the immediate range of their interest. By this I mean to say that the very absence of the Swaminarayanis from studies such as Farquhar's is not due to a simple deficit of information; it actually speaks to the fact that the Swaminarayanis have been considered, but just as quickly excluded, from the narrative. In this way, they actually do find a place in our logics—confirming the frame by marking its limits. One indication of this can be found in the fact (just noted) that Farquhar was not unaware of the Sampraday; it seems most likely that he consciously chose not to consider them. One response to this fact might of course be to argue that if hitherto the Sampraday has been omitted from narratives on Hindu reform, then a compromise solution can be reached simply by widening the scope of how we understand reform. This seems to account for Williams's decision to construe the Swaminarayan Sampraday as both a vestige of medieval Hinduism and a first instance of modern reform.[8]

Recently Williams has returned to this interpretive strategy. He and Paramtattvadas have written that Sahajanand "revived, refined, and reinterpreted aspects of classical Hindu thought." This in a sense only rephrases the idea that Sahajanand represented the "last of the medieval." The problem is that now this claim is explicitly linked to that other vestige from the empire of reform: the trope of revival. Not only is revival itself a teleologically determined concept (suggesting back pressure against progress); more importantly perhaps, it must surely remain problematic to claim that Sahajanand was interested in reviving the past. The interpretation I have tried to develop here seeks to emphasize instead his creative role in articulating a new polity within the multiscalar world of overlapping polities he found in early colonial Gujarat. In his outreach to local lords, his promulgation of new codes, and his construction of new edifices and institutional structures, there is little sense of reclaiming something he feared had been lost. One senses instead a kind of innovative energy to his work.

When it comes to the idea of Sahajanand being a modern reformer, in a recent essay Paramtattvadas and Williams add a measure of nuance to this claim, even while embedding it just as firmly in existing characterizations of Sahajanand as a useful handmaid of empire. They suggest that Sahajanand's activities "caused" his British acquaintances—men such as Heber and Malcolm—"to interpret him as a religious and social reformer whose reforms contributed to social order and welfare."[9] To their credit, Paramtattvadas and Williams pay close attention to the kind of comparative reflection on Sahajanand that was beginning to color his reception among colonial officials (as we saw in Chapter 8). In this way, Paramtattvadas and Williams gesture toward the possibility that it was the early British who viewed Sahajanand through the lens of reform, even if Paramtattvadas and Williams are less eager to claim him as a reformer themselves.

Here I sense an almost anxious distancing from the rubric of reform, which may correlate to a perceived need in the early twenty-first century to say something above all about the Sampraday as being authentically Hindu. Once again the subtle operation of reform's logic can be sensed even as the label is more or less eschewed—something like the inverse of what we saw with Farquhar. If the latter had used the litmus test of Christian influence to decide where "fresh" reform made its inroads in India, Paramtattvadas and Williams turn the tables and suggest that, in a sense, Farquhar read the situation correctly: there was no appreciable influence in this case; if anything, Sahajanand worked at recovery and revival. Except that now, in the hands of Paramtattvadas and Williams, the claim is rendered into something like a boast: Sahajanand was not really a modern reformer!

Transition and Acculturation

The aporias thrown up around the application of reform-based logics are just as evident if we turn to another relatively recent and authoritative survey of socioreligious movements in South Asia, first published around the time of Williams's pioneering monograph on the Sampraday. I refer to Kenneth Jones's monograph, *Socio-Religious Reform Movements in British India*. When elaborating the "conceptual framework" that would guide his study, Jones proposed a distinction between two modes of religious change in modern India: "acculturative" and "transitional." According to Jones, we should think of acculturative movements as those led by figures who were "products of cultural interaction."[10] As Jones would go on to show, this was the appropriate category by which to understand Rammohun, whom he credits with the first Indian "unfolding" of acculturative change. He stresses that Rammohun was the product of "diverse cultural influences," sketching in short order his family's status as Persianized Brahmin elites, his varied training, his early challenges to religious orthodoxy, and his service under the East India

Company.[11] These were to become the backdrop to Rammohun's work of reform, announced most forcefully in his famous challenge to suttee.

For Jones, such patterns of acculturation and reform cannot be applied in the case of the Swaminarayan Sampraday. This he prefers to construe as a transitional movement, by which he means to say that the Sampraday remained firmly rooted in the precolonial world. Sahajanand's teachings represented the ongoing salience of "indigenous" modes of religious life as opposed to those of an "intrusive" Western culture.[12] Whereas acculturative movements like the Brahmo Samaj sought active accommodation with British rule and European culture, transitional movements like the Swaminarayan Sampraday were characterized by the absence of anglicized leaders and a pronounced lack of interest in adjusting their concepts and structures to the norms of the colonial world.[13] In his analysis of the Sampraday, Jones stressed the fact that Sahajanand had commenced his public career as a renouncer, had taken initiation under Ramanand Swami, and (after the latter's death) had propagated a form of Krishna devotion that was both "popular and well-established" in Gujarat.[14] Coming into play in this epitome of Sahajanand's life are thus a series of assumptions about traditional Hinduism, the power of the guru, and the role of the Swaminarayan Sampraday in reinforcing existing Hindu norms and practices.[15]

For all that I respect the effort and the monumental task of surveying two centuries of religious change in this fashion, I find Jones's framework ultimately unsatisfactory. Although he was eager to offer scholars a new set of tools for thinking about religious change under colonial conditions, his critical framework remained all too embedded in the key categories, tropes, and culturalist binaries that have long shaped discourse on religious reform: reform as emancipation; indigenous versus intrusive cultural forms; the distinction between traditional modes of communal solidarity and modern modes of voluntary association; celebration of reason coupled with anxiety over charisma and religious authority. Finally, Jones's two operative categories for understanding modern socioreligious movements are themselves all too clearly predicated on an unstated teleology of the modern. There is little doubt as to which movements are the more modern and may thus be reckoned the best suited to represent the religious spirit of postindependence India.

The acculturative and the transitional are, in this respect, not so much two modes of change as a ratification of the perennial distinction between medieval and modern.

We see this reflected in Jones's treatment of categories like *sampraday* and *samaj*. Although he does not make this point explicitly, he tends to frame the Brahmo Samaj as a kind of modern voluntary association, encouraging us to think of its emergence as coeval with the colonial public sphere.[16] This naturalizing of *samaj* as a kind of modern social organization is facilitated by the fact that, from Rammohun's day onward, the term would increasingly be used to translate the term "society." Thus, almost tautologically, the modernity of the Brahmos inheres in their own organizational descriptor: *samaj*. By contrast, the term *sampraday*—though it had found use early on in places like Calcutta as a translation equivalent for society—remains locked in the embrace of assumptions about sectarianism, guru-based authority, and tradition itself.[17] For Jones to invoke the idea of *sampraday* was to conjure something very much like a premodern religious order: something medieval, cloistered, and resistant to change.

Here it is important to note that it is possible to interrogate concepts like *samaj / sabha* and *sampraday* as deployed in the early colonial moment and arrive at a very different sort of conclusion—one that would in fact emphasize what Sahajanand and Rammohun shared rather than how they differed. To do this we must first agree to postpone freighting a term like *samaj* with the modern meaning of "society," especially if by that we mean to signal something like the celebrated transition from "status" to "contract."[18] We have already seen that, rather than thinking of *samaj* as modern society, there is good reason to think of it in the sense of court society. In Rammohun's case I have tried to emphasize the importance of his having constituted a *darbar* of dedicated participants who gathered under his lordship and gave symbolic weight through their loyalty to his status as raja.[19] Viewed in this way, the conditions of possibility that first supported the emergence of the Brahmo Samaj are not so different from those that supported Sahajanand's articulation of his own polity; in both cases the articulation of a new polity was grounded in what Robert Travers refers to as a common precolonial "culture of assembly."[20] Rather than bifurcating the idioms of *samaj* and *sampraday* along lines of modernity and tradition, we should recognize what both reveal about the articulation of religious authority in the early colonial moment.

Sahajanand and Rammohun each sought to develop, promulgate, and operationalize their religious mastery to the ends of promulgating new sets of norms and practices that would frame the polities they respectively referred to as *sampraday* and *samaj*. Whether under the rubric of a court-based *samaj/sabha* or that of a devotional *sampraday*, the two leaders sought to draw on and repurpose modes of premodern scriptural knowledge, moral regulation, and social organization; and both men worked assiduously to situate their polities within an early colonial scale of forms, while remaining attentive—and deferential—to the overlapping layers of power in their regions. Thus *pace* Jones, one could just as well argue that Sahajanand and Rammohun were in their respective ways acculturative *and* transitional. It is nothing but a distinction without a difference. Furthermore, by questioning the utility of the dichotomy in this way we solve another problem: we are able now to dispense with the underlying spatiotemporal logic according to which Bengal represented the first advent of those cultural encounters that would be central to modernity in South Asia, while Gujarat remained distant in both space and time. We know enough by now to say that this is itself a problematic assumption. At the turn of the nineteenth century, both regions were, to borrow again from Travers, "unstable, precarious but also politically generative" contexts.[21]

Back to the Mountains

We need a different model, one that can make sense of religious innovation in such contexts without framing it in terms of the expectations associated with hegemonic norms of religious modernity. Thankfully, as I have argued throughout, Inden has shown us how to proceed. In the present context it might be helpful to consider what he has to say in his concluding remarks to *Imagining India*. Here he pulls together some of the key categories I have drawn on in my own analysis, to wit, lordship, mastery, polity, scale of forms, and complex agency. As we know, the central category for Inden is polity, which he employs as a way to escape all the deeply ingrained conceptual habits shaping Western theories of state and society. The problem with such theories, he argues, is that they tend to treat state and / or society as ideal types that are "self-centered, unitary, homogeneous and permanent." Whether articulated through individualist or socialist theories, this framing has produced systems of representation wherein the ideal state is inevitably contrasted with some "imperfectly realized" society at the actual level.

Inden turns away from such idealism by invoking Collingwood's idea of polity, encouraging us to think anew about state and society in terms of the activities of a wide range of more or less complex agents, not least royal courts, assemblies, and councils. At the highest level Inden speaks of the "imperial formation" within which claims of universal sovereignty are articulated within a scale of overlapping polities; these latter are never necessarily opposed to one another nor are they mutually exclusive; instead they should be thought of as "continually being completed, contested and remade."[22] In premodern India, this understanding of imperial formation was captured in concepts like the "circle of kings" (raja-mandala). What the circle of kings suggested was that sovereignty was never achieved through the elimination of all enemies and others; it was constructed instead by incorporating these others within an encompassing scale of topographic and epistemic forms that served to express and embody universal lordship.

Inden's preferred example for such an imperial formation was the Rashtrakuta polity of the eighth to tenth centuries.[23] There is something particularly apt about the name for this polity, since it may be translated as "summit of the realm." Sure enough, Inden shows how, just like a towering peak set amid a vast mountain range, the Rashtrakutas imagined their imperial formation in terms of a vast scale of forms, a range of polities within which we might speak of greater and lesser peaks of sovereignty. The metaphorics here are particularly apt, since the Rashtrakutas (like so many South Asian polities) understood the Himalayas as both a sacred landscape in their own right and a kind of metonymic backdrop for the articulation of their political rule. Thus in the Rashtrakuta imaginary, Mount Kailash—the abode of the great god Shiva—formed both the center and summit of Sanskritic cosmology. This helps explain why a polity based in the Deccan Plateau expended the vast resources it did in order to create the massive rock-cut Kailashanatha Temple at Ellora—this temple to Shiva as "Lord of Kailasa" gave material expression to the Rashtrakuta's symbolic claims to mastery over Bharatvarsha.[24]

The point to bear in mind is that one cannot conjure the Himalayas without imagining a vast range composed of countless mountain peaks. In just the same way, it should be impossible to imagine the Rashtra-kutas standing alone and isolated. They did not rule in a political vacuum. And as much as they strived both materially and symbolically to con-struct the kind of world over which they sought to rule, they did so in relation to a plural scale of existing political formations. That is to say, there were other peaks on the horizon. In fact, of great concern to the Rashtrakutas were the competing kingdoms of the Gujaras and the Palas. As Inden puts it, the Rashtrakuta concern to situate themselves within a range of such existing polities speaks to the basic "theological realism" inherent in South Asian discourse on kingship. In this realistic world-view, there is always room for lesser gods to reign as lesser gods, and for lesser kings to reign as lesser kings.[25] All the Rashtrakutas hoped to assert was that they were the "summit of the realm." Surely Inden appreciates how the root metaphor here is supported by the facts of geomorphology: no less than existing mountain ranges, imperial for-mations are inherently unstable; it is always possible that a peak might topple, thereby altering the landscape in consequential ways.

I have tried to argue that Rammohun and Sahajanand both lived during a moment when this kind of pluralist vision of sovereignty was just beginning to give way to new notions of a consolidated empire and, latterly, the vision of an integrated Indian nation, or *rashtra*. We can see now, in particular, how Rammohun's conception of Bharatvarsha, with its various regions and shifting borders, was not so different from that of the Rashtrakuta imperial imagination. No less than Sahajanand, Ram-mohun was aware of, conversant with, and attentive to a world of over-lapping polities. And as I have tried to argue, the articulation of the Swaminarayan Sampraday and the Brahmo Samaj involved the canny and creative attempt by both men to identify and occupy a place for their new polities within the multiscalar world of overlapping polities found in regions like Gujarat and Bengal around the beginning of the nineteenth century.

We might say that both Sahajanand and Rammohun sought to promote their theological and organizational goals in a contrapuntal fashion, seeking neither to drown out nor to harmonize too closely with other existing religious formations that made up the religious and political landscape of their day. As we have seen, Sahajanand was more than willing to promote a useful synergy with communities like the Vallabhites and with the newest and most consequential political power in the region, the British. In Rammohun's case, the colonial city of Calcutta offered him the perfect environment in which to advance his own court assembly-cum-voluntary association, drawing on the support of his *purohit* and acharya and seeking expansive new ties with European actors and institutions. In both cases, lordship over a new polity—even if this sounds odd when applied to a quasi-republican figure like Rammohun—can serve as a useful shorthand for thinking about the emergence of both the Swaminarayan Sampraday and the Brahmo Samaj. And unlike standard frameworks of reform, with their normative judgments about progress, or dichotomies predicated on chronotopes of tradition and modernity, this way of viewing things allows us to situate the Swaminarayanis and Brahmos within a single interpretive frame that is attentive to a shared historical moment.

If the metaphor of the mountain range proves useful for conceptualizing a world of multiscalar polities, in my analysis the mountains themselves serve as an important cosmological and experiential landscape for Sahajanand and Rammohun. Within the shared Puranic cosmology and theological systems that were operative for both men, the Himalayas retained their status as the realm of gods and sages, the site for undertaking arduous spiritual work, and the ideal location in which to seek self-transformation. I do not think it stretches the available evidence too much to say that the Himalayas played just such a transformative role for both Sahajanand and Rammohun. For both men, in their youth, the mountains had provided a place in which to wander as well as a kind of religious laboratory in which to experiment with new visions of themselves and their world. By drawing on a number of existing hagiographies and biographies, in Chapters 4 and 5 I was able to insert both

Sahajanand and Rammohun in the "confluent" worlds of trans-Himalayan life.[26] By so doing, I was able to point toward what they drew from interactions with a wide range of religious actors, while speculating on ways this polycentric universe might have informed their acquisition of different modes of religious mastery.

Is There Room in This Approach for Difference?

Having found a way to examine the emergence of the Swaminarayan Sampraday and the Brahmo Samaj within a single analytical frame, it would be fair to ask, Have I left room for identifying any important differences between the two, not least as expressions of modern Hinduism? Perhaps one way to tackle this question is to pick up where I left off at the end of Chapter 5. In that context I cautioned against drawing overly hasty distinctions between Sahajanand and Rammohun on the basis of the fact that their lives have come down to us via hagiography, on the one hand, and historical narrative, on the other. My goal at that point had been to place the two men in a shared religio-cultural landscape and within a single analytical frame that would support an examination of just how they went about constructing their polities. In the spirit of critical postponement, my chief concern then was to defer the application of normative judgments about reform that claimed to be based on prima facie distinctions between the two literary genres.

But perhaps I went too far in postponing the search for difference. After all, in the case of the Swaminarayan Sampraday, we do have to deal with a mythicizing hagiography framed with the purpose of manifesting and affirming the divine authority of a new Vaishnava Lord. If a text like the *Satsangi Jivanam* takes no interest in the minutiae of the landscapes through which Nilakantha moved, this is consonant with its own cosmic perspective and larger theological agenda. Here perhaps we can find a meaningful point of difference with the case of Rammohun. After all, in the latter's autobiographical comments, as well as in the work of his early biographers, the goal was to plant Rammohun firmly in history and to use that context to account for his personality and accomplishments. If in Rammohun's case there was any kind of advent to highlight, it was not divine but strictly human. Texts about Rammohun promote his status as a liberal reformer.

The textualization of these two figures then, while similar in terms of serving to authenticate and characterize the inaugural work of Sahajanand and Rammohun, is geared toward the ratification of two different sorts of religious polities. Here we need only look again at two texts that have hitherto had much to tell us about the work of these two men—the *Shikshapatri* and the Brahmo Trust Deed. Both are documents that embody the polity-making aspirations of these early colonial religious lords; as such, both articulate rules and disciplinary structures for the polities in question. In Hodgson's terms, these texts reach out to new followers while providing specific codes of conduct and institutional frameworks intended to be self-sustaining over time; they offer rules for life.[27]

But the rules of life and organizational forms promoted in these texts suggest differences in how Sahajanand and Rammohun extended their influence beyond a group of dedicated followers in order to cultivate relationships with other ruling powers. Sahajanand sought to insert his community within an existing milieu of devotional and temple-based Hinduism that was rapidly conforming some of its own norms to the ruling authority of the British. His own devotion to Ramanand Swami and the newfound reverence he received from local rulers and peasant groups meant that Sahajanand could articulate his authority in close conformity to patterns already established by devotional polities like the Vallabhites. Rammohun's early experiences, not least his service to various East India Company officials, suggested to him patterns of opportunity of another kind. If the *Shikshapatri* reveals an author looking for direct inspiration from the Vallabhites, the Trust Deed speaks to the earlier experiences of a young man who began reading European newspapers while serving under Digby in Rangpur and who later found himself drawn to the values of republicanism, free trade liberalism, and, eventually, Unitarianism.

Here we might turn to Philip Gorski's concept of a "disciplinary revolution," which offers a useful interpretive angle for thinking about the kinds of difference we see enshrined in texts like the *Shikshapatri* and the Trust Deed. If we take the case of Sahajanand's ideal of *satsang*, we encounter what Gorski might call a revolution from below. That is to say, we see the attempt by a local religious leader to operationalize a potent combination of individual and communal discipline that would end up having (as Gorski's model predicted) profound and long-lasting effects for the Sampraday.[28] This disciplinary order was not dependent on either state authority or the judgments of legal courts; instead, the discipline of the *satsang* presumed the regular embrace of the values of *satsang* and a near-constant scrutiny of both individual behavior and communal comportment. As itself an object of daily recitation and reflection, the *Shikshapatri* is the embodiment of this disciplinary ideal. The order enunciated in the text and enacted daily by Satsangis proved to be an invaluable aid in ensuring the stability of the Sampraday, especially in the volatile first decades of the nineteenth century in Gujarat. When viewed against the backdrop of the *longue durée,* the text has lent a sort of confessionalized disciplinary solidity to the Sampraday. It is precisely this communal disciplinary revolution from below that has led the Swaminarayan to be framed as a puritanical, sectarian, and traditionalist Hindu group.

In Gorski's terms, Rammohun's deployment of religious mastery also constituted a revolution from below, since it required no state for its initial articulation or the enforcement of its moral code. It too was predicated, like Sahajanand's polity, on the internalization of self-discipline and restraint. But, unlike Sahajanand, Rammohun did not find inspiration in the realm of devotional polities as much as in the mannered world of the elite court or *darbar.* At least initially, he predicated his authority and prestige on the enactment of shared codes of comportment that were characteristic of cultured life within the Indo-Persian ecumene. Although Rammohun relied on his performance of courtly mastery to establish the first lineaments of his new Brahmo polity, he also drew into his moral and theological system additional norms associated with Vedic scripture and European philosophy. This proved to be a unique combination, yielding a kind of Brahmo ethic of self-restraint grounded in the Upanishads but paired with an Enlightenment skepticism of religious authority. We notice, as a result, that norms of communal discipline are attenuated among Brahmos when compared with those of Swaminarayanis. The Trust Deed, in particular, with its tenor as modern legal document, is grounded more in what Gorski identifies as a judicial or institutional mode of discipline. Less communally regimented, but still socially constrained, the world of the Brahmo polity looks like what Gorski might characterize in terms of an individual-normative self-discipline expressed within a social-institutional public frame. This is what prompted me in my earlier work to characterize post-Rammohun Brahmo religiosity as a form of "bourgeois Hinduism."[29]

No doubt Gorski would be the first to caution that this way of categorizing in terms of disciplinary types remains ideal-typical; he would remind us that the "greatest effect of all" occurs when multiple modes of discipline come into play—when communal discipline is reinforced by social norms, and self-discipline is backed up by the potential for coercive or corrective discipline.[30] Such a warning in fact proves helpful, since it directs our attention toward another important difference between the Sampraday and the Samaj—especially when viewed across the longer history of modern Indian public culture. As much as the ideal of *satsang* required a profound internal disciplinary reorientation that was backed up by rigorous communal discipline (and even surveillance), it also came to be integrated with a powerful social ethic. This ethic grew from strength to strength as the Swaminarayanis began to draw into their fold Gujarati agricultural communities and found points of contact with the worlds of urban commerce, politics, and (in time) diasporic religion. Never dependent on the state for the management or enforcement of its particular form of life, the Sampraday could also (as late as 1966) make the case to the Indian Supreme Court that it was in fact something other than Hinduism, at least as the modern court was coming to define that tradition.

In the Brahmo case, as we have seen, the polity did not require a strict communal ethic; one result of this fact is that the bourgeois social ethic that came to be associated with the Brahmo "lifestyle" almost quietly morphed into a mode of social etiquette that was gaining increased acceptance among the middling, newly aspirational classes of colonial Calcutta. One might even think of it not as the empire of reform tended to do—as evidence of Britain's overall civilizing mission—but in terms of what Elias so famously characterized as a "civilizing process"; which is to say, a set of developments that constituted neither a rational plan intended in advance by particular agents (the British or Rammohun) nor yet something irrational that defies understanding.[31] To see this we need only begin with the original courtly polity context of the Brahmo Samaj and then consider how the world of the *sabha* gave birth over time to the ideal of modern *sabhyata* or "civilization." That this was a gradual and far-from-linear process is suggested by considering two facts: First, the values of this new *sabhyata*, sometimes associated with the extreme liberalism of the Young Bengal faction during the 1830s and 1840s, were met with suspicion as something unbounded and uncouth, whereby debauchery took shelter under the flag of freedom. The classic critique came in Michael Madhusudan Datta's 1859 play, "You Call This Civilization?" (*Ekei ki bole sabhyata?*). Second, an illustration of just how gradual this civilizing process proved to be can be found in the fact that some members of the Young Bengal group who were the target of Datta's satire thought nothing of turning to the royal authority of a local zamindar lord to get the play shut down before it could be staged![32]

Even Datta himself can be seen as an embodiment of the same civilizing process whose excesses he sought to lampoon, suggesting that over time the values of *sabhyata* would prove transformative compared with the lingering sovereignty of local ruling lords. Here another claim about difference begins to emerge, insofar as while participation in the Swaminarayan polity was predicated on deference to a divine lord through the embrace of his rules, the Brahmos after Rammohun came to pledge their allegiance not to an absent guru-lord but to the power of a sovereign law, associated in part with an abstract (some would say almost otiose) unitary God but also with a natural law inscribed in the universe.[33] What Rammohun had called a "simple code of religion and morality" thus became the backbone of discourse around rights, freedoms, and moral responsibility.[34] And so, at the risk of making a long story short, we arrive inevitably at Kopf's observation that the Brahmos had a direct role in shaping the "modern Indian mind." With their bourgeois ethic, their recourse to liberal norms, and their consistent attempt to guide the reformist project of the colonial and postcolonial state, the Brahmos would become synonymous with the aspirational project of the Indian nation.

By beginning with attention to the role of lordship in the articulation of religious polities we thus equip ourselves to frame some comparative conclusions about the difference between Swaminarayanis and

Brahmos, not least in relation to conceptions of sovereignty.[35] In the Swaminarayan case, the earthly lord Sahajanand came to be revered as the supreme deity; the immanent charisma of the ruling lord was thereby translated (figuratively and theologically) into the cosmic authority of Bhagavan Swaminarayan. His heavenly court then came to be celebrated and affirmed over time by honoring the disciplinary codes and hierarchical form of life first promulgated when Lord Swaminarayan lived and taught in Gujarat—as well as by the regular performance of those temple rituals and acts of personal devotion he enjoined.

By contrast, Rammohun's efforts went toward the promotion of a scripturally valid and rationally defensible monotheistic creed; his sovereignty in turn became like that of a righteous ruler who had all along been bound to laws that were higher than himself. Never a god himself, he was only primus inter pares. But for the very reason of his being the Fürst, he was also qualified to be "the man at the helm," the father of the Indian nation.[36] That the precise nature of Brahmo identity remained unclear even at the time of his death is suggested by the fact that the next generation of Brahmos would apply themselves to framing the simple code by which Brahmos should be guided in relation to their memories of who Rammohun had been. In time this would lead to the creation of the first Brahmo "scripture"—the *Brahmo Dharmah*, created in 1850 under Debendranath—and to important acts of collective memory in which Rammohun began to figure as the founding reformer.[37]

If we want to make sense of the difference between the two early polities in this regard, customary church / sect models will be of little use. Picturing Hinduism as a centralized institution that manages to weather the winds of change over time is simply untenable; there is no such Hinduism to be found. Furthermore this sort of formulation requires the equally problematic assertion that sects (or reform movements) exist at the far end of a "tension axis;" as if they represent attempts to either cause or resist change at the institutional (or church) level.[38] This model not only requires essentializing Hinduism in ways we need to avoid; but also, to adopt it is to recommit ourselves to the discourse of reform. As we have seen, this is the way we arrive at misleading comparisons of the Swaminarayan Sampraday and the Brahmo Samaj in terms of a purported tension between *sampradayikatva* and *sabhyata*—communalism versus liberal community. We have seen enough by now to realize how problematic such a simple contrast proves.

How then should we understand the latter-day transformation of groups like the Swaminarayanis and the Brahmos into the kinds of organizations we think of today—defined increasingly in relation to affect-laden and politically charged tensions between the claims of primordial Hindu identity and the values of the liberal public sphere? Reading Nussbaum, one might reply that the answer lies in the need to address the manifest failure of reform. In this view, the national poetics of freedom and justice originally offered by the Brahmos has increasingly been compromised by the persistence of communalized allegiances, themselves fueled by the forces of manipulative leadership and corporate ritual habits. And yet does this way of seeing things not simply threaten to double down on the tropes of colonial reform? Does it not threaten to view contemporary religious life in terms of older anxieties surrounding popery and priestcraft, all the while underwriting one particular understanding of bourgeois selfhood? I think we can see today how tenuous it becomes to continue down this track, especially since recent scholarship around the discussion of secularism and tolerance in South Asia has undercut the myth of secularism's distance from the claims of religion. In this regard, even as a great deal continues to be made of Indian secularism as a model of tolerance—which Gandhi framed as equal regard for all religions (*sarva-dharma sama-bhava*)—Cassie Adcock has shown that this very ideal is itself the legacy of an imperial discursive regime deeply rooted in notions of religious discord, sectarianism, and intolerance.[39] For there to be some prospect of rethinking the place of religion in modern India, we need another way to construe the differences among groups like the Swaminarayan Sampraday and the Brahmo Samaj, an approach that does not fall back on the discursive legacy of the empire of reform. We can now see how that discourse is rife with ambiguity and founded on deeply culturalist assumptions about the very meaning of religion.

Here the work of Philip Gorski may be of some help, not least because his work suggests that what two polities like the Swaminarayan Sampraday and the Brahmo Samaj originally shared is also what might allow us think further about their late colonial and even postcolonial histories. As we have seen, Gorski's work offers us a means to construe both polities in terms of the concept of disciplinary revolution. The disciplinary revolution of the Swaminarayan Sampraday was at once both individual and communal, a form of life predicated on self-discipline and obedience to the rules of *satsang*. Needing no support from the state, the Sampraday developed as a self-constituting polity existing within the British imperial formation, neither entirely sheltered from nor actively engaged in the project of empire or nation. By contrast, the self-discipline of the Brahmo Samaj (no less predicated on the individual embrace of self-restraint) did not constitute itself in a communal mode; its disciplinary energies went toward refiguring the realm of the social. It came, as we have seen, to embody a culture of bourgeois aspiration and sensibility that effectively paired personal moral restraint with public respectability, spiritual aspiration with social cohesion (albeit a liberal one). Because of the trajectory that led the Brahmos to become the moral educators for an emerging Indian public, Nussbaum is not wrong to see in their overall political poetics—not least those of Rabindranath Tagore—the historical template for one version of Indian national belonging. Her chief error may have been to excessively laud the superiority of the Brahmo project in this regard, without attending fully to the limits of its own project of liberal, androcentric, high-caste hegemony.

Where, then, does this leave us? In light of the crisis of communalism highlighted by Nussbaum—not to mention the ongoing spatialization of chauvinist claims about Hindu history—how might one wish to see the commitments of Swaminarayanis and Brahmos rearticulated in the future? Would it be too much to issue a basic challenge to groups like the Swaminarayan Sampraday, such that even as the validity of their form of life is recognized, the community is enjoined to reach beyond *satsang* in order to situate themselves effectively within a religious and political landscape shaped by the values of pluralism, individual rights, justice, and the rule of law? The *Shikshapatri* might even serve as a kind of guide here, especially when we recall Sahajanand's injunction that Satsangis adjust their religious practices and worldly affairs to the norms of place, time, and context.[40] As we saw in Chapter 6, it had never been Sahajanand's goal to place his *sampraday* in complete opposition to other existing polities; his was a project of emplacement, not replacement.

Viewed in this light, might there be a way to move away from frameworks that construe the Sampraday as narrowly "sampradayik" in order to recover an older understanding of *sampraday* wherein reverence for the guru's rules and the practice of *satsang* do not run counter to the norms and goals of contemporary democracy?

Of course, if we are going to ask questions like these we must do no less when it comes to the Brahmos. Here our attention might likewise turn to the role and legacy of their regulatory habitus in the contemporary moment. That legacy is scarcely rendered harmless by virtue of its unmarked operation in so much of public life. Indeed, as the unmarked ideal of reformed religion, perhaps Vedantic modes of tolerant religion have been given too much of a pass when it comes to addressing some of the unintended consequences of universalist discourse—which for all its apparent tolerance rests on powerful hierarchies and exclusions.[41] What is more, the sheer fact of Brahmo hegemony in terms both of regulating interiorized religious subjectivity and governing the body politic, suggests a very real need to interrogate the operation of its sovereign power.

As the work of J. Barton Scott has shown, the development of colonial understandings of a self-regulating bourgeois subject depended on the reform-based critique of other modes of South Asian religious life, not least as found in bhakti-oriented polities such as the Vallabhites— or, we may add, the Swaminarayanis. But where the empire of reform posited an either/or choice between Protestant self-rule or popish enslavement, Scott suggests the possibility of an exit from this false bind in order to consider both the Satsangi and the Brahmo disciplinary projects as two modern regimes of self-rule.[42] That being the case, if it is time to reframe our understanding of *satsang*, then it is likewise time to reframe Brahmo dharma.

In the end, it may be that an awareness of how both the Swaminarayan Sampraday and the Brahmo Samaj first arose as distinctive disciplinary polities—neither one more modern than the other—might open up new comparative perspectives from which to begin framing responses to the ongoing inequities and injustices India faces in terms of religion, caste, class, gender, and sexuality.

ABBREVIATIONS

NOTES

BIBLIOGRAPHY

INDEX

Abbreviations

BC	Nishkulanand, Swami. *Bhaktachintamani.*
HLA	Viharilalji, Maharaj. *Harililamrita.*
Lekh	Sahajanand, Swami. *Desh-Vibhag-no Lekh.*
MBh	Sinha, Kaliprasanna. *Mahabharata.*
PP	Deshpande, N. A. *Padma Purana.*
RR	Roy, Rammohun. *Rammohun-Rachanabali: Samagra Bangla rachana, Samskrita o Pharasi rachanar anubad, patrabali evam pradhan Inreji rachanasaha ek khande sampurna.*
RRBV	Roy, Rammohun. *Raja Rammohan Ray-pranita granthabali.*
RRET	Roy, Rammohun. *The English Works of Raja Rammohun Roy with an English Translation of "Tuhfatul Muwahhiddin."*
RRGift	Roy, Rammohun. *Tuhfatul Muwahhiddin or A Gift to Deists.*
RV	Vidyavagish, Ramchandra. *Parameshvarer upasanabishaye prathama byakhyana abadhi dvadasha byakhyana paryanta.*
SPE	Monier-Williams, Monier. "Sanskrit Text of the Siksha-Patri of the Svami-Narayan Sect."
SPMs	Sahajanand Swami. *Shikshapattri.*
SPNM	Sahajanand Swami. *Sri Sahajananda Swamina lakheli Siksapatri: Nityananda Munini lakheli Gujarati tikasathe.*
SPS	Sahajanand Swami. *Shikshapatri.*
SSJ	Shatanand, Muni. *Satsangijivanam: Shatananda Muni Virachitam.*
SSJM	Muktananda, Swami. *Satsangijivanam Mahatmyam: Shatananda Muni Virachitam.*

SSJSum	Jani, Jaydev A., and Peter Schreiner. *The Satsangijivanam by Satananda.*
SV	Gunatitanand, Swami. *Swamini vato.*
TP 21	*Tattvabodhini Patrika* Vol. 21.
TP 50	*Tattvabodhini Patrika* Vol. 50.
VA	Swaminarayan, Bhagwan. *Vachanamrut: The Spiritual Discourses of Bhagwan Swaminarayan.*
VAG	Sahajananda Swami. *Vachanamrtani.*
WHMill	"Two Months Journal from Poona to Neemuch (via Surat, Baroda, Ahmedabad & Segwaree)."

Notes

Introduction

1. There are discrepancies in the birthdates for both figures. For Sahajanand, see Williams 2001: 13n1; for Rammohun, see Killingley 1993, 1n2, and Sen 2012, who prefers 1774.
2. Drawing on Chatterjee 2012.
3. Since my focus is on early colonial origins, I employ only the generic names of the Swaminarayan Sampraday and the Brahmo Samaj and do not explore the many subsequent permutations and debates over leadership within each community.
4. On saffronization, see Lele 1995 and Hansen 1999; on the Swaminarayanis and Hindu nationalism, see Mukta 2000.
5. Marshall 1987.
6. On the Brahmos generally, see Kopf 1979; on the Punjab, see Jones 1976 and 1989.
7. On the region and these two designations, see Tambs-Lyche 2010: 101.
8. The Sampraday had achieved so little visibility by the early twentieth century that important works on religion from the period fail to mention it; Farquhar 1915.
9. Borrowing from Younger 2009. A look at the BAPS "Global Network" of religious sites reveals the dispersion of this branch of the Swaminarayan community; see http://www.baps.org/Global-Network.aspx (accessed June 23, 2017).
10. See Hatcher 2008.
11. Kopf 1979: 333–334. Charles Heimsath subsumed Brahmo influence within the larger category of reform, noting its impact on the "mental processes" of Indians and the "structure of their society" (1964: 4).

12. Banerjee 2018: 121.
13. Kopf 1979: 209.
14. Hardiman 1988. In 1948, Swaminarayan leaders resisted pressures toward pluralism and inclusion, fighting for a legal injunction to exclude untouchable (or Dalit) communities from a temple in Ahmedabad. This moment gets only passing mention in Williams and Trivedi 2016: 43–44; for more detail, see Mehta 2002: 12–13.
15. See Zavos et al. 2012.
16. I borrow the coinage of Mukta 2000.
17. Williams 1984; revised as Williams 2001.
18. Tavakoli-Targhi 2001; see also Ali 2012.
19. See Auber 1837.
20. On prolepsis and narrativity, see Prince 1982: 157.
21. For a similar critical approach, see Duara 1995.
22. Tavakoli-Targhi 2001: 9.
23. The Bartlett temple is affiliated with the BAPS branch of the Sampraday; for background, see Williams 2001.
24. Nussbaum 2007: 303.
25. Referring to the much-argued thesis in Huntington 1996.
26. Nussbaum 2007: 2 and 51. On the pogrom in Ahmedabad, see Ghassem-Fachandi 2012.
27. Nussbaum 2007: ix.
28. A recent monograph on the region begins by noting the lack of historical study around Gujarat, which in the wake of Godhra left scholars "scrambling for academic work" to help them make sense of things (Sheikh 2010: 2).
29. House Resolution 227 of April 26, 2005, is reproduced in Nussbaum 2007: 302.
30. Nussbaum 2007: 328.
31. See Dhingra 2012: 4–5 and 225n22.
32. See Dhingra 2012: 183 on the importance of the Sampraday for many Gujarati-American hotel owners.
33. Nussbaum 2007: 324.
34. On Swaminarayan temples and the representation of Hinduism, see Singh 2010 and Kim 2011.
35. Nussbaum 2007: 322.
36. Nussbaum 2007: 302–303.
37. Nussbaum 2007: 303.
38. Bose 1884: 14: "The Brahmos . . . move from a degenerate toward a better faith. Their system may justly be characterized as a reform."
39. See Hatcher 2016.
40. Mallison (1973: 8) speaks of Sahajanand's reforming spirit.
41. Nussbaum (2007: 322) overstates the nature of Sahajanand's "campaign" against female infanticide; cp. Mehta 2016: 42. For an assessment of tensions in Sahajanand's views on caste, see Fuller 2004: 173–174.

42. Williams 1984: 24; cp. Mallison 1973: 11; Parekh 1980: ix; and Williams and Trivedi 2016: passim.
43. Fuller (2004: 174) uses "partially modernized"; cp. Mehta 2016: 41.
44. See Monier-Williams 1877:146 and Monier-Williams 1885: 148 and 155.
45. Nussbaum 2007: 323.
46. Monier-Williams 1885: 155; cp. Mallison 1973: 8.
47. Nussbaum 2007: ix.
48. Nussbaum 2007: 79.
49. See Chakrabarti 1935.
50. See Nussbaum 2007: 93–94.
51. Nussbaum 2007: xiii.
52. Nussbaum 2007: 79.
53. See Nussbaum 2007: 77.
54. Das 2002: 302. Das wins accolades from the likes of Nandan Nilekani, Fareed Zakaria, and Tom Friedman; see gurcharandas.org (accessed June 9, 2017).
55. Or call it "bourgeois Hinduism" (Hatcher 2008).
56. Tellingly, Nussbaum avoids addressing the eventual success of the Swamina-rayan Sampraday among mercantile groups in India, not to mention among the diaspora middle class.
57. See Kanungo 2002.
58. Nussbaum 2007: 296.
59. See Kopf 1979 and Sarkar 2008.

1. Before Reform

1. On the waves sweeping over Bengal, see Chattopadhyay 1880: 37. On *andolan* and nation, see Hawley 2015: passim. *Prabuddha Bharata* was the title of an important journal launched in 1896 in association with the Vedantic nation-alism of Swami Vivekananda.
2. See Sen 2013: np: "The Punjab was the last to come under the spell of modern Hindu reformism."
3. On chronotope, see Bakhtin 1983.
4. Goswami 2004: 45 and 171–172.
5. On this, see Sinha 2012.
6. In Kane 1962, vol. 5.2: iv.
7. Kane 1962, vol. 5.2: v.
8. Kane 1962, vol. 5.2: v.
9. Graham 1990 and Jaffrelot 1996.
10. For representative studies, see Hansen 1999, Chatterjee 1993, and Sarkar 2002.
11. See Hatcher 1999 and Chandra 2014.
12. See Tavakoli-Targhi 2001.
13. Shapiro 1994.
14. Shapiro 1994: 498 and 494.

15. Shapiro 1994: 482.
16. It is worth noting that at the time of India's Independence, J. Reid Graham concluded his study of the Arya Samaj by reminding readers that the story of the Samaj was bound to "the future of India" (1942: 603).
17. Zaehner 1980: 1.
18. Zaehner 1980: 150.
19. Zaehner 1980: 149.
20. Zaehner 1980: 8.
21. Zaehner 1980: 187.
22. Monier-Williams 1877: 2.
23. Quoted in Mukherjee 2010: 72.
24. Zaehner 1980: 198.
25. Farquhar 1915: 1.
26. Chirol 1910: xv.
27. See Tweed 2006: 13.
28. On this, see Ludden 2003.
29. O'Hanlon 2007: 364.
30. Asher and Talbot 2006; on the book, see O'Hanlon 2007.
31. On nationalist "frames," see Sarkar 2002.
32. On the co-emergence of linear history and the territorial nation-state, see Duara 1998: 77.
33. Asher and Talbot 2006: 2. On enumerated communities, see Kaviraj 2010.
34. Scholars had been warned off crude images of precolonial anarchy by Stokes 1975, only to be reminded in works like Bayly 1983 and 1988.
35. For a review of trends, see Chatterjee 2012: 73–76. On global intellectual history, see Moyn and Sartori 2013; on transcolonial perspectives, see Dodson and Hatcher 2012.
36. Chatterjee 2012: 75.
37. Chaudhuri 2012 views it as the period between 1760 and 1859.
38. On the last, in particular, see McDermott 2011.
39. On associational life in the early colonial moment, see Hatcher 2018.
40. Chatterjee 2012; cp. an earlier formulation in Chatterjee 2008.
41. Chatterjee 2012: 76; see also Chatterjee 2008.
42. Bayly 1983: 34.
43. Bayly 1983: 2.
44. See Sharma 2002.
45. Chaudhuri 2012.
46. See Hatcher 2018; see Bose 1874.
47. An important early work is Banerjee 1989.
48. See Robb 2014 and Hatcher 2018.
49. Chatterjee 2012: 157.
50. Haberman 1993: 48–49.
51. See Hatcher 2018.

52. Chaudhuri 2012a: 197.
53. See Chaudhuri 2012a: 194–198; compare the discussion in Chaudhuri 2012b: ch. 2.
54. Derozio started the journal *Kaleidoscope* in 1829.
55. Milinda Banerjee actually notes that "tropes of global unity" played a more important role in Rammohun's thought than did those of "national unity" (2018: 177).
56. Chatterjee 2012: 155.
57. Chatterjee 2012: 76.
58. RRET: 224.
59. RRET: 224.
60. See Ludden 2003 and 2012; Goswami 2004.
61. See Goswami 2004: 262 on the late colonial as a "specific historical juncture and geopolitical field."
62. Tavakoli-Targhi 2001 and my comments in the Introduction.
63. González-Reimann 2009 and Inden 2006.
64. For Sahajanand, see the letter he composed in November of 1806; VA: 786–792.
65. On the Sampraday's early view of Bharata-khanda and its sacred sites, see SSJ 1.8.9. On the land of Bharata as blessed (*dhanya*) by the touch of Lord Narayana's feet, see SSJ 1.5.51.
66. Sahajanand knew Badrikashram as the abode of Lord Narayana, a mythic place where souls lingered before taking birth as humans; see VA 544 (Gadadha II.45.3).
67. From "Preliminary Remarks" to Rammohun's 1832 *Exposition of the Practical Operation of the Judicial and Revenue Systems of India*; RRET: 231.
68. C. T. E. Rhenius, as quoted in Ramaswamy 2013: 373.
69. Rennell 1776; on maps and empire, see Ramaswamy 2013: 359.
70. See Ramaswamy 2017: 26.
71. See RRET: 232.
72. RRET: 233.
73. On the affective dimensions of precolonial Indic space and the shift toward colonial objectification, see Sinha 2012: ch. 1.
74. RRET: 233.
75. From R. Venkat Ratnam's 1906 address, "The Spirit of Rammohun Roy," in Collet 1914: 266.

2. Fluid Landscapes

1. Sheikh 2010 complicates such typologies with respect to Gujarat; for a sophisticated view of Mughal sovereignty, see Bayly 1983.
2. Bayly 1988: 43–44.
3. Asher and Talbot 2006: 8.
4. See Asher and Talbot 2006: 8; on alternate ways to conceptualize frontiers, see Eaton 1993.

5. See Lorenzen 1978 and Pinch 2006.
6. On this, see Gilmartin 1988.
7. Ewing 1997: 49.
8. It may seem strange to refer to the "father of modern India" as King Rammohun, but the usage (consistent with his title of Raja) is not unknown; see Giri 2002: 42.
9. On the phenomenon of sacred kingship, see Hocart 1927.
10. Bayly 1988: 43–44.
11. See Spear 1951. As the authors of one new textbook put it, the diversity of regional political movements and the dynamism of the late Mughal era are no proof of the collapse of that regime; if anything, they are its very fruit (Metcalf and Metcalf 2012).
12. This logic is laid out succinctly in Metcalf 1994.
13. Heber (1829: 3.27) comments on the frequent "forays and plundering excursions" of marauding groups in Gujarat.
14. A standard colonial-era account is Ghosh 1930, but others have sought to complicate matters; see especially Cohn 1964, Kolff 1971, Pinch 2006.
15. Duff 1840: 301.
16. Hausner 2007.
17. On Dasnami *mathamnayas*, see Clark 2006.
18. Wilson 1846: 173.
19. For the rules shaping Dasnami monastic life, see Clark 2006.
20. Gosain "corporations" sought to adapt to the new economic order of the early nineteenth century. Up to the 1840s, Gosains remained property holders in cities like Allahabad, Mirzapur, and Nagpur; see Bayly 1983: 241–242 and 452.
21. Bayly 1988: 42.
22. Lorenzen 1978: 71.
23. From a letter by Maj. James Rennell, written in August 1766 after being injured in a skirmish with armed fakirs near the Bhutan frontier (British Library, OIOC H / 765, 155–166).
24. Chatterjee 2013.
25. See Chatterjee 2015.
26. Shapiro 1994: 498 and 494.
27. On Hariharananda, see Bandyopadhyay 1939.
28. Hariharananda apparently died in Kashi (Varanasi) in 1832.
29. On regional differences in the colonial era, see Shodhan 2001 and Carson 2012.
30. On Gujarat's regional history, see Sheikh 2010.
31. On Pax Britannica, see Wilberforce-Bell 1916: x. This and other colonial accounts routinely describe eighteenth-century Gujarat using terms like chaos, confusion, and disorder (see *Gazetteer of the Bombay Presidency* 1883: 167).
32. On the discourse of priestcraft in relation to colonial-era reform, see Scott 2016.
33. See Hatcher 2018.
34. Alam 1991: 68–69.

35. Tambs-Lyche 2002: 204, building on Skaria 1999.
36. On the "turbulent and incorrigible tribes" of Kathiawar, see Raval 1987: 14. Even a cautious scholar like Pocock (1973: 152) invokes the "turbulent" lower castes of Saurashtra.
37. Tambs-Lyche 2002: 187. Nadri (2009: 20) points out that Kathiawari chieftains took to piracy as a way to express their power. See also Skaria 1998 and Peabody 2001.
38. Tambs-Lyche 2002: 188. As Tambs-Lyche points out, whether a ruler went to war was often more a calculation based on risk assessment than a function of morality per se (197). Kolff (1990: 193–199) discusses how Rajput lives were structured around cycles of warrior aggression and settled home-building.
39. Tambs-Lyche 2004: 12.
40. See Williams and Trivedi 2016: 40. On the Kathis, see Mallison 1974: 443.
41. Smith 1987: 104.
42. Given Brahmin-Bania dominance at the center, the region of Saurashtra may have proved a more promising place for a "foreign" teacher to consolidate support. On this see, Tambs-Lyche 2010: 103.
43. Mukundcharandas 1999: 52. Only about 17 percent of the *Vachanamrut* discourses were delivered on the mainland at places like Ahmedabad or Vartal.
44. VA sect. 44 (Gadhada 1.44): 83; cp. (Kariyani 1): 223. Local styles for turbans and garments are discussed in Mukundcharandas 1999: 81–94.
45. So significant is Dada Khachar's courtyard that site plans are often included in Swaminarayan publications; see Mukundcharandas 1999.
46. See Mukundcharandas 1999: 223–224.
47. See Mukundcharandas 1999: 223.
48. See Nadri 2009: 151–153; see also Nadri 2008.
49. On the concept of religious franchises, see Green 2011. On Vallabhites, Sants, and Ismailis (Satpanth), see Mallison 2016 and Purohit 2012.
50. See Subramaniam 1996; see also Chaudhury 1975 and Nadri 2009, which cites an eighteenth-century Persian document listing fifteen ports and sixty-three wharves along the Gulf of Gujarat (160n4).
51. See Mallison 2016.
52. See Pocock 1973: 152.
53. Mallison 2016: 54; see also Mehta 2016. Sheikh 2010 discusses Indo-Muslim polities in the region.
54. Tambs-Lyche 2011; cp. Mallison 2016.
55. Haynes 1987.
56. Bayly 1988: 160.
57. Fuller 2004: 174.
58. For an exploration of these themes together in relation to modern western India, see Purohit 2012.
59. On the *bhadralok* as "sentinels of culture" during the nineteenth and early twentieth centuries, see Bhattacharya 2005.

60. D'Oyly 1848.
61. Biswas 1984 and Santra 2014.
62. See LMS 1821: 41.
63. See the comments of Santra 1980: 115–116; also Sanyal 1981 and McCutchion 1972.
64. On Durga Puja, see McDermott 2011.
65. On Burdwan, see McLane 1993; for Burdwan and support of Kali devotion, see McDermott 2001.
66. On Tarakeshwar, see Morinis 1984; on Gajan, see Nicholas 2008.
67. On the Dasnamis generally, see Clark 2006, which has little to say about this region or this moment.
68. These sites are the focus of my own ongoing research project on Dasnami monastic settlements in the districts of southwestern Bengal.
69. On Mangal-kabyas, see Bhattacharya 1964.
70. Collet 1914: 2.

3. Polities before Publics

1. On the use of deliberate anachronism, see Novetzke 2016: 42.
2. Borrowing from Mukta 2000.
3. On bordered histories, see Tavakoli-Targhi 2001.
4. See "Shantiniketan Brahmacharyashram," in Tagore 1995: 14.299–308.
5. On Debendranath, see Hatcher 2008 and 2006.
6. See Shapiro 1994, and discussion in the Introduction.
7. Tagore 1995: 14.304.
8. Tagore 1995: 14.299.
9. See Zavos 2000: 32.
10. Tagore 1995: 14.299.
11. Tagore 1995: 14.301.
12. Tagore 1995: 14.302–303.
13. I speak of Rammohun as Debendranath's guru only loosely, since succession within the Samaj was never understood in these terms; see Hatcher 2006.
14. Referring to Hodgson's comments on the "dialectic of a cultural tradition" (1977: 1.79–83).
15. Hodgson 1977: 1.81.
16. See Hatcher 2006, drawing on Hervieu-Léger 2000.
17. For Rabindranath's version of bordered history, see his 1902 essay "Bharat-varsher itihaser dhara," in Tagore 1995.
18. I want to thank Bart Scott for flagging this issue for me.
19. Hodgson 1977: 1.80.
20. Hodgson 1977: 1.81.
21. Two models for considering life under the discipline of a polity may be found in Agamben 2013 and Gorski 2003.

22. Hodgson 1977: 1.82.
23. Hodgson 1977: 1.82.
24. On the historiography of the medieval, see Ali 2012.
25. On this, see Inden et al. 2000: 13.
26. Collingwood 1942: 20:36.
27. See Collingwood 1942: 20:33.
28. Inden 1990: 29.
29. Inden 1990: 28. Collingwood defines authority as, "The relation between a society and a part of that society to which the society assigns the execution of a part of its joint enterprise" (1942: 20.48).
30. Collingwood 1942: 24.55.
31. Shodhan 2001: 37.
32. Shodhan 2001: 37.
33. Shodhan 2001: 196.
34. For background on the Aga Khan case, see Purohit 2012; for the Maharaja libel case, see Haberman 1993 and Scott 2016: ch. 4.
35. For more, see Yelle 2012.
36. Thapar 1997.
37. We see something like this in Parsi *panchayat*s under colonial rule; see Briggs 1852: Section IV.
38. Shodhan 2001: 58–59.
39. Shodhan 2001: 37, citing evidence from the Bombay Regulations between 1819 and 1827.
40. Shodhan 2001: 44–75.
41. Shodhan (2001: 73) highlights factors such as the assumption of rule by the Crown in 1858 and the emerging discipline of colonial sociology under Henry Sumner Maine during the 1860s.
42. Stoker 2016: 11. Fisher (2017: 5) also tackles the legacy of scholarly reflection on Hindu "sectarianism" in relation to "emic" ways of understanding Hindu pluralism in premodern South India.
43. Thus a leader like Vyasatirtha (1460–1539) should be seen not as a religious head (like a pontiff) but as an administrator, intellectual, patron of public works, temple donor, and state agent; see Stoker 2016: 12 and 134.
44. On how this has shaped modern reflections on Hinduism, see Wilson 1846, Monier-Williams 1877, and Griswold 1934: vii. Griswold states, "In both Europe and India movements of 'protest' against the dominant 'catholic' form of religion broke out, the reformed sects of India—Brahmo Samaj, Arya Samaj, etc.—corresponding to the Protestant churches of the West" (vii).
45. Shodhan 2001: 31.
46. See Shodhan 2001: 33. For more on Mulji, see Scott 2016: ch. 4.
47. See Kaviraj 2010.
48. Fisher 2017.
49. Fisher 2017: 19.

50. Fisher 2017: 27.
51. Fisher 2017: 20.
52. Fisher 2017: 192–194.
53. Scott and Ingram 2015 offer a review of two decades of writing on South Asian publics.
54. See the special issue of *South Asia* dedicated to "Aspects of 'the Public' in Colonial South Asia," especially the essay by Freitag 1991.
55. See Copley 2003, Reddy and Zavos 2010, and Stark 2011.
56. See Bayly 1999, Novetzke 2008 and 2016, and Pernau and Jaffrey 2009.
57. Hasan 2005: 87.
58. Hasan 2005: 103–104.
59. Novetzke (2016: 313n79) cites some relevant work.
60. Warner 2005, qtd in Novetzke 2007: 261.
61. See Warner 2005.
62. Fisher 2017: 23–24.
63. Novetzke 2016: 34.
64. Novetzke 2016: 42; for a prompt critical response to this idea, see Sherman 2018.
65. Ali 2004: 6. For Inden, see esp. his contributions to Inden et al. 2000.
66. Ali 2004: 6–7.
67. See the review of Heesterman in Inden 1986.
68. See "Lordship and Caste in Hindu Discourse," in Inden 2006: 160–178; and Inden et al. 2000: 13. For an attempt to rethink Gupta-era sovereignty along these lines, see Willis 2009.
69. Inden's interpretation draws on the work of Hocart 1927 and 1950; see Ali 2004: 6n8.
70. On this see Ali 2004: 3. We shall see that the Persianate world also had a court-centered understanding of royal authority, etiquette, scholarship, and aesthetics; see Hodgson 1977: 2.159–160 and 299.
71. Price 1991 does not factor into the critical discussion found in either Fisher 2017 or Novetzke 2016.
72. Novetzke 2016: 91.
73. Ali 2004: 43.
74. Novetzke 2016: 92.
75. Fisher 2017: 136.
76. I do not want to misread Fisher or Novetzke, nor discount the valuable efforts they make toward understanding dimensions of performance, material display, textual transmission, and affective experience.
77. See Daud Ali's introduction to Inden 2006: 3.
78. Novetzke 2016: 42.
79. Novetzke (2016: 179–180) refers to the role of one particular woman devotee in memorizing the text of the *Lilacharitra* and thus preventing its disappearance.
80. On these issues, see Novetzke 2016: 57–73.

81. Novetzke 2016: 203.
82. Novetzke 2016: 206; the trial is recounted on 205.
83. On this see Novetzke 2016: 43. I share the critical concerns of Sherman 2018.
84. Novetzke 2016: 207, with a note suggesting a parallel with the Sixth Amendment of the US Constitution.
85. Discussion of the trial can be found in Novetzke 2016: 201–210.
86. See Manu 8.11: *yasmindeshe nisidanti vipra vedavidastrayah / Rajnashca prakrito vidvan brahmaṇastaṃ sabhaṃ viduh*; translated in Olivelle 2005: 123.
87. Novetzke 2016: 205.
88. Novetzke 2016: 205.
89. On the court as "an arena of activity and knowledge," see Ali 2004: 5.
90. Inden 1992: 575n23.
91. See Briggs 1852 for a sense of the early colonial moment when Parsi *panchayat*s in Bombay began to articulate themselves in relation to the new legal and bureaucratic authority coming into view in relation to British power.

4. On the Road with Nilakantha

1. I first viewed the film, produced by BAPS Charities, at the New Delhi Akshardham complex in 2013.
2. Shrivastava 1981: 86.
3. Nilakantha is none other than Swaminarayan, the highest Lord: *swaminarayano nilakantho narayano harih | harikrishnashca sahajanandah krishno 'stu me hrdi*; SSJ 1.4.2.
4. Schreiner 2001: 159; on *satsang*, see Parekh 1980: 98.
5. The text comprises more than sixteen thousand Sanskrit verses.
6. Schreiner 2001: 167. I am not suggesting that Burgess was correct in saying that Sahajanand was an "imposter" who played on the "credulity" of his followers (1872: 331).
7. On the theological agenda of the text, see Dave 1974: 228–234.
8. Schreiner 2001: 164–166.
9. At SSJ 2.37.18, the place name is given as Chuppaya. Mallison gives the parents' names as Hari Prasad and Premavati (1973: 2).
10. See SSJ 2.37.22.
11. See SSJ 2.37.25.
12. Quoting from Burgess 1872: 332, which appears to refer to an account originally found in BC: chs. 22–23.
13. See SSJ 1.2.21 and Dave 2006: 71. On the authorship of the text, see Jani and Schreiner 2016.
14. I refer both to ancient Indian tropes for renunciation and to the work of Tavakoli-Targhi 2001.
15. SSJ 2.24.12.
16. See BC: ch. 26.

17. On such activity, see Cohn 1964 and Kolff 1971.
18. Manilal Parekh quoted in Williams 2001: 14.
19. See Eck 2012: 22.
20. SSJ 2.37.27–29. See Schreiner 2001: 164.
21. SSJ 1.44.11–13.
22. SSJ 1.45.28–29.
23. SSJ 1.45.35.
24. See Tambs-Lyche 2001: 267.
25. David Curley explores how the premodern *Gauri Mangala* sheds light on routes linking sites like Baidyanath in Jharkhand to temples in Bengal such as Tarapith (Curley nd).
26. The vitality of trade, commerce, and travel during this period is depicted with great detail in Bayly 1983. On Mughal urbanization and roadways, see Naqvi 1972.
27. Eck 2012 highlights the integrative quality of South Asian sacred geography but maps that sacred geography only in relation to the boundaries of the Indian nation-state.
28. Dasgupta 1982: 50.
29. Letter dated "Bengall March 31st 1771." Oriental and India Office Collections H/765, 220–221. On revenue collection by fakirs, see Dasgupta 1982: 26–27.
30. Letter to the Reverend Thomas Burrington, dated August 30, 1766. Oriental and India Office Collections H/765, 155–166. Majnu Shah was involved in an important conflict at Bogra in 1777; see Lorenzen 1978: 74.
31. On British fears of sedition, see Bayly 1999: 147. On the discursive legacy of the Sannyasi, see Ghosh 1930 and Bhattacharya 2014, along with Pinch 2006.
32. Quoted in Dasgupta 1982: 46–74, from Ghosh 1930.
33. See Ghosh 1930, Dasgupta 1982, and Bhattacharya 2012.
34. See Dasgupta 1982 and references in Ludden 2012: 495–496.
35. Beveridge 1878: 91.
36. More than a century ago the river was reported to be "an insignificant stream" that was "scarcely navigable" except during the rainy season (Beveridge 1878: 88).
37. Beveridge 1878: 89. The PP lists the Karatoya as one of Bharatvarsha's great rivers (III.6.1.27–30). The river is celebrated in the Mahabharata, where it is identified with the Kingdom of Virata where the Pandavas hid themselves from the Kauravas; see Beveridge 1878: 90; also MBh 3.85.3 and Hazra 1987: 162.
38. In Varanasi, Rani Bhabani helped renovate existing Shiva temples and constructed the famous Durga Mandir; see Desai 2017: ch. 4.
39. On these and related developments, see McDermott 2011.
40. Gupta 1910: 119.
41. Gupta 1910: 162.
42. The text refers to thousands who worshipped "inferior deities" (*kshudra-devata*); SSJ 1.46.3.

43. The Rani was a patron of the famous Kali temple at Tarapith, a well-known center for Tantra.
44. In the *Satsangi Jivanam*, along with black arts, Bengal is associated with torrential rains, which play a part in the eventual defeat of the yogis; see SSJ 1.46.15.
45. The scene is retold in SSJ 1.24, which features an "ugly, black-limbed priest" (*dushpratigrahakrishnanga vipra*) and "proud spiritual adepts" (*siddhabhimanishakta*).
46. See SSJ 1.46.46: *ananyasiddham nijasadhubhavam nodricyate sma prathayan harih sah.*
47. The English translation of the first *prakarana* of the *Satsangi Jivanam* employs loaded phrases like "black magic powers" (*siddhatamasamantra*; SSJ 1.46.4) and "unholy association" (*kaulasanga*; SSJ 1.47.6).
48. For brief details, see Beveridge 1878: 94. On sannyasis in the area around Bogra and Mahasthan, see Dasgupta 1992: 44; see also the tables in Ghosh 2014: 287–294.
49. Pinch 2003 offers a compelling reading of George Grierson's role in promoting a Protestant vision of reformed Indian religion in the late colonial era.
50. The SSJ depicts Nilakantha traveling with larger groups (SSJ 1.47.1).
51. On the Dasnamis generally, see Clark 2006. On the Dasnami Sannyasis and Madari Sufi fakirs, see Ghosh 1930 and 2014.
52. Beveridge mentions two other rulers living in the vicinity of Jogir Bhaban (1878: 94–95).
53. SSJ 1.47.4–6.
54. SSJ 1.47.8.
55. SSJ 1.47.13: *eka eva hi siddho 'smi sampratam bhuvi napara.*
56. SSJ 1.47.57.
57. Nilakantha's time in Navalaksha is recounted in SSJ 1.48.
58. See VA Partharo: 16.
59. Sen 1884: 3.
60. Lewin (1869: 6) speaks of "inflammable gas" rising in great quantity.
61. These sites are not indicated on Eck's map of Hindu sacred geography (2012: xii).
62. O'Malley 1908:189–190.
63. The site is mentioned in modern Bengali *tirtha* manuals, such as Ghosh 1910: 94–95.
64. Sen 1884: 7.
65. Nilakantha often pauses for three days in specific locales. This is the length of time he undertakes fasting, either intentionally or through lack of available food. In texts like the *Padma Purana*, pilgrims are enjoined to undertake three-day fasts at major *tirthas*, including beside the Karatoya River (see PP III.39). Fasting in Sahajanand's later teaching supports the goal of calmness or tranquility (*upasham*), which is necessary in order to overcome the dominance of the senses and the dangers of rebirth; see VA Amdavad 8.28.

66. Sen 1884 provides extensive quotation from a range of such sources.

67. Dev 2007.

68. The dispute is mentioned briefly in Sen 1884: 8.

69. Quoting a colonial-era petition discussed by Thomas Newbold (unpublished ms). I am grateful to him for sharing his paper and directing me to Sen 1884.

70. There is some ambiguity here, since the SSJ tells us that when he left Barava Kund he headed in a southeasterly direction (*agnidisha*); that would take him into present day Myanmar. For the direction to be true, Nilakantha would have to have set off from somewhere in northwestern Bengal or Bihar. Although there are hot springs near Bakreshwar and Gaya, these do not fit with the rest of Nilakantha's itinerary along the far eastern frontier.

71. The *Padma Purana* indicates that one who fasts at Ganga Sagar receives ten times the fruits of performing the royal Ashvamedha sacrifice (PP III.39.4).

72. SSJ 1.48.13.

73. SSJ 1.48.77.

74. VA, Gadhada I.10.1–7.

75. Drawing on ideas developed in Hegarty 2009.

76. Quoting from Inden's essay, "Hierarchies of Kings in Early Medieval India," in Inden 2006: 156; see also Inden et al. 2000: 30; see also Inden 1985: 54.

77. On mastery and lordship, see his "Lordship and Caste in Hindu Discourse" in Inden 2006: 160–178.

5. Upcountry with Rammohun

1. See his essay on Rammohun from *Charitra-puja* in Tagore 1995: 2.

2. Chakrabarti 1935.

3. On this, see Hatcher 2001.

4. See Collet 1914: 7.

5. Chanda and Majumdar 1938: xxviii.

6. Brajendranath Bandyopadhyay refers to such reports as *kimvadanti*, or "hearsay" (1972: 13). On the kinds of records Carpenter had on hand, see Carpenter 1833b: 100.

7. See the preface to RRGift.

8. See RRET 223–225. Carpenter gives his age as fifteen, while acknowledging that the letter indicates he was sixteen (1833b: 101).

9. The letter in which Rammohun's statement appears was published in the *Athenaeum* on October 5, 1833. It is reprinted in RRET: 223–225. The authenticity of the letter was questioned by Collet (1914: 7 and 249), but it has been defended by Killingley (1993: 20).

10. Quoted in Collet 1914: 5.

11. Following data found in Arnot 1833 and Carpenter 1833b; see Ghani 2015.

12. See Carpenter 1833b: 100–101 and Mitter 1845; refracted in later works like Chattopadhyay 1880 and Collet 1914.

13. Sen (2012: 33) has questioned these claims about time spent studying in Patna and Varanasi, but I don't find his refutation compelling enough to reject this portion of Rammohun's biography.
14. RRET: 224.
15. See Ghose 1978: 37.
16. RRET: 223.
17. Quoting from RRET: 223.
18. On this era in Bengal, see Ray 1979.
19. Quoting from RRET: 223.
20. See Kumkum Chatterjee 2008 and 2010.
21. See for example, Nandy 1991.
22. Carpenter 1833b: 100. Rammohun was a Brahmin of the Bandyopadhyay clan, many of whom would have employed the surname Sharma for official purposes.
23. See Chanda and Majumdar 1938.
24. See Calkins 1970. On the Burdwan Raj, see McLane 1993.
25. Desai 2017 stresses the role played by Mughal and later Indo-Islamic traditions in shaping the lived space of a city like Varanasi.
26. Boyk 2015: ix.
27. See Ghani 2015: 60.
28. Boyk 2015: 58.
29. Carpenter 1833b: 101.
30. Ghani 2015: 59–60.
31. See Alam 2004: 98.
32. An important early study is Seal 1933; Sarkar 1985 remains important.
33. On this, see Killingley 1993: 20.
34. Tavakoli-Targhi 2001.
35. Tavakoli-Targhi 2001: 9. See also Tavakoli-Targhi 2011.
36. For a translation, see RRGift, first published in 1884.
37. Banerjee 2015: 89.
38. Ghani 2015: 58, though I disagree that the work is primarily a critique of Hinduism as Ghani suggests.
39. RRGift: 1.
40. RRGift: 2.
41. RRGift: 24–25.
42. Collet 1914: 11.
43. See Scott 2016.
44. Arnot 1833: 198.
45. See Ghani 2015: 59–60. This is different from concluding that *Tuhfat* is an immature work, as Rajnarain Bose does in his preface to RRGift.
46. Ray 1976: 69.
47. See Ernst 2003.
48. Ray 1976: 73 contrasts the emotional language of *Jawab* with the cooler reasoning of *Tuhfat*.

49. For more on *Jawab*, see Ghani 2015: 73–74 and Biswas 1983: 581.

50. Rammohun's respect for Islam may be gauged by the number of Arabic sayings of Muhammad, including the *shahada* or "profession of faith," he cites; RRET: 598–600. See also Collet 1914: 14.

51. RRGift: 25. Notice that Rammohun closes *Tuhfat* by saying he had to rush it into print so as "to avoid any future change . . . by copyists."

52. Another Persian text of importance to Rammohun was the Sufistic Masnavi; see Mitter 1845: 366.

53. RRGift: preface. On the *Dabistan,* see Ali 1999 and Behl 2011.

54. Robertson 1995: 97–109 and Sarkar 1985.

55. Gould 2016 focuses on Akhundzada (1812–1878), who shared with Rammohun the borderless world of Indo-Iranian intellectual life.

56. RRGift: 6.

57. Dasgupta 2016: 31. For Tusi's *Akhlaq-i Nasiri,* see Wickens 1964.

58. See Dasgupta 2016: 157–158, drawing on Kinra 2015 and Alam 2004.

59. Dasgupta 2016: 159.

60. Alam 2004: 66.

61. RRGift: 24–25.

62. Quoting Alam 2004: 66 and RRGift: 6.

63. Wickens 1964: 78. On Tusi as someone who fostered scientific inquiry alongside ethics and metaphysics, see Hodgson 1977: 2.475.

64. *Amal,* "clerk," *sheristadar,* "head writer"; *munshi,* "teacher"; and *diwan,* "minister," or, in this case, perhaps, "secretary"; see Robertson 1995: 18–22; at this time appointments to such positions depended on the patronage of particular employers (Dasgupta 2016: 85).

65. Dasgupta 2016: 84.

66. See Bray 2009. Robertson suggests the Bhutan mission may have been the trip to Tibet that Rammohun mentioned to Lant Carpenter in later years (1995: 22).

67. Sen 1942: iii.

68. See Chatterjee 2013 for a masterful mapping of this world.

69. Dasgupta 1992: 76.

70. See Sen 1942: 15, on the properties acquired by Sarbananda in collusion with his royal patron.

71. Dasgupta 1992: 78–79. A classic case would be the Dasnami sadhu Puran Gir, who assisted Warren Hastings efforts to open diplomatic relations with Lhasa.

72. Leonard 1879: 23; see Hunter 1876, vol. 7: 224.

73. On Tibet, see Mitter 1845: 361. Bandyopadhyay says Rammohun nowhere mentions having spent time in Tibet (1972: 14).

74. Chatterjee 2013: 102–103.

75. Adopting a phrase from Bergmann 2016, speaking of the colonial history of a trans-Himalayan community.

76. On Rangpur as *preparatio reformata,* see Sarma 1944: 74; see Shastri 1911: 21.

6. The Guru's Rules

1. See Schreiner 1999. There are nods to texts like the Mahabharata as well; see SSJM 1.4.5.
2. I read the *Satsangi Jivanam* in light of Inden's thoughts on the *Vishnudharmottara Purana*; see Inden et al. 2000: 29–98.
3. See Hawley 2015: 60 and 67–68 on the *Bhagavata Mahatmya*.
4. SSJM 1.1.11.
5. See SSJM 1.1.30: giving guidance in all matters of observance (*sakaladharmavinirnaya*).
6. SSJM 1.2.42 and 1.1.53–54.
7. See Patel 2017.
8. Modern hagiographers differ on how to treat the two years between Sahajanand's arrival in Gujarat and his assumption of leadership over the Sampraday; some, like Dave 1974, pay no attention to this period, as is pointed out by Tambs-Lyche (2001: 271).
9. SSJ 2.7.3–5.
10. At this time Sahajanand purged his community of two women ascetics who had contested his views on segregation of the sexes.
11. See SSJ 1.3.47–48. Chapter colophons describe the work as a life of the Lord and a code of duty (*shri satsangi-jivana narayana-charitra dharmashastra*).
12. SSJ 2.7.74; compare *na svatantryena kartavyam* (Manu 5.147) at (SSJ 2.7.75).
13. SSJ 2.7.101.
14. SSJ 2.7.107–108. When the Rev. William Mill met a member of the Sampraday in 1822 he noted that the latter brought with him the "Narayana Gita textbook in Sanscrit slogans"; MSMill: folio 24. This suggests the text originated during Sahajanand's day.
15. SSJ 2.16.31. Elsewhere Sahajanand speaks of "our Satsang"; VA, sect. 252 (Gadhada 3–30): 642.
16. SSJ 2.16.51. Mirroring the *dharmashastra* tradition, Sahajanand allows Brahmins to perform such rites in cases of emergency (*apad*).
17. Brahmbhatt (2018: 13) views this as one of two texts given "scriptural" status, alongside the *Vachanamrut*.
18. However, it now appears there was an earlier recension composed in 1823, which was later supplanted; see Chag 2016.
19. *Likhami sahajanandasvami sarvan nijashritan nanadeshasthitan shikshapatrim;* SPS: 15 (v. 2). This is the same as SSJ 4.44.2. On the presence of a version of the *Shikshapatri* within the *Satsangi Jivanam* (at 4.44) see Jani and Schreiner 2016. They venture the possibility that what Sahajanand originally composed could have been a Gujarati prose work that was later re-created in Sanskrit *anustubh* meter by Shatanand Muni. Though Jani and Schreiner do not mention it, this would be consistent with the fact that Shatanand Muni

translated Sahajanand's Gujarati discourses in the *Vachanamrut* into Sanskrit under the title *Harivakyasudhasindhu*; see Dave 2006.

20. Brahmbhatt 2018: 4–5.
21. *Sacchashtranam samuddhrtya sarvesham saram atmana*; SPS: 607; cp. SPE: 771.
22. SPE: 771.
23. Chag 2016: 176.
24. SPS v. 209, translation by Dave 1974: 258. Monier-Williams glosses *rupa* as "representative" (SPE: 772); Briggs chooses the language of "image" (1849: App. E, xxiv).
25. SPNM from 1862 includes as frontispiece an image of the seated Sahajanand framed by the words, "This is the very form of the author of the Siksapatri, Sahajanand."
26. We know Sahajanand wrote often; see HLA 9, chapters 7–10 and SSJ 1:54.43.
27. See Briggs 1849: App. E, xxiv.
28. SPE: 733; cp. Monier-Williams 1877: 146n1; see also Chag 2016: 195.
29. An account is given in the late-nineteenth-century HLA; see Williams and Trivedi 2016: 86–89. Both Chag (2016: 183) and Patel (2017: 81n36) note the importance of this moment within the Sampraday's historiography and visual culture.
30. On acknowledging the sovereignty of rulers, see VA, sect. 202 (Vartal 2.5): 524.
31. Parekh 1980: 87 (no source provided for the quotation).
32. See v. 23 in SPE: 753.
33. See v. 149 in SPE: 766.
34. See v. 46 in SPE: 755.
35. Nor does it make sense to invoke anodyne notions of religious tolerance, as one finds in Desai 1970: 12–13.
36. See v. 120, quoting from the translation in Briggs 1849: App. E, xx.
37. See SPS: 455.
38. Mallison 1973: 5 and Tambs-Lyche 2001: 274.
39. See v. 120; SPE: 763.
40. See vv. 81–82 in SPS: 235 and SPE: 759.
41. See v. 121 in SPE: 763. Sahajanand also situates his authority in relation to the Vedas, Upanishads, Bhagavad Gita, various Smriti texts, and the Puranas; see vv. 93–95; on this, see Brahmbhatt 2018: 14.
42. On religion and place, see Smith 1987.
43. See v. 69, following the Sanskrit terms found in SPS: 221.
44. See VA, sect. 135 (Loya 17): 320–324. While I have consulted the Gujarati original, VAG is not paginated for easy citation.
45. VA: 321.
46. VA: 324.
47. One of few occasions in the *Vachanamrut* when Sahajanand refers to the presence of British rulers in western India; see also VA, sect. 129 (Panchala 3) and sect. 236 (Gadhada III.13).

48. SSJ 2:34.31–36; cp. SSJ 1:21.
49. SSJ 2:34.38–43, the last verse of which proclaims, "This is the ten-fold dharma protected by that greatest of kings."
50. SSJ 2:34.45.
51. See SSJ 2.35. Jani and Schreiner suggest the figure may have been Col. Ballyntine, who is mentioned in records from the period; see SSJSum: 176n228.
52. SSJ 2:36.57–58: *dhrtaveshah sukhenaiva bhumau vicaratanaghah!*
53. This manuscript, with the alternate spelling *Shiksapattri* (see SPMs), is said to have made its way into the collection of the Bodleian Library at Oxford, and contemporary Satsangis view it as what Avni Chag calls a modern "relic." However, Chag reveals that the Bodleian manuscript was not copied until after Sahajanand's death and so therefore could not bear the traces of contact with the guru (Chag 2016).
54. The interplay among different scales of authority is registered in a comment quoted by William Hodge Mill in his diary wherein a member of the Swaminarayan community told him that when Satsangis complained to the Gaekwad court about being persecuted, they were told, "If it is an affair of you Vaishnavas—*look ye to it*'; WHMill: folio 24.
55. On Malcolm and Sahajanand, see Purohit 2012. As we shall see, the young community formed relationships with many Britons; for details, see Williams and Trivedi 2016: 58–93.
56. Williams 2001: 5.
57. See for instance, Hardiman 1988.
58. Patel 2017: 81n36.
59. Heber 1829: 3, 38.
60. Patel 2017: 50.
61. See SSJ 1.10, wherein demonic actors are identified with Shakta and Shaiva teachers of false doctrines, who promote the use of alcohol and animal sacrifice; with people who dress like ascetics but carry weapons; and with those who craft new books that corrupt the teachings of the Veda.
62. Patel 2017: 66.
63. See Agamben 2013. In Philip Gorski's terms, *satsang* involves two types of discipline: self-discipline and communal discipline. As he notes, the communal dimension tends to ensure the most long-lasting effects (2003: 32–33).
64. VA, sect. 8 (Gadhada I.8): 8.
65. VA, sect. 236 (Gadhada III.13): 598.
66. SV:6.4.
67. VA, sect. 129 (Panchala 3): 346. The five vows for sadhus are celibacy, nongreed, detachment from pleasures of taste, detachment from bodily pleasure, and humility. For householders, the five vows are no theft, no adultery, no meat eating, no alcohol, no forcing of anyone to change their duties of social class or station in life.
68. VA, sect. 129 (Panchala 3): 346.

69. Agamben 2013: 86.
70. Agamben 2013: 26.
71. SSJM 1.2.2.
72. Patel 2017: 68.
73. Agamben 2013: 58.
74. VA, sect. 252 (Gadhada 3–30): 642; and VA, sect. 217 (Vartal 17): 556.
75. SSJ 2.7.100: *snanam dhyanam hareh puja japashcha gunakirtanam / satsangash-cheti sarvesham shatkarmani dinedine.*
76. Schreiner 2001: 159, referring only to SSJ, but usefully applied here to all three texts. Paramtattvadas (2017: 45) views the VA as the most authoritative source for Swaminarayan theology.
77. Brahmbhatt 2018 examines evidence from later texts like the *Shri Hari Digvijaya* (mid-nineteenth century) regarding attacks on the Sampraday's scriptural bona fides.
78. VA sect. 218 (Vartal 18.3): 556; see Dave 1974: 226–227.
79. VA sect. 218 (Vartal 18.14): 560.
80. *Lekh* 1826 is an online version (in Gujarati and English); the text may not be definitive.
81. The document, in Devanagari, was signed by both Ayodhyaprasad and Raghuvir and witnessed by the copyist Shukamuni, two other local leaders, and several sadhus.
82. On Dwarka as a point of reference in the articulation of royal and spiritual power, see Sheikh 2017: 126.
83. See Inden 1990: 231–232.
84. Mallison 1973: 9.
85. Mallison 2016: 51. For more on the acharyas, see Williams 1984: 25–27.
86. By way of contrast, the Vallabha Sampraday owed its "distinctive forms" not to the original work of Vallabha as much as to the achievements of his son Vittalnath (Hawley 2015: 187).
87. See *Lekh*, v. 12.
88. See *Lekh*, v. 15.
89. See *Lekh*, v. 13.
90. Quoting Inden 1990: 220.
91. Williams 1984: 25.
92. Overall, Sahajanand established six temples during his lifetime, in Ahmedabad, Bhuj, Vartal, Junagadh, Dholera, and Gadhada.
93. Williams denies that Sahajanand took the idea of "dioceses" from the British (1984: 28), but the very use of this term is curious.
94. H. T. Dave wrongly gives the impression that Sahajanand only reluctantly turned to temple-building as a concession to the lower faculties of ordinary beings; see 1974: 163.
95. Or perhaps nearly simultaneously with the promulgation of the *Shikshapatri*, a recension of which may have existed as early as 1823; see Chag 2016: 200.

96. See SSJ 4.25.5, where the people of Ahmedabad (called Shrinagar in the text) come to him and say, *Bhagavan! Puramasmakam kripaya ayatumarhasi | vidhatum mandiram tatra sarveshamasti manasam.*

97. Heber expressed dismay at being petitioned by Sahajanand for assistance in acquiring land for a temple he hoped to build in Kheda (1829: 3.51).

98. Dunlop appears to be the source of that report; see Paramtattvadas and Williams 2016: 68.

99. As before, SSJ 4.27.6 records the direct speech of the residents of Vartal, indicating their gift of land for construction of a temple to Lord Krishna.

100. Dave comments on the "tough characters" Sahajanand brought around to his views (1974: 111).

101. See SSJ 2.19 on promoting nonviolence among the *mahashaktas*.

102. Mallison 1973: 11.

103. I allude to Shodhan 2001: 30–39.

104. Inden 1990: 221.

7. The Raja's *Darbar*

1. See Hatcher 2014.

2. Crawford 1987: 232.

3. Müller 1884: 29.

4. Ali 2004: 108.

5. Inden 2006.

6. Ali 2004: 108.

7. Ramkanta's role at Burdwan is reviewed in McLane 1993: ch. 13.

8. Relevant official records may be found in Chanda and Majumdar 1938.

9. Ramakanta's fortunes crashed around 1799–1800, and he died in 1803. By this time Rammohun was in service with the British, and his fortunes were strong enough to celebrate his father's *shraddh* in Calcutta.

10. The land near Burdwan was acquired in 1799; see Crawford 1987: 9.

11. On this see the relevant chapters in Hatcher 1996a and 2014.

12. Bandyopadhyay reports an early colonial publication that listed Rammohun as a prominent Baniyan in Calcutta (1972: 39).

13. The list of leaders who paid calls on Rammohun after he established himself in Calcutta is impressive; see TP 50: 90 and Bandyopadhyay 1972: 39.

14. Quoting from an unpublished paper by Mukhopadhyay 2017; for more on *baithak-khana*, see Hatcher 2018: 83.

15. Chakrabarti 1935: 174. For Rammohun's evocation of the courtly demeanor of a just ruler, see the short piece entitled *Itihas* [History] he wrote for the newspaper *Sambad Kaumudi* (RRBV: 787).

16. On the importance of a ruler's self-discipline, see Ali 2004: 240. Gorski's work, which draws on Norbert Elias, suggests there is a top-down element to this mode of self-discipline, with its roots in the ethos of a mannered court; see 2003: 29–31.

17. Sanskrit pandits attended the meetings of the Atmiya Sabha to receive the gifts typically given by rulers to Brahmins. Later, some denigrated Rammohun for his pretensions; see TP 50: 90.

18. Ali 2004: 135–136.

19. Ali 2004: 102.

20. See Ali 2004: 164. Rabindranath made much of Rammohun's *tejas*; see Tagore 1995: 2.791.

21. Ron Inden commented (personal communication) on the obvious parallel here between Rammohun's stately home in Calcutta and the culture of gentlemen and country houses in Georgian Britain, which in Rammohun's day was still characterized by an obsession with social rank, titles, and recognition at court.

22. Chakrabarti 1935: 175.

23. Chakrabarti 1935: 175.

24. Macdonald 1879: 20.

25. Bandyopadhyay (1972: 40–41) tells us Rammohun lived in "Persian style."

26. Mitter 1845: 364.

27. Mitter 1845: 365.

28. See Chattopadhyay 1880: 29 and Collet 1914: 21.

29. Crawford 1987: 16.

30. Rammohun's propertied status led some to question his ability to adequately address zamindar oppression before Parliament; see the *Bengal Hukaru* as quoted in Sarkar 1985: 11.

31. See Chattopadhyay 1880: 26.

32. Collet 1914: 17.

33. Chattopadhyay 1880: 27.

34. Evidence from Jyotirmoy Dasgupta, qtd in Crawford 1987: 16.

35. Ali 2004: 44; Willis 2009: 169–182; Inden 1992.

36. Bandyopadhyay 1939: 192; see also Bandyopadhyay 1980.

37. See Willis 2009: 169; on the secret role of the *purohit*, see 181.

38. Nandakumar was twelve years Rammohun's senior and hailed from Palpara, a town nearby Rammohun's birthplace.

39. Robertson (1995: 13n10) views this as unlikely. In any case Nandakumar was originally initiated into the Dasnami Sampraday, as suggested by his title Tirtha. Later he was initiated into the Avadhuta order of tantric asceticism, taking the additional title of Kulavadhuta.

40. See Biswas 1960. The Mahanirvana Tantra (Avalon 1929) occupied an important place in Rammohun's theological repertoire. When the Brahmo Samaj published a version of the text in 1876 it was accompanied by the commentary of Hariharananda.

41. Willis refers to the merger of the roles of *purohit* and guru in classical courts (2009: 317n66).

42. Shastri 1911: 21.

43. For an important attempt to query the trope of the break, see Sarkar 1985.

44. Ghose (1978: xi) refers to Rammohun emerging from "rural obscurity" in 1815.
45. An early Baptist missionary publication from 1816 describes Rammohun as a "very rich" Brahmin and Sanskrit scholar; (qtd in Collet 1914: 29).
46. Collet notes that the "fame of his provincial discussions" preceded Rammohun's shift to Calcutta (1914: 29).
47. Mukherjee 1977: 3; on voluntary associations in Calcutta, see Sanyal 1980.
48. Mukherjee 1977: 43. See Bandyopadhyay 1935: 416, which construes the Atmiya Sabha as a "debating body" in which a group of friends discussed "the religious problems facing them and tried to promulgate a doctrine of Hindu monotheism."
49. On the shift from royal court to elite salon in eighteenth-century France, see Elias 1983: 79.
50. Ali 2004: 65.
51. On Dwarkanath, see Kling 1976.
52. On the tensions and eventual failures of this combination, see Sarkar 1985: 11.
53. The classic study on this topic remains Mukherjee 1977.
54. For an early Bengali account, see TP 50. For a short version in English that lists the same early participants, see Shastri 1911: 24.
55. In 1818 the *Monthly Repository* reported that a meeting of the Atmiya Sabha "was crowded with a great number of natives of great respectability"; quoted in Bandyopadhyay 1935: 416.
56. Shastri 1911: 25. Collet (1914: 30) follows this pattern.
57. On courtiers seeking to establish lasting familial bonds with their rulers, see Ali 2004: 36.
58. Mukherjee 1977: 43; there was a "Secretary" (*nirbahaka*); for more, see Hatcher 2018.
59. For a list of his earliest bhaktas, see Chattopadhyay 1880: 38–39. Bipin Chandra Pal remarked that most were attracted by Rammohun's "powerful and fascinating personality" (Pal 1973: 451).
60. See Inden et al. 2000: 31.
61. Bandyopadhyay (1970, vol. 1: 428) construes Krishnamohan Majumdar as Rammohun's "bhakta" (SPSK, 428). Collet indicates Hariharananda was "bound to Rammohun by love" (1914: 33).
62. Collet 1914: 32; on the court, see Ali 2004: 183.
63. On Ramchandra's life, see TP 21.
64. In the ancient Indian court, the *purohit* was charged with rites of well-being, while a second Brahman priest was responsible for knowledge of the Veda; see Inden 1992: 562–563.
65. Collet 1914: 35. One Bengali account uses the equivalent, *chayavat* (TP 50: 90).
66. See the lectures printed in RV.
67. See Inden et al. 2000: esp. 38.
68. See TP 21:166.
69. On this later period, see Hatcher 2008.

70. *Gayatrir artha, om tat sat* of 1818 in RR: 176–179.
71. Tagore 1909: 79; on the role of the Gayatri in initiation, Olivelle 2005: ch. 2.
72. Collet 1914: 132.
73. For details, see Collet 1914: 74–75 and Hatcher 2008: 25–26.
74. One early Bengali account credits Tarachand Chakravarti and Chandrashekhar Deb with asking Rammohun to find a "general place" (*sadharana sthana*) for worship; TP 50: 91.
75. Following TP 50: 91; cp. Collet 1914: 129.
76. The title page of RV identifies the group as the Brahmo Samaj.
77. In Bandyopadhyay 1970, vol. 1: 3.
78. See Hatcher 2018: 81.
79. See, for instance, Ward 1817.
80. Sankara Sastri as quoted in RRET: 90.
81. Rammohun's reply to Sankara Sastri, in RRET: 91.
82. Sources have it that Rammohun once expressed a fear that after his death disputes would break out over which "sect" would claim him as its leader; see the Introduction to RRET: xiii.
83. Leonard 1879: 4.
84. I have not located this tract, but Bose 1882 communicates the message alluded to by Leonard.
85. Collet 1914: 159.
86. Quoting here and below from RRET: 214.
87. For a related exploration of such developments, see Hatcher 2018.
88. See the text of RV.
89. Hatcher 2008: 54.
90. Hatcher 2008: 50.
91. We should speak principally of *bhadralok* identity, since Brahmo values remained largely restricted to members of high-caste, educated, and urbane Hindu society; see Bhattacharya 2005.
92. See Hatcher 2006.

8. The Empire of Reform

1. See Lavan 1977 and Zastoupil 2010.
2. Citing from Carpenter 1833b: 21 and 34, respectively.
3. Carpenter 1833b: 34–35.
4. Carpenter 1833b: np.
5. See Hatcher 2001:139–140.
6. Müller 1884: 29.
7. Banerjee 2018: 91.
8. See Hatcher 2016.
9. Though still unverified, there may be evidence that one British official met Sahajanand as early as 1818; see Paramtattvadas and Williams 2016: 69.

10. On Mill, see Amaladass and Young 1995. Almost a decade later, Rammohun would criticize Mill's approach to translating biblical terms into Sanskrit (see Young 1981: 41–42).

11. See Paramtattvadas and Williams 2016: 60, which draws from Mill's diaries, now preserved in the Bodleian Library, Oxford.

12. On Dunlop's appointment, see Briggs 1849: 213.

13. This memoir may have been the source for the earliest printed account of the Swaminarayan Sampraday, "Memorandum Respecting a Sect lately introduced by a Person calling himself Swamee Naraen," published in the *Bombay Courier* in 1822. The text of Dunlop's memoir is reprinted in Paramtattvadas and Williams 2016: 82–84.

14. My transcription of WHMill: folio 20, dated June 10, Ahmedabad. This differs only slightly from what is found in Paramtattvadas and Williams 2016: 60. I want to thank Richard Fox Young and Raymond Brady Williams for sharing their own work on the diary.

15. These details are found in Paramtattvadas and Williams 2016: 61; cp. 83.

16. WHMill: folios 22–23; cp. Paramtattvadas and Williams 2016: 64.

17. I am indebted to Richard Fox Young for sharing his thoughts on this matter in an email communication from October 29, 2018. On the trope of priestcraft in colonial accounts of reform, see Scott 2016.

18. See Hatcher 2016.

19. WHMill: folio 24.

20. WHMill: folio 25.

21. Paramtattvadas and Williams 2016: 64–66.

22. WHMill: folio 20.

23. Chapter 25 of volume 3 of Heber 1829 includes one of the earliest published European depictions of Sahajanand Swami.

24. Heber 1829: 3.29.

25. See Paramtattvadas and Williams 2016: 73–74.

26. Heber commented wistfully that he once might have commanded a similar degree of devotion from congregants back home; Heber 1829: 3.35.

27. Heber 1829: 3.52.

28. Heber 1829: 3.42.

29. See Paramtattvadas and Williams 2016: 80.

30. Heber discusses his encounter with "Swaamee Narain" early in volume 3, whereas "Ram Mohun Roy" comes up only in some of Heber's correspondence reproduced in the latter half of the same volume.

31. Often this is stated as a kind of truism: "British records show that East India Company officials respected Swaminarayan and his followers because they contributed to social order in a troubled territory" (Paramtattvadas and Williams 2016: 58).

32. Empire fostered a similar ambivalence around the idea of an Indian renaissance. For Brahmos (Shastri 1911), Rammohun had initiated the rebirth of

Indian culture, while for imperialists (Chirol 1910) the only outcome of renaissance was unrest.

33. On Briggs, see Buckland 1906: 52.
34. Briggs 1849: "Prefatory."
35. Briggs 1849: 1–2.
36. See Spurr 1993.
37. Briggs 1849: 3.
38. Briggs 1849: 3.
39. Briggs 1849: 403–404.
40. Allen 2016: 7.
41. Briggs 1959: 2.
42. On Bentinck as an enlightened, liberal, imperial reformer, see Rosselli 1974: 79; on reform as the key to progress in everything from public works to morality, see Sinha 2012.
43. In 1831, one editor in Calcutta sought to parse the distinctive styles among "Hindoo reformers" including Ultra-Radicals, Half-Radicals, and Moderate Reformers; see the selection from *Bengal Hurkaru* (October 26, 1831) in Ghose 1978: 131–132.
44. Auber 1837: 610–615.
45. Auber 1837: 621.
46. Briggs 1849: 336.
47. Briggs 1849: 326.
48. Briggs 1849: 326 (emphasis in original).
49. Briggs 1849: 393.
50. Briggs 1849: 393.
51. See Mufti 2007 and Scott and Ingram 2015.
52. Reproduced in Hill 1753: 217–242.
53. Hill 1753: 225. In quoting Hill, I do not replicate the original typography, in which italics are employed freely.
54. Hill 1753: 224.
55. Hill 1753: 225.
56. See especially Chidester 2014.
57. Hill 1753: 226. Compare the list of religious types he provides on another occasion, from Muftis, Popes, and "Lhamas" to Rabbis, Marabouts, and "Bonzees" (222).
58. Hill 1753: 228.
59. Hill 1753: 231.
60. Hill 1753: 233–234. Hill most likely uses "mopes" to refer to the fabled forest ascetics of India, while his reference to Columbia gestures toward the peoples of the Americas or the "New World."
61. Hill 1753: 235.
62. Hill 1753: 242. Hill warns against being "sure of all" when "knowing nothing" (237).

63. For a short overview of the Radical Enlightenment, see Israel 2017.
64. Hill 1753: 220.
65. Hill 1735: 227, referring directly to the devious tactics employed by the "Papal Pontiff" when fishing for souls.
66. Hill 1735: 235.
67. For the relevant passage, see Briggs 1849: 235–243.
68. See Hatcher 2016.
69. Briggs 1849: 191.
70. Discussed at the end of Chapter 6.
71. Briggs 1849: 235.
72. Briggs 1849: 235.
73. See Pullen 1870. One of the reasons John Malcolm approved of the Maratha ruler Mahadji Shinde was because he stood alone "amid all the mummery" of Indian despotism (qtd in Harrington 2010: 115).
74. Briggs 1849: 235.
75. Briggs 1849: 235.
76. Briggs 1849: 236.
77. See, for instance, Briggs 1849: 311 and 349.
78. Briggs 1849: 237.
79. Briggs 1849: 238.
80. Briggs 1849: 238–239.
81. Briggs 1849: 240.
82. Briggs 1849: 241.
83. Quoted by Briggs 1849: 241.
84. Briggs 1849: 241.
85. Briggs 1849: 241–242.
86. Williams (2001: 29) memorably pairs Pax Britannica with Pax Sahajananda.
87. Briggs wrote in the wake of anxieties around the Reform Bill and at the moment when the Radical Enlightenment was drawing its last breath; on the latter, see Israel 2017: 15.
88. Malcolm, qtd in Harrington 2010: 100.
89. Briggs 1849: 241–242.
90. On Sahajanand's "mesmerism," see Briggs 1849: 236. Dunlop reported on Sahajanand's ability to induce trance (or *samadhi*) in devotees; see Paramtat-tvadas and Williams 2016: 82.
91. Briggs 1849: 242.
92. Briggs 1849: 242.
93. Briggs 1849: 243.
94. Müller 1899: 107.
95. Hill fell prey to the same limitations. In his account of travels through the Ottoman Empire, he praised his patron for balancing admiration for the Turks with recognition of Britain's imperial needs in the region (1709: xxiii).

278 NOTES TO PAGES 225–242

9. Old Comparisons and New

1. Banerjee 2009: 105.
2. For more on this argument and the relevant sources, see Hatcher 2016.
3. Hatcher 2016: 30; see Williams 1984.
4. Ingram 2009 questions the analytic precision of reform, seeing it as an umbrella category subsuming a "multitude of movements, agendas and ideologies" (482).
5. An idea announced with authority in Müller 1899: 83–84.
6. Farquhar 1915: 16.
7. Curiously, in a slightly later work Farquhar gave a one-paragraph summary of the Sampraday as an "active reforming sect" (1920: 318–319).
8. Williams 1984: 24.
9. Paramtattvadas and Williams 2016: 59.
10. The framework is laid out in Jones 1989: 1–4.
11. Jones 1989: 30.
12. Jones 1989: 47.
13. Jones 1989: 3.
14. Jones 1989: 125.
15. Jones 1989: 128.
16. Jones 1989: 38. On the Brahmo Samaj as the first modern Indian voluntary association, see Mukherjee 1977: 43.
17. For more, see Hatcher 2018. One classic definition of *sampraday* can be found in the Amarakosha: *guru-paramparagate sadupadese upacharat tadupadesha-yute jane ca* (see Shodhan 2001: 31).
18. Maine 1861: 170.
19. Curley 2002 discusses the role of the Brahmin *samaj* in articulating ruling polities in the eighteenth-century zamindaris of Nadia and Dacca.
20. Citing from an unpublished manuscript with the author's permission.
21. Travers (unpublished manuscript) is describing Bengal, but the description fits both contexts well.
22. Quoting passim from Inden 1990: 263–267.
23. See Inden 1990: 257.
24. See Inden 1990: 256–262.
25. Inden 1990: 269.
26. Borrowing a term from Bergmann 2016.
27. On Hodgson's model, see Chapter 3.
28. Gorski 2003: 32–33.
29. Hatcher 2008.
30. Gorski 2003: 33.
31. Elias 2000: 366.
32. On this, see Datta 2004: 30–31; on Young Bengal, see Chaudhuri 2012.
33. See the discourses translated in Hatcher 2008: ch. 8.

34. RRET: 485.
35. Here I offer some reflections informed by conversation with Azfar Moin about structures and transformations within modes of sacred kingship. Needless to say, he is not responsible for how I have developed these points.
36. Müller 1884: 29.
37. See Hatcher 2008: ch. 3; see also Hatcher 2006.
38. Quoting from a classic essay by Stark and Bainbridge 1979.
39. See Adcock 2014.
40. See SPS v. 120; SPE: 763.
41. On this, see Hatcher 1999.
42. See Scott 2016: ch. 4.

BIBLIOGRAPHY

Primary Sources

Deshpande, N. A. 1990. *Padma Purana*. [English]. Ancient Indian Tradition and Mythology Series. New Delhi: Motilal Banarsidass.

Gunatitanand, Swami. *Swamini vato*. [Gujarati]. http://anirdesh.com/vato (accessed May 23, 2018).

Mill, W. H. 1822. "Two Months Journal from Poona to Neemuch (via Surat, Baroda, Ahmedabad & Segwaree)." MS Mill 205. Bodleian Library, Oxford University.

Monier-Williams, Monier. 1882. "Sanskrit Text of the Siksha-Patri of the Svami-Narayan Sect." [Sanskrit]. *Journal of the Royal Asiatic Society of Great Britain and Ireland* 14.4: 733–772.

Muktananda, Swami. 1930. *Satsangijivanam Mahatmyam: Shatananda Muni Virachitam*. [Sanskrit]. Vartal: Swami Narayan Temple.

Nishkulanand, Swami. 1969. *Bhaktachintamani* [Gujarati]. Ahmedabad: Swaminarayan Aksharpith. http://www.anirdesh.com/chintamani/# (accessed September 28, 2017).

Roy, Rammohun. 1880. *Raja Rammohan Ray-pranita granthabali* [Bengali]. Edited by Rajanarayan Basu and Anandachandra Vedantavagisha. Calcutta: Adi Brahmo Samaj Press.

———. 1906. *The English Works of Raja Rammohun Roy with an English Translation of "Tuhfatul Muwahhidin."* [English]. Allahabad: Panini Office.

———. 1949. *Tuhfatul Muwahhiddin or A Gift to Deists*. [English]. Translated into English by the Moulavi Obaidullah El Obaide. Calcutta: Adi Brahmo Samaj Press.

————. 1973. *Rammohun-Rachanabali: Samagra Bangla rachana, Samskrita o Pharasi rachanar anubad, patrabali evam pradhan Inreji rachanasaha ek khande sampurna* [Bengali]. Edited by Ajitkumar Ghosh. Calcutta: Haraph Prakashani.

Sahajanand, Swami. 1826. *Desh-Vibhag-no Lekh* [Gujarati]. np. http://www
.swaminarayanvadtalgadi.org/literature/scripture/desh-vibhag-no-lekh/
(accessed August 6, 2018).

————. 1830. *Shikshapattri.* [Sanskrit]. MS. Ind.Inst.Sansk. 72. Bodleian Library, Oxford University. Permalink: https://digital.bodleian.ox.ac.uk/inquire/p
/d8ef0051-3bc6-4589-9353-e40d1921bb1c.

————. 1862. *Sri Sahajananda Swamina lakheli Siksapatri: Nityananda Munini lakheli Gujarati tikasathe* [Sanskrit and Gujarati]. Mumbai: Education Society Press.

————. 1877. *Vachanamrtani.* [Gujarati]. Mumbai.

————. 1924. *Shikshapatri.* [Sanskrit]. With the commentary of Shatanand Muni. Bombay: Nirnaya Sagara Press.

Shatanand, Muni. 1930. *Satsangijivanam; Shatananda Muni Virachitam.* [Sanskrit]. Vartal: Swami Narayan Temple.

Sinha, Kaliprasanna. 1987. *Mahabharata* [Bengali]. Reprint ed. Two Parts. Calcutta: Tuli-Kalam.

Swaminarayan, Bhagwan. 2006. *Vachanamrut: The Spiritual Discourses of Bhagwan Swaminarayan.* [English]. 3rd ed. Ahmedabad: Swaminarayan Aksharpith.

Tattvabodhini Patrika [Bengali]. Vol. 21. Ashvin 1767 [1845].

Tattvabodhini Patrika [Bengali]. Vol. 50. Ashvin 1769 [1847].

Vidyavagish, Ramchandra. 1836. *Parameshvarer upasanabishaye prathama byakhyana abadhi dvadasha byakhyana paryanta.* [Bengali]. Calcutta: np.

Viharilalji, Maharaj. 2011. *Harililamrita* [Gujarati]. Four Parts. 2nd ed. Baroda: Swaminarayan Mandir. http://www.swaminarayanbhagwan.com/wp-content
/uploads/2017/07/HariLilamrut-Part-1.pdf.

Secondary Sources

Adcock, C. S. 2014. *The Limits of Tolerance: Secularism and the Politics of Religious Freedom.* New York: Oxford University Press.

Agamben, Giorgio. 2013. *The Highest Poverty: Monastic Rules and Form-of-Life.* Stanford, CA: Stanford University Press.

Alam, Muzaffar. 1991. "Eastern India in the Early Eighteenth Century 'Crisis': Some Evidence from Bihar." *Indian Economic and Social History Review* 28.1: 43–71.

————. 2004. *The Languages of Political Islam: India, 1200–1800.* Chicago: University of Chicago Press.

Alam, Muzaffar, and Sanjay Subrahmanyam. 2011. "The Making of a Munshi." In *Forms of Knowledge in Early Modern South Asia: Explorations in the Intellectual*

History of India and Tibet, 1500–1800, edited by Sheldon Pollock, 185–209. Durham, NC: Duke University Press.

Alexander, Claire, Joya Chatterjee, and Annu Jalais, eds. 2016. *The Bengali Diaspora: Rethinking Internal Migration.* New York: Routledge.

Ali, Daud. 2004. *Courtly Culture and Political Life in Early Medieval India.* New York: Cambridge University Press.

———. 2012. "The Historiography of the Medieval in South Asia." *Journal of the Royal Asiatic Society* (Third Series) 22.1: 7–12.

Ali, M. Athar. 1999. "Pursuing an Elusive Seeker of Universal Truth: The Identity and Environment of the Author of the Dabistan-i Mazahib." *Journal of the Royal Asiatic Society* 3.9: 365–373.

Allen, Amy. 2016. *The End of Progress: Decolonizing the Normative Foundations of Critical Theory.* New York: Columbia University Press.

Amaladass, Anand, and Richard Fox Young. 1995. *The Indian Christiad: A Concise Anthology of Didactic and Devotional Literature in Early Church Sanskrit.* Anand, Gujarat: Gujarat Sahitya Prakash.

Aquil, Raziuddin, and Partha Chatterjee. 2008. *History in the Vernacular.* Delhi: Permanent Black.

Arnot, Sanford. 1833. "Ram Mohun Roy." *Asiatic Journal and Monthly Register* 12: 195–213.

Asad, Talal. 1993. *Genealogies of Religion: Discipline and Reasons of Power in Christianity and Islam.* Baltimore, MD: Johns Hopkins University Press.

———. 2001. "Reading a Modern Classic: W. C. Smith's *The Meaning and End of Religion.*" *History of Religions* 40.3: 205–222.

Asher, Catherine B., and Cynthia Talbot. 2006. *India before Europe.* New York: Cambridge.

Auber, Peter. 1837. *The Rise and Progress of British Power in India.* 2 vols. London: W. H. Allen.

Avalon, Arthur, ed. 1929. *Mahanirvaṇa Tantra with the Commentary of Hariharananda Bharati.* Tantrik Texts. Vol. 13. Madras: Ganesh and Co.

———. 1972. *The Tantra of the Great Liberation (Mahanirvana Tantra).* New York: Dover Books.

Bakhtin, Mikhail. 1983. *Dialogic Imagination: Four Essays.* Austin: University of Texas Press.

Bandyopadhyay, Brajendranath. 1935. "Societies Founded by Rammohun Roy for Religious Reform." *Modern Review* (January–June): 415–419.

———. 1939. "Hariharananda Tirthaswami Kulavadhuta." *Sahitya-Parishad-Patrika* 46: 192–195.

———. 1970. *Sambad patre sekaler katha.* 2 vols. Calcutta: Bangiya Sahitya Parishad.

———. 1972. "Rammohana Raya." *Sahitya-Sadhak-Charitmala.* No. 16. Calcutta: Bangiya Sahitya Parishad.

———. 1980. "Ramchandra Vidyavagish, Hariharanandanath Tirthaswami." *Sahitya-Sadhak-Charitmala.* No. 9. Calcutta: Bangiya Sahitya Parishad.

Bandyopadhyay, Sekhar. 2004. *Caste, Culture and Hegemony: Social Domination in Colonial Bengal*. New Delhi: Sage.

Banerjea, K. M. 1845. "Transition States of the Hindu Mind." *Calcutta Review* 3: 102–147.

Banerjee, Milinda. 2009. *Rammohun Roy: A Pilgrim's Progress—Intellectual Strands and Premises in Rammohun Roy's Pursuit of Reason, God and Common Sense in Early Modern India*. Kolkata: Centre for Archaeological Studies and Training.

———. 2015. "All This Is Indeed Brahman": Rammohun Roy and a 'Global' History of the Rights-Bearing Self." *Asian Review of World Histories* 3.1: 81–112.

———. 2018. *The Mortal God: Imagining the Sovereign in Colonial India*. New York: Cambridge University Press.

Banerjee, Sumanta. 1989. *The Parlour and the Streets: Elite and Popular Culture in Nineteenth Century Calcutta*. Calcutta: Seagull Books.

Bayly, C. A. 1983. *Rulers, Townsmen and Bazaars: North Indian Society in the Age of British Expansion, 1770–1870*. New York: Cambridge University Press.

———. 1985. "The Pre-History of Communalism: Religious Conflict in India, 1700–1860." *Modern Asian Studies* 19.2: 177–203.

———. 1988. *Indian Society and the Making of the British Empire*. The New Cambridge History of India, II.1. New York: Cambridge University Press.

———. 1999. *Empire and Information: Intelligence Gathering and Social Communication in India, 1780–1870*. New York: Cambridge University Press.

———. 2012. *Recovering Liberties: Indian Thought in the Age of Liberalism and Empire*. New York: Cambridge University Press.

Behl, Aditya. 2011. "Pages from the Book of Religions: Encountering Difference in Mughal India." In *Forms of Knowledge in Early Modern South Asia: Explorations in the Intellectual History of India and Tibet, 1500–1800*, edited by Sheldon Pollock, 210–239. Durham, NC: Duke University Press.

Bergmann, Christoph. 2016. "Confluent Territories and Overlapping Sovereignties: Britain's Nineteenth-Century Indian Empire in the Kumaon Himalaya." *Journal of Historical Geography* 51: 88–98.

Beveridge, H. 1878. "The Antiquities of Bagura (Bogra)." *Journal of the Asiatic Society of Bengal* 47.1: 88–95.

Bhargava, Rajeev, and Helmut Reifeld, eds. 2005. *Civil Society, Public Sphere and Citizenship*. Delhi: Sage Publications.

Bhattacharjee, Malini. 2016. "*Seva*, Hindutva, and the Politics of Post-Earthquake Relief and Reconstruction in Rural Kutch." *Asian Ethnology* 75.1: 75–104.

Bhattacharya, Ananda. 2012. "Reconsidering the Sannyasi Rebellion." *Social Scientist* 40.3/4: 81–100.

———. 2014. "The Peripatetic Sannyasis: A Challenge to Peasant Stability and Colonial Rule?" *Indian Historical Review* 41.1: 47–66.

Bhattacharya, Asutosh. 1964. *Bangla Mangalkabyer Itihas*. Calcutta: Mukherjee.

Bhattacharya, Tithi. 2005. *Sentinels of Culture: Class, Education, and the Colonial Intellectual in Bengal (1848–85)*. New York: Oxford University Press.
Biswas, Dilip Kumar. 1960. "Rammohan Rayer dharmamata o tantrashastra." *Vishva Bharati Patrika* 4: 225–247.
———. 1983. *Rammohan-samiksha*. Calcutta: Sarasvat Library.
———. 1989. "Rammohaner dharmacinta." In *Rammohan Smarana*, edited by Pulinbihari Sen et al., 349–371. Calcutta: Rammohan Ray Smritiraksha-samiti.
Biswas, Liny. 1984. "Evolution of Hindu Temples in Calcutta." *Journal of Cultural Geography* 4.2: 73–85.
Bose, Rajnarain. 1874 [1976]. *Se kal ar e kal*. Edited by B. Bandyopadhyay and S. Das. Calcutta: Bangiya Sahitya Parishad.
———. 1882. "Hindu Theism." *The Theosophist* 3.33 (June): 215–216.
Bose, Ram Chandra. 1884. *Brahmoism; or, History of Reformed Hinduism*. New York: Funk and Wagnalls.
Boyk, David Sol. 2015. "Provincial Urbanity: Intellectuals and Public Life in Patna, 1880–1930." PhD dissertation, University of California, Berkeley.
Brahmbhatt, Arun. 2018. "Scholastic Publics: Sanskrit Textual Practices in Gujarat, 1800–Present." PhD dissertation, University of Toronto.
Bray, John. 2009. "Krishnakanta Basu, Rammohan Ray and Early-Nineteenth Century Contacts with Bhutan and Tibet." *Tibet Journal* 34 (Special Issue): 1–28.
Briggs, Asa. 1959. *The Age of Improvement*. London: Longmans.
Briggs, Henry George. 1849. *The Cities of Gujarashtra: Their Topography and History Illustrated in the Journal of a Recent Tour*. Bombay: Printed at the Times' Press by James Chesson.
———. 1852. *The Parsis or, Modern Zerdusthians: A Sketch*. Bombay: Andrew Dunlop.
Buckland, C. E. 1906. *Dictionary of Indian Biography*. London: Swan Sonnenschein.
Burgess, James. 1872. "Narayan Swami." *Indian Antiquary*. Vol. 1: 331–336.
Calkins, Philip. 1970. "The Formation of a Regionally-Oriented Ruling Group." *Journal of Asian Studies* 29.4: 799–806.
Carpenter, Lant. 1833a. *Brief Notes on the Rev. Dr. Arnold's "Principles of Church Reform"; addressed to the author*. London: Browne and Reid.
———. 1833b. *A Review of the Labours, Opinions, and Character of Rajah Rammohun Roy: In a Discourse, on occasion of his death*. London: Browne and Reid.
Carson, Penelope. 2012. *The East India Company and Religion, 1698–1858*. Rochester, NY: Boydell Press.
Chag, Avni. 2016. "Manuscript as Relic: The Svaminarayana Siksapattri Manuscript in the Bodleian Library, Oxford." *Bodleian Library Review* 29.2: 170–210.
Chakrabarti, Satis Chandra. 1935. *The Father of Modern India: Commemoration Volume of the Rammohun Roy Centenary Celebrations 1933*. Calcutta: Rammohun Roy Centenary Committee.
Chakrabarty, Dipesh. 2000. *Provincializing Europe: Postcolonial Thought and Historical Difference*. Princeton, NJ: Princeton University Press.

Chanda, Ramaprasad, and Jatindra Kumar Majumdar. 1938. *Selections from Official Records and Documents Relating to the Life of Raja Rammohun Roy*. Vol. 1: 1791–1830. Calcutta: Calcutta Oriental Book Agency.

Chatterjee, Indrani. 2013. *Forgotten Friends: Monks, Marriages, and Memories in Northeast India*. New Delhi: Oxford University Press.

———. 2015. "Monastic 'Governmentality': Revisiting 'Community' and 'Communalism' in South Asia." *History Compass* 13.10: 497–511.

Chatterjee, Kumkum. 2008. "The Persianization of 'Itihasa': Performance Narratives and Mughal Political Culture in Eighteenth-Century Bengal." *Journal of Asian Studies* 67.2: 513–543.

———. 2010. "Scribal Elites in Sultanate and Mughal Bengal." *Indian Economic and Social History Review* 47.4: 445–472.

Chatterjee, Partha. 1993. *The Nation and Its Fragments*. Princeton, NJ: Princeton University Press.

———. 2008. "Introduction: History in the Vernacular." In *History in the Vernacular*, edited by R. Aquil and P. Chatterjee, 1–24. Delhi: Permanent Black.

———. 2012. *The Black Hole of Empire: History of a Global Practice of Power*. Princeton, NJ: Princeton University Press.

Chattopadhyay, Nagendra Nath. 1880. *Mahatma Raja Rammohan Rayer Jivanacharita*. Calcutta: Ray Press.

Chaudhuri, Rosinka. 2012a. "Three Poets in Search of History: Calcutta, 1752–1859." In *Trans-colonial Modernities in South Asia*, edited by M. S. Dodson and B. A. Hatcher, 189–207. New York: Routledge.

———. 2012b. *Freedom and Beef Steaks: Colonial Calcutta Culture*. New Delhi: Orient Blackswan.

Chaudhury, Sushil. 1975. *Trade and Commercial Organization in Bengal, 1650–1720*. Calcutta: Firma KLM.

Chidester, David. 1996. *Savage Systems: Colonialism and Comparative Religion in Southern Africa*. Charlottesville: University Press of Virginia.

———. 2014. *Empire of Religion: Imperialism and Comparative Religion*. Chicago: University of Chicago Press.

Chirol, Valentine. 1910. *Indian Unrest*. London: Macmillan.

Clark, Matthew. 2006. *The Dasanami-Sannyasis: The Integration of Ascetic Lineages into an Order*. Leiden: Brill.

Coburn, Thomas B. 1991. *Encountering the Goddess: A Translation of the Devi-Mahatmya and a Study of Its Interpretation*. Albany: State University of New York Press.

Cohn, B. S. 1964. "The Role of the Gosains in the Economy of Eighteenth and Nineteenth Century Upper India." *Indian Economic and Social History Review* 4: 175–182.

Collet, Sophia Dobson. 1914. *Life and Letters of Raja Rammohun Roy*. 2nd ed. Edited by Hem Chandra Sarkar. Calcutta: np.

Collingwood, R. G. 1942. *The New Leviathan, or Man, Society, Civilization and Barbarism*. New York: Oxford University Press.

Copley, Antony, ed. 2003. *Hinduism in Public and Private*. New Delhi: Oxford University Press.

Crawford, S. Cromwell. 1987. *Ram Mohan Roy: Social, Political, and Religious Reform in 19th Century India*. New York: Paragon House Publishers.

Curley, David L. nd. "Goddess Worship and Hindu Kingship in the *Gauri-mangal* by Raja Prithvichandra." Unpublished ms.

———. 2002. "Maharaja Krisnacandra, Hinduism and Kingship in the Contact Zone of Bengal." In *Rethinking Early Modern India*, edited by Richard B. Barnett. 85–117. Delhi: Manohar.

Damen, Frans L. 1983. *Crisis and Religious Renewal in the Brahmo Samaj (1860–1884): A Documentary Study of the Emergence of the "New Dispensation" under Keshab Chandra Sen*. Louvain: Catholic University.

Das, Gurcharan. 2002. *India Unbound: The Social and Economic Revolution from Independence to the Global Information Age*. New York: Random House.

———. 2009. "The Dharma of Capitalism." *Wall Street Journal*, April 21.

———. 2010. *The Difficulty of Being Good: On the Subtle Art of Dharma*. Delhi: Penguin.

Dasgupta, Atis. 1982. "The Fakir and Sannyasi Rebellion." *Social Scientist* 10.1: 44–55.

———. 1992. *The Fakir and Sannyasi Uprisings*. Calcutta: K. P. Bagchi.

Dasgupta, Shomik. 2016. "Ethics, Distance and Accountability: The Political Thought of Rammohun Roy, c. 1803–32." DPhil dissertation, King's College, London.

Datta, Michael Madhusudan. 2004. *The Slaying of Meghanada: A Ramayana from Colonial Bengal*. Translated by Clinton B. Seely. New York: Oxford University Press.

Dave, H. T. 1974. *Life and Philosophy of Shree Swaminarayan*. Edited by Leslie Shepard. London: George Allen and Unwin.

Dave, Jyotindra. 2006. "Sri Harivakyasudhasindhu of Sri Satananda Muni: A Critical Study with Reference to the Original Structure of the Philosophy of Lord Swminarayana as Reflected in Vacanamrtam." PhD dissertation, University of Baroda.

De, Barun. 1977. "A Historiographical Critique of Renaissance Analogues for Nineteenth Century India." In *Perspectives in Social Sciences*, vol. 1, edited by Barun De, 178–218. Calcutta: Oxford University Press.

De, S. K. 1919. *History of Bengali Literature in the Nineteenth Century: 1800–1825*. Calcutta: University of Calcutta Press.

Desai, B. G. 1970. *Ethics of the Shikshapatri*. Baroda: Maharaja Sayajirao University of Baroda.

Desai, Madhuri. 2017. *Banaras Reconstructed: Architecture and Sacred Space in a Hindu Holy City*. Seattle: University of Washington Press.

Dev, Prem Ranjan. 2007. "Sitakunda Shrine and Shiba Chaturdarshi Festival." *New Nation* February 16. https://web.archive.org/web/20070927175457/http://nation.ittefaq.com/artman/exec/view.cgi/62/34085.

Dhingra, Pawan. 201. *Life behind the Lobby: Indian American Hotel Owners and the American Dream*. Albany: Stanford University Press.

Dodson, Michael Sinclair, and Brian A. Hatcher, eds. 2012. *Trans-Colonial Modernities in South Asia*. New York: Routledge.

D'Oyly, Charles. 1848. *Views of Calcutta and Its Environs*. London: Dickenson and Co.

Duara, Prasenjit. 1995. *Rescuing History from the Nation: Questioning Narratives of Modern China*. Chicago: University of Chicago Press.

———. 1998. "The Critique of Modernity in India and China." In *Across the Himalayan Gap: An Indian Quest for Understanding China*, edited by Tan Chung, 77–90. New Delhi: Indira Gandhi National Centre for the Arts.

Duff, Alexander. 1840 [1839]. *India and India Missions*. 2nd ed. Edinburgh: John Johnstone.

———. 1845. "Vedantism, What Is It?" *Calcutta Review* 4.7: 50–61.

Dumont, Louis. 1980 [1960]. "World Renunciation in Indian Religions." In *Homo Hierarchicus: The Caste System and Its Implications*, by Louis Dumont, translated by Mark Sainsbury, Louis Dumont, and Basia Gulati, 267–286. Chicago: University of Chicago Press.

Duncan, Jonathan. 1873. *Selections from the Duncan Records*. Vol. 2, edited by A. Shakespear. Benares: Medical Hall Press.

Eaton, Richard M. 1993. *The Rise of Islam and the Bengal Frontier, 1204–1760*. Berkeley: University of California Press.

Eck, Diana L. 2012. *India: A Sacred Geography*. New York: Three Rivers Press.

Elias, Norbert. 1983. *The Court Society*. Translated by Edmund Jephcott. New York: Pantheon Books.

———. 2000. *The Civilizing Process: Sociogenetic and Psychogenetic Investigations*. Translated by Edmund Jephcott. Revised edition by Eric Dunning, Johan Goudsblom, and Stephen Mennell. Malden, MA: Basil Blackwell.

Ernst, Carl. 2003. "Muslim Studies of Hinduism? A Reconsideration of Arabic and Persian Translations from Indian Languages." *Iranian Studies* 32.3: 173–196.

Ewing, Katherine. 1997. *Arguing Sainthood: Modernity, Psychoanalysis, and Islam*. Princeton, NJ: Princeton University Press.

Farquhar, John Nicol. 1913. *The Crown of Hinduism*. London: Oxford University Press.

———. 1915. *Modern Religious Movements in India*. New York: Macmillan.

———. 1920. *An Outline of the Religious Literature of India*. Oxford: Oxford University Press.

Fisher, Elaine. 2015. "Public Philology: Text Criticism and the Sectarianization of Hinduism." In *Scholar Intellectuals in Early Modern India*, edited by C. Minkowski, P. O'Hanlon, and A. Venkatkrishnan, 50–69. New York: Routledge.

———. 2017. *Hindu Pluralism: Religion and the Public Sphere in Early Modern South Asia*. Berkeley: University of California Press.

Fox, Richard J. 1992. "East of Said." In *Edward Said: A Critical Reader*, edited by
    M. Sprinker, 144–156. Oxford: Blackwell.
Fraser, Nancy. 1993. "Rethinking the Public Sphere: A Contribution to the Critique
    of Actually Existing Democracy." In *Habermas and the Public Sphere*, edited by
    Craig Calhoun, 109–142. Cambridge, MA: MIT Press.
Freitag, Sandria B. 1989. *Collective Action and Community: Public Arenas and the
    Emergence of Communalism in North India*. Berkeley: University of California
    Press.
———. 1991. "Introduction: 'The Public' and its Meanings in Colonial South Asia."
    South Asia: Journal of South Asian Studies 14.1: 1–13.
———. 2015. "Postscript: Exploring Aspects of 'the Public' from 1991 to 2014." *South
    Asia: Journal of South Asian Studies* 38.3: 512–523.
Fuller, C. J. 2004. *The Camphor Flame: Popular Hinduism and Society in India*.
    Rev. ed. Princeton, NJ: Princeton University Press.
Fuller, Jason. 2009. "Modern Hinduism and the Middle Class: Beyond *Reform* and
    Revival in the Historiography of Colonial India." *Journal of Hindu Studies* 2:
    160–178.
Gazetteer of the Bombay Presidency. 1883. Volume 7. Baroda: Government Central
    Press.
Ghani, Kashshaf. 2015. "Vestige of a Dying Tradition: Persian Tract of *Tuhfat
    ul-Muwahhidin* in Nineteenth Century Bengal." *Studia Iranica* 44: 55–81.
Ghassem-Fachandi, Parvis. 2012. *Pogrom in Gujarat: Hindu Nationalism and
    Anti-Muslim Violence in India*. Princeton, NJ: Princeton University Press.
Ghose, Benoy. 1978. *Selections from English Periodicals of 19th Century Bengal*.
    Vol. 1: 1815–1833. Calcutta: Papyrus.
Ghosh, Benoy. 2010. *Pashchim Banger Sanskriti*. Reprint ed. 2 vols. Calcutta:
    Prakash Bhavan.
Ghosh, Jamini Mohan. 1930. *Sannyasi and Fakir Raiders in Bengal*. Calcutta:
    Bengal Secretariat Depot.
———. 2014. *Sannyasi and Fakir Rebellion in Bengal: Jamini Mohan Ghosh
    Revisited*. Edited by Ananda Bhattacharya. Delhi: Manohar.
Ghosh, Suresh Chandra. 1910. *Guru Kripay Tirtha Darshan*. Calcutta: np.
Gilmartin, David. 1988. *Empire and Islam: Punjab and the Making of Pakistan*.
    Berkeley: University of California Press.
Giri, Satyeswarananda. 2002. *Biography of a Yogi*. San Diego, CA: Sanskrit Classics
    Library.
González-Reimann, Luis. 2009. "Cosmic Cycles, Cosmology, and Cosmography."
    In *Brill's Encyclopedia of Hinduism*, vol. 1, edited by Knut Jacobsen, 411–428.
    Leiden: Brill.
Gorski, Philip S. 2003. *The Disciplinary Revolution: Calvinism and the Rise of the
    State in Early Modern Europe*. Chicago: University of Chicago.
Goswami, Manu. 2004. *Producing India: From Colonial Economy to National
    Space*. Chicago: University of Chicago.

Gould, Rebecca. 2016. "The Critique of Religion as Political Critique: Mirz Fatḥ 'Ali Akhundzda's Pre-Islamic Xenology." *Intellectual History Review* 26.2: 171–184.

Graham, Bruce D. 1990. *Hindu Nationalism and Indian Politics: The Origins and Development of the Bharatiya Jana Sangh.* Cambridge, UK: Cambridge University Press.

Graham, J. Reid. 1942. "The Arya Samaj as a Reformation in Hinduism with Special Reference to Caste." PhD dissertation, Yale University.

Green, Nile. 2011. *Bombay Islam: The Religious Economy of the West Indian Ocean, 1840–1915.* New York: Cambridge University Press.

Griswold, H. G. 1934. *Insights into Modern Hinduism.* New York: Henry Holt.

Guha, Ranajit. 1999 [1983]. *Elementary Aspects of Peasant Insurgency in Colonial India.* Durham, NC: Duke University Press.

Gupta, J. N. 1910. *Bogra: District Gazeteers of Eastern Bengal and Assam.* Allahabad: Pioneer Press.

Gupta, Svarupa. 2007. "Samaj, Jati and Desh: Reflections on Nationhood in Late Colonial Bengal." *Studies in History* 23.2: 177–203.

Haberman, David. 1993. "On Trial: The Love of the Sixteen Thousand Gopees." *History of Religions* 33.1: 44–70.

Habermas, Jürgen. 1991. *The Structural Transformation of the Public Sphere.* Translated by Thomas Burger. Cambridge, MA: MIT Press.

Hansen, Thomas Blom. 1999. *The Saffron Wave: Democracy and Hindu Nationalism in Modern India.* Princeton, NJ: Princeton University Press.

Hardiman, David. 1988. "Class Base of Swaminarayan Sect." *Economic and Political Weekly* 23.37: 1907–1912.

Harrington, Jack. 2010. *Sir John Malcolm and the Creation of British India.* New York: Palgrave.

Hasan, Farhat. 2005. "Forms of Civility and Publicness in Pre-British India." In *Civil Society, Public Sphere and Citizenship,* edited by Rajeev Bhargava and Helmut Reifeld, 84–105. Delhi: Sage.

Hatcher, Brian A. 1996a. *Idioms of Improvement: Vidyasagar and Cultural Encounter in Bengal.* Calcutta: Oxford University Press.

———. 1996b. "Indigent Brahmans, Industrious Pandits: Bourgeois Ideology and Sanskrit Pandits in Colonial Calcutta." *Comparative Studies of South Asia, Africa and the Middle East, Special Issue: Divergent Modernities* 16.1: 15–26.

———. 1999. *Eclecticism and Modern Hindu Discourse.* New York: Oxford University Press.

———. 2001. "Great Men Waking: Paradigms in the Historiography of the Bengal Renaissance." In *Bengal: Rethinking History. Essays in Historiography,* edited by Sekhar Bandyopadhyay, 135–163. International Centre for Bengal Studies, no. 29. New Delhi: Manohar.

———. 2004. "Contemporary Hindu Thought." In *Contemporary Hinduism: Ritual, Culture, and Practice,* edited by Robin Rinehart, 179–211. New York: ABC-CLIO.

———. 2006. "Remembering Rammohan: An Essay on the (Re-)emergence of Modern Hinduism." *History of Religions* 46.1: 50–80.

———. 2007. "Sanskrit and the Morning After: The Metaphorics and Theory of Intellectual Change." *Indian Economic and Social History Review* 44.3: 333–361.

———. 2008. *Bourgeois Hinduism, or the Faith of the Modern Vedantists: Rare Discourses from Early Colonial Bengal.* New York: Oxford University Press.

———. 2013. "The Brahmo Samaj and Keshub Chunder Sen." *Brill Encyclopedia of Hinduism*, vol. 5: 437–444. Leiden: E. J. Brill.

———. 2014. *Vidyasagar: The Life and After-life of an Eminent Indian.* New Delhi: Routledge.

———. 2016. "Situating the Swaminarayan Tradition in the Historiography of Modern Hindu Reform." In *Swaminarayan Hinduism: Tradition, Adaptation, and Identity*, edited by R. B. Williams and Y. Trivedi, 6–37. New Delhi: Oxford University Press.

———. 2017a. "India's Many Puritans: Connectivity and Friction in the Study of Modern Hinduism." *History Compass* 15.1: 1–12.

———. 2017b. "Take Me to the River: Religion Seen and Unseen in Early Colonial Bengal." In *In Quest of the Historian's Craft: Essays in Honour of Professor B. B. Chaudhuri*, part 2: Polity, Society and Culture, edited by Arun Bandyopadhyay and Sanjukta Das Gupta, 593–616. New Delhi: Manohar.

———. 2017c. "Translation in the Zone of the Dubash: Colonial Mediations of *Anuvada.*" *Journal of Asian Studies* 76.1: 1–28.

———. 2018. "Imitation, Then and Now: On the Emergence of Philanthropy in Early Colonial Calcutta." *Modern Asian Studies: Special Issue, Charity and Philanthropy in South Asia* 52.1: 62–98.

———. 2019. "Intervening on the Indian Renaissance, or a User's Guide to the Dreary Sands of Dead Habit." *Sophia: International Journal of Philosophy and Traditions* 58.1: 13–17.

Hausner, Sondra. 2007. *Wandering with Sadhus: Ascetics in the Hindu Himalayas.* Bloomington: Indiana University Press.

Hawley, John Stratton. 1991. "Naming Hinduism." *Wilson Quarterly* 15.3: 20–34.

———. 2015. *A Storm of Songs: India and the Idea of the Bhakti Movement.* Cambridge, MA: Harvard University Press.

Haynes, Douglas. 1987. "From Tribute to Philanthropy: The Politics of Gift Giving in a Western Indian City." *Journal of Asian Studies* 46.2: 30.

———. 1991. *Rhetoric and Ritual in Colonial India: The Shaping of a Public Culture in Surat City, 1852–1928.* Berkeley: University of California Press.

Hazra, R. C. 1987. *Studies in the Puranic Records on Hindu Rites and Customs.* Delhi: Motilal Banarsidass.

Heber, Reginald. 1829. *A Journey through the Upper Provinces of India.* 4th ed. 3 vols. London: John Murray.

Hegarty, James M. 2009. "On Platial Imagination in the Sanskrit Mahabharata." *History of Religions* 13.2: 163–187.

Heimsath, Charles H. 1964. *Indian Nationalism and Hindu Social Reform.* Princeton, NJ: Princeton University Press.

Hervieu-Léger, Danièle. 2000. *Religion as a Chain of Memory.* Cambridge, UK: Polity Press.

Hill, Aaron. 1709. *A Full and Just Account of the Present State of the Ottoman Empire in all its Branches, with the Government, and Policy, Religion, Customs, and Way of Living of the Turks, in General.* London.

———. 1753. *The Works of the Late Aaron Hill, Esq.; in Four Volumes.* Vol. 4. London.

Hirst, Jacqueline Suthren, and John Zavos. 2011. *Religious Traditions in Modern South Asia.* New York: Routledge.

Hocart, A. M. 1927. *Kingship.* Oxford: Oxford University Press.

———. 1950. *Caste: A Comparative Study.* London: Methuen.

Hodgson, Marshall. 1977. *Venture of Islam: Conscience and History in a World Civilization.* 3 vols. Chicago: University of Chicago Press.

Hunter, W. W. 1876. *A Statistical Account of Bengal.* London: Trübner and Co.

Huntington, Samuel B. 1996. *The Clash of Civilizations and the Remaking of World Order.* New York: Simon and Schuster.

Inden, Ronald. 1979. "The Ceremony of the Great Gift (Mahadana): Structure and Historical Context in Indian Ritual and Society." In *Asie du Sud, traditions et changements,* 131–136. Paris: Éditions du Centre Nationale de la Recherche Scientific.

———. 1985. "The Temple and the Hindu Chain of Being (Kashmir)." *Purushartha* 8: 53–74.

———. 1986. "Tradition against Itself." *American Ethnologist* 13.4: 762–775.

———. 1990. *Imagining India.* New York: Basil Blackwell.

———. 1992. "Changes in the Vedic Priesthood." *Ritual, State and History in South Asia.* nv: 556–577.

———. 2006. *Text and Practice: Essays on South Asian History by Ronald Inden.* Delhi: Oxford University Press.

Inden, Ronald, Daud Ali, and Jonathan Walters. 2000. *Querying the Medieval: Texts and the History of Practices in South Asia.* New York: Oxford University Press.

Ingram, Brannon. 2009. "Sufis, Scholars and Scapegoats: Rashid Ahmad Gangohi (d. 1905) and the Deobandi Critique of Sufism." *Muslim World* 99: 478–501.

Israel, Jonathan I. 2017. "'Radical Enlightenment': A Game-Changing Concept." In *Reassessing the Radical Enlightenment,* edited by Steffen Ducheyne, 15–47. New York: Routledge.

Jacobsen, Knut A. 2013. *Pilgrimage in the Hindu Tradition: Salvific Space.* New York: Routledge.

Jaffrelot, Christophe. 1996. *The Hindu Nationalist Movement and Indian Politics: 1925 to the 1990s: Strategies of Identity-Building, Implantation and Mobilisation.* London: Hurst.

Jani, Jaydev A., and Peter Schreiner. 2016. "Authorship and Authority in the Sanskrit Literary Tradition of the Swaminarayana Movement: Sikṣapatri and Satsangijivanam." *Asiatische Studien* 70.2: 467–487.

Jani, Jaydev A., and Peter Schreiner. 2017. *The Satsangijivanam by Satananda: The Life and Teachings of Swaminarayan. An English Summary of Contents with Index.* Heidelberg: CrossAsia-eBooks.

Jones, Kenneth W. 1976. *Arya Dharm: Hindu Consciousness in 19th-Century Punjab.* Berkeley: University of California Press.

———. 1989. *Socio-Religious Reform Movements in British India.* The New Cambridge History of India, III.1. New York: Cambridge University Press.

Kane, P. V. 1962. *History of Dharmasastra.* 5 vols. Poona: Bhandarkar Oriental Research Institute.

Kanungo, Pralay. 2002. *The RSS Tryst with Politics: From Hedgewar to Sudarshan.* Delhi: Manohar.

Kaviraj, Sudipta. 1998. *The Unhappy Consciousness: Bankimchandra Chattopadhyay and the Formation of Nationalist Discourse in India.* Delhi: Oxford University Press.

———. 2010. *The Imaginary Institution of India: Politics and Ideas.* New York: Columbia University Press.

Killingley, D. H. 1976. "Vedanta and Modernity." In *Indian Society and the Beginnings of Modernization, c. 1830–1850,* by C. H. Philips and M. Wainwright, 127–140. London: School of Oriental and African Studies.

———. 1981. "Rammohan Roy on the Vedanta Sutras." *Religion* 11:151–169.

———. 1993. *Rammohun Roy in Hindu and Christian Tradition.* The Teape Lectures, 1990. Newcastle upon Tyne: Grevatt and Grevatt.

Kim, Hanna. 2010. "Public Engagement and Personal Desires: BAPS Swaminarayan Temples and Their Contribution to the Discourses on Religion." *International Journal of Hindu Studies* 13.3: 357–390.

———. 2011. "Steeples and Spires: Exploring the Materiality of Built and Unbuilt Temples." *Nidan* 23: 37–52.

Kinra, Rajeev. 2015. *Writing Self, Writing Empire: Chandar Bhan Brahman and the Cultural World of the Indo-Persian State Secretary.* Berkeley: University of California Press.

Kling, Blair. 1976. *Partner in Empire: Dwarkanath Tagore and the Age of Enterprise in Eastern India.* Berkeley: University of California Press.

Kolff, Dirk. 1971. "Sannyasi Trader-Soldiers." *Indian Economic and Social History Review* 8.2: 213–218.

———. 1990. *Naukar, Rajput and Sepoy.* Cambridge, UK: Cambridge University Press.

Kopf, David. 1969a. "Rammohan Roy's Historical Quest for an Identity in the Modern World: The Puritanization of a Hindu Tradition in Bengal." In *Bengal: Regional Identity,* edited by D. Kopf. East Lansing: Michigan State University.

———. 1969b. *British Orientalism and the Bengal Renaissance: The Dynamics of Indian Modernization 1773–1835.* Berkeley: University of California Press.

———. 1970. "The Brahmo Samaj Intelligentsia and the Bengal Renaissance: A Study of Revitalization and Modernization in Nineteenth Century Bengal." In *Transition in South Asia: Problems in Modernization*, edited by R. I. Crane, 7–48. Durham, NC: Duke University Press.

———. 1979. *The Brahmo Samaj and the Shaping of the Modern Indian Mind.* Princeton, NJ: Princeton University Press.

Kurien, Prema. 2006. "Multiculturalism and 'American' Religion: The Case of Hindu Indian Americans." *Social Forces* 85.2: 723–741.

Lavan, Spencer. 1977. *Unitarians and India: A Study in Exposure and Response.* Boston: Beacon Press.

Lele, Jayant. 1995. "Saffronization of the Shiv Sena: The Political Economy of City, State, and Nation." In *Bombay: Metaphor for Modern India*, edited by Sujata Patel and Alice Thorner, 185–212. Delhi: Oxford University Press.

Leonard, G. S. 1879. *A History of the Brahma Samaj, from Its Rise to the Present Day.* Calcutta: W. Newman.

Lewin, T. H. 1869. *The Hill Tracts of Chittagong and the Dwellers Therein; with Comparative Vocabularies of the Hill Dialects.* Calcutta: Bengal Printing Company.

Llewellyn, J. E. 2005. *Defining Hinduism: A Reader.* New York: Routledge.

LMS. 1821. *27th Report of the London Missionary Society.* London: LMS.

Lorenzen, David. 1978. "Warrior Ascetics in Indian History." *Journal of the American Oriental Society* 98.1: 61–75.

Lovett, Richard. 1899. *The History of the London Missionary Society, 1795–1895.* 2 vols. London: Henry Frowde.

Ludden, David. 2003. "Presidential Address: Maps in the Mind and the Mobility of Asia." *Journal of Asian Studies* 62.4: 1057–1078.

———. 2012. "Spatial Inequality and National Territory: Remapping 1905 in Bengal and Assam." *Modern Asian Studies* 46.3: 483–525.

Macdonald, K. S. 1879. *Rajah Ram Mohun Roy: The Bengali Religious Reformer.* Calcutta: The Herald.

Maclean, Kama. 2008. *Pilgrimage and Power: The Kumbh Mela in Allahabad, 1765–1954.* New York: Oxford University Press.

Maine, Henry Sumner. 1861. *Ancient Law.* London: John Murray.

Majumdar, Rochona. 2012. "A Conceptual History of the Social: Some Reflections out of Colonial Bengal." In *Trans-colonial Modernities in South Asia*, edited by M. S. Dodson and B. A. Hatcher, 165–188. New York: Routledge.

Malcolm, John. 1812. *Sketch of the Sikhs; a Singular Nation who inhabit the provinces of the Penjab.* London: John Murray.

Mallison, Françoise, trans. 1973. *L'épouse idéale: La* sati-gita *de Muktananda.* Paris: Institute de civilisation indienne.

———. 1974. "La Secte Krishnaïte des Svami-Narayaṇi au Gujarat." *Journal Asiatique* 262.3/4: 435–471.

———. 2016. "Gujarati Socio-religious Context of Swaminarayan Devotion and Doctrine." In *Swaminarayan Hinduism: Tradition, Adaptation and Identity,* edited by Raymond B. Williams and Yogi Trivedi, 49–57. New Delhi: Oxford University Press.

Marriott, McKim, ed. 1990. *India through Hindu Categories.* New Delhi: Sage.

Marshall, P. J. 1987. *Bengal: The British Bridgehead. Eastern India 1740–1828.* The New Cambridge History of India, II.2. New York: Cambridge University Press.

Masuzawa, Tomoko. 2005. *The Invention of World Religions: Or, How European Universalism Was Preserved in the Language of Pluralism.* Chicago: University of Chicago Press.

Maurice, Frederick Denison. 1852 [1846]. *The Religions of the World and Their Relation to Christianity.* Cambridge, UK: Macmillan.

McCutchion, David J. 1972. *Late Medieval Temples in Bengal.* Calcutta: Asiatic Society.

McDermott, Rachel. 2001. *Mother of My Heart, Daughter of My Dreams: Kali and Uma in the Devotional Poetry of Bengal.* New York: Oxford University Press.

———. 2011. *Revelry, Rivalry and Longing for the Goddesses of Bengal.* New York: Columbia University Press.

McLane, J. R. 1993. *Land and Local Kingship in Eighteenth-Century Bengal.* New York: Cambridge University Press.

Mehta, Makrand. 2002. "The Dalit Temple Entry Movements in Maharashtra and Gujarat, 1930–1948." In *The Other Gujarat: Social Transformations among Weaker Sections,* edited by Takashi Shinoda, 1–21. Mumbai: Popular Prakashan.

———. 2016. "Sahajanand Swami's Language and Communication." In *Swaminarayan Hinduism: Tradition, Adaptation, and Identity,* edited by R. B. Williams and Y. Trivedi, 38–48. New Delhi: Oxford University Press.

"Memorandum respecting a Sect lately introduced by a Person calling himself Swamee Naraen." *Asiatic Journal* (1823); reprinted from an article in the *Bombay Courier* (1822).

Metcalf, Barbara D., and Thomas R. Metcalf, eds. 2012. *A Concise History of Modern India.* 3rd ed. New York: Cambridge University Press.

Metcalf, Thomas R. 1994. *Ideologies of the Raj.* The New Cambridge History of India, III.4. New York: Cambridge University Press.

Minkowski, Christopher, Rosalind O'Hanlon, and Anant Venkatkrishnan, eds. 2015. *Scholar Intellectuals in Early Modern India.* New York: Routledge.

Miscellaneous Notices. 1845. *Calcutta Review* 3.2: 266–277.

Mitter, K. C. 1845. "Rammohun Roy." *Calcutta Review* 4 (July–December): 355–393.

Monier-Williams, Monier. 1877. *Hinduism.* London: Society for Promoting Christian Knowledge.

———. 1882. "The Vaishnava Religion, with Special Reference to the Siksha-patri of the Modern Sect called Svami-Narayaṇa." *Journal of the Royal Asiatic Society of Great Britain and Ireland* (New Series) 14.4: 289–316.

———. 1885 [1883]. *Religious Thought and Life in India.* 2nd ed. London: John Murray.

Moor, Edward. 1810. *The Hindu Pantheon.* London: J. Johnson.

Morinis, E. Alan. 1984. *Pilgrimage in the Hindu Tradition: A Case Study from West Bengal*. Delhi: Oxford University Press.

Moyn, Samuel, and Andrew Sartori, eds. 2013. *Global Intellectual History*. New York: Columbia University Press.

Mufti, Aamir. 2007. *Enlightenment in the Colony: The Jewish Question and the Crisis of Postcolonial Culture*. Princeton, NJ: Princeton University Press.

Mukherjee, Mithi. 2010. *India in the Shadows of Empire: A Legal and Political History, 1774–1950*. New Delhi: Oxford University Press.

Mukherjee, S. N. 1977. *Calcutta: Myths and History*. Calcutta: Subarnarekha.

Mukhopadhyay, Urvi. 2017. "The Islamicate Traces in the Nineteenth Century Bengali Elite Culture." Unpublished ms.

Mukta, Parita. 2000. "The Public Face of Hinduism." *Ethnic and Racial Studies* 23.3: 442–466.

Mukundcharandas, Sadhu. 1999. *Handbook to the Vachanamrutam*. Amdavad: Swaminarayan Aksharpith.

Mullens, Joseph. 1852. *Vedantism, Brahmism, and Christianity Examined and Compared. A Prize Essay*. Calcutta: Calcutta Christian Tract and Book Society.

Müller, F. Max. 1884. *Biographical Essays*. New York: Scribners.

———. 1899. *Auld Lang Syne. Second Series: My Indian Friends*. New York: Charles Scribner's Sons.

Nadri, Ghulam A. 2008. "Exploring the Gulf of Kachh: Regional Economy and Trade in the Eighteenth Century." *Journal of the Economic and Social History of the Orient* 51.3: 460–486.

———. 2009. *Eighteenth-Century Gujarat: The Dynamics of Its Political Economy, 1750–1800*. Leiden: Brill.

Nandy, Ashish. 1991. *At the Edge of Psychology: Essays in Politics and Culture*. Delhi: Oxford University Press.

Naqvi, Hameeda Khatoon. 1972. *Urbanisation and Urban Centers under the Mughals, 1556–1707: An Essay in Interpretation*. Vol. 1. Simla: Institute for Advanced Study.

Nicholas, Ralph. 2008. *Rites of Spring: Gajan in Village Bengal*. New Delhi: Chronicle Books.

Nongbri, Brent. 2013. *Before Religion: A History of a Modern Concept*. New Haven, CT: Yale University Press.

Novetzke, Christian Lee. 2007. "Bhakti and Its Public." *International Journal of Hindu Studies* 11.3: 255–272.

———. 2008. *Religion and Public Memory: A Cultural History of Sant Namdev in India*. New York: Columbia University Press.

———. 2016. *The Quotidian Revolution: Vernacularization, Religion, and the Premodern Public Sphere in India*. New York: Columbia University Press.

———. 2018. "Vernacularization." In *Hindu Law: A New History of Dharmasastra*, edited by Patrick Olivelle and Donald R. Davis, Jr. New York: Oxford University Press.

Nussbaum, Martha. 2007. *The Clash Within: Democracy, Religious Violence, and India's Future*. Cambridge, MA: Harvard University Press.

Oddie, Geoffrey A. 2006. *Imagined Hinduism: British Protestant Missionary Constructions of Hinduism, 1793–1900*. New Delhi: Sage.

O'Hanlon, Rosalind. 2007. "Cultural Pluralism, Empire and the State in Early Modern South Asia—A Review Essay." *Indian Economic and Social History Review* 44.3: 363–381.

O'Hanlon, Rosalind, and David Washbrook, eds. 2012. *Religious Cultures in Early Modern India*. New York: Routledge.

Olivelle, Patrick, trans. 2005. *The Law Code of Manu*. New York: Oxford University Press.

O'Malley, L. S. S. 1908. *Chittagong*. Eastern Bengal District Gazetteers. Calcutta: Bengal Secretariat Book Depot.

Orsini, Francesca. 2002. *The Hindi Public Sphere, 1920–1940*. Delhi: Oxford University Press.

Pal, Bipin Chandra. 1973. *Memories of My Life and Times*. 2nd rev. ed. Calcutta: B. C. Pal Institute.

———. 2012. *Navayuger Bangla*. Reprint ed. Kolkata: Chirayat Prakashan.

Pal, Nimaichandra, ed. 2012. *Shivayan: Ramkrishna Kavichandra Virachita*. Kolkata: Vivekananda Book Center.

Pandey, Gyandendra. 2001. *Remembering Partition: Violence, Nationalism and History in India*. New York: Cambridge University Press.

Paramtattvadas, Sadhu. 2017. *Introduction to Swaminarayan Theology*. New York: Cambridge University Press.

Paramtattvadas, Sadhu, and Raymond B. Williams. 2016. "Swaminarayan and British Contacts in Gujarat in the 1820s." In *Swaminarayan Hinduism: Tradition, Adaptation, and Identity*, edited by R. B. Williams and Y. Trivedi, 58–93. New Delhi: Oxford University Press.

Parekh, Manilal C. 1980 [1936]. *Sri Swami Narayana: A Gospel of Bhagwat-dharma or God in Redemptive Action*. 3rd ed. Bombay: Bharatiya Vidya Bhavan.

Patel, Shruti. 2017. "Beyond the Lens of Reform: Religious Culture in Modern Gujarat." *Journal of Hindu Studies* 10: 47–85.

Peabody, Norbert. 2001. "Cents, Sense and Census: Human Inventories in Late Pre-colonial and Early Colonial India." *Comparative Studies in Society and History* 43.4: 819–850.

Pennington, Brian K. 2005. *Was Hinduism Invented? Britons, Indians, and the Colonial Construction of Religion*. Oxford: Oxford University Press.

Pernau, Margrit, and Yunus Jaffery, eds. 2009. *Information and the Public Sphere: Persian Newsletters from Mughal Delhi*. Oxford: Oxford University Press.

Pinch, William. 2000. "Killing Ascetics in Indian History, 1500–2000." *PoLAR* 23.2: 134–140.

———. 2003. "Bhakti and the British Empire." *Past and Present* 179: 159–196.

———. 2006. *Warrior Ascetics and Indian Empires*. New York: Cambridge University Press.

Pocock, David. 1973. *Mind, Body and Wealth: A Study of Belief and Practice in an Indian Village*. Oxford: Basil Blackwell.

Pollock, Sheldon. 2001. "New Intellectuals in Seventeenth-Century India." *Indian Economic and Social History Review* 38.1: 3–31.

———. 2002. "Introduction: Working Papers on Sanskrit Knowledge-Systems on the Eve of Colonialism." *Journal of Indian Philosophy* 30: 431–439.

———. 2006. *The Language of the Gods in the World of Men: Sanskrit, Culture, and Power in Premodern India*. Berkeley: University of California Press.

———. 2011. *Forms of Knowledge in Early Modern Asia: Explorations in the Intellectual History of India and Tibet, 1500–1800*. Durham, NC: Duke University Press.

Price, Pamela. 1991. "Acting in Public versus Forming a Public: Conflict Processing and Political Mobilization in Nineteenth Century South India." *South Asia: Journal of South Asian Studies* 14.1: 91–121.

Prince, Gerald. 1982. *Narratology: The Form and Functioning of Narrative*. New York: Mouton.

Pullen, H. W. 1870. *Medieval Mummery in 1870: A Few Words about Cathedral Installations*. 2nd ed. London: Simpkin, Marshall and Co.

Purohit, Teena. 2012. *The Aga Khan Case: Religion and Identity in Colonial India*. Cambridge, MA: Harvard University Press.

Radhakrishnan, Sarvepalli. 1927. *The Hindu View of Life*. London: George Allen and Unwin.

Ramaswamy, Sumathi. 2013. "Global Encounters, Earthly Knowledges, Worldly Selves." *Purusartha* 31: 359–391.

———. 2017. *Terrestrial Lessons: The Conquest of the World as Globe*. Chicago: University of Chicago Press.

Ranade, M. G. 1902. *Religious and Social Reform: A Collection of Essays and Speeches*. Bombay: Gopal Narayen and Co.

Rao, Velcheru Narayana, David Shulman, and Sanjay Subrahmaniyam, eds. 2003. *Textures of Time: Writing History in South India, 1600–1800*. New York: Other Press.

Raval, R. 1987. *Socio-Religious Reform Movements in Gujarat during the Nineteenth Century*. New Delhi: Ess Ess Publications.

Ray, Ajit. 1976. *The Religious Ideas of Rammohun Roy*. New Delhi: Kanak.

Ray, Ratnalekha. 1979. *Change in Bengal Agrarian Society c. 1760–1850*. Delhi: Manohar.

Reddy, Deepa, and John Zavos, eds. 2010. "Temple Publics: Religious Institutions and the Construction of Contemporary Hindu Communities." *International Journal of Hindu Studies* 13.3: 241–260.

Rennell, James. 1776. *An Actual Survey of the Provinces of Bengal, Bahar, etc. by Major James Rennell, Esq*. London: Andrew Drury.

Robb, Peter. 2014. *Useful Friendship: Europeans and Indians in Early Calcutta*. New Delhi: Oxford University Press.

Robertson, Bruce C. 1995. *Raja Rammohun Roy: The Father of Modern India*. New Delhi: Oxford University Press.

Rosselli, John. 1974. *Lord William Bentinck: The Making of a Liberal Imperialist, 1774–1839*. Berkeley: University of California Press.

Rudolf, Lloyd, and Susanne Rudolf. 1967. *The Modernity of Tradition: Political Development in India*. Chicago: University of Chicago Press.

Said, Edward. 1978. *Orientalism*. New York: Vintage Books.

Santra, Tarapada. 1976. *Haora jelar purakirti*. Calcutta: Pashchim Banga Sarkar.

———. 1980. *Medinipur: Sanskriti o Manavasamaj*. Howrah: Kaushiki.

———. 2014. *Kalikatar Mandir-Masjid*. Kolkata: Ananda Publishers.

Sanyal, Hiteshranjan. 1981. *Social Mobility in Bengal*. Calcutta: Papyrus.

Sanyal, Rajat. 1980. *Voluntary Associations and the Urban Public Life in Bengal*. Calcutta: Riddhi-India.

Sarkar, Jadunath. 1928. *India through the Ages: A Survey of the Growth of Indian Life and Thought*. Calcutta: M. C. Sarkar.

Sarkar, Mahua. 2008. *Visible Histories, Disappearing Women: Producing Muslim Womanhood in Late Colonial Bengal*. Durham, NC: Duke University Press.

Sarkar, Sumit. 1985. "Rammohun Roy and the Break with the Past." In *A Critique of Colonial India*, by Sumit Sarkar. Calcutta: Papyrus.

———. 2002. *Beyond Nationalist Frames: Postmodernism, Hindu Fundamentalism, History*. Bloomington: Indiana University Press.

Sarma, D. S. 1944. *The Renaissance of Hinduism*. Benares: Benares Hindu University.

Schreiner, Peter. 1999. "The Bhagavatapurana as Model for the Satsangijvanam." In *Composing a Tradition: Concepts, Techniques and Relationships*, edited by M. Brockington and P. Schreiner, 257–278. Zagreb: Croatian Academy of Sciences and Arts.

———. 2001. "Institutionalization of Charisma: The Case of Sahajanand." In *Charisma and Canon: Essays on the Religious History of the Indian Subcontinent*, edited by Vasudha Dalmia, 155–170. New Delhi: Oxford University Press.

Scott, J. Barton. 2015. "Aryas Unbound: Print Hinduism and the Cultural Regulation of Religious Offense." *Comparative Studies in South Asia, Africa and the Middle East* 35.2: 294–309.

———. 2016. *Spiritual Despots: Modern Hinduism and the Genealogies of Self-Rule*. Chicago: University of Chicago Press.

Scott, J. Barton, and Brandon Ingram. 2015. "What Is a Public? Notes from South Asia." *South Asia: Journal of South Asian Studies* 38.3: 357–370.

Seal, Brajendranath. 1933. "Rammohun Roy: The Universal Man." Reprinted in *Rammohun Roy: The Man and His Work*. Calcutta: Satish Chandra Chakravarti.

Sen, Adharlal. 1884. *The Shrines of Sitakund in the District of Chittagong in Bengal*. Calcutta: Thacker and Spink.

Sen, Amiya P. 2012. *Rammohun Roy: A Critical Biography*. New Delhi: Viking Penguin.

———. 2013. "Reform Hinduism." *Oxford Bibliographies Online*. www
.oxfordbibliographiesonline.com/ (accessed June 10, 2018).

Sen, Asok. 1977. *Vidyasagar and His Elusive Milestones*. Calcutta: RDDHI India.

Sen, Kshitimohan. 1936. *Medieval Mysticism in India*. Translated by Manomohan
Ghosh. London: Luzac.

Sen, Surendranath. 1942. *Prachin Bangala Patra Sankalana*. Calcutta: University of
Calcutta.

Shapiro, Michael. 1994. "Moral Geographies and the Ethics of Post-Sovereignty."
Public Culture 6:479–502.

Sharma, Arvind. 2002. *Modern Hindu Thought: Essential Texts*. Delhi: Oxford
University Press.

Shastri, Shivnath. 1911. *History of the Brahmo Samaj*. 2 vols. Calcutta: R. Chatterji.

Sheikh, Samira. 2008. "Alliance, Genealogy and Political Power: The Cudasamas of
Junagadh and the Sultans of Gujarat." *Medieval History Journal* 11.1: 29–61.

———. 2010. *Forging a Region: Sultans, Traders, and Pilgrims in Gujarat, 1200–1500*.
New York: Oxford University Press.

———. 2017. "Ruling Dvaraka: Krsna's Capital in Later Times (ca. 1450–1950)."
International Journal of Hindu Studies 10: 112–130.

Sherman, William E. B. 2018. "Karma in the Public Sphere: Habermas in Ancient
India." *Marginalia: LA Review of Books*, March 16. https://marginalia
.lareviewofbooks.org/karma-public-sphere-habermas-ancient-india/.

Shodhan, Amrita. 2001. *A Question of Community: Religious Groups and Colonial
Law*. Delhi: Samya.

———. 2010. "Caste in the Judicial Courts of Gujarat, 1800–60." In *The Idea of
Gujarat: History, Ethnography and Text*, edited by Edward Simpson and Aparna
Kapadia, 32–49. Delhi: Orient Blackswan.

Shrivastava, S. P. 1981. "Swaminarayan and Hindu Renaissance." In *New Dimensions in Vedanta Philosophy*, Part 1. Ahmedabad: BAPS, 1981.

Simpson, Edward. 2005. "The 'Gujarat' Earthquake and the Political Economy of
Nostalgia." *Contributions to Indian Sociology* 39.2: 219–249.

Simpson, Edward, and Aparna Kapadia, eds. 2010. *The Idea of Gujarat: History,
Ethnography and Text*. Delhi: Orient Blackswan.

Singh, Kavita. 2010. "Temple of Eternal Return: The Swaminarayan Akshardham
Complex in Delhi." *Artibus Asiae* 50.1: 47–76.

Sinha, Nitin. 2012. *Communication and Colonialism in Eastern India: Bihar,
1760s–1880s*. New York: Anthem Press.

Sircar, D. C. 1973. *The Sakta Pithas*. 2nd ed. Delhi: Motilal Banarsidass.

Skaria, Ajay. 1998. "Being *jangli*: The Politics of Wildness." *Studies in History* 14.2:
193–215.

———. 1999. *Hybrid Histories: Forests, Frontiers and Wilderness in Western India*.
Delhi: Oxford University Press.

Smith, Jonathan Z. 1987. *To Take Place: Toward Theory in Ritual*. Chicago:
University of Chicago Press.

Smith, Wilfred Cantwell. 1979. *Faith and Belief.* Princeton, NJ: Princeton University Press.

Spear, Percival. 1951. *Twilight of the Mughuls: Studies in Late Mughul Delhi.* Cambridge, UK: Cambridge University Press.

Spurr, David. 1993. *The Rhetoric of Empire: Colonial Discourse in Journalism, Travel Writing, and Imperial Administration.* Durham, NC: Duke University Press.

Stark, Rodney, and William Sims Bainbridge. 1979. "Of Churches, Sects, and Cults: Preliminary Concepts for a Theory of Religious Movements." *Journal for the Scientific Study of Religion* 18. 2: 117–131.

Stark, Ulrike. 2011. "Associational Culture and Civic Engagement in Colonial Lucknow: The Jalsah-e Tahzib." *Indian Economic and Social History Review* 48.1: 1–33.

Stewart, Charles. *History of Bengal from the First Mohammedan Invasion to the Virtual Conquest of That Country by the English A.D. 1757.* London: Black, Perry and Co.

Stoker, Valerie. 2016. *Polemics and Patronage in the City of Victory: Vyasatirtha, Hindu Sectarianism, and the Sixteenth-Century Vijayanagara Court.* Berkeley: University of California Press.

Stokes, Eric J. 1975. "Agrarian Society and the Pax Britannica in Northern India in the Early Nineteenth Century." *Modern Asian Studies* 9.4: 505–528.

Subrahmanyam, Sanjay. 2001. *Penumbral Visions: Making Polities in Early Modern South India.* Ann Arbor: University of Michigan Press.

———. 2005. *Mughals and Franks: Explorations in Connected History.* New Delhi: Oxford University Press.

Subramaniam, Lakshmi. 1996. *Indigenous Capital and Imperial Expansion: Bombay, Surat, and the West Coast.* Delhi: Oxford University Press.

Tagore, Debendranath. 1909. *The Autobiography of Maharshi Devendranath Tagore.* Translated from the original Bengali by Satyendranath Tagore and Indira Devi. Calcutta: S. K. Lahiri.

———. 1975 [1850]. *Brahma Dharmaḥ.* Calcutta: Sadharana Brahmo Samaj.

Tagore, Rabindranath. 1995. *Rabindra-racanabali.* 15 vols. Calcutta: Vishvabharati Press.

———. 1996 [1923]. "A Vision of India's History." In *The English Writings of Rabindranath Tagore*, vol. 3, edited by Sisir Kumar Das, 439–459. New Delhi: Sahitya Akademi.

———. 2000. *Rabindra-rachanabali.* Vol 17. Calcutta: Vishvabharati Press.

Tambs-Lyche, Harald. 2001. "Svami Narayan: Une hagiographie récente au Gujarat." In *Constructions hagiographiques dans le monde indien*, edited by Françoise Mallison, 257–281. Paris: Editions Champion.

———. 2002. "Townsmen, Tenants and Tribes: War, Wildness and Wilderness in the Traditional Politics of Western India." In *Contemporary Society: Tribal Society*, edited by G. Pfeffer and D. K. Behera, vol. 5, 186–207. Delhi: Concept Publishing.

——. 2004. *The Good Country: Individual, Situation and Society in Saurashtra.* Delhi: Manohar.

——. 2010. "Reflections on Caste in Gujarat." In *The Idea of Gujarat: History, Ethnography and Text,* edited by Edward Simpson and Aparna Kapadia, 100–119. Delhi: Orient Blackswan.

——. 2011. "The Quest for Purity in Gujarat Hinduism: A Bird's Eye View." *South Asia: Journal of South Asian Studies* 34.3: 333–353.

Tavakoli-Targhi, Mohamad. 2001. *Refashioning Iran: Orientalism, Occidentalism and Historiography.* New York: Palgrave.

——. 2011. "Early Persianate Modernity." In *Forms of Knowledge in Early Modern South Asia: Explorations in the Intellectual History of India and Tibet, 1500–1800,* edited by Sheldon Pollock, 257–290. Durham, NC: Duke University Press.

Thapar, Romila. 1997. "Syndicated Hinduism." In *Hinduism Reconsidered,* edited by G. Sontheimer and H. Kulke, 54–81. Delhi: Manohar.

Tweed, Thomas. 2006. *Crossing and Dwelling: A Theory of Religion.* Cambridge, MA: Harvard University Press.

Van der Veer, Peter. 2001. *Imperial Encounters: Religion and Modernity in India and Britain.* Princeton, NJ: Princeton University Press.

——. 2014. *The Modern Spirit of Asia: The Spiritual and the Secular in China and India.* Princeton, NJ: Princeton University Press.

Van Spengen, Wiim. 2000. *Tibetan Border Worlds: A Geohistorical Analysis of Trade and Traders.* London: Kegan Paul.

Vertovec, Steven. 2000. *Hindu Diaspora: Comparative Patterns.* New York: Routledge.

Ward, William. 1817. *A View of the History, Religion and Literature of the Hindoos.* 2 vols. London: Baptist Missionary Society.

Warner, Michael. 2005 [2002]. *Publics and Counterpublics.* Cambridge, MA: Zone Books.

Washbrook, David. 1993. "Economic Depression and the Making of Traditional Society in Colonial India, 1820–1855." *Transactions of the Royal Historical Society* 3: 237–263.

White, David Gordon. 2006. *Kiss of the Yogini: "Tantric Sex" in Its South Asian Contexts.* Chicago: University of Chicago Press.

Wickens, G. M., trans. 1964. *The Nasirean Ethics.* London: Routledge.

Wilberforce-Bell, H. 1916. *The History of Kathiawad from the Earliest Times.* London: Walter Heinemann.

Williams, Raymond Brady. 1984. *A New Face of Hinduism: The Swaminarayan Religion.* New York: Cambridge University Press.

——. 2001. *An Introduction to Swaminarayan Hinduism.* New York: Cambridge University Press.

Williams, Raymond Brady, and Yogi Trivedi, eds. 2016. *Swaminarayan Hinduism: Tradition, Adaptation and Identity.* New Delhi: Oxford University Press.

Willis, Michael. 2009. *The Archaeology of Hindu Ritual: Temples and the Establishment of the Gods*. New York: Cambridge University Press.

Wilson, H. H. 1840. *Two Lectures on the Religious Practice and Opinions of the Hindus*. London: W. H. Allen.

———. 1846. *Sketch of the Religious Sects of the Hindus*. Calcutta: Bishop's College Press.

Wilson, Jon E. 2005. "'A Thousand Countries to Go To': Peasants and Rulers in Late-Eighteenth Century Bengal." *Bengal Past and Present* 189: 81–109.

Yang, Anand A. 1998. *Bazaar India: Markets, Society, and the Colonial State in Gangetic Bihar*. Berkeley: University of California Press.

Yelle, Robert. 2012. *The Language of Disenchantment: Protestant Literalism and Colonial Discourse in British India*. New York: Oxford University Press.

Young, Richard Fox. 1981. *Resistant Hinduism: Sanskrit Sources on Anti-Christian Apologetics in Early Nineteenth-Century India*. Leiden: E. J. Brill.

Younger, Paul. 2009. *New Homelands: Hindu Communities in Mauritius, Guyana, Trinidad, South Africa, Fiji, and East Africa*. New York: Oxford University Press.

Zaehner, R. C. 1980 [1962]. *Hinduism*. New York: Oxford University Press.

Zastoupil, Lynn. 2010. *Rammohun Roy and the Making of Victorian Britain*. New York: Palgrave Macmillan.

Zavos, John. 1999. "The Arya Samaj and the Antecedents of Hindu Nationalism." *International Journal of Hindu Studies* 3.1: 57–81.

———. 2000. "Patterns of Organization in Turn of the Century Hinduism: An Examination with Reference to the Punjab." *International Journal of Punjab Studies* 7.1: 29–52.

———. 2001. "Defending Hindu Tradition: Sanatana Dharma as a Symbol of Orthodoxy in Colonial India." *Religion* 31: 109–123.

Zavos, John, P. Kanungo, D. Reddy, M. Warrier, and R. Williams, eds. 2012. *Public Hinduisms*. New Delhi: Sage Publications India.

INDEX